INVISIBLE WAR

INVISIBLE WAR

THE UNITED STATES AND THE IRAQ SANCTIONS

Joy Gordon

HARVARD UNIVERSITY PRESS

Cambridge, Massachusetts

London, England

First Harvard University Press paperback edition, 2012

Library of Congress Cataloging-in-Publication Data

Gordon, Joy.
    Invisible war : the United States and the Iraq sanctions / Joy Gordon.
        p. cm.
    Includes bibliographical references and index.
    ISBN 978-0-674-03571-3 (cloth : alk. paper)
    ISBN 978-0-674-06408-9 (pbk.)
    1. Economic sanctions—Iraq. 2. United Nations—Iraq. 3. United Nations. Security
Council. 4. United States—Foreign relations—Iraq. 5. Iraq—Foreign relations—
United States. I. Title.
HF1586.3.G67 2010
327.1'17—dc22   2009050639

She urged the delegation to look at the situation facing children now, and how these economic problems caused by sanctions will have a major impact on their future. She pointed to examples of civil unrest in Africa and elsewhere, usually caused by disaffected youth with no hope of education, job, or a future. There is just such a generation of Iraqis growing up now, she said, with no hope, no connection to the outside world, isolated. And that will be very dangerous.

Iraq Trip Report, written by congressional staff,
summarizing discussion with Anupama Rao Singh,
the head of UNICEF in Iraq, September 1999

CONTENTS

This book is a study of the ways in which the United States shaped the character and extent of the sanctions imposed on Iraq by the United Nations (UN) Security Council. The United States exercised a singular influence in determining these policies, and often did so in the face of vehement opposition from the majority of the Security Council, UN agencies, and the UN General Assembly. Consequently, this book is in part a case study of how the United States projected influence within the UN Security Council at a specific historical juncture.

It is also the story of a bureaucracy (or rather a set of bureaucracies) and the enormous human damage that was done, not out of hatred but out of indifference, and because the decision-making process itself was so diffuse and abstract. In the course of telling this story, the book raises legal and moral issues about both U.S. policy and international law: What do we make of a policy generated by an institution of international governance, intended to address aggression and human rights violations, which is itself a source of indiscriminate and large-scale human damage? How do we attribute responsibility, given that decisions were made collectively, or politically, or bureaucratically? How do we approach the question of the U.S. intent in regard to a policy that was formulated by a complex arrangement of technicians, politicians, and diplomats?

This book covers the period from August 1990, when Iraq invaded Kuwait and sanctions were first imposed, to the conclusion of the sanctions after the second Persian Gulf War in May 2003. It is not intended to provide a comprehensive description of all the UN Security Council resolutions or their implementation, or the sanctions structure overall; nor is it a complete review of the impact of the sanctions on public health, education, and mortality. However, Chapter 2 contains summaries of both.

It might be asked of this book: Why focus on the United States? Why are both sides of the issue not represented? Should there not be a greater focus on the dilemma in which U.S. policymakers found themselves? In part, the answer is that the role of the United States has not been at all clear. In general, the sanctions and their implementation appeared as simply the decisions and policies of the UN Security Council, and the role of any particular Council member was generally not visible. There is a need to understand clearly what part the United States played.

At the same time, the U.S. government's side of the story is already extremely well known: the U.S. government (along with the British government) made many statements to the press regarding the sanctions, and the State Department and other U.S. agencies gave congressional testimony and released detailed position statements. All of these articulated the U.S. government's view that Saddam Hussein was exaggerating the humanitarian impact, or was himself responsible for it in various ways; that the sanctions would end if Hussein complied with UN requirements; that only dual-use or military goods were being blocked; that the Iraqi government had failed to spend the funds available to it; that the Iraqi government was stockpiling humanitarian goods rather than distributing them; and that the United States was doing its best, but was helpless to improve the plight of the Iraqi people. Many of these reports and statements are cited throughout the book.

The story begins, in the first chapter, by placing these events in the context of the intractable dilemma in which U.S. policymakers found themselves: throughout all three administrations there was a hope that regime change would take place, but little likelihood that it would come about. In the meantime, the United States calculated that the next best option was containment. Containment, in turn, was fraught with difficulties and compromises; and U.S. policymakers were faced with the erosion of support within the Security Council and, beginning in the latter part of the 1990s, growing public pressure.

While the U.S. views, and the U.S. predicament, are well known, what is not well known is the complexity of the internal debate that took place within the Security Council and among different branches of the UN, how the compromises were negotiated, and the political and diplomatic means by which the outcomes of these debates were determined. From the beginning there were deep tensions within the UN concerning the sanctions regime, as many felt it to be antithetical to the fundamental mission of the organization. There was considerable anguish on the part of many within the UN, and there were early and continuous attempts at reform. Within the Security Council the disputes became increasingly bitter and angry. In the face of all of this, the United States remained largely intransigent, making compromises only where there were no political options, then finding ways to undermine even those compromises.

Some of this is publicly known, but it has not been documented. This is in large measure because the meetings where these matters were resolved took place in committees that met behind closed doors or informally between individual members of the Security Council. Where there were minutes, their circulation was restricted. Many of the documents were internal to the UN agencies and were not publicly distributed.

In doing the research I conducted interviews with many of the diplomats and UN officials involved with the sanctions process. Within the U.S. government, I interviewed a number of the people who were involved with the Iraq sanctions, ranging from senior policy-making positions to those working with technical implementation. Because the research took place over an extended period and the sanctions underwent changes during that time, I interviewed several key people multiple times. For the most part I used these interviews for my own background, to understand the programs accurately and to identify which additional documents would be helpful. Whenever possible I relied on documentary sources and publications. I cited interviews only when I could not find a document or publication containing the same information.

In addition to the Security Council processes, there are certainly other factors that played a role in Iraq's fate in recent years, most notably oil interests. However, that is an issue that has been widely discussed elsewhere, and I do not explore its significance here.

I should mention that, as of this writing, I have never traveled to Iraq myself and I only occasionally cite observations by visitors. In describing Iraq's economy, its infrastructure, and the overall condition of the Iraqi population, I have relied primarily on the information available from humanitarian monitors, relief organizations, and other sources reflecting systematic and long-term observation throughout the country and across the different sectors.

CASI	Campaign Against Sanctions in Iraq
CIA	Central Intelligence Agency
CRS	Congressional Research Service
DHA	United Nations Department of Humanitarian Affairs
ECOSOC	United Nations Economic and Social Council
EPIC	Education for Peace in Iraq
FAO	Food and Agricultural Organization
GAO	General Accounting Office (up to July 2004)
GAO	Government Accountability Office (after July 2004)
GRL	Goods Review List
HELP	Humanitarian Exports Leading to Peace Act
HST	Harvard Study Team
IAEA	International Atomic Energy Association
IAMB	International Advisory and Monitoring Board for Iraq
IASC	Interagency Standing Committee
ICC	International Criminal Court
ICESCR	International Covenant on Economic, Social and Cultural Rights
ICJ	International Court of Justice
ICRC	International Committee of the Red Cross
ICTR	International Criminal Tribunal for Rwanda
IIC	Independent Inquiry Committee
ILA	Iraq Liberation Act
INA	Iraqi National Accord
IST	International Study Team
ITU	International Telecommunications Union
MDOU	Multidisciplinary Observation Unit

MIF	Multinational Interception Force
MOU	Memorandum of Understanding
NGO	Nongovernmental organization
OIP	Office of the Iraq Programme
SC	Security Council
SDI	Samara Drug Industries
TSWG	Telecommunications Sector Working Group
UNCC	United Nations Compensation Commission
UNDP	United Nations Development Programme
UNESCO	United Nations Educational, Scientific and Cultural Organization
UNICEF	United Nations Children's Fund
UNMOVIC	United Nations Monitoring, Verification and Inspection Commission
UNOHCI	United Nations Office of the Humanitarian Coordinator for Iraq
UNOPS	United Nations Office for Project Services
UNSCOM	United Nations Special Commission
USDA	United States Department of Agriculture
WFP	World Food Programme
WHO	World Health Organization

INVISIBLE WAR

1

THE POLICY OF CONTAINMENT

Surely the U.S.-led invasion and occupation of Iraq in 2003 will be viewed as one of the catastrophes of contemporary U.S. foreign policy. With U.S. casualties numbering in the thousands, Iraqi deaths in at least the tens of thousands, and years of daily reports portraying Iraq's descent into a hellish and chaotic state, it seems astonishing to recall that George W. Bush's administration envisioned a domino effect where a free and democratic Iraq would be followed by political reform in one Arab country after another. The U.S. presence in Iraq came a long way from the "liberation" of 2003 and the toppling of Saddam Hussein's statue to the suicide bombings and dozens of makeshift bombs daily targeting U.S. and allied soldiers and contractors.

How did this come about? Part of the answer lies with the killing of Iraqi civilians in the war of 2003, and the period thereafter, which included attacks on insurgents, intrusive searches of Iraqi homes, the arbitrary arrest of Iraqis labeled as suspected terrorists, and the infamous abuses of Abu Ghraib. But it is important to remember that the U.S. presence in Iraq, and the harm done by the United States to the Iraqi population, did not begin in 2003. Starting in August 1990, the United States was instrumental in imposing the cruelest sanctions in the history of international governance. While the United Nations (UN) Security Council was within its mandate to respond to Iraq's invasion of Kuwait, the sanctions regime it imposed, in conjunction with the massive bombing campaign of 1991, destroyed nearly all of Iraq's infrastructure, industrial capacity, agriculture, telecommunications, and critical public services, particularly electricity and water treatment. For the next twelve years the sanctions would prevent Iraq from restoring any of these to the level Iraq had achieved in the 1980s and would devastate the health, education, and basic well-being of almost the entire Iraqi population. The situation was

1

worsened by the corruption in the Iraqi government, and the Iraqi government was not particularly effective in mitigating the harm done by the UN measures. But it was the extraordinary harshness of the sanctions, coming on top of the massive bombing of 1991, that was primarily responsible for the collapse of Iraq's economy and the deterioration of public services.

The United States, and to some extent the UN, attributed Iraq's economic collapse in the 1990s to the callousness and corruption of Saddam Hussein. All three U.S. administrations maintained, for example, that the sanctions did not prevent Saddam from buying food for his people. But what was not said was that while food arrived in Iraq, Iraq's ability to distribute it was crippled by the lack of transportation, and the United States alone on the Security Council was consistently responsible for preventing Iraq from importing trucks, tires, and repair parts. Blame was often placed as well on the corruption of the Iraqi government, on the grounds that Hussein was using Iraq's funds, illicit income from smuggling, and proceeds from the Oil-for-Food Programme to buy luxury goods for himself, his cronies, and privileged groups in Iraq. But in fact these practices had only a marginal effect on Iraq's economy. The real damage to Iraq's economy and society was not from Hussein's neglect or corruption but from the systematic impoverishment of the entire nation.

The role of the United States in this process was sometimes criticized, particularly with regard to incidents such as its refusal in 2001 to allow Iraq to import child vaccines. But in general, the U.S. role in the sanctions is not widely known. The entire sanctions regime was overseen by a committee of the Security Council that met behind closed doors, did not circulate minutes of its meetings, and had little transparency or accountability. The sanctions regime involved a Byzantine set of bureaucratic structures, and was at the same time fraught at every juncture with political posturing. While there was from the beginning a process to allow for humanitarian exemptions, the politics of the process were such that humanitarian imports were badly compromised throughout the thirteen years of the sanctions regime. The United States held a central role in this: lobbying aggressively for procedural rules that gave the United States the power to unilaterally block Iraq from importing humanitarian goods; maneuvering to discredit the reports on the humanitarian situation submitted by UN agencies; maneuvering to exclude external legal opinions that might influence the committee to grant access to humanitarian goods; delaying urgent goods, sometimes for years at a time; and changing the criteria for approval or flatly refusing to state what criteria the United States used in granting or denying approval. As the humanitarian situation worsened and public pressure increased, there were demands for reform. The United States, often accompanied by Britain and occasionally by other nations, found ways to ensure that each of those reforms was compromised in turn.

Throughout the sanctions regime, reports poured in from UN agencies and international organizations documenting the dramatic increase in child mortality, water-borne diseases, and malnutrition. Both within and outside the UN there were accusations that the sanctions were themselves human rights violations, and arguably genocidal, even though they were established by the UN Security Council. A UN human rights rapporteur, Andreas Mavrommatis, charged with reporting on only the violations of the Iraqi government, nevertheless reported as well on the human rights impact of the sanctions.[1] Three career UN officials—Denis Halliday, Hans von Sponeck, and Jutta Burghardt—resigned their positions in protest against the sanctions, maintaining that to work for the UN in Iraq, even in a humanitarian capacity, was to participate in an immoral and indefensible policy. The UN Commission on Human Rights commissioned a study by Belgian jurist Marc Bossuyt on the circumstances in which economic sanctions would violate international human rights law. His report highlighted the situation in Iraq,[2] and the Commission passed a resolution condemning the economic situation in Iraq as a human rights violation.[3]

Despite all of this, it was the consistent policy of all three U.S. administrations, from 1990 to 2003, to inflict the most extreme economic damage possible on Iraq. This was true even though each administration insisted that it was committed to the well-being of the Iraqi population. Secretary of State Madeleine Albright once said, "I care more about the children of Iraq than Saddam Hussein does." But the truth was that in implementing the policy on sanctions, the human damage was never a factor in U.S. policy, except insofar as it presented a political liability for U.S. administrations.

The same was true of Congress. It was true of both parties, and it was true irrespective of which party controlled Congress. However severe the humanitarian impact was, there were few in Congress who had any substantial interest in the issue. In the early 1990s, when the Democrats controlled both houses, they sought to distance themselves from Iraq and the Gulf War, which was seen as an unequivocal victory for the Bush

3

administration. Nor did the Democrats want to raise any humanitarian concerns for fear they would be accused of being sympathetic to the Iraqi government. After 1995, when the Republicans controlled Congress, there was even less room to introduce the topic of Iraq's humanitarian issues in any context, such as congressional hearings, much less in legislation. Consequently, in regard to Iraq, both the Democrats and the Republicans focused almost exclusively on issues of disarmament and regime change. In the late 1990s there were a number of individual members of Congress who were vocal in bringing attention to the humanitarian situation. But the leadership, of both parties, had little tolerance for any advocacy regarding the humanitarian issues in Iraq.

The sole concern of the U.S. government, through strategies that were overly broad in the extreme, was to prevent Iraq from rebuilding its military. The first strategy was simply to bankrupt the nation as a whole to prevent the state from rearming. The second was disarmament, which included a prohibition on "dual-use" goods, interpreted in the broadest possible sense. Invoking "dual use," the United States unilaterally blocked goods including child vaccines, water tankers during a period of drought, cloth, the generator needed to run a sewage treatment plant, radios for ambulances—any goods that could even conceivably be used by the military, for any possible purpose. The problem, of course, is that there is precious little that is used by a civilian population that is not also used by the military: window glass, brake fluid, telephones, light switches—the list is absolutely without end.

Regardless of the U.S. government's public posturing, the officials who formulated and implemented the U.S. government's policy literally gave no weight to the humanitarian cost of their actions. "It was not part of our skill set," said one State Department official. "That was supposed to be the responsibility of the UN." But in this regard the UN did its job very well. UNICEF, UNESCO, the World Health Organization, the Food and Agriculture Organization, the World Food Programme—all of these agencies documented the situation from the beginning, documented the harm being done by the sanctions in general and documented the specific damage being done by U.S. policies. All of this information was known to U.S. officials. Rather than taking these concerns seriously, the United States dismissed them as the claims of those who were "siding with Saddam" and sought to discredit or suppress the reports of Halliday, von Sponeck, and other humanitarian officials in Iraq.

4

The Genocide Convention and the Rome Statute of the International Criminal Court define genocide as including "acts committed with intent to destroy, in whole or in part, a national, ethnical, racial or religious group, as such . . . [by d]eliberately inflicting on the group conditions of life calculated to bring about its physical destruction in whole or in part."[4] Some have argued that the U.S. role in shaping the sanctions on Iraq turned an act of international governance into a genocidal enterprise; that U.S. officials deliberately and knowingly brought about the indiscriminate destruction of life as well as destroying the means to sustain life in Iraq.

The possibility that economic sanctions could be a human rights violation, or even a form of genocide, was not something that anyone imagined when the sanctions were first imposed on Iraq in 1990. Sieges and blockades in time of war, such as the siege of Leningrad, caused terrible loss of life. But economic sanctions, as a form of political pressure outside the context of war, had not. If nations of comparable size imposed sanctions on each other, as was the case with the United States and the Soviet Union, then the impact was little more than symbolic. If the United States sanctioned a small nation, such as Cuba, then the targeted nation could shift its trade to the Soviet bloc. Consequently, economic sanctions during the Cold War were never devastating. In fact, they were viewed as a "middle route": they were seen as nonviolent, in contrast to military intervention, but also as having more of a bite than diplomatic efforts. As of the late 1980s there was little concern about the ethics or humanitarian impact of sanctions. For the most part, those who wrote about sanctions were concerned with whether they were likely to succeed in getting the target state to change its policies, or with the difficulty of keeping sanctions in place when the members of an alliance were losing trade opportunities.

Not only were sanctions seen as innocuous, but the case of South Africa made them seem quite attractive. The Black South African population itself—the population most likely to be harmed by economic sanctions—called for sanctions against South Africa as an act of international solidarity. The sanctions imposed on South Africa were effective for a combination of reasons. They were accompanied by international diplomacy and social isolation of the apartheid regime within the international community. In addition to the international pressure, there was growing domestic opposition from labor, students, and political organizations, which

5

emerged as forces within South Africa's increasing urbanization and industrialization. One commentator noted that the "hurting stalemate" resulted in moderates from both sides negotiating with each other, and there were also reformist elites that emerged within the Afrikaner-dominated National Party.[5] In any event, there was little ground to claim that the sanctions were hurting an innocent population against its will. In the end the apartheid regime gave way to democracy and sanctions were viewed as having an important and effective role in accomplishing this.

But the sanctions regime imposed on South Africa was anomalous in every regard: typically there is little support from the population that is harmed, and sanctions rarely induce the targeted state to change its practices. On the contrary, the more typical response is a "rally 'round the flag" effect in which the population supports the state in the face of what is seen as aggression by a foreign power.[6] Furthermore, the most optimistic studies of sanctions in the twentieth century found that sanctions influence the target nation only about one-third of the time.[7] Critics have argued that even this number includes cases that are overdetermined, and that if we look only at the number of cases where sanctions are clearly the determinative factor in changing a state's policies, sanctions were clearly effective in only about 5 percent of the cases in the twentieth century.[8]

But while the South Africa case may have been anomalous, it was also deeply influential: by the late 1980s, economic sanctions were very much identified as an effective, nonviolent tool that was successful in bringing about democratic change. In 1990, after Iraq invaded Kuwait, much of the support for economic sanctions came from those who opposed military intervention and advocated a nonviolent response. Many of these groups came to have misgivings, not only because they saw the sanctions cause such suffering in Iraq later on but also because it seemed that, in retrospect, the George H. W. Bush administration had only introduced sanctions as an intermediate measure, to lay the groundwork for a military incursion.[9] The Iraq sanctions changed the views of many peace activists and organizations: "Economic sanctions and the UN Charter, rather than serving as the 'threshold for peace,' became a 'trap door to war.'"[10]

For the first few months of the sanctions regime in 1990 the first Bush administration insisted that sanctions were proving to be an effective tool for pressuring Iraq to withdraw from Kuwait, with senior Bush administration officials maintaining they were "increasingly convinced that economic sanctions are seriously hurting Saddam Hussein's economy and military."[11] Media coverage described how the sanctions were blocking Iraq's access to raw materials and spare parts, and how the shortages in Iraq undermined industrial production and forced the state to begin rationing gasoline.[12] The gasoline shortages, in turn, meant that Iraq's military capacity would be compromised.[13]

But in November 1990 the administration changed position, insisting that the sanctions were failing and that the Security Council must authorize military intervention. Secretary of Defense Richard Cheney argued that the sanctions were having little effect on the Iraqi regime and were giving Iraq "breathing space" to expand its military—"[Saddam Hussein] can ride them out."[14] The administration's about-face was obvious:

> Some White House and State Department officials who two months ago said the international embargo was "working" and would force Iraq to withdraw from Kuwait, have shifted their public predictions of its success. Now, they say, the cutoff of trade may not work or may take so long that the US-led coalition opposed to Iraq could crumble.[15]

The Bush administration got what it wanted. In late November the Security Council passed Resolution 678, which authorized member states to use "all necessary means" against Iraq if it did not withdraw from Kuwait by January 15. For the next two months there was an intensive lobbying campaign within the United States, coming from several sources, to maintain the sanctions rather than go into a U.S.-led war against Iraq. The leading scholars on economic sanctions testified at congressional hearings and published op-ed articles saying that the sanctions were likely to work: "The sanctions against Iraq were imposed so swiftly, decisively, and comprehensively that together with a credible military threat, there is a high probability they can contribute to an Iraqi withdrawal."[16]

Members of Congress openly questioned the necessity of going to war, arguing that sanctions should be given more time to work. In a Senate committee hearing, Senator Joseph Biden asked Secretary of State James Baker to explain

> what you told this committee just 3 months ago. You said that the sanctions policy is, "the only peaceful path to meeting the objectives set by the President." You continued by stating, "What we ask most of the American people is to stand firm, be patient and

remain united." What we are now hearing from some of the administration is that the American people do not have such patience, yet I find not one single, solitary shred of evidence to sustain that claim.[17]

In December 1990 the Senate Armed Services Committee held a set of hearings that included testimony from an impressive array of speakers with military and security credentials. Two former chairmen of the Joint Chiefs of Staff, William J. Crowe Jr. and David C. Jones, both suggested waiting for a year or more to see if the situation could be resolved through sanctions rather than rushing to war. William E. Odom, who had been director of Army Intelligence and had served as head of the National Security Agency, testified as well that the sanctions would reduce Iraq's military capacity while possibly providing a peaceful solution to the conflict.[18] Former secretary of defense James Schlesinger testified that "lack of spare parts will force Iraq to begin to cannibalize its military equipment. Military industry, as yet significantly unaffected, will follow the downward path of civilian industry. In short, the burden on both Iraq's economy and her military strength will steadily increase."[19] Former secretary of defense Robert McNamara testified that the United States should be prepared to continue sanctions for twelve to eighteen months, "if that offers an opportunity to achieve our political objective without the loss of American lives. Who can doubt that a year of blockade will be cheaper than a week of war?"[20]

William Webster, the director of the Central Intelligence Agency (CIA), testified that the sanctions had already made a substantial impact on Iraq's economy.

> All sectors of the Iraq economy are feeling the pinch of sanctions and many industries have largely shut down . . . The blockade and embargo have worked more effectively than Saddam probably expected. More than 97 percent of imports and 90 percent of exports have been shut off . . . Iraq's efforts to break sanctions have thus far been largely unsuccessful.

Webster testified as well that the sanctions were likely to degrade Iraq's military capacity over time: "The embargo will eventually hurt Iraqi armor by preventing the replacement . . . and creating shortages of [critical parts]."[21] House Majority Leader Richard Gephardt maintained that economic sanctions should be given "about a year" to work before military action was considered.[22] Senator Sam Nunn, the chair of the Senate Armed Services Committee, had a leading role in Congress in advocating for the continuation of sanctions and withholding authority for U.S. military action.[23]

When Colin Powell, then chairman of the Joint Chiefs of Staff, testified that waiting out the sanctions was "not without cost," Senator Nunn confronted him with a statement from General Norman Schwartzkopf, the commander in the field, who had said, "At present, I think time is on the side of the world coalition. I really don't think there is going to come a time when time is on the side of Iraq, as long as the sanctions are in effect." Rather than urging military action, according to Nunn, Schwartzkopf had said, "If the alternative to dying is sitting out in the sun for another summer, that's not a bad alternative."[24]

The skepticism toward the sudden urgency of going to war and the attractiveness of continuing sanctions was also heard outside Washington as well. A letter to the editor of the *New York Times* argued that "sanctions just may prevent a war with Iraq. The uncertainties and risks that go along with sanctions are certainly no greater than those that go along with war."[25] The Catholic theologian and human rights scholar Robert F. Drinan wrote that sanctions "have not yet been tried and found wanting."[26] Citing the Bible, one person wrote in a letter to the editor, "'We look for peace, but find no good, for a time of healing, but there is terror instead' (Jeremiah 8:15) . . . every day we became more baffled by President Bush's unwillingness to allow sanctions to squeeze the economic life out of the Iraqi regime."[27] Even conservative columnists such as George Will shared this view: "Do not bet on military victory delivered from the air, with no American blood on the ground. A better bet is to give today's sanctions, which have sharp teeth, time to bite."[28] There was also widespread support in other nations for the sanctions. In Canada, for example, a November 1990 poll showed that two in three Canadians believed that sanctions should be "given more time to work" before Canada considered participating in any military undertaking.[29]

During this debate in 1990 there were no criticisms of the sanctions on humanitarian grounds. This was in part because the impact of the sanctions at that juncture was not severe, or at least not particularly visible. Although food prices had gone up in Iraq and industry had started to slow, there were none of the dramatic humanitarian effects that would come about six months later. But the support for sanctions from the liberal and humanitarian perspectives came about primarily because the

Bush administration was clearly moving toward the "military option," and continuing sanctions seemed a far less bloody alternative.

But while theologians, antiwar activists, and academics argued in 1990 for giving sanctions "more time to work," it was also true that these were different sanctions from any that had been seen before. They were comprehensive in every regard. Because these sanctions were imposed by the Security Council, binding every member of the UN, Iraq did not have the option of shifting trade to another bloc. The sanctions were not limited to weapons or strategic goods but affected the entire economy. Because Iraq was so highly dependent on oil exports for its income and on imports for every part of its economy and social services, it was particularly vulnerable to these measures.

The sanctions initially imposed in August 1990 caused considerable disruption to the economy. But if nothing more had occurred, Iraq might well have increased its agriculture and industrial production enough to compensate for much of the loss. Iraq had a highly educated society with a substantial middle class and well-trained professionals in most fields. The government of Iraq also took some measures to respond to the situation. Immediately after the sanctions were imposed the Iraqi government established food rations, which prevented starvation, and also put into place a number of measures to stimulate agricultural production. But the Persian Gulf War in 1991 undermined any possibility that Iraq might have expanded domestic production enough to compensate. The blanket destruction of the coalition's bombing campaign, combined with the sanctions already in place, meant that Iraq was limited to restoring electricity, agriculture, and industry only with cannibalized parts and jerry-rigging, and eventually those measures collapsed as well. Even with the relief work done by UN agencies, as well as the Oil-for-Food Programme, Iraq never recovered from the devastation, and never came close to restoring the standard of living that most Iraqis had had up to 1990.

If the sanctions regime imposed on Iraq was unique in some ways, in others it was quite typical. The history of economic sanctions suggests that they often turn into a stalemate from which none of the parties can extract themselves. On one hand, the sanctions are unlikely to be successful, since the target state rarely changes its actions or policies in response. So the "sender" state is in something of a dilemma: if it lifts the sanctions, it will be a clear admission of failure. But if the sanctions are left in place, even for years, the sender state can say, "we are giving the sanctions time to work." And there are few costs to leaving the sanctions in place. Economic sanctions do not have the same political costs as sending troops. While some companies may suffer losses from the missed trade opportunities, those do not present direct economic costs to the sender state. Consequently, there is often a very real problem of extrication: it is unlikely the sender will ever be able to claim victory, and the sender state will lose face by conceding failure; so there is no motivation to remove them, and little cost to keeping them in place. The sanctions on Iraq were characterized at every moment by this problem of extrication. Saddam Hussein was not the only one who was a prisoner of the sanctions regime. Because of its policy of containment, accompanied by an insistence on regime change, the United States was also in an untenable situation from which it could see no way out.

Even so, in looking back on the U.S. policy in Iraq prior to 2003, a number of U.S. officials feel quite vindicated: the fundamental goal of sanctions, after all, was containment. The inspections did effectively disarm Iraq; the sustained collapse of the Iraqi economy did prevent Iraq from rebuilding its military capacity; and in the end, Iraq had no weapons of mass destruction.

One senior State Department official commented:

> The American government never really understood that the Oil for Food Program was Saddam Hussein's nightmare. Now it's being criticized, but it locked up his treasury completely. It doesn't matter if he imported Mercedes—he couldn't control the money. On the whole, the program worked with integrity to deny Saddam billions of dollars. He was looking for ways to target payoffs on oil, etc. But if you look at the overall operation of the program, he didn't import much. The decrepit condition of Iraq in 2003 was testimony to that . . . The most effective sanctions consisted of the denial of hard currency to the regime.[30]

Madeleine Albright wrote:

> Our policy of pressuring Iraq to disarm while containing its military was apt: each time Saddam had tested us, we had tightened his leash. Allied troops enforced no-fly zones over 40 percent of the country. A multinational Maritime Interception Force was striving to prevent illicit shipments from reaching Iraq through the Persian Gulf. UN weapons inspectors had by then destroyed more weapons

11

of mass destruction capacity than had been eliminated during the Gulf War. The Iraqi armed forces were less well equipped and modern with each passing year . . . I remain convinced that ours was the right approach for Iraq for its place and time.[31]

If in fact the United States had only sought containment, and if the United States had been willing to lift the sanctions, had Iraq complied with the disarmament requirements, the situation might have been less intractable. But the U.S. policy was much muddier than that: it involved an ongoing commitment to regime change, but without the capacity or will to achieve that. At the same time, its goal of regime change put the United States at odds with the rest of the Security Council, and indeed, with the UN Charter, while ensuring that Saddam Hussein had no incentive to comply with disarmament demands. In the end, the U.S. government found itself wishing for regime change while scrambling to shore up the continual erosion of international political support for the sanctions, and at the same time fending off domestic criticism that called for more aggressive measures than containment. How did the United States find itself in this dilemma?

The humanitarian situation in Iraq deteriorated rapidly after the massive bombing campaign of the Persian Gulf War. Iraq's capacity to generate electricity had been crippled, and as a result Iraq's economy and social services—industrial production, agriculture, water treatment, health care, and so on—were all severely compromised. The UN Secretary-General sent an envoy in the summer of 1991, who reported that the basic conditions for sustaining human life were at risk and estimated that the cost for restoring Iraq's infrastructure to its prewar condition would come to over $22 billion.[32] The Secretary-General proposed an initial oil-for-food arrangement, which would have provided $2 billion per year to be used for humanitarian imports. The United States has often claimed that Iraq's rejection of this proposal was proof that Saddam Hussein had no regard for the welfare of his people, and that his refusal to accept the proposal meant that he bore responsibility for the suffering that followed. However, even if Iraq had accepted the proposal, the amount was so inadequate that the humanitarian situation would not have been significantly improved. In any case, Hussein rejected the proposal, gambling that Iraq would be able to manage without it and that the sanctions would have to be lifted soon.

Within Iraq the situation deteriorated rapidly. Although the Iraqis were initially able to restart water treatment and other critical services, the economy as well as state services had largely collapsed. Hyperinflation set in. By August 1991 the inflation rate was 2,000 percent and earnings had fallen to one-tenth of the prewar figures.[33] In September 1994 food rations were cut by one-third.[34] In May and June of 1995 the dinar lost nearly half its value.[35] Between August 1990 and December 1995, food prices increased by 4,000 to 5,000 times; by January 1996 the dinar had fallen to 3,000 to the dollar from a prewar rate of about three dollars to the dinar.[36]

During the same period there were several defections and coup attempts against the regime. There was a coup attempted in July 1992.[37] In 1993 there was a revolt by a part of the al-'Ubayd tribe, on which the regime relied heavily.[38] In December 1993 there was an attempt to assassinate Saddam Hussein in his motorcade.[39] In late 1994 the head of the Iraqi Intelligence Service defected and provided U.S. intelligence services with information about Iraq's weapons programs.[40] In 1995 Hussein learned of another planned coup attempt, this time involving an Iraqi general.[41] In August 1995 Hussein's son-in-law, Hussein Kamel, defected to Jordan.[42]

U.S. officials as well as others expected the imminent collapse of the regime. One former British official described it as "a race against time": there was optimism on the part of the United States and Britain that Hussein would be overthrown. Meanwhile, there was a rapid erosion of support for the sanctions. The urgent hope of the United States and Britain was that Hussein would be removed before the United States and Britain had to give in to international pressure to remove the sanctions.

However, Hussein survived the assassination and coup attempts. The Iraqi National Accord (INA), which included current and former members from the Iraqi military and security forces, was penetrated by Iraqi intelligence. In June 1996 more than 100 INA supporters in the military were arrested or executed.[43] In August 1996 one of the Kurdish factions asked the Iraqi military to assist in capturing the city of Irbil from a rival faction. Iraq used the opportunity to attack the base of the Iraqi National Congress in the north, reportedly executing 200 members of the opposition and arresting as many as 2,000 others.[44]

It was at this juncture that both the United States and Iraq agreed to the Oil-for-Food Programme. For Iraq, while there had been considerable international opposition to the sanctions, it had not been sufficient to get them lifted; and in light of the frequent attacks on the regime from

13

within Iraq, the state needed to take measures to shore up its own legitimacy and respond to the growing internal dissent. For the United States, while Hussein's regime had been repeatedly attacked from within, the attacks had not been successful at removing Hussein from power; and in light of the growing criticism of the impact of sanctions on the Iraqi population the United States needed to make concessions or risk losing the sanctions altogether.

The U.S. policy on Iraq was problematic in part because the U.S. goal of regime change was in conflict with the Security Council's position, and it had the effect of undermining the possibility of Iraqi compliance with Security Council demands. The situation was made even more complicated because the United States' own objectives—regime change and containment—were both fraught with contradictions.

Although from the beginning the United States had hoped for regime change in Iraq, at the same time there was a considerable ambivalence and reluctance to take on the risks of pursuing regime change directly and aggressively.[45] At each juncture—prior to the events of September 2001—where the question was revisited the outcome was not much different. In the end, partly by design and partly by default, the policy that was implemented was containment.

As one insider describes it, the "moderate hawks"

> favored an aggressive form of containment that would require the United States to play an active role in maintaining the diplomatic consensus to keep Saddam tightly contained, the regular use of military force to smack Saddam down whenever he mounted a serious challenge to some element of containment . . . Because both wings of the hawkish factions favored pressing ahead with regime change while maintaining a confrontational approach on containment, for most of the Bush Sr. and Clinton administrations, the two groups were virtually indistinguishable.[46]

Meanwhile,

> the "doves" never apologized for Saddam or argued that he was not a problem; they simply believed that Saddam could be handled in a less confrontational manner that would free up resources for what they considered higher priority issues . . . Somalia, Bosnia, Haiti, Kosovo, etc.[47]

14

There were similar debates within all three administrations—Bush Sr., Clinton, and Bush Jr.—up to 9/11. According to Madeleine Albright, during the Clinton administration,

> no serious consideration was given to actually invading Iraq. The senior President Bush had not invaded when given the chance with hundreds of thousands of troops already in the region during the Gulf War. If President Clinton had proposed doing so in 1998, he would have been accused of being reckless and opposed by friends in the Gulf, our allies, most senior officers in our own military, and leading Republicans.[48]

When George W. Bush took office in January 2001, his top officials were divided on how to address Saddam Hussein. At the State Department, Colin Powell argued for an improved containment policy, while "the hegemons"—Vice President Richard Cheney, Secretary of Defense Donald Rumsfeld, and Deputy Secretary of Defense Paul Wolfowitz—focused on regime change.[49] The administration of George W. Bush was expected to pursue a more aggressive policy, but initially it did not, opting instead for reforming the sanctions regime.[50]

> In truth, every administration chose what it believed was the "least bad" option, and interestingly, before September 11, 2001, every administration ended up with the dovish version of containment even though three of the four (Bush, Sr., second Clinton administration, and Bush, Jr.) all started off wanting to pursue one of the harder-line options.[51]

While the United States chose not to risk its own military to pursue regime change prior to 2003, the U.S. government nevertheless encouraged regime change from within Iraq,[52] and the United States formally declared this policy in 1998.[53] But the Iraqi experience was that the United States was an unreliable ally for efforts along these lines. President Bush had called for the Iraqi people to overthrow the regime in mid-January 1991, prior to the beginning of the Persian Gulf War.[54] On February 15, 1991, during the war, President Bush urged Iraqis to "take matters into their own hands, to force Saddam Hussein, the dictator, to step aside." Similar language was used in the CIA-funded Voice of Free-Iraq: "We are with you, in every heartbeat, in all your feelings, and in every move you make."[55]

Many Iraqis placed great weight in this, believing that the United States would provide support once insurrections took place. Shortly after the war came to a close, at the end of February 1991, there were large-scale uprisings by the Shi'a in the south and by the Kurds in the north. The insurrections took over most of the provinces in Iraq and reached to the suburbs of Baghdad.[56] The United States, however, provided no military support and did nothing as the Iraqi government responded brutally to put down the insurrections. By one account the Bush administration took this posture because it was afraid that the Shi'a would be aligned with Iran, and preferred that Saddam Hussein remain in place rather than see Iran gain a foothold in Iraq.[57] In addition, it seems that the United States wanted a military coup, not a popular insurrection that might break up the country.[58] In the end the Kurds were left with autonomy over the northern region; but the Shi'a were targeted for terribly bloody retribution by the Iraqi government, and never forgot what they saw as a betrayal by the United States after they responded to U.S. urgings to rebel.[59]

Even so, the U.S. government continuously supported opposition groups and encouraged insurrections. In May 1991 Bush authorized covert action "to create the conditions for the removal of Saddam Hussein from power."[60] A few months later the funding for covert action and support for opposition groups was nearly tripled, from $15 million to $40 million.[61] In the early 1990s alone, the United States spent over $100 million to support insurrections and coup attempts.[62] In the late 1990s the U.S. Congress explicitly adopted a policy of seeking the removal of Saddam Hussein from power. In October 1998 Congress overwhelmingly passed the Iraq Liberation Act,[63] giving the president authority to spend up to nearly $100 million in military support to opposition groups as well as broadcasting and other activities. As he signed the law, President Clinton stated that his administration had pursued the objectives of a democratically supported regime and a "normal international life" for Iraq through Security Council resolutions; but "the evidence is overwhelming that such changes will not happen under the current Iraqi leadership." In the meantime, "the United States is providing support to opposition groups from all sectors of the Iraqi community that could lead to a popularly supported government."[64] In January 1999 the position of "Coordinator for the Transition in Iraq" was created within the State Department, and Frank Ricciardone was appointed to the position.[65] In early 1999 Kenneth Pollack was hired to develop a plan to bring about the removal of Saddam Hussein's government.[66] From 1998 to 2002 Congress appropriated a total of $78 million for covert action, support for opposition groups, and other efforts toward regime change.[67]

Although the United States repeatedly called for regime change, it was clear that this was grossly unrealistic. This was the case in part because of the stranglehold by the regime and the certainty of retribution for anyone involved in such an attempt. But it was made even more unlikely because, however frequently the United States repeated its demands or offered funding for insurrection and covert action, anyone who might have engaged in these efforts knew of the United States' own track record and its failure to support an insurrection when it did occur.

But while regime change was unlikely, from the beginning all three U.S. administration officials stated in a variety of contexts that regime change was a prerequisite for lifting sanctions. In early May 1991 deputy national security advisor Robert Gates said: "Saddam is discredited and cannot be redeemed. His leadership will never be accepted by the world community . . . All possible sanctions will be maintained until he is gone . . . Any easing of sanctions will be considered only when there is a new government."[68] According to Secretary of State Madeleine Albright, "The senior president Bush had vowed that sanctions would never be lifted as long as Saddam remained in power."[69] In 1993, Clinton began his term by saying, "There is no difference between my policy and the policy of the [Bush] Administration . . . I have no intention of normalizing relations with [Saddam Hussein]."[70] This policy continued throughout both terms of the Clinton administration. In March 1997 Albright gave a major policy speech on Iraq, in which she said, "We do not agree with the nations who argue that if Iraq complies with its obligations concerning weapons of mass destruction, sanctions should be lifted."[71]

But this policy in turn undermined any likelihood that Iraq would comply with the Security Council's objective, which was disarmament. As Madeleine Albright noted afterward, "the problem with [the U.S. commitment to regime change] was that it appeared to eliminate any incentive for Iraq to comply with Security Council resolutions." According to Albright, the Clinton administration "didn't say it was impossible [that the sanctions could be lifted while Hussein was in power], but we expressed our doubts."[72] In fact, the Clinton administration *did* say this, as did the second Bush administration. The problem was not that this "appeared" to eliminate incentive for compliance; it was that

17

this position in fact undermined any motivation for Saddam Hussein to comply.

The United States frequently blamed Saddam Hussein for the sanctions on the grounds that all he had to do was comply with Security Council resolutions and the sanctions would be lifted. Albright wrote, "Saddam Hussein could have prevented any child from suffering simply by meeting his obligations."[73] But in actuality the U.S. administrations maintained an irrebuttable presumption that Saddam Hussein would never comply. On the occasions when Iraq did so, the United States denounced it as mere manipulation. U.S. administrations maintained that, in any event, compliance was not sufficient to lift sanctions; only regime change was. Given Hussein's commitment to his own political survival, he had nothing to gain by complying with the Security Council resolutions, and given that he could expect the United States to support further coup attempts and insurrections, he evidently had good reason to maintain his military forces and security apparatus.

The divergence between the U.S. position—that regime change was the only acceptable outcome—and the terms of the Security Council resolutions was a source of tension within the Council. This was apparent early on. In 1992, the ambassador from Zimbabwe, one of the elected members of the Council, pointedly said that

> while my delegation will insist that Iraq meet its obligations called for in Council resolutions, it is also important for the Security Council, while undertaking its reviews, to avoid the temptation to shift the goalposts. Where compliance has occurred . . . the Security Council [must] remain continuously focused on the legitimate goals and objectives for which the sanctions regime was imposed.[74]

In the fall of 1994 Russia challenged the U.S. position, saying that the Council "must be ready to take 'Yes' for an answer" regarding whether sanctions could ever be removed. "If Iraq really complies with all the demands in all the resolutions, the current sanctions regime will cease to have any sense."[75]

Because of the U.S. insistence on regime change, the Security Council's position was fundamentally untenable. If Saddam Hussein was supposed to be motivated by self-interest, and wanted sanctions to end, then there was no reason for him to comply with the demands of the Security Council, since sanctions could not be removed without U.S. agreement and the United States repeatedly made clear that it would never remove them while Hussein was in power. There was a similar problem with the notion that Hussein should be moved to comply with UN demands by the terrible plight of his people, given that he was also portrayed as callous and indifferent to the suffering of Iraqis. A former UN consultant noted that discussions about compliance

> went in strange contradictory circles. Saddam was a highly irratio-nal ruler in whose hands weapons of mass destruction would un-failingly spell disaster for his neighbours and for the world. Why then was the only exit option out of sanctions left to this man? How come all this trust was invested into him rationally calculating his stakes and eventually complying? Saddam was a ruthless dictator to be blamed for whatever human hardship sanctions generated or aggravated. Why should concern for the fate of the population guide his decisions and move him to comply?[76]

In the end, the contradictions within the United States' own policy, as well as the disparity between the goals of the United States and those of the UN, did much to create a dilemma from which no one could see a way out. While it was the United States that led the response to Iraq's aggression, it was the U.S. policies thereafter that did much to make the resulting situation so intractable.

2

HOW THE SANCTIONS WORKED

The economic sanctions imposed on Iraq by the UN Security Council were not only the most extreme measures ever imposed in the context of international governance but the most complex as well. They involved a labyrinth of UN agencies as well as the establishment of an entirely new agency within the UN. They required the active participation of dozens of nations in determining policies, as well as thousands of decisions on individual items. There was a maritime interception force, involving dozens of nations and hundreds of ships, as well as two agencies for weapons inspection within the UN, in addition to the International Atomic Energy Association (IAEA). There were over sixty Security Council resolutions regarding Iraq's invasion of Kuwait and the aftermath, of which dozens concerned the establishment and modification of the sanctions regime. Thousands of pages of information were generated in reports by the Secretary-General, by the numerous UN agencies involved, by special envoys, and by investigatory panels.

To understand the role of the United States in all of this, it is important to have some familiarity with the basic chronology and the institutions involved.

The Structure of the Sanctions Regime

On August 2, 1990, Iraq invaded Kuwait. On the same day, the UN Security Council passed Resolution 660, which demanded that Iraq withdraw its forces, and called upon Iraq and Kuwait to negotiate their differences. The resolution was passed 14 to 0, with Yemen abstaining. Four days later the Security Council passed Resolution 661, invoking Chapter VII, the chapter of the UN Charter that authorized the Security Council to act in situations of aggression, breaches of the peace, and threats to peace. In Resolution 661, the Security Council imposed a broad array of the economic measures available to it under Chapter VII of the Charter, requiring that all UN member states prevent the importation of any goods into their territories from Iraq or Kuwait (which was under Iraqi control), and that they prohibit their nationals from shipping goods to Iraqi or Kuwait or transferring funds to either country. Resolution 661 prohibited the sale or supply of any goods to Iraq or Kuwait, "not including supplies intended strictly for medical purposes, and, in humanitarian circumstances, foodstuffs."[1] The resolution was passed with thirteen votes, no votes opposing, and two abstentions by Cuba and Yemen.

With the narrow exceptions of medicine and, conditionally, food, Iraq could import nothing, could export nothing, could receive no funds; and every member state of the UN—virtually every country in the world— was obligated to enforce these restrictions. Any nation subject to these measures would have been severely affected, but Iraq's economy was particularly vulnerable because of its extraordinarily heavy reliance on trade. Oil exports constituted approximately 60 percent of Iraq's gross domestic product (GDP) and 95 percent of its foreign currency earnings.[2] At the same time, Iraq was highly dependent on imports to meet basic needs. Iraq produced only one-third of the food it consumed, relying on imports for the remainder.[3]

The impact of Resolution 661 was immediate and severe. By all estimates, Iraq's GDP declined precipitously. In 1997, economists at the London School of Economics found that real GDP had probably fallen on the order of 50 percent, due to the loss in real production, and then fell by a factor of seven in the price of foreign exchange, due to scarcity.[4] Others estimated that Iraq's GDP had declined by two-thirds.[5] After the Persian Gulf War in 1991, the economy was compromised further. In 1989 Iraq's GDP was $66.2 billion; by 1996 it was $10.8 billion.[6] Per capita annual income went from $3,510 in 1989 to $450 in 1996.[7] Iraqi economists estimated the loss in opportunities for economic growth, comparing actual GDP with estimates of what Iraq's GDP would have been without sanctions. They calculated this loss to be about $265.3 billion for 1990–1995, of which $98.7 billion was in the oil sector and the remaining $166.6 billion was in other sectors.[8]

Despite the imposition of sanctions, by January 1991 Iraq had not yet withdrawn from Kuwait. A coalition of countries led by the United States conducted a massive bombing campaign against Iraq. The coalition air forces flew a total of 118,000 sorties and dropped more than 170,000 bombs, aimed at nearly 800 targets.[9] These included not only military targets but also Iraq's infrastructure and industrial capacity.[10] Although the war of 1991 lasted only forty-two days, the massive bombing campaign "resulted in widespread devastation of all service facilities such as electricity, water, sewerage, telecommunications, radio and television stations, some dams, some large productive enterprises, and it was the direct cause of the collapse of economic activity in Iraq in 1991."[11] The overall cost to Iraq of the destruction from the 1991 Gulf War has been estimated at $190 billion.[12]

In March 1991 UN Secretary-General Javier Perez de Cuellar sent special envoy Martti Ahtisaari to Iraq to assess the humanitarian situation. In July 1991 the Secretary-General sent a second envoy, Sadruddin Aga Khan. They described the situation as one of devastation and imminent humanitarian catastrophe. The water purification plants and distribution systems were badly damaged, reducing access to water by 75 percent; the price of basic foods such as rice and wheat flour had increased by as much as 4,500 percent; and nearly half the telephone lines in the country were damaged beyond repair. Eighty-five to 90 percent of Iraq's national power grid and twenty power stations had been damaged or destroyed in the Gulf War. In December 1990 Iraq had a generating capacity of 9,000 megawatts (MW); by March 1991 this had been reduced to 340 MW.[13]

Ahtisaari stated bluntly that "Most means of modern life support have been destroyed or rendered tenuous."[14] Aga Khan's delegation estimated that the cost of restoring electrical generation would be $12 billion, let alone the costs of restoring water treatment plants, food imports, and agriculture.[15] Aga Khan urged that the Security Council consider permitting Iraq to sell enough oil to have the funds to restore the infrastructure and meet the needs of the population. The result was the first proposal for an oil for food program.

In August 1991 the Security Council passed Resolution 706, which permitted Iraq to export up to $1.6 billion worth of oil in a six-month period to fund the importation of food, medicine, and essential civilian needs. Of the $1.6 billion, 30 percent would be applied to the UN Compensation Fund,[16] and funds would also be subtracted to pay the costs of UN activities in Iraq. Thus Resolution 706 permitted Iraq to spend, at most, approximately $1 billion on the country's urgent humanitarian needs for a six-month period—a one-time arrangement, amounting to about $73 per person. However, as the Secretary-General's envoy noted in his report, Iraq would need more than three times that amount to meet even the most basic needs to sustain human life.[17] Iraq rejected this proposal on the grounds that it constituted an impermissible intrusion on Iraqi sovereignty by intervening in Iraq's economic decisions. The Iraqi government also maintained that such an arrangement provided legitimacy to the sanctions by appearing to meet humanitarian needs, while in fact institutionalizing a condition of extreme deprivation. In addition to its political objections, Iraq consistently argued in negotiations that it would get almost nothing from cooperating with the proposed program because the proceeds would be subject to so many costs and other deductions.[18] The proposal was so patently inadequate that some suggested that the United States and Britain deliberately chose a ceiling that was insufficient to meet Iraqi needs in order to trigger Iraqi defiance, allowing the United States and Britain to then blame Saddam Hussein for the humanitarian situation in Iraq.[19]

While this early proposal for an "oil for food" program was not implemented, Iraq was permitted to buy humanitarian goods through a different route. It was allowed, at least in principle, to use funds it had on hand to buy humanitarian goods, with each purchase approved on a case-by-case basis by the "661 Committee." When the sanctions were imposed, Resolution 661 provided for the creation of a committee of the Security Council to implement the sanctions regime.[20] It came to be known as the "Iraq Sanctions Committee," or more commonly the "661 Committee." It consisted of fifteen members, mirroring the Security Council itself. The committee's initial mandate was quite modest: it was to review the Secretary-General's reports concerning the other provisions of Resolution 661; and to seek information from other states regarding the implementation of Resolution 661's provisions.[21] What actually happened is that the committee came to take on extremely broad responsibilities for the overall implementation of the sanctions regime. The 661 Committee determined what goods Iraq could import as humanitarian exemptions, responded to allegations of smuggling, determined what goods the UN agencies engaged in humanitarian work could bring into Iraq, addressed issues involving the no-fly zones, and took upon itself the task of interpreting Security Council resolutions regarding Iraq.

From 1990 to 1995 much of the 661 Committee's time was occupied with determining the parameters of the humanitarian exemptions and reviewing individual applications for exemptions. For the 661 Committee this mandate was shaped by two competing mandates: it was charged with enforcing the sanctions regime imposed on Iraq, and also with granting exemptions to it. The committee operated by consensus, and when any member of the committee objected to any purchase, the committee's default position was denial. There was no transparency and little consistency on the part of the committee. The large majority of requests were denied without explanation. From 1990 to 1995 this procedure of the 661 Committee was the sole legal means for Iraq to import any goods.

During this period UN agencies maintained a presence in Iraq, providing some amount of humanitarian goods and in some cases monitoring humanitarian supplies, such as chlorine for water purification, to meet the demands of the Security Council. In 1991 and 1992, the UN High Commission for Refugees as well as the UN Disaster Relief Organization provided some humanitarian relief. The United Nations Children's Fund (UNICEF) contributed to water and sanitation and children's health care and the World Food Programme (WFP) contributed some foodstuffs,[22] while other UN agencies played smaller roles. In May 1991 the UN established the Inter-Agency Humanitarian Programme to coordinate the work of the various UN agencies present in Iraq. UNICEF, WFP, and other UN agencies provided services focusing on the vulnerable sectors of the Iraqi population. Funded by the UN, these programs cost nearly $1 billion from 1991 to 1996.[23] In the early 1990s, the UN also established the Department of Humanitarian Affairs (DHA) to coordinate its emergency humanitarian work around the globe.[24] In 1998 it was restructured as part of a UN reorganization and was renamed the Office for the Coordination of Humanitarian Affairs.

Beginning in 1996, the UN's humanitarian agencies were involved in Iraq in two capacities: they continued to run relief programs but also had roles in the Oil-for-Food Programme. In 1996 the Office of the Iraq Programme (OIP) was established within the Secretariat to house both the UN's country programs in Iraq and the Oil-for-Food Programme. Each agency had specific areas of responsibility, in both its own programs and in the context of the Oil-for-Food Programme. UNICEF was the UN agency that had primary responsibility for water and sewage treatment in Iraq and also had programs for primary school education and vaccinations. The World Health Organization (WHO), WFP, and the Food and Agriculture Organization (FAO) operated programs in the areas of health, nutrition, and agriculture. The UN Development Programme (UNDP) had responsibility for infrastructure, particularly electricity. The UN Office for Project Services (UNOPS) conducted de-mining operations. The International Telecommunication Union worked to rehabilitate the telephone system. UN-Habitat was involved in building housing. The United Nations Educational, Scientific and Cultural Organization (UNESCO) had programs to support schools and education. Some areas required the involvement of more than one agency; for example, in the education sector, UNICEF was involved with primary education while UNESCO had responsibilities for secondary and postsecondary education. In addition, under the Oil-for-Food Programme the position of UN Office of the Humanitarian Coordinator for Iraq (UNOHCI) was established to coordinate the work of the agencies. Overall, the UN employed approximately 1,100 international staff in Iraq, as well as 2,000 Iraqi nationals.[25]

Although the UN and some international nongovernmental organizations were providing relief efforts from 1990 to 1995, and Iraq was able to buy some goods with assets on hand, none of these were sufficient to prevent the collapse of Iraq's economy and social systems. By 1995 the situation in Iraq had deteriorated so badly that the ration system could only provide 1,100 calories per person per day,[26] and the conditions were present for imminent, large-scale famine. In April 1995 the Security Council passed Resolution 986, the second "oil for food" program. A year later, in May 1996, the Security Council and Iraq arrived at an agreement regarding the operation of the program, articulated in a Memorandum of Understanding (MOU).

Resolution 986 and the MOU provided that Iraq could sell up to $1 billion worth of oil each ninety days.[27] Thirty percent of the oil proceeds went to the compensation fund for Kuwait, and 4 percent was used to pay all the costs of UN weapons inspectors, as well as the UN's administrative costs for the program.[28] Thus, of the income from these sales, only 66 percent of the proceeds from the oil sales were actually available for humanitarian imports. Of this amount, 53 percent of the proceeds went to the south/central region of Iraq; and 13 percent was earmarked for the Kurdish area in the north. Under the best of circumstances, the program as initially designed would not have gone far toward restoring Iraq's economy. The Oil-for-Food Programme originally allowed imports totaling $130 per person per year. Together with existing imports, which averaged $20 per person per year, total imports came to $150, well below the level of the poorest Arab countries.[29] In February 1998 the amount of oil Iraq was permitted to sell was increased to $5.26 billion each six months,[30] and in December 1999 the Security Council lifted the ceiling on oil sales.[31]

The Oil-for-Food Programme in effect consisted of two separate operations: one for the three northern governorates where the Kurdish population lived, and one for the fifteen central and southern governorates. In the north, the program was administered directly by the UN itself "on behalf of" the government of Iraq. In the south/central governorates, the Iraqi government performed the normal governmental functions, such as food distribution, education, and health care, and UN agencies provided assistance and oversight. The program in the northern governorates had more funding, relative to the population, than the south/central program. Fifty-nine percent of the funds went to the south/central region, with 86.5 percent of the population, while 13 percent went to the north, with 13.5 percent of the population. The program in the north also had far more flexibility; for example, a portion of the funds was available as a "cash component" that could be used to hire and pay local workers, and could be used to buy locally produced goods. By the time the program terminated in 2003, this came to $20 million per month. The program in the north was also given far more authority to rehabilitate or construct infrastructure, such as power plants, than the Iraqi government was allowed in the south/central region. As a result, while the Kurdish population had suffered badly under the Ba'athist regime, under economic sanctions the conditions of life for the Kurds actually improved significantly, in contrast to the rest of Iraq where the standard of living declined precipitously.

Resolution 986 and the MOU provided an elaborate structure of oversight, giving the Iraqi government very little direct control and requiring UN and 661 Committee approval over every aspect of Iraq's economic decisions. The Security Council and an array of UN agencies not only monitored the payments and contracting process. In addition, they monitored the program's implementation in Iraq to determine whether goods were distributed equitably and efficiently, and to gauge the adequacy of the program.

The Oil-for-Food Programme operated in six-month phases. Within each phase, before Iraq was permitted to purchase any goods the Iraqi government was first required to submit a "distribution plan" for the upcoming phase. The distribution plan presented a detailed description of the areas of need in each sector (nutrition, health care, water treatment, and so forth), for each part of the country. On the basis of this overview, the plan then allocated funds from the expected oil proceeds to each sector. The plan then listed every single item to be purchased, how it would be used, and where it would be used: every piece of equipment for electrical production, and the specific power plant where it would go; every chemical or instrument for water treatment, and the specific laboratory or plant where they would be used; every dose of vaccine for poultry and cattle, and every syringe, needle, and scissors for veterinarians; and so forth. OIP then circulated the distribution plan to the UN agencies with expertise in each area: for example, the FAO reviewed the proposals regarding agriculture, UNICEF reviewed the proposals regarding elementary education, UNDP looked at electricity purchases, and WHO looked at purchases for health care and water treatment. Once the plan was reviewed (and sometimes modified), OIP would then approve it.

Iraq could then negotiate contracts with vendors for the approved items. However, once the contract was signed it was subject to a series of additional procedures before it could be approved. Most contracts were circulated to the United Nations Special Commission (UNSCOM) and the International Atomic energy Agency (IAEA); and later the United Nations Monitoring, Verification and Inspection Commission (UNMOVIC), as well as IAEA, to determine if there were any prohibited items, or any goods on the "1051 list," the list of items that had possible military uses, as identified in Resolution 1051. Contracts were also circulated to each member of the 661 Committee for approval, and each member could block the contract, put a hold on it, or ask for further information before approving it. In December 1999 the Security Council passed Resolution 1284, which mandated the 661 Committee to set up "fast-track" procedures that would allow contracts for food and medicine, as well as basic educational and agricultural supplies, to bypass the 661 Committee.[32] This was known as the "green list." The 661 Committee gradually added items to the green list. However, the bulk of humanitarian goods (including nearly everything related to electricity and Iraq's infrastructure) continued to go through the full approval process of OIP, the 661 Committee, and UNMOVIC.

Once the contracts were approved, letters of credit were drawn up and vendors were paid out of a UN-controlled escrow account. Independent inspection agents (Lloyd's Register and later Cotecna) confirmed the arrival of the goods in Iraq. For most goods, UN staff in Iraq monitored the distribution—for example, by conducting thousands of spot checks at food distribution centers—to determine if goods were arriving at their proper destination. Where there were security concerns or the 661 Committee requested additional monitoring, UN staff also tracked individual items from arrival in Iraq to consumption and disposal. Chlorine, for example, was essential to water purification, but could also be used to produce chemical weapons. For this reason UNICEF provided monitors who tracked each canister of chlorine from arrival in Iraq, to transport to its destination, to installation of the canister and disposal of empty canisters.

Because Resolution 986 and the MOU also required that the program be monitored for equity, adequacy, and efficiency,[33] the Secretary-General provided the Security Council with reports each ninety days addressing these criteria in regard to all categories of goods, throughout Iraq. These reports were quite extensive, containing detailed information on every aspect of the program. They provided information on the volume of oil loadings at each oil platform during the three-month period, and on each of the escrow accounts held in each of several banks, letters of credit, and encumbered funds. The Secretary-General reported on the status of every category of contracts outstanding, for every phase of the program. The reports provided information on the number of holds placed on humanitarian import contracts, the monitoring mechanisms, and the contracts approved under the green list process. The reports provided information about the contracts and delivery of goods in every sector: food, health care, water and sanitation, agriculture, electricity, education, telecommunications, housing, and de-mining. The reports provided data from the UN monitoring teams concerning the final delivery and consumption of goods by the population. They also discussed issues and problems and made recommendations for streamlining or adjusting priorities.

The process of oil sales was likewise subject to an elaborate structure of oversight and monitoring. The 661 Committee was required to approve all sales of Iraqi oil, including the price and the transportation route,[34] and to ensure that oil was sold at fair market value. The MOU established a group of "oil overseers," experts from the petroleum industry, appointed by the Secretary-General with the approval of the 661 Committee, to assist the 661 Committee.[35] In addition, there were inspection agents (from Saybolt, a Dutch company) at the loading facilities who monitored the quantity and quality of the oil shipped.[36] Each month the 661 Committee set the price of Iraqi oil for the upcoming month, based upon the recommendations of the oil overseers. This procedure was followed until the introduction of "retroactive oil pricing" in 2001, in which the committee withheld its approval of the price until after the sale had taken place, and then retroactively assigned what it deemed to be the fair market value for the prior month.

Once the oil sale was complete the proceeds were deposited into the escrow account controlled by the UN. Under the terms of the program, Iraq handled none of the funds at any point. The proceeds of all oil sales were deposited in this account and all payments to vendors were made from this account.

A substantial portion of the funds from the Oil-for-Food Programme (25 to 30 percent) went into the UN Compensation Commission (UNCC), which was charged with awarding damages to those who had suffered losses as a result of Iraq's invasion of Kuwait, as envisioned by Resolution 687. Ultimately, the UNCC paid close to $20 billion in claims from Oil for Food funds.[37]

The first year of the Oil-for-Food Programme's operation mostly involved the importation of food and medicine. The imports were largely uncontroversial, and few members of the Security Council blocked or delayed purchases. However, it quickly became clear that importing food and medicine was not enough. Without adequate water and sewage treatment, for example, there would be widespread water-borne diseases and increases in infant and child mortality, regardless of whether Iraq was allowed to import medicine. Without trucks, food could not be distributed; without electricity, it was not possible to maintain the cold chain for medicines. After the first year, Iraq was permitted to submit distribution plans that included a broader range of goods. However, this did not mean that the actual contracts to buy them would be approved, since any member of the 661 Committee could still block or delay any import or export contract. U.S. "holds" on import contracts grew enormously over the course of the program: from about $150 million in 1998, to $5 billion of goods on hold in July 2002. Britain occasionally blocked contracts. No other country blocked any goods under the Oil-for-Food Programme.

As the media and members of the Security Council began to report publicly on the humanitarian impact of the holds in the winter of 2001, the United States and Britain pressed for a new system, which they called "smart sanctions." They described their proposal as a tool for targeting the sanctions more effectively on the goods that presented security concerns, while allowing Iraq to import civilian humanitarian goods more freely. However, under this proposal the list of goods that were still subject to the committee's review was very broad, and included most goods that were related to the infrastructure. Russia refused to agree. In the fall there was another attempt to reform the approval process, and the Security

Council passed Resolution 1382. It provided that the Council would adopt a "Goods Review List" (GRL) that would establish categories of goods and modified procedures. In May 2002, the Council passed Resolution 1409, which actually implemented the GRL and the new procedures. Under the old procedures everything outside the very limited green lists had been sent to the entire committee for review (as well as UNMOVIC, IAEA, and OIP). Under the new procedures future contracts (as well as contracts then on hold) would be reviewed by UNMOVIC and IAEA to determine if they were on the GRL. Only if these weapons agencies found a security concern would the contract be sent on to the 661 Committee for review. The result was that UNMOVIC forwarded far fewer contracts to the committee than the committee had received in the past. In addition, UNMOVIC immediately removed most of the holds that were then in place.

Other UN measures included the disarmament regime and military enforcement of the economic sanctions. In late August 1990 the Security Council passed Resolution 665, which invited member states with naval forces in the area to inspect cargoes to prevent violations of the embargo on imports and exports. What emerged was a loose coalition of ships, primarily those of the U.S. Fifth Fleet, which came to be known as the Multinational Interception Force.

In November 1990 the Security Council passed Resolution 678. It invoked Chapter VII, the section of the UN Charter authorizing the use of force. Resolution 678 authorized member states to use "all necessary means" to enforce Resolution 660 if Iraq did not withdraw from Kuwait by January 15, 1991. Iraq did not withdraw from Kuwait, and in mid-January a group of nations led by the United States began the bombing campaign against Iraq. The war continued for six weeks. In early March the Iraqi government formally accepted the terms of the cease-fire. In April 1991 the Security Council passed Resolution 687, which contained a number of provisions. It required Iraq to respect Kuwait's boundaries and to renounce the use of chemical and biological weapons. Under Resolution 687, Iraq agreed to a disarmament regime that would involve the destruction of chemical and biological weapons and materials for their production, as well as the destruction of all conventional missiles with a range of more than 150 kilometers. Nuclear materials were to be turned over to IAEA. In addition, Resolution 687 established UNSCOM, the agency that would conduct the inspections.

The disarmament process began immediately after the war's end. In April and May 1991 Iraq provided its initial declaration of all materials that could be used in the production of chemical, biological, and nuclear weapons. In June 1991 UNSCOM sent its first chemical weapons inspection team, and in August sent a biological weapons inspection team.[38] Also in the summer of 1991, IAEA began sending inspectors as well.

From 1991 to 1998, UNSCOM conducted inspections in Iraq, although UNSCOM complained frequently that the Iraqi government was not providing the cooperation required by the Security Council resolutions. In mid-December 1998, UNSCOM withdrew its personnel from Iraq. The United States and Britain conducted an intensive bombing campaign for several days. The following month the United States altered the rules of engagement for planes flying over Iraq, conducting bombing strikes in a much broader range of circumstances. However, Iraq did not allow UNSCOM inspectors to return to the country. In December 1999 the Security Council passed Resolution 1284, which replaced UNSCOM with UNMOVIC (and maintained the role of IAEA). Iraq did not allow UNMOVIC inspectors into the country until fall of 2002, when it gave UNMOVIC unlimited access. Between November 2002 and the end of February 2003 UNMOVIC conducted 550 inspections at 350 different sites.[39]

UNSCOM, UNMOVIC, and IAEA also had roles in monitoring imports into Iraq. Security Council Resolution 715, passed in October 1991, envisioned a system for the long-term monitoring of goods imported into Iraq. In March 1996 the Security Council passed Resolution 1051, which laid out the structure for the import/export mechanism. It required Iraq to provide notification of any imports on a list of goods that were necessary for the civilian economy or the infrastructure, but also had possible military uses (the "1051 list"). While UNSCOM inspectors were in Iraq, Iraq was permitted to import some items on the 1051 list, which UNSCOM then monitored. After UNSCOM withdrew its personnel, the United States routinely blocked any contracts containing 1051 items.

In April 1991, in the face of a refugee crisis in Iraq and the suppression of a civil uprising, the Security Council passed Resolution 688. It demanded that Iraq give access to humanitarian agencies, and "appeal[ed] to all Member States and to all humanitarian organizations to contribute to these humanitarian relief efforts." The United States and Britain took the position that this language authorized the creation and enforcement of "no-fly zones," banning all flights by Iraqi aircraft, although the resolution contained no language concerning such measures. The United States and Britain (and France, until 1996) established and patrolled the no-fly zone in

31

northern Iraq at the 33rd parallel. In August 1992, the United States, Britain, and France established the southern no-fly zone at the 32nd parallel (France withdrew in 1998).

In general, the United States exercised extraordinary influence over every aspect of the measures imposed by the Security Council, although Britain had a key supporting role. While Britain often joined or supported the United States, the United States clearly held the leadership position. The initial resolutions were drafted by the United States, and it lobbied aggressively for their passage, offering loans, investment, or diplomatic favors to those willing to vote for the measures; and canceling International Monetary Fund loans and threatening retaliation against those reluctant to support the resolutions. In the Persian Gulf War of 1991, the forces were predominantly American. Of the 2,400 coalition aircraft involved in the Persian Gulf War, 1,800 were from the United States.[40] The Multinational Interception Force for its entire history was under the command of U.S. naval officers,[41] while the deputy commanders were British. Although approximately two dozen countries contributed or participated, the United States contributed the overwhelming majority of naval vessels.

The United States and Britain (initially joined by France) were alone in insisting that Resolution 688 authorized the creation of no-fly zones. By 1998 France had ended its participation, and only the United States and Britain continued to operate overflights and bombing sorties.[42] In shaping the sanctions regime, the overwhelming majority of holds on humanitarian imports were imposed by the United States unilaterally; Britain was usually responsible for 5 percent of the holds and the remainder were imposed by the United States. The retroactive pricing policy was a U.S.-British initiative that was imposed with no support from other members of the Security Council, and over the vociferous objections of many.

The Humanitarian Situation

Prior to the Persian Gulf War, the Iraqi government had invested heavily in social and economic development, both before and during the Iran-Iraq war. Prior to the Gulf War, Iraq had made impressive strides in health, education, and development of the infrastructure. At least 80 percent of the population had access to safe water.[43] In 1980 the Iraqi government initiated a program to reduce infant and child mortality rates by more than half by 1990. The result was a rapid and steady decline in childhood mortality.[44] Prior to the Gulf War there was good vaccination coverage; the majority of women received some assistance from trained health professionals during delivery; the majority of the adult population was literate and there was nearly universal access to primary school education; and the vast majority of households had access to safe water and electricity.[45]

Prior to the Gulf War, Iraq "had one of the highest per-capita food-availability ratings in the region, due to its relative prosperity and capacity to import large quantities of food."[46] Iraq imported 70 percent of cereals, legumes, oils, and sugar prior to 1991.[47] A 1988 survey in Baghdad conducted by the Food and Agriculture Organization noted that undernourishment was no longer a public health problem; in fact, 7 percent of Iraqi children were obese.[48]

In the late 1970s, Iraq had initiated a highly effective campaign to eradicate illiteracy, focusing on women, for which it won an award from UNESCO.[49] At the time sanctions were imposed, female literacy was 85 percent.[50] At the beginning of the 1990s, 93 percent of primary school-age children attended school.[51] Prior to the embargo, 93 percent of the population had access to health care.[52] The majority of Iraqi physicians were trained in Europe or the United States, and one-quarter were board certified.[53]

However, the Iraqi economy was particularly vulnerable to the kind of disruption that comprehensive sanctions brought about, since it was highly dependent on income from oil exports and on foreign imports for food and other basic goods. By 1991, GDP had dropped by about three-quarters of its 1990 value to approximately that of the 1940s.[54] Iraq's GDP in 1960 was $8.7 billion; in 1979, it was $54 billion; in 1993 it had dropped to $10 billion. The annual value of imports in 1980 was $11.5 billion; in 1996 it was $0.492 billion. The annual value of exports in 1980 was $28.3 billion; in 1996 it was $0.502 billion.[55] The extreme and relentless economic collapse, as one commentator noted, brought about "the nullification of nearly half a century of growth and improvement in the living standards."[56] By 1991, 18 percent of children under five years of age were malnourished; by 1996 that figure had increased to 31 percent; and by 1997, one million children under five were malnourished.[57] As of 1998, 70 percent of Iraqi women were anemic.[58]

In response to the situation, the government implemented various measures, but they could not come close to reconstructing the economy or restoring adequate public services. In April 1991 the government initiated a three-month campaign to repair roads, bridges, telecommunications, electricity, and water facilities.[59] Although these emergency repairs were accomplished quickly, they could not restore the infrastructure to a sustainable and adequate level of operation.

> Unexpected success was achieved in the short run using cannibalised parts, but cumulatively these "solutions," however ingenious, caused a further deterioration in services after a couple of years. As an aid agency official put it: "If two facilities are damaged, one has been rebuilt using parts from each. This means that repaired installations are forced to run well over capacity, with no fallback facilities at all."[60]

The destruction from the 1991 bombing campaign of electric generating plants, water purification, and sewage treatment facilities resulted in cholera and typhoid epidemics.[61] In 1990 the incidence of typhoid was 11.3 per 100,000 people; by 1994 it was more than 142 per 100,000. In 1989 there were zero cases of cholera per 100,000 people; by 1994 there were 1,344 per 100,000.[62]

In March 1991, Martti Ahtisaari, Under-Secretary-General for Administration and Management, visited Iraq with a UN delegation of personnel from the major humanitarian agencies, including UNICEF, WHO, UNDP, FAO, and UNHCR. In his report, Ahtisaari observed that "the recent conflict has wrought near-apocalyptic results upon the economic mechanized society . . . Iraq has, for some time to come, been relegated to a pre-industrial age, but with all the disabilities of post-industrial dependency on an intensive use of energy and technology."[63] Ahtisaari described in some detail the extensive breakdown in infrastructure, including water purification and sewage treatment, agricultural production and food supplies and distribution, the destruction of the telephone system and all modern means of communication, and the large number of refugees whose homes were destroyed in the air war. He identified the particular urgency of energy needs. Without the production of electricity, he noted,

> food that is imported cannot be preserved and distributed; water cannot be purified; sewage cannot be pumped away and cleansed; crops cannot be irrigated; medicaments cannot be conveyed where they are required; needs cannot even be effectively assessed. It is

unmistakable that the Iraqi people may soon face a further imminent catastrophe, which could include epidemic and famine, if massive life-supporting needs are not rapidly met.[64]

A few months later, a second UN mission was sent to Iraq to assess
the humanitarian situation, led by Sadruddin Aga Khan from the office
of the Secretary-General. Aga Khan noted that the Iraqi government had
already established a food rationing system,[65] and made major efforts to
restore the infrastructure to the extent possible.[66] However, there was
little more that could be done with the existing resources. The reserves of
food were nearly exhausted.[67] Electrical generation capacity was operating at less than half of prewar capacity, and even that was unlikely to be
sustained, since it relied on makeshift repairs, cannibalized parts, and continuous operation without any maintenance. Aga Khan recommended a
set of measures that would provide minimum life support: 20 percent of
the prewar level of clean drinking water, food rations at the WFP minimum level provided to disaster-stricken populations, one-half the electrical power of prewar capacity, and so on.[68] He estimated the cost of these
services, well below their prewar levels, to be $6.8 billion for one year.[69]
However, the UN's appeal for humanitarian assistance for the region had
only brought in $210 million, most of which was already committed to
assisting refugees. The funding dilemma was one of the first indicators of
the tension between the UN's humanitarian missions and the enforcement of sanctions: as Aga Khan noted in the 1991 report, Iraq was now
competing for aid with "a continually lengthening list of other emergency
situations around the world with very compelling needs."[70]

The comprehensive nature of the embargo resulted in complex problems, in which one emergency situation triggered others, and there were
no means to intervene in a way that could stop the chain of events. In
response to the food shortages, for example, Iraq increased rice production. However, the conditions for the production of rice resulted in water
stagnation; this in turn generated mosquitoes and malaria; but there was
neither insecticide available to control the mosquitoes nor drugs available for treatment of the malaria.[71] There were complex ongoing crises in
Iraq throughout the entire sanctions period.

In Aga Khan's 1991 report, he notes that in Basrah, only one-quarter
of the sewage pumping stations were operating; and city authorities had
to choose whether to use the pumps to satisfy drinking water need, or to
limit the flow of water until repairs could be made. By 1993 the situation

had worsened. The emergency repairs were no longer adequate, and critical public utilities were barely functioning. A UNICEF report in April 1993 found that water production was less than 50 percent of the prewar level due to the loss of electricity and infrastructure damage. Industrial unemployment was estimated at 70 percent.[72] The loss of electricity "meant the destruction of all refrigerated medicines and laboratory reagents. Most local drug production, estimated at 25 percent of total consumption, ceased before the war due to a lack of imported raw materials." Much of the medical equipment no longer functioned, due to the lack of maintenance and spare parts, and to the fluctuations in electricity supply.[73] The UNICEF report noted that "damage to the water infrastructure is so vast, and the parts are so expensive to procure, that it will take years before the water supply network is rehabilitated to pre-war levels.[74] In 1993 an FAO report found that large numbers of Iraqis had food intakes lower than those of the populations in drought-stricken Africa.[75] The FAO found that the availability of food throughout the country had deteriorated considerably. There were numerous indicators that famine was imminent: extremely high food prices, collapse of private incomes, depletion of personal assets, and rapidly increasing numbers of the destitute. There was an "unprecedented imbalance between income and the price of basic commodities."[76]

In 1995 the crisis continued. Major surgeries were at only 30 percent of the presanctions level, and pharmacies and hospitals had shortages of critical medicines.[77] FAO noted that there was "a strong possibility of an outright collapse in the food and agriculture economy which would cripple the goods rationing system and lead to widespread famine and hunger."[78]

Although the sanctions regime had allowed Iraq to purchase medicines since the beginning, medicines alone were not sufficient to address the public health needs because hospitals and clinics required considerably more than that in order to function. As of April 1998, UNICEF reported that based on its survey, one-third of all hospital beds were closed; more than half of all diagnostic and therapeutic equipment was not working; all hospitals visited lacked proper illumination, hygiene, water supplies, or waste disposal; postoperative care and pain management in some hospitals was limited to aspirin; and rural hospitals were unable to serve their populations because of a lack of ambulances.[79]

Even after the Oil-for-Food Programme began operating, the situation improved only incrementally. In 1998 UNICEF was reporting the same set of problems: water treatment plants lacked spare parts, equipment, treatment chemicals, proper maintenance, and adequate qualified staff; electricity was critical and the extended power cuts undermined the capacity of the water treatment plants to operate effectively. Imported chlorine was highly limited because of embargo restrictions but local supplies of chlorine and aluminum sulphate were minimal. Manufacturing plants for chlorine were unable to produce even one-tenth of the amounts required because of frequent breakdowns; and locally produced aluminum sulphate was so impure as to ruin the water treatment equipment.[80] Because treatment chemicals were unavailable, while demand for drinking water remained high, plants often simply pumped untreated water. Thus the population often had no choice but to obtain water directly from contaminated rivers, resulting in turn in the massive increases in water-borne diseases such as typhoid and cholera.[81]

The collapse of all of these systems—water treatment, electricity, health care, transportation, agriculture—was reflected in the "excess mortality rate" of children under the age of five; that is, the number of young children who died during sanctions who would not have died without them. Although the data available from Iraq have not always been reliable, and this figure has been the subject of much debate, the majority of the studies over the course of the sanctions regime strongly suggest that, for the period from 1990 to 2003, that figure is at least 500,000.[82] Sustained increases of child mortality in the twentieth century were extremely rare, and the kind of increases of child mortality that were seen in Iraq are almost unknown in the public health literature. Epidemiologist Richard Garfield has maintained that Iraq is the only instance of a sustained, large increase in mortality in a stable population of more than 2 million in the last 200 years.[83]

The social impact was no less severe. Two-thirds of the conscripts in Iraq's enormous army were demobilized, with limited education and with no jobs, since Iraqi industry was idled by lack of inputs, equipment, and electricity. As hyperinflation set in, the salaries from both the remaining state sector jobs and private sector jobs were able to buy very little, outside of the ration system. The increasing desperation was particularly visible as families sold off their possessions—furniture, electrical goods, clothing, even parts of their houses, such as doors, windows, and cement blocks.[84] Among professionals with family abroad, and enough assets to pay the necessary exit fees and bribes, there was a mass exodus. Following the pattern common in economic sanctions, small sectors of the population did very well. For those with considerable wealth, or access to resources via smuggling or relatives living abroad, the situation provided opportunities to acquire anything imaginable at fire-sale prices, or to make huge profits from black-market sales. A 1995 FAO report estimated that 7–9 percent of the population was doing very well as a result of domestic trade, while 70 percent of the population was in a precarious condition. Although the middle class experienced the most extreme decline in living standards, the urban poor suffered the worst hardship in terms of their ability to feed their families, loss of education, and incidence of childhood illness and mortality.[85]

As the value of salaries eroded, teachers left the profession or took on multiple jobs. Between 1990 and 1994, it was reported that some 12,000 teachers left their jobs. There were chronic shortages of paper, books, and school supplies. Primary school attendance had been quite high in Iraq, even in rural areas, but that declined as family income deteriorated due to unemployment and inflation and the cost of sending children to school increased, since students were now required to pay for their own paper, pencils, and school supplies. At the same time there was a significant increase in the number of children working as vendors on the street.[86] There was also a substantial increase in crime, including thefts, prostitution, and violent crimes. This was due in part to the flood of soldiers demobilized after the Gulf War; in 1988, 21 percent of young men were in the armed forces, many of whom were released after 1990.[87] But they rejoined domestic society with few skills other than fighting, having had little contact with their families, and with few prospects for employment.[88]

By the mid-1990s, Iraq's economic collapse had a broad impact on domestic society: as professionals fled the country, access to education was severely degraded, and unemployment and impoverishment brought about not only malnourishment and disease but crime and a deterioration in the social fabric. One official from WFP noted, "If help does not come soon, the survivors will be the sanctions-breakers, the black marketeers, and the thieves."[89]

3

THE INFLUENCE OF THE UNITED STATES

In many regards the structure of the sanctions regime tells us less about Iraq, its policies, and its decisions than it does about the policies and decisions of the United States and its capacity to project influence within an institution of international governance in the post–Cold War world, at a juncture when no member of the Security Council could provide a counterweight. The basic conflicts within the sanctions regime, the bureaucratic and political problems, the legal issues, and the humanitarian problems were all resolved—or went unresolved—in this context.

The United States exercised singular influence over every aspect of the structure and extent of the sanctions. Using a variety of means, the United States determined the outcome of many of the most basic issues, and did so in the face of vehement, widespread opposition within the Council, as well as from many sectors of the UN, and in the face of broad, intense public criticism. The United States, often joined by Britain, had enormous weight in determining the parameters of the economic restrictions; in determining the outcome of the conflict between security and humanitarian interests; in determining the length of the sanctions; in first drafting then interpreting critical Security Council resolutions; in determining the applicability of international law; in influencing the votes of other members; in shaping the procedures of the 661 Committee; in determining the criteria for granting humanitarian exemptions; in determining Iraq's output of oil—including the condition of the oil industry, the pricing mechanisms, the availability of spare parts—and consequently the amount of funds available for humanitarian goods; in limiting the 661 Committee's access to information presented by UN staff and diplomats; in unilateral decisions to override the findings of United Nations Monitoring, Verification and Inspection Commission (UNMOVIC); in establishing and enforcing "no-fly zones" in opposition to other members of the Council;

and in preventing testimony before panels charged with reforming the sanctions regime.

The United States used direct measures, such as explicit vetoes, as well as indirect means, such as insisting on ambiguous or subjective standards that compromised the approval process without the political cost of formal vetoes. Both sorts of practices were in turn insulated from accountability by other measures put in place by the United States and its allies, which prevented visibility or oversight by any entity outside the Security Council, and to some extent even by the Security Council and its members.

The Initial Imposition of Sanctions

The structure of the sanctions regime imposed on Iraq cannot be separated from the structure of the Security Council as a political body. This structure makes it possible for the Council to adopt measures that may be inconsistent with international law, and at the same time makes it possible for those measures to evade both judicial review and political restraint by the broader international community.

Within the Security Council, there are five permanent members (the "P5") who were the leading nations among the Allies in World War II: the United States, Britain, France, Russia,[1] and China. Each of the permanent members holds veto power over any Security Council measure. There are ten elected members representing every region in the world. The elected members serve for two years each and do not hold veto power.

There is a basic tension regarding the counter-majoritarian nature of the decision making. While Security Council actions in accordance with the Charter's procedures may be legal, the structure of decision making is such that the Security Council may well authorize actions that do not at all reflect the will of the broader international community. The five permanent members disproportionately represent wealthy Western nations, and include no nations that are small and poor. In addition to the power wielded by the P5 via the vehicle of the veto, there is a second feature that gives the P5 greater influence within the Council than the elected members: institutional memory. Whereas the P5 can maintain their own sets of records going back to prior years and have diplomatic staff with extensive experience on the Council, a country that sits on the Council for two years has neither of those.

On the face of it, the Security Council operates in a highly politicized way, with neither the neutrality and independence of a judicial body such as the International Court of Justice (ICJ) nor the features of broad representation, such as the General Assembly. While the General Assembly may discuss or make recommendations concerning peace and security,[2] the UN Charter authorizes the Security Council to determine whether there is a threat to the peace, a breach of the peace, or an act of aggression, and to decide what to do in response.[3] The Charter then obliges every member nation of the UN to carry out the decision of the Council.[4] If there is a question about whether the Security Council has acted illegally under the Charter or in violation of international law, it is unclear who would judge such a situation. While the Council itself can seek an advisory opinion from the ICJ about the legality of the Council's rulings, it has rarely been the case that the Council voted for a particular policy and then voted to question the legality of its decision.[5] The General Assembly could seek such an advisory opinion, but that would require a majority vote.[6]

Because of the structure of the Security Council, the basic conflicts within the sanctions regime—the bureaucratic problems, the legal issues, and the humanitarian problems—were all highly politicized. Other than the debates that took place within the Council itself, there was little accountability and even less transparency. Almost all Security Council meetings are closed, as were the meetings of the sanctions committees, and minutes of the 661 Committee's proceedings were restricted. Consequently, during the period of the Iraq sanctions there was almost no opportunity for public scrutiny of the Council's internal proceedings, or even for the provision of basic information to the UN member states who did not sit on the Council. The sanctions regime was shaped as well by the absence of any Council members who were in a position to challenge the United States. Once the Soviet Union was dissolved it was possible for the United States to forward its agenda within the Security Council much more aggressively, with U.S. goals now carrying the force and legitimacy of international governance.

Although Iraq had clearly violated international law when it invaded Kuwait, it was not at all obvious that Iraq's actions against Kuwait in 1990 would ordinarily have brought a response from the Security Council. Prior to 1990, the Security Council had rarely invoked Chapter VII measures, even in cases of violations of sovereignty. The Security Council did not use Chapter VII measures to intervene, for example, in 1956, when the Soviet Union invaded Hungary; in 1957, when France and England invaded Egypt to protect their interests in the Suez Canal; in the crisis in Congo during the early 1960s; in Indonesia's occupation of East Timor, which began in 1975; in the Falklands War in 1982; and in the U.S. invasion of Granada in 1983. Nor had the Security Council adopted Chapter VII measures in the face of genocidal acts against the Aché Indians in Paraguay, the Bengalis in East Pakistan, the Bangsa Moro in the Philippines, or the Ibos in Nigeria.[7] Although Iraq's human rights record was cited as part of the justification for the sanctions regime, there was no resolution of disapproval or denunciation by the Security Council at the time that the Iraqi government used chemical weapons against Kurds in northern Iraq in the late 1980s or against Iranian soldiers in the Iran-Iraq War. Indeed, the United States had opposed any Security Council statements even castigating Iraq on that occasion.[8] Thus the extreme response of comprehensive sanctions followed by massive military action was an abrupt departure from Security Council practice.

Although these measures received the votes of nearly every member of the Council, U.S. officials drafted many of the major resolutions establishing the sanctions on Iraq.[9] During the Gulf War itself, as well as in the military operation Provide Comfort in northern Iraq and in all subsequent military strikes in Iraq, it was the United States that provided the military command, not the UN.[10] In regard to the initial resolutions mapping out the comprehensive measures, the United States influenced the vote through political pressure and economic rewards. The original resolution imposing the sanctions, Resolution 661, had broad support within the Council, but only after the United States had offered incentives to several members. Colombia, Ethiopia, and Zaire were offered new economic aid, and Colombia was offered diplomatic rehabilitation and an economic development package. Arab countries not on the Security Council were offered attractive packages of military and economic aid for their support. According to one researcher, the United States provided $7 billion in debt relief to Egypt and used its leverage with the International Monetary Fund and the World Bank such that those institutions made loans to Jordan, Turkey, and Egypt on unusually favorable terms.[11] The United States made elaborate deals as well with China and the Soviet Union.[12]

The U.S. offer to Yemen was said to involve a promise to support the appointment of a Palestinian ombudsman in the Israeli-occupied territories.[13] When Yemen ultimately voted against the resolution (one of two negative votes cast, along with that of Cuba), a U.S. diplomat informed Yemen's ambassador, Abdallah Saleh al-Ashtal, that "that will be the most expensive 'no' vote you ever cast." Three days later the United States cancelled its $70 million aid program to Yemen, which is one of the poorest countries in the region.[14]

The "Reverse Veto"

But the support for sanctions within the Security Council, as well as in the broader international community, deteriorated considerably over the course of the sanctions regime. By the mid-1990s, the humanitarian situation in Iraq had worsened, and as Iraq haggled with the United Nations Special Commission (UNSCOM) over inspections, the end of the sanctions regime seemed to be nowhere in sight. The very limited range of humanitarian goods that Iraq was permitted to import legally provided little help; the inability to legally export oil prevented Iraq from importing even permitted goods in quantities sufficient to meet humanitarian needs; and Iraq's illicit trade was not sufficient to have much impact on the economy. The United States disputed claims of massive increases in child mortality and civilian suffering, and the United States and Britain took the position that Iraq was flatly responsible for whatever suffering there was, on the grounds that if Iraq simply cooperated fully with the UNSCOM inspectors the sanctions would have been lifted. But by the mid-1990s, other members of the Council were far less sanguine and began insisting that, regardless of who was responsible for the humanitarian impact, the Council should institute reforms in the sanctions regime that would lessen the humanitarian cost.

In the latter part of the 1990s, several countries began to ignore the no-fly zones and sent in both passenger flights and flights with humanitarian goods. Trade between Iraq and its neighbors continued, in defiance of the sanctions resolutions. Several members of the Council proposed measures, such as Resolution 1284, to make the sanctions less restrictive, to impose a time limit, or to remove them altogether. "Sanctions fatigue" was even more visible in UN humanitarian agencies such as UNICEF, the General Assembly's Economic and Social Council, and the Secretariat, which was increasingly burdened by the administration of the sanctions regime.

Despite the deteriorating support for the sanctions within the Security Council, and the UN in general, the sanctions were at the most fundamental level kept in place through the "reverse veto" of the United States.[15] The initial imposition of sanctions had required the support of nine of the fifteen members of the Council and the support or abstentions of all five permanent members. But because the sanctions were open-ended in duration, a new resolution would be required to lift the sanctions and such a resolution could be vetoed by any single member of the P5. Thus the sanctions on Iraq could not be removed, no matter how much opposition there was in the Council, as long as the United States (or any other permanent member) wished them to remain in place. Because of the "reverse veto," the sanctions would simply continue as long as the United States chose, even if the sanctions had ceased to reflect the will of every other member of the Council, much less the other sectors of the UN or the broader international community. While the Security Council itself is a counter-majoritarian institution, the reverse veto is even more so: it allows a single permanent member to force the continuation of a policy, even after it is clear that the majority, including other permanent members, oppose it.

The reverse veto was problematic not only because it meant that the Council's decisions could reflect the will of a single Council member. In the case of the Iraq sanctions, this was problematic in particular because the U.S. conditions for ending the sanctions differed significantly from those established by the Security Council, and arguably were not even permissible under the Charter. The United States consistently maintained that the sanctions would be in place as long as Saddam Hussein's government was in power. Indeed, it was common to hear U.S. officials describing the future of the UN sanctions on Iraq very much as a U.S. policy decision: lifting sanctions "will probably be discussed at some time, but the US hasn't agreed to anything"; and "We do not agree with the nations who argue that if Iraq complies with its obligations concerning weapons of mass destruction, sanctions should be lifted."[16] In addition, the United States funded and supported Iraqi opposition groups beginning immediately after the Persian Gulf War. The Central Intelligence Agency engaged in covert action to overthrow Hussein and provided funds to support military attacks from the northern region and to finance and train Iraqi opposition. The United States also specified the requirements for a replacement government and its foreign policies. During the Clinton administration, Secretary of State Madeline Albright held that if the new Iraqi government were to cooperate with arms inspections and comply with the UN mandates, the United States would support Iraq's "reintegration," but only if it found Iraq to be "independent, unified and free from external influence, for example, from Iran."[17]

None of those measures—demanding the removal of the Iraqi leadership, conducting a campaign of covert action to achieve that goal, financing and training opposition groups, or setting conditions for what would constitute an acceptable replacement for Saddam Hussein—were measures that were authorized by the Security Council. The Security Council resolutions only required Iraq to withdraw from Kuwait, implement partial disarmament, and provide information and access to UN arms inspectors. Under the terms of these resolutions, the sanctions regime on Iraq would no longer be warranted if Iraq were to comply fully with these requirements, regardless of who headed the Iraqi government. Indeed, the Security Council resolutions repeatedly reiterated the Council's commitment, and the obligation of all member states of the UN, to respect Iraq's sovereignty.[18] Yet the reverse veto meant that the Council in effect (if involuntarily) came to adopt these goals as well, since in practice the Security Council sanctions would not be lifted until the U.S. goals were met.

The U.S. position was problematic because its own conditions for lifting the sanctions were not those authorized by the Security Council, but also because it appears that the U.S. goals for the sanctions could not legally have been authorized by the Council at all, even if there had been political support for such measures. The Security Council may act only pursuant to the authority granted it under the Charter, and Article 24 states that "In discharging these duties the Security Council shall act in accordance with the Purposes and Principles of the United Nations." Although Chapter VII authorizes the use of force to address aggression or threats to the peace, there is no explicit authorization to remove or replace a government or political leaders. At the same time, the Charter is quite clear, in general terms, in its insistence on the sovereignty and self-determination of all member states. Chapter I, "Purposes and Principles," refers to the UN commitment to "equal rights and self-determination of peoples," and states that the UN is based upon "the principle of the sovereign equality of all its Members." Article 2(4) provides that "All members shall refrain in their international relations from the threat or use of force against the territorial integrity or political independence of any state." Chapter VII itself, which authorized the Security Council's use of force, does not explicitly authorize the Council to remove a government or political leader it finds unacceptable but rather identifies specific acts which the Council is to address: threats to the peace, breaches of the peace, and acts of aggression.

Thus the reverse veto not only allowed the United States to substitute its own conditions for lifting the sanctions in place of those articulated by the Security Council, but arguably had the effect of installing a policy—regime change—that is incompatible with the language of the Charter, which in turn is the source of the Council's authority.

At the same time, there was effectively no recourse to a judicial venue to review the legality of imposing sanctions in such circumstances; or recourse to a venue that could override the vote of the permanent members if that vote violated the Charter or other sources of international law. The ICJ is empowered to issue only an advisory ruling regarding the Security Council, and then only upon request by the Security Council or General Assembly.[19] Yet the United States would presumably have vetoed any attempt by other members of the Security Council to seek judicial review of those policies of the Council which the United States had authored; and member states in the General Assembly would presumably have had good cause to fear retribution by the United States, in the face of the severe punishment imposed on Yemen for its opposition.

The reverse veto also raised another set of legal issues as well: the conflict between the Charter's mandates of security, on one hand, and economic development on the other. Although scholars have argued about how such a conflict should be resolved, in fact there is no explicit guidance within the Charter. Article 24 of the Charter provides that "In discharging [its] duties the Security Council shall act in accordance with the Purposes and Principles of the United Nations." While Chapter VII grants the Council the power to use force, the Charter does not suggest that these powers could exceed or override Chapter I, the statement of purposes and principles, since its powers are granted for the purpose of fulfilling the Council's duties under Chapter I.

Article 1 provides for the achievement of security, stating that one purpose of the UN is "to take effective collective measures for the prevention and removal of threats to the peace, and for the suppression of acts of aggression or other breaches of the peace." Chapter VII provides that the Council is responsible for determining the occurrence of aggression, breaches of the peace, and threats to the peace.[20] At the same time, the stated purposes of the UN include the achievement of international cooperation in "solving international problems of an economic, social, cultural, or humanitarian character."[21] The social and economic goals are spelled out in Article 55:

With a view to the creation of conditions of stability and well-being which are necessary for peaceful and friendly relations among nations based on respect for the principle of equal rights and self-determination of peoples, the United Nations shall promote:

a. higher standards of living, full employment, and conditions of economic and social progress and development;
b. solutions of international economic, social, health, and related problems; and international cultural and education cooperation; and
c. universal respect for, and observance of, human rights and fundamental freedoms for all without distinction as to race, sex, language, or religion.

There is no language that suggests that the social and economic goals of the UN are subordinate to the security aims, or vice versa. Arguably, Article 55 in conjunction with Article 1 could well preclude measures by the Security Council that undermine economic development, or create or worsen social and economic problems. It is difficult to reconcile the Charter's mandate to achieve health, education, and economic development with comprehensive, long-term economic sanctions that effectively undermine a population's living standard; reverse decades of economic development; and create extensive economic, social, and health problems. At the same time it is unclear how to resolve a conflict between two competing fundamental interests put forward by the Charter: security and economic well-being.

While the Security Council theoretically could have sought an advisory opinion from the ICJ, it did not do so. Because the matter was not resolved judicially, or in any other venue outside the Council, it was effectively resolved by the reverse veto: even though there were serious questions about the fundamental legality of the sanctions regime under the terms of the Charter, the United States' and Britain's power to maintain the sanctions indefinitely, or until their own goals were met, constituted the dispositive resolution of the matter.

The 661 Committee

Once economic sanctions were imposed on Iraq in 1990 there was from the beginning a process by which Iraq could seek exceptions for humanitarian purposes from the 661 Committee. At the same time, however, the committee adopted procedures that systematically impeded approval of any goods, even those that were clearly both permissible and urgent. Furthermore, because its procedures and decision making in turn operated without transparency or consistent standards, the result was that the committee operated in a way that was arbitrary and unpredictable. This in turn compromised any possibility that the government of Iraq could plan or use humanitarian imports effectively. The United States played a critical role in every aspect of this process.

The 661 Committee, like the Security Council itself, operated as a political body in a number of ways. The Council's resolutions were often drafted in response to a crisis, or as the outcome of political compromise, both of which contributed to language which was often imprecise or contradictory.[22] As a political body, the committee's members often had disparate and competing agendas, which were resolved by political pressure and negotiation rather than by reference to any standing principles or standards. The closed meetings and lack of public statements meant that there could be no public scrutiny. Decisions in the 661 Committee were made by "consensus," effectively giving every member veto power. The consensus structure meant that the will of the majority could be blocked by one or a few members without the need to provide any plausible justification.

The procedures of the 661 Committee had the effect of maximizing restrictions and minimizing humanitarian exemptions at each juncture. Even for food and medicine—goods that were clearly permissible under the sanctions—the notification procedures slowed the import process. For everything else, there were considerable obstacles for any company that wanted to sell humanitarian goods to Iraq, and of these attempts, most were denied.

The possibility of any effective humanitarian program in Iraq was even more deeply compromised when the 661 Committee established procedures that created and maintained confusion and inconsistency; and in the resulting vacuum of structures of accountability and transparency, the agendas of the members with the greatest political power operated largely without obstruction.

The authorizing resolution, Resolution 661, certainly did not envision that the committee would have nearly the scope of the activities that it in fact undertook. The committee was established under Rule 28 of the

Council's Provisional Rules of Procedure, which provides for a special rapporteur to study a matter or conduct research, and report back to the Council.[23] The authorizing language provides only for a committee to examine reports on the implementation of the sanctions measures and to gather information from the member states concerning implementation.[24]

In fact, it was the case that the committee had little to do with information gathering and instead primarily involved the administration of humanitarian waivers, something that was unknown in prior sanctions regimes.[25] This task turned out to involve a huge amount of work: because the sanctions were nearly comprehensive, every item that Iraq sought to import to sustain a population of 22 million people had to go through a process of either approval or notification; and Iraq was a country whose economy had been heavily dependent on imports in nearly every area.

It was clear from the beginning that the committee was in general quite poorly suited for the tasks it came to take on. The fifteen delegates of the 661 Committee,

> most of them severely overburdened, under-resourced, and disin-
> terested, came to be making more than 6,000 decisions a year . . .
> most of them on banal routine matters. The 724 Yugoslavia Com-
> mittee, largely with the same decision-makers and with hardly any
> greater resources, was making close to 30,000 such decisions a
> year.[26]

Thus, even if the 661 Committee had been genuinely committed to facilitating the flow of humanitarian goods into Iraq, it was crippled from the beginning by a lack of adequate staffing.

The administration and resources available to the 661 Committee stood in stark contrast with those of UNSCOM. Whereas the structure and operations of the 661 Committee reflected a deep reluctance to facilitate the flow of goods into Iraq, the structure of UNSCOM suggested an unequivocal commitment to maximizing its effectiveness. Although the 661 Committee had responsibility for approving every contract for humanitarian goods for a country of 22 million people, it had only a total of fifteen diplomats as members, all of whom had extensive obligations in addition to their work on the 661 Committee, and few of whom had expertise in economic development, emergency relief, oil, or any other of the committee's substantive areas of work. There was effectively no access to prior committee decisions, except for the P5's private records. The constant turnover of elected members precluded any possibility of consistency or continuity. However, the Security Council's support of UNSCOM was quite the opposite. UNSCOM had extensive resources available to it on all levels. It had, for example, a comprehensive computerized system for handling data from the beginning of its operations.[27] In contrast to the staffing of the 661 Committee, UNSCOM had 160–180 full-time staff.[28] It was given great flexibility in staffing its work on the basis of expertise and continuity. One commentator notes that UNSCOM was quite atypical as a UN organization in this regard, in that the executive chair was able to request additional staff with specific skills very quickly from supporting governments without having to go through the usual UN procedures for recruiting staff,[29] giving it far greater flexibility and speed in acquiring expertise and staffing than most UN organizations.[30] In addition to the weapons experts who served on UNSCOM, there were also full-time, long-term administrators who provided the organization with continuity: Rolf Ekeus served as executive chair from 1991 to 1997, and over half of those appointed to UNSCOM in 1991 were still serving as of 1998.[31]

That the Security Council prioritized disarmament over humanitarian concerns was certainly clear. But the 661 Committee's inconsistent policies, its refusal to articulate criteria, and its aversion to any form of transparency or accountability went beyond simply an overriding commitment to security concerns. Paul Conlon, the Secretariat's administrator for the 661 Committee for the first several years of its operation, suggests that the 661 Committee presented a "classic case of poor management," in that its procedural rules "were geared to solving complex and largely unforeseen political problems, yet ultimately more than 95 percent of its activities were of a routine and repetitive nature."[32] Given the nature of the committee's work—the large volume of contracts to review, the repetition of the same issues again and again, and the frequent need to address technical questions—it would seem that the committee would have been well served by functioning on the model of a regulatory agency: developing procedures and standards that would achieve some measure of efficiency, expertise, and consistency. There was also a sense in which the 661 Committee served a quasi-judicial function in that it resolved competing factual claims put forward by its members, humanitarian agencies, the government of Iraq, vendors, and the vendor states; and in that it performed a variety of interpretive functions, including the interpretation of the authorizing resolutions and their application. However, the committee did not adopt the procedures of a well-functioning regulatory agency; nor did it follow any of the norms found in the judiciary under the rule of law, such as fairness, consistency, application of stated principles, or the use of impartial decision makers. Indeed, the United States aggressively opposed all attempts to establish precedents or any other procedures that would provide consistency and predictability. If the function of the committee was to process exemption waivers with consistency or efficiency, then it was indeed a case of poor management. However, if the function of the committee was political rather than regulatory, it in fact functioned quite well insofar as it served as a vehicle for the United States and its allies to effectuate their own political agendas.

The Consensus Rule

At its inception in August 1990, the 661 Committee adopted a practice of decision making by consensus, effectively giving each member state a veto over every decision. Thus the consensus rule in some sense equalized the members, in contrast to the Security Council itself, where only the permanent members held veto power. But since much of the committee's work involved requests for humanitarian waivers, a failure to agree meant that the waiver was denied. Consequently, the consensus rule had the effect of implementing the most restrictive procedure possible in regard to humanitarian approvals. In practice, the United States, Britain, and (for the first several years) France were the countries responsible for nearly all the "failures to achieve consensus," joined occasionally by Japan or other elected members.

Furthermore, as is the case with the Security Council, the members did not need to offer any reasons for their positions. The primary justification given by delegates for their positions was "the opinion of my government" and "the view of my delegation," with little opportunity to verify the factual assertions and little substance to even the arguments that were couched in terms of law or legal reasoning.[33]

It was obvious from the beginning that the consensus requirement would lead to paralysis. Consequently, there was some initial suggestion by elected members that "consensus" should be taken to mean a "broad majority."[34] But that was quickly overridden.

Food Imports and "Humanitarian Circumstances"

The impact of the consensus rule was first apparent when Iraq sought permission to import food immediately after the sanctions were imposed. Resolution 661 provided that Iraq could import medicine freely but could import food only in "humanitarian circumstances." Although Iraq had imported two-thirds of its food prior to August 1990, the United States and a few others on the 661 Committee were adamant in insisting that "humanitarian circumstances" were not present. Disputing the interpretation of "humanitarian circumstances," and using the veto power implied by consensus decision making, the United States, sometimes accompanied by others, effectively prevented Iraq from importing food for eight months.

One striking example was a dispute regarding whether Iraq could import powdered milk. In the fall of 1990 Bulgaria asked the committee for permission to deliver a cargo of powdered milk that had already been scheduled for delivery to Iraq when the Security Council passed Resolution 661. There was disagreement about the legal interpretation of the resolution and whether it applied to the situation. The chairman proposed to circulate a draft request to the Office of Legal Counsel for guidance. The U.S. delegate adamantly opposed granting Bulgaria permission to deliver the milk, and likewise opposed seeking a legal opinion outside the committee. He argued that

> the purpose of Security Council resolution 661 (1990) was clear: to prevent the supply of any products, including foodstuffs, unless justified by humanitarian circumstances . . . The products in question were clearly covered by resolution 661 (1990). It was regrettable that hardships would be imposed, but the resolution was perfectly clear and there was no need to seek the opinion of the Legal Counsel.[35]

The British delegate agreed with the United States.[36] But other members of the committee held that the delivery of powdered milk should be permitted as a humanitarian measure. The Canadian representative argued that the resolution "should not be interpreted inhumanely,"[37] and the delegates from Colombia, Cuba, and Yemen took similar positions.[38] Some suggested that if the committee could not agree on whether the resolution permitted this, then the Office of Legal Counsel should be consulted. The delegate from Malaysia "urged the United States and United

Kingdom representatives, for the good of the Committee, to accept refer-ral of the question to the Legal Counsel."[39] They refused, and in the end their very extreme interpretation—shared by no one else—prevailed.

Thus the United States not only used the consensus requirement to block specific shipments of goods into Iraq but then went to some length to prevent the committee from even hearing a nonbinding legal opinion that might conflict with the position of the United States.[40]

The U.S. position on powdered milk was consistent with its position on food imports in general. In a memorandum recording the dispute, an administrator for the 661 Committee noted:

> The P-3 held that food-deprivation as applied to national econo-mies was permissible whereas only food-deprivation as applied to human beings was subject to strictures under humanitarian law. This means that depriving a national economy of food inputs from the outside was acceptable in order to put pressure on the target state, e.g., by forcing it to redeploy resources from other sectors into food production, food preparation or food distribution. This presupposes that the target state's leadership prioritizes food and then opts to deploy its resources in this manner, and/or that this tactic succeeds in warding off food deprivation for its people ...
>
> The western countries (P-3 plus Canada) were not too explicit but seemed to feel that only severe food shortages such as in a fam-ine would constitute [humanitarian] circumstances. Cuba argued that it had to be "construed in the larger context of the basic hu-man right to decent nourishment," i.e., even marginal undernour-ishment of children would be prohibited. Finland also cautioned against limiting humanitarian circumstances to outright famine ... Western countries (as defined above) all held that resolution 661 had not declared foodstuffs as such to be humanitarian items *per se*, nor did the resolution exclude foodstuffs as it had done with medicines.[41]

From August 1990 until February 1991, the United States consis-tently objected to the attempts of others on the committee to find that there were "humanitarian circumstances" present—thereby allowing Iraq to import food—arguing that this "might undermine the very purpose of the resolution."[42] When Russia noted that the media impression was that the Council intended to use starvation as a weapon, the United States responded that there was "no need for an urgent decision."[43] On other occasions, with or without a plausible rationale, the United States simply invoked the consensus rule to block requests by Iraq to import food.[44] Five months into the embargo, the United States continued to block infants' milk on the grounds that it "could not be considered medicine," and humanitarian circumstances still had not been shown.[45] Even when no Iraqis would benefit from food imports, the United States objected. The United States delayed shipment of food to Pakistani nationals living in Iraq, even though none of the food would have gone to Iraqis. The United States was particularly reluctant to allow food to be delivered to Pakistanis if they were in Iraq voluntarily, and demanded to know whether the Pakistanis were being held against their will in Iraq before agreeing to allow Pakistan to ship food to its nationals in Iraq.[46]

In the end, while the United States often claimed that Iraq was never formally prohibited from buying food, in fact it was the case that Iraq was not permitted to import food from August 1990 to March 1991. However, for the duration of the sanctions regime the United States denied that Iraq had ever been prevented from buying food. A UN diplomat observed, "The sanctions weapon when applied to food is a double-edged sword. We want Iraq to hurt, but cannot be seen to use famine to bring the country down."[47] In March 1991, after the Gulf War ended, the Ahtisaari report documented the crisis in every aspect of Iraq's economy, public health, and infrastructure. At that point, the United States could no longer dispute that "humanitarian circumstances" were present. Three days later, the 661 Committee made "a general determination that humanitarian circumstances apply with respect to the entire civilian population of Iraq in all parts of Iraq's territory." Iraq's food purchases no longer went through the "no objection" procedure, which had allowed Iraq to import food only if no one on the committee objected. Instead, food was subject to "simple notification," with no procedural opportunity for the United States to prevent Iraq from importing food.[48]

Even after the 661 Committee found in March 1991 that "humanitarian circumstances" were present and that food would be allowed on the basis of simple notification to the committee, the United States and Britain often found other ways to interfere with Iraq's food access, especially in the early 1990s. For example, the United States blocked Iraq from importing materials to produce plastic bottles for juice;[49] Britain blocked materials to manufacture tomato paste in Iraq on the grounds that this would enhance Iraq's infrastructure;[50] the United States blocked the purchase of salt on the grounds that it could be used for the salinization of leather, which contributed to Iraqi industry;[51] and Britain opposed Iraq's request to import aluminum lids for canning food on the grounds that "aluminum was a strategic metal which could be used as an input for that country's industrial infrastructure."[52]

Although contracts related to food generally bypassed the committee once the Oil-for-Food Programme was in place, on the occasions that they did come before the committee, the United States and Britain challenged them aggressively. In May 2000 Syria asked the committee to approve a contract to mill flour for Iraq. Whereas Iraq ordinarily purchased food directly, in this case Iraq was growing wheat but did not have adequate facilities to process it into flour. This was in part because the 661 Committee had on occasion prohibited items such as nylon cloth for filtering flour.[53] Earlier that year, in March, Anupama Rao Singh, the UNICEF official in charge of Iraq operations, had made the first direct presentation to the committee on the humanitarian situation that the United States and Britain had permitted since the sanctions had been imposed. She informed the 661 Committee that 25 percent of children in south and central governorates suffered from chronic malnutrition, which was often irreversible, and 9 percent from acute malnutrition. She described the child mortality rates as "alarming," noting that mortality for children under five had gone from 56/1,000 prior to sanctions to 131/1,000 in the 1990s.[54] In discussing the Syrian proposal two months later, the Russian delegate argued that, in light of the report the committee had received on Iraq's flour mills and the fact that flour was an essential element of the Iraqi diet, the committee had no choice but to approve the request on humanitarian grounds.[55]

The delegate from China weighed in, in support, as did the delegates from France and Argentina. But the U.S. representative argued that "there should be no hurry" to move on this request: he noted that the flour requirement under Security Council Resolution 986 had been met; that, in general, the number of requests on hold were "relatively low"; and that the committee should wait for the results of a study being conducted by WFP first.[56] Ironically, he even argued against the flour milling contract on the grounds that "the focus should be on capacity-building within the country," even though that represented a stark reversal of U.S. policy, which consistently opposed any form of economic development within Iraq. The delegate from Britain likewise produced a flurry of objections. He argued that it had not been shown "how the request would fit into the Iraqi food programme" and that there were questions about transport and insurance. In the end, despite the extreme malnutrition of which the committee was aware, the U.S. delegate insisted it would be "premature" to grant such a request, and the British representative joined him blocking the project from going forward.

Relief versus Reconstruction

Not only were Iraq's imports subject to restriction. In addition, UN agencies could only engage in relief programs and were blocked from any activities that the Security Council viewed as "rehabilitation." The United States and Britain insisted that whatever goods Iraq was allowed to import could only be used for relief or emergency aid, and not for reconstruction or rehabilitation of buildings or infrastructure.[57] Thus, in 1992, even though most of Iraq's power plants had been badly damaged or destroyed in war and the Ahtisaari report had emphasized that restoring electrical capacity was an urgent priority, the United States insisted that there could be no new construction of power plants, only emergency repairs on existing ones.[58] When the United Nations Development Programme asked for authorization to train Iraqi personnel in addressing humanitarian problems in the face of Iraq's enormous losses of skilled personnel in all fields, the United States vetoed it, claiming this was a "long term development issue," not "vital humanitarian aid," even though others, such as the German delegate, argued this was humanitarian.[59] Hans von Sponeck, the UN's humanitarian coordinator in Iraq, noted that this bias in favor of relief directly compromised efforts toward development or even rehabilitation.[60] This was built in as well to the authorization structure for the Oil-for-Food Programme because the Security Council authorized extensions only in six-month periods. In effect, the entire program functioned as a short-term emergency relief program, which was renewed each six months, making it impossible to plan effectively for the immediate and long-term needs, such as housing construction for displaced persons or import of agricultural inputs for the next growing season.

Transparency

Within the structure of the 661 Committee, there was little opportunity for scrutiny or for accountability. At its first meeting, the committee decided that all further meetings would be closed.[61] Other member states of the UN had no access to the meetings, and the circulation of the minutes was highly restricted. Meetings were not only closed to the press or public observers, but for the first several years of its operation the committee had no spokesperson and rarely authorized the chair to speak to the press about any of its decisions.[62] The ostensible justification for holding closed meetings was that the committee needed to maintain confidentiality in dealing with situations where states conducted trade with Iraq in violation of the sanctions. The secrecy was necessary to "[discuss] alleged violations of the sanctions, because Governments might not be willing to offer information on alleged violations if they had to fear publicity."[63] Yet these cases were infrequent and accounted for very little of the committee's work. Conlon notes that in the first 117 meetings of the committee there were only eleven cases of alleged sanctions violations, taking up a total of approximately 2.5 percent of the committee's time.[64]

Not only were the committee's activities inaccessible to outsiders, the committee was, in a sense, not even transparent to itself. For years, the agendas for the meetings were not only unavailable to those outside the committee, including the parties involved in the agenda items; the agendas were actually not available to the committee members themselves. The chair conducted the meetings, introduced items, and then explained them from a "brief" prepared by the Secretariat in consultation with the chair. These "briefs," in turn, were made available to Secretariat officials attending the meeting, to the brief writer, and to the interpreters, but not to the members themselves.[65] There were no verbatim minutes kept of the meetings, only a "summary record" paraphrasing and shortening each speaker's comments.[66] Furthermore, the committee's prior decisions were effectively unavailable to any of the elected members. The records for the cases before the committee—by 1994, there had been 7,000—were not filed in an organized system and were not computerized.[67] As a result, if the committee was considering a request to approve ambulance helicopters, for example, and a new member wanted to know the committee's prior rulings concerning ambulance helicopters, the new delegate would literally have had to sift through thousands of documents. Because there was no viable mechanism for institutional memory established by the committee itself, the permanent members had a considerable advantage: they could maintain their own archives of any records they chose, organize them in an accessible way, and invoke them in disputes later, while the elected members had no such materials to draw on.

In addition to excluding observers or disinterested parties from attending, the meetings were also closed to all of the parties to the transactions. Thus, for any given contract for humanitarian goods, the exporters themselves could not appear before the committee to answer questions or offer clarification, or to ask the reasons for a delay or rejection; nor could any representatives from their UN missions, which were the bodies that formally submitted the application; nor was any representative of Iraq ever permitted to do so. Thus, because there could be no direct communication between those seeking humanitarian waivers and those granting them, there were continual delays, even for goods that were urgent and permissible, simply by making it impossible for vendors or the Iraqi government to address questions.

There was no transparency even for something as basic as providing the vendors with the reasons their contracts had been denied. As a result, the vendor had no idea whether the contract had been denied because someone on the committee believed it to present a security threat that would never be approved under any circumstances, or because the printing on the fax was smudged and the problem could be fixed by re-sending it. There was initially a short-lived practice in which the chair would informally tell the requesting mission why the contract had been rejected. But, predictably, there were many requests for these explanations. The response of the committee was not to develop a system to provide the vendors with the reasons but rather to adopt the policy of flatly refusing to provide any reasons to anyone. Once a contract was blocked, the chairman would notify the requesting mission "that the [661 Committee] had been unable to agree," and that was that.[68]

The Security Council's rules of procedure specify that all meetings should be public unless it decides otherwise, to allow governments that are not members of the Council to participate. In the case of Iraq, the meetings where Iraq policy was decided were almost without exception classified as "informal," effectively barring Iraq from participating.[69] Iraq was not permitted to send a representative, either to address questions about specific items or to discuss policy or procedural issues without a special invitation to attend. While Iraq was permitted to send letters to the committee, there was no opportunity to address concerns or questions raised during the meetings or to be heard on policy changes before the committee made its decision. Tono Eitel, the German ambassador and a former chair of the 661 Committee, criticized not only the general lack of transparency but the loss of the rights of the concerned parties, such as

Iraq, to address the Council while it was still deliberating and before it had arrived at a final decision.[70]

These practices continued throughout much of the sanctions regime, despite multiple calls for reform and for greater transparency. Paul Conlon noted that the secrecy "inhibit[ed] the development of coherent practice":

> There is no self-assessment on the part of the decision-makers, no basis for fulfillment of accountability obligations (if they were ever to be introduced) and none of the involved actors has any overview of the scope of practice . . . The lack of decent legal and administrative procedures delegitimises the decisions of the sanctions committees, whatever their constitutional status might be under other circumstances.[71]

Conlon argued that the Committee's procedures were so counter to basic principles of the rule of law as to jeopardize their legal validity.

> It can also be asked on the basis of what strange legal doctrines the Committee as a source of authority can simultaneously require the non-disclosure of its decisions and then assert pretensions to their universally binding nature? In most legal systems the validity of laws and decisions is directly dependent on their proper promulgation.[72]

In 1995 a UN consultant cited complaints because of the sanctions committee's "penchant for secrecy, their seemingly arbitrary and unpredictable humanitarian waiver practices and because they took forever to decide cases."[73] In 1997 the French delegate criticized the ambiguity of the committee's procedures and criteria, and called for an increase in transparency.[74] By January 1999 the Security Council agreed that the countries affected or targeted by sanctions should have greater opportunity to present their points of view. However, after almost a decade there was still no direct mechanism to even inform Iraq of the outcome of the committee meetings, let alone provide minutes or permit Iraq to come to meetings to present its position. When Iraq asked to attend meetings and to present its point of view, citing this decision, the United States refused to allow Iraq to even receive the committee's minutes, much less attend or participate in its meetings.[75]

In the end, all of these things—the reverse veto, the consensus rule, the lack of transparency, the impossibility of public scrutiny—enabled the United States to shape the initial terms of the sanctions regime and to determine its duration, as well as impose its will in many regards on the implementation of the sanctions by the Security Council's 661 Committee. This was the case even in the face of reluctance or outright opposition by some or even most of the members of the Security Council. The procedural maneuvering of the United States, along with measures such as vetoing food shipments, were all directed toward the same outcome: doing as much damage as possible to Iraq's economy, in every regard, however indiscriminate it might be.

4

THE PROBLEM OF HOLDS

As the humanitarian impact of sanctions became more visible in the 1990s, a number of political scientists and ethicists proposed criteria for their ethical use, including humanitarian exemptions to protect the most vulnerable members of the population. These exemptions were ostensibly provided when the 661 Committee took on the task of reviewing requests for humanitarian imports. But while this protection existed in principle, it was compromised in many ways.

The United States insisted that Iraq seek permission for each item, rather than approving categories of permitted goods, and the United States insisted as well that each item be judged on a case-by-case basis, without the use of precedent or criteria for approval. Each approval was an exception to the general prohibition on trade; consequently, because of the consensus decision-making rule, each approval required the agreement of the entire committee. Any single member of the committee could unilaterally block the purchase of any contract for humanitarian goods by withholding its approval.

Taken as a whole, the approval process demonstrated the damage that could be done simply because each item, however urgent, had to be approved by a bureaucracy that was cumbersome and opaque. However, the holds were also a stark illustration of the level of detail, and the degree of effort, that went into crippling Iraq, one item at a time. They make evident how deliberate and consistent the U.S. practices were: it required constant attention and political maneuvering, on a daily or weekly basis, regarding each item and request—of which there were thousands annually—in order to deny each in turn, in the face of constant and vocal skepticism.

The use of holds also speaks to one of the fundamental issues for sanctions imposed by the UN: when there is a conflict between the UN's commitment to humanitarian principles and its commitment to security, which one trumps? In the case of the holds, the answer was that any security risk, however speculative or slight, was given absolute credence and overrode any humanitarian harm, however extensive and certain.

The holds on contracts were not the sole impediments to the flow of humanitarian goods into Iraq. The Iraqi government was sometimes slow to submit proposed contracts and sometimes did not contract for the goods that were most needed. Contractors were sometimes slow to respond to requests for details about their products. Once in the country, difficulties with transportation, warehousing, and administration sometimes delayed the distribution of goods. But those factors were relatively minor compared to the fundamental constraints on the flow of critical humanitarian goods into Iraq: the limited amount of funds available to the program overall and the massive amount of those goods that were blocked or delayed by the United States, through the 661 Committee.

The holds placed on contracts provide a roadmap of the U.S. practices that ensured that the sanctions would keep Iraq in a state of destitution, regardless of any attempt to provide humanitarian exemptions. They were a source of tension between the United States and the other members of the Security Council, as well as between the Council and the other organs of the UN: the Secretariat, the humanitarian agencies, and even the weapons inspectors. They were shaped at every turn by an unequivocal policy of the United States, shared by no one else, even Britain. After March 1991, Iraq was permitted to buy humanitarian goods with funds it had on hand, subject to 661 Committee approval, although it was not allowed to sell oil to generate foreign exchange until 1996, when the Oil-for-Food Programme began. The 661 Committee permitted Iraq to import food and medicine for the most part without objection. However, from 1991 to 1995 almost everything else was denied, as either an "input to industry" or on the grounds that they were not essential civilian goods. The U.S. interpretation of these standards was arbitrary and often absurd.

On one occasion the United States agreed to allow black fabric for nuns but blocked white cloth as an input to industry.[1] Some months later, when the United States objected to cloth for burial shrouds, others objected; the United States justified its position on the grounds that the cloth was an input to industry and therefore prohibited by the sanctions.[2] Britain blocked equipment for food processing on the grounds that it "would enhance the basic infrastructure"[3] and blocked tissue paper as an input to industry.[4] The United States blocked materials to make shoes,[5] glue for manufacturing cigarettes,[6] sewing thread,[7] materials to package food,[8] raw cotton for the production of medical gauze and fabric to make hospital bed covers—all on the grounds that they supported Iraqi industry.[9] On one occasion, in response to the extreme positions of the United States, other members of the 661 Committee challenged the U.S. decision to block a request from Turkey to export a shipment of glue to Iraq. The U.S. delegate replied that "his delegation objected to the request in the interest of saving horses."[10]

The Oil-for-Food Programme began in 1995. In many ways the holds under the Oil-for-Food Programme mirrored the denials of contracts for humanitarian goods under the 661 Committee's humanitarian exemption process from 1991 to 1995: there was little transparency, the approval process was inconsistent and arbitrary, and the overall result was that humanitarian contracts were denied in large numbers. But the Oil-for-Food Programme was managed by a UN agency outside the Security Council (the Office of the Iraq Programme [OIP]), and for this reason alone the member states were forced to be more explicit. Even so, there was little public knowledge about the holds and how they actually worked.

Under the Oil-for-Food Programme there were in theory several points at which Iraq could increase its access to goods: when the Security Council allowed oil sales to increase; when the ceiling on oil sales was lifted altogether; and when the Security Council began authorizing Iraq to sign contracts for equipment to generate electricity, provide water treatment, and rehabilitate the infrastructure. In spite of these, the amount of goods that actually arrived in Iraq remained low; every time reforms were implemented to streamline the process, the United States simply invoked the consensus rule and blocked more contracts, circumventing the reforms. As of November 1998, holds on humanitarian contracts totaled $147.5 million;[11] by August 1999 that figure had grown to about $500 million,[12] by April 2000 to $1.7 billion,[13] by December 2000 to $2.5 billion,[14] by July 2001 to $3.3 billion,[15] and by May 2002 to over $5 billion.[16] So many of Iraq's contracts were blocked that, from the time the program began operating in 1996 until March 2003, a total of only $27 billion in humanitarian goods were actually delivered to Iraq.[17] That came to about $204 per person per year for all goods, including food, medicine, and the reconstruction of the infrastructure, since the program began operation; or about one-half the per capita income of Haiti, the poorest country in the Western Hemisphere.

The Oil-for-Food Programme operated in six-month phases. For each phase, the United States generally imposed 90 percent of the holds unilaterally; Britain would place holds on 3–5 percent unilaterally; and the remainder of holds were placed jointly by the United States and Britain. Under the Oil-for-Food Programme, no other country placed holds on humanitarian goods. This was the case from the beginning of the program to the end of the sanctions regime, and it was true for all types of goods.

U.S. policies in this period varied with the type of goods involved. In general there were few holds on food imports. In regard to health care, water and sanitation, education, and housing, the United States blocked part of Iraq's purchases but allowed a portion of these contracts to be approved. However, in some areas, such as electricity and telecommunications, nearly all goods were blocked until the last two or three years, when the United States agreed to allow Iraq to bring in very limited amounts of equipment and supplies.

The United States often would not relent, even when UN agencies and international monitoring organizations documented at great length the damage being done specifically by the blocked contracts. In the areas of water and sanitation, for example, in June 2000 the director of UNICEF identified eighteen high-priority contracts that were on hold, totaling about $65 million. These contracts were for equipment including chlorinators and related equipment for 300 water treatment plants, affecting 1.5 million people; water tankers, which were particularly urgent during the drought that was taking place; and water purification chemicals, which were indispensable. Of the eighteen priority contracts, eleven were on hold by the United States alone, one was on hold by Britain, and the other six were jointly blocked by the United States and Britain.[18] The following year, in September 2001, UNICEF again reported to the 661 Committee that the situation regarding water and sanitation in Iraq was quite urgent. UNICEF stressed that there were numerous contracts for goods that were urgently needed, but that these had been blocked by the committee: equipment for three particular sewage treatment plants, which served approximately 1 million people;[19] equipment for compact water treatment units for rural areas;[20] sewage pumps and water pumps;[21] water tankers for rural areas; drilling rigs in areas dependent on groundwater; and chemicals for water treatment and equipment for their use.[22] The United States was responsible for blocking nearly every one of these items. At that time, of the contracts for water and sewage treatment equipment, there were 125 on hold. Of these, Britain had blocked one contract on its own; the United States and Britain had jointly put holds on nine contracts; and the remaining 115 holds were placed by the United States alone.

This happened continually. In 2002 the UN staff documented the specific need for water pumps to be used in the plant that treated raw water from the Tigris, all of which were being blocked by the United States.[23] In their report on an observation visit to the Basrah Sewage Treatment Plant, UN staff noted that

> more then 50% of the sewage generated is indiscriminately discharged and polluting many densely populated areas in Basrah, [and] even the flows discharged to the treatment facility do not receive necessary treatment and only contribute to polluting a concentrated area. The efforts of the local authorities are rendered totally ineffective simply because the vital [mechanical and engineering] equipment requested is on hold.[24]

Eleven pumping stations in Basrah could not operate due to a block on mechanical and electrical equipment that had been ordered.[25] The United States had blocked the equipment, citing security concerns, even though UN personnel maintained that it could easily be monitored through "full tracking . . . from the date of arrival to installation at facility and thereafter as necessary."[26]

Because the sewage system was not functioning, raw water had in some cases more than 100 times the World Health Organization (WHO) standard for fecal contamination.[27] Of the water that was treated and pumped through water pipes for distribution, about 40 percent was lost due to breaks in the pipes. A UN consultant reported that to repair these breaks, it was necessary to have trucks, cranes, and other construction equipment.[28] However, the United States routinely blocked water pipes and earthmoving equipment.

In its report on the health sector in March 2002, WHO described in detail the pervasive shortages of essential drugs, medical supplies, and equipment. It reported that as a result of these shortages a number of diseases that had previously been under control, such as cholera, polio, and malaria, had reemerged.[29] The capacity of the health care system to provide medical services was badly compromised: the number of surgical operations plummeted in the 1990s,[30] as did the amount of laboratory work.[31] In 1989 the number of major surgeries performed averaged

15,125 per month; by 1992 this number had dropped to 5,477, and remained around 5,000 or below for the rest of the decade.[32]

But while the need for medical supplies was obviously urgent, WHO reported that the holds on medical goods had not gone down. On the contrary, they had tripled in two years, from about $150 million in February 2000 to $450 million in February 2002.[33] Blood bank refrigerators had been blocked, as well as laboratory equipment and materials, machinery, and spare parts for local drug production.[34] Of the 182 contracts in the health sector on hold as of March 2002, four were placed on hold by Britain alone, nineteen were placed jointly by the United States and Britain, and the remaining 159 were placed by the United States alone.[35] In a report on sterilizers and autoclaves, UN staff found a pattern of infections related to reusable medical devices that had not been adequately disinfected or sterilized. This was in part due to a lack of autoclaves, which UN personnel found were old, in poor condition, and required spare parts. The autoclaves, sterilizers, and spare parts ordered by the Ministry of Health had been blocked by the United States.[36]

The United States often justified its denials by citing suspicions that the Iraqi government could divert goods to military uses, such as when the United States blocked electrical generators and cables for the health system.[37] The United States maintained this position, even when UN staff were given full access to production sites and confirmed that the goods were being properly used. For example, UN staff supported efforts by SDI, Iraq's state enterprise for production of pharmaceuticals and medical equipment, to produce goods domestically in order to reduce dependence on imports. However, a request for a production line to produce medical ampules was denied,[38] even though the UN team had been given free access to the factory and to all records they requested,[39] and visited and inspected the installation and operations of equipment and materials obtained through the Oil-for-Food Programme, confirming that the goods had not been diverted to other uses.[40]

The following year the United States again blocked spare parts for equipment to produce pharmaceuticals, even though "the UN team again physically observed the machines that were in use . . . and they were shown the worn out parts."[41] Later that year, a UN field report on Salah Al-Din, the main plant for pharmaceutical production, noted that a contract for refrigerated trucks needed to transport medicines without spoilage was on hold. The United States had blocked them on the grounds that a cold storage truck could be used to transport biological agents for weapons of mass destruction (WMD).[42] The United States took this position even though the UN staff documented the urgency of the need and the legitimacy of the factory's medical production, based on "unimpeded access" to the factory as well as to ledgers and record books, and all other information they requested.[43]

In regard to agriculture, the United States followed the same practices, despite the large-scale chronic malnutrition in Iraq. In an assessment of agricultural machinery, the UN's Agriculture Sector Working Group for Iraq (ASWG) found that the Iraqi government was fairly quick and efficient in distributing farm equipment once it arrived, and that all equipment that had been received was being used. The ASWG found that the distribution was equitable, in that the equipment was directed to large farms with higher yields. However, there were serious shortages; for most types of machinery, the equipment available met less than 45 percent of the need.[44] Despite the shortages, the United States, and occasionally Britain, continued to block Iraq from importing agricultural equipment and supplies. There were holds on diesel generators,[45] heavy machinery, and vehicles.[46] There were a large number of agricultural holds that impacted the resources necessary for Iraq to increase its own domestic production, such as equipment for repairs on a fertilizer production plant.[47] When the United States expressed concerns about civilian goods being diverted to the military, the UN put observers in place to monitor the actual use of the goods and ensure that this did not happen. Once the monitors were in place, OIP pressed for approval of goods, such as animal vaccines and pesticides. Instead, the number of holds in this area increased.[48]

A study done by the ASWG in May 2001 looked at the impact of the Oil-for-Food Programme on rehabilitating the veterinary cold chain, refrigerating vaccines and medicines during delivery, distribution, and storage. This was critical to Iraq's ability to produce poultry, milk, and meat. The ASWG found that, to the extent Iraqi orders for generators and refrigerated trucks had arrived, they had been helpful, but again, the holds were an impediment. The United States, for example, blocked an order for 250 compressors that were necessary to restore the cold chain for veterinary medicines.[49] The ASWG conducted a study of the Iraqi government's efforts to increase local food production. The Oil-for-Food Programme had improved production of vegetables and fruits to some extent, but production was still limited, in part due to lack of irrigation water.[50] However, in 2000, the largest number of agriculture holds were on irrigation equipment.[51] As late as 2003 the same problems continued.

The UN Humanitarian Coordinator for Iraq issued a report noting that Iraq's agricultural production was still compromised by the delays and holds on equipment related to water and the drought, including water tankers, drilling rigs, pumps, and spare parts.[52]

To increase food production, the Iraqi government worked with UN personnel to import vaccines for enterotoxaemia, a disease found in small ruminants, such as sheep and goats, that is endemic in Iraq.[53] The Iraqi government prioritized this program and began ordering the vaccines early on. When the vaccination program was operating, UN personnel found that it had been implemented in accordance with the plan and on the basis of need, and that the program had been successful—there were no outbreaks of the disease, to the extent that vaccines had been available. However, UN staff noted that at least 6 million doses were necessary for the next vaccination campaign. The United States had blocked all of these.[54]

Iraq's capacity to generate electricity was also undermined by holds, and this in itself compromised Iraq's infrastructure and critical public services overall; even when a water treatment plant had sufficient equipment and parts, without electricity it would be at a standstill. In 2001 the humanitarian coordinator in Iraq referred to the "deplorable condition of the power network."[55] A UN report the same year indicated that electricity production was still compromised by the holds on equipment. The 2001 report cited almost $300 million of equipment for electricity production, all blocked by the United States. While the United States often claimed that it blocked goods because the vendor or the Iraqi government had not provided adequate information, in some cases all information requested by the United States had been provided but the United States would still neither approve the contract nor formally reject it.[56] In a number of cases, the applications were on hold by the United States for over a year.[57] A contract for aluminum ingots for the electrical system was kept on hold for a year and a half, then finally approved. But at that point the prices had changed and the supplier was no longer willing to deliver the goods at the same price, requiring the contract to be renegotiated and reviewed all over again. A state company that manufactured cables, telephone wires, and copper wires could not produce these goods because of a lack of raw materials.[58]

In a study of the impact of the holds on housing and construction, the Housing Sector Working Group (HSWG) listed the blocked goods that were critical for construction, such as equipment for paving roads and for asphalt production. They had been blocked by the United States,[59] along with laboratory equipment to monitor stress on concrete, described as "essential in the construction industry."[60] The United States blocked equipment for drilling through rock and earth-moving equipment needed to maintain sewer lines and drain flooded areas. The United States also blocked cranes on the grounds that they could be used to launch missiles.[61] The HSWG noted that while the construction of private homes did not necessarily require specialized equipment, the construction of roads, public buildings, and infrastructure, with their different types of foundations, did require earth-moving equipment such as bulldozers, equipment to produce and deliver concrete, and trucks that could transport them.[62] At that point, nearly half the contracts for construction equipment were on hold.[63] The HSWG noted that transport equipment, such as flatbed semitrailers, were "indispensable for the development of road networks and maintenance.[64]" Nevertheless, the United States blocked tractor-trailers on the grounds that they were "dual use/WMD" and could be used to transport missiles.[65]

The same held true for telecommunications, which in turn affected everything from Iraq's agriculture to its ability to contact vendors from the Oil-for-Food Programme. A report by the International Telecommunications Union (ITU) noted that two years into the Oil-for-Food Programme, "communication by phone and fax was nearly impossible" and that rehabilitation of the network would require an investment of more than $1 billion. Three years later, it reported that "Iraqi telecommunications network conditions have not improved"[66]—"the level of service is so low that the system as a whole cannot be said to be functioning."[67] At that point there were holds on $215 million in contracts for telecommunications and meteorological equipment, or about two-thirds of all the applications that had been submitted.[68] The ITU report also identified some of the consequences of the blocks on particular equipment. One contract was for equipment that was necessary for international phone lines and for national phone lines among major cities. The result was the "non possibility of contacting overseas firms." In addition, "an outdated national exchange will make it impossible for the local population to get basic services such as Emergency Medical Services."[69] The holds on equipment linking Baghdad and Basra impeded communication with Um-Qasr, the major entry point for bulk humanitarian supplies; interfered with the transfer of data by UN observers from southern governorates to Baghdad; and created security concerns for UN staff.[70] Holds on equipment for small mobile networks undermined communication to emergency vehicles.[71] Holds on meteorological equipment meant that accurate information was not available for the forecasts needed for agriculture and irrigation or for warnings to the population regarding water levels in the rivers or coming storms.[72] In all of these cases the contracts were blocked by the United States, although Britain joined it in a few instances.[73]

Similarly, transportation was critical to every sector. A report by the UN's humanitarian coordinator noted that, while there was efficient distribution of goods from the central warehouse to the warehouses in each governorate, the distribution from those warehouses to the local facilities was compromised by lack of transportation.[74] Vehicles in general were targeted by the United States on the grounds, for example, that a vehicle that could carry a bulldozer could conceivably be used by the military to carry a tank. Trucks in general were routinely blocked on this reasoning, along with items necessary to repair and maintain them. Sixty percent of the transportation contracts on hold were for accessories such as tires, car batteries, or spare parts,[75] making it impossible to maintain or repair whatever vehicles there were.

Vehicles of all types were blocked. A report in May 2001 by the UN humanitarian coordinator noted that the firefighting equipment available in Iraq was inadequate, and pressed for lifting the holds on four contracts for firefighting vehicles.[76] The United States had blocked all four contracts.[77]

Boats and related equipment were blocked as well. In a report on the Um Qasr port, where many of the goods for the Oil-for-Food Programme were delivered, the wreckage in the channel caused serious safety hazards for ships and impeded the delivery of humanitarian goods. However, the service contract with a Turkish company to clear the wreckage was blocked.[78] Cranes, diesel engines, and even an ambulance boat were on hold.[79] A port cannot function without cranes and forklifts, but these were blocked.[80]

For transportation contracts, as in other areas, the situation was worsened because the United States refused to provide vendors or UN agencies with any guidelines about the information required, instead imposing inconsistent and unpredictable demands for information; and even when those demands were met, in many cases the United States simply refused to respond at all, either to approve or to explicitly disapprove.

In February 2002 U.S. holds on transportation contracts grew, accompanied by greater demands on the part of the United States for information about the end user. The vendors, the Iraqi government, and UN agencies went to considerable lengths to provide the information requested, but the United States often then asked for additional information or did not respond for months after the new information had been submitted. On multiple occasions, UN staff asked the United States to simply tell them what information would be needed for various types of goods so that the information could be provided up front. A report in February 2002 noted that "OIP would appreciate a feedback from the holding mission as to the level of detail that is required."[81] For the functioning of the port, UN staff reported that Iraq badly needed tugboats and dredgers to clear the port and to dock ships. A total of $18 million in contracts for these were on hold. The Office of the Iraq Programme asked that the holds be released for these high-priority contracts, "especially in cases where the requested information has already been provided. [In addition,] we would appreciate if, at least, a more specific reason for holds could be given on four [contracts] that remain on hold only for 'pending further evaluation/consideration.'"[82]

The United States invoked "dual use" and "WMD" to block every imaginable type of vehicle. The United States blocked a contract for 1,000 water tankers on the grounds that they were lined with stainless steel and therefore were "WMD dual use." Vehicles containing equipment used to empty cesspools were also blocked because of the material used to line the tanks.[83] There were holds on a variety of vehicles necessary for an airport to function: machinery to sweep debris off the runway, firefighting trucks and emergency trucks in case of crashes, vehicles to remove wastewater and to supply drinking water to civilian aircraft, elevators, and even a catering truck.[84] The United States blocked the road sweeper on the grounds that the tank was fiberglass, and blocked the firefighting vehicles because the tanks, which held foam to put out fires, were corrosion resistant. The wastewater truck was considered a "possible dual use application," and the catering truck was blocked because it was refrigerated.

The holds often targeted a specific piece of equipment that was indispensable for the functioning of an entire transportation system. For example, the United States blocked a switching system, the equipment that links an airport with air traffic controls at other airports.[85] The same was true with regard to the railroads. UN staff reported that "Without a reliable railways signalling and communications system the risk of accidents, e.g. head on and rear end collisions, increases dramatically . . . These types of accidents cause loss of human lives, cause substantial losses in equipment, disrupt the normal train traffic." They noted that the Iraqi railway authority had placed orders for equipment in response to "the desperate need to have an immediate working and minimum reliable railway signalling and communication system."[86]

The Iraqi railway authority had ordered a fiber-optic cable system that would provide reliable centralized traffic control to replace the damaged communication and signalling cables. That order was blocked. In the absence of this equipment, the Iraqi railway authority had ordered regular cables to repair the 255 kilometers of damaged cables, to provide at least a short-term solution. Those were also on hold. With neither the current equipment functioning nor upgraded equipment permitted, the railway authority had ordered 100 radio sets, to be placed at railway stations, allowing the staff to radio ahead when a train was coming to ask if the track was clear. Even that would have been a considerable improvement over the existing method, which was to send staff, by taxi, from station to station to clear the line. Each time a train arrived at a station, it had to wait for the rail personnel to drive to the next station and clear the track before the train could depart. However, the radio sets were also blocked.[87]

The losses from the holds were magnified when some goods would arrive but could not be put to use because there were complementary parts needed, and *those* had been blocked. For example, in 2002 UN staff noted that "Al-Shimal and Salah al-Din power stations are both under construction. Programme materials worth $81 million of materials that have arrived cannot be utilized because applications for main equipment are not approved."[88] A 2002 report by the humanitarian coordinator found that production by domestic pharmaceutical plants was compromised when some of the equipment that had arrived could not be used for lack of other parts that had been blocked. For example, inhalers could not be produced because the propellant necessary to make them had been blocked.[89]

Many of the holds were justified on the grounds that these were contracts for dual-use goods, goods that were on the "1051 list," or goods that could be used to produce WMD. Resolution 1051, passed by the Security Council in 1996, identified a list of goods that were not prohibited but that required notification to UNSCOM. After UNSCOM withdrew in 1998, the United States generally blocked 1051 goods across the board. In March 2002 about one-quarter of the holds on medical goods were justified on the grounds that they could be used to produce WMD.[90] Of the equipment for water and sanitation blocked in the fall of 2001, half of the contracts blocked were justified as dual use or on the 1051 list.[91] In November 2001 there were holds on about $1 billion in contracts relating to electricity—one-third of all the funds allocated to electricity in the first five years of the program.[92] The justifications for many of these were dual-use concerns or the claim that they were on the 1051 list.[93]

However, while the United States invoked security concerns and WMD as the rationale for blocking huge quantities of humanitarian goods, its views were rarely shared by others on the Council, and in some cases were disputed by the weapons inspectors themselves. This was the case, for example, when the United States blocked Iraq's contracts for vaccines to treat infant hepatitis, tetanus, and diphtheria. The United States reasoned that the very weak viruses contained in the vaccines might conceivably be extracted and strengthened, then might be grown to produce a biological agent, which then might be used as a biological weapon, if and when Iraq was able to develop the technology for that. Other members of the Security Council disagreed vehemently with these very speculative "security concerns," as did the weapons inspectors for the United Nations Monitoring, Verification and Inspection Commission (UNMOVIC).[94]

Similarly, the United States claimed that certain goods it blocked were contained in the 1051 list, even when that was contradicted by the weapons experts at UNMOVIC and the International Atomic Energy Association. These came to be known as "1051 disagreements." There were, for example, $130.5 million worth of these "1051 disagreements" regarding electrical equipment blocked by the United States in November 2001.[95] But there were also 1051 disagreements in nearly every area—water, electricity, agriculture, and so forth—from 1998 until 2002.

When the United States had no articulated objections, it still blocked goods by simply delaying them without any particular justification. The United States often requested more information, ostensibly in order to gauge the security risk, but once the information was provided in many cases the United States still did not lift the hold. For example, in November 2001, nearly half a billion dollars in holds on critical equipment for electricity—43 percent of all electricity applications on hold—were still blocked by the United States, even though all information that it had requested had already been provided.[96]

In the area of food handling, a report from February 2002 discussed the holds that were frequently placed on trucks and other vehicles, as well as food processing equipment, electrical generators, and laboratory equipment. At the time of the report, $115 million of food processing equipment was on hold, mainly due to requests for "additional information." However, in a third of those cases, all information requested had already been provided but the holds remained in place. Twenty applications for raw materials were on hold, even though in half of the cases all information requested by the United States had been provided.[97]

Over the course of the Oil-for-Food Programme there was a growing number of contracts where the United States received all the information it had requested and still did not respond for months, either to ask for more information or to lift the hold. In February 2002 the total goods on hold were $5.32 billion. For about a third of those ($1.86 billion) all the information requested by the United States had been provided months before and the United States had simply never responded.[98] These included goods in nearly every area, including agriculture, education, food handling, housing, health care, electricity, and oil production. Over 600 contracts were still on hold—months or even years after all the U.S.-requested information had been provided—including everything from olive oil plants to water tankers, furniture, dental equipment, yogurt making equipment, and firemen's suits.[99]

In addition, the United States often demanded that the suppliers provide detailed information about exactly the same items that had been approved before, and then refused to approve the contract until that was done. At a November 2001 briefing to the 661 Committee, technical experts noted that in over 70 percent of the electricity contracts that were on hold, every item questioned by the United States was something that had previously been approved.[100]

In some cases, such as chlorine, the U.S. claim that the goods had dual-use WMD capabilities was quite sound. In response to these concerns, OIP and the UN agencies put in place elaborate monitoring systems that tracked the goods at every point: from the time of contracting, to arrival in Iraq, to delivery at the intended site, to installation of each item, to disposal of the empty or broken items being replaced. In every area, UN and international agencies offered to monitor each item that had dual-use capability or in some other way raised security concerns[101] and then reported in detail on their findings.[102]

For the most part, UN observers found that there was little indication that imported goods were diverted or misused. For example, in a May 2001 report, the humanitarian coordinator for Iraq noted that "End-use/user observations of hospital equipment revealed that all the tracked items were accounted for at every level of the distribution chain."[103] When the United States did allow, for example, water pumps for agricultural irrigation, UN staff found that the pumps "were distributed efficiently and equitably and [Iraqi] staff carried out their installation, operation and maintenance properly."[104] The UN's humanitarian coordinator noted in a May 2001 report that the electrical and mechanical equipment, spare parts, and firefighting vehicles that had been received were equitably distributed.[105]

But even with these systems in place to address U.S. security concerns, and little credible evidence of actual misuse, holds did not decrease. In every area, they increased. For water and sanitation equipment, for example, in July 2000 about $1 million in holds were released but another $15 million of contracts were blocked. In August 2001 $80 million in holds were released, but another $180 million of holds were placed on other contracts.[106] This was the practice throughout the entire Oil-for-Food Programme.

Not surprisingly, the U.S. practices regarding holds were a matter of considerable concern to the other sectors of the UN. In their reports to the 661 Committee the UN agencies repeatedly implored the committee to recognize the urgency of the contracts blocked and to find ways to address the problem of the holds. Under the heading of "immediate requirements" for the water and sanitation sector, UNICEF lists "relax 'hold' criteria, give serious consideration to WatSan priority list [priority contracts to be released from hold]."[107] WHO's report on the health sector concludes, "We strongly urge the 661 Committee to consider the release of holds . . . as an effective observation mechanism is in place."[108]

On a few occasions, for goods that were critical for the civilian population and for which there were no adequate substitutes, after extensive lobbying and negotiating, UN staff were eventually able to persuade the United States to allow these goods into Iraq. For example, in the course of negotiating the items on the Goods Review List (GRL), the United States objected to allowing Iraq to import atropine and insisted on categorizing it as "dual-use," which would ensure considerable delays and would make the drug subject to outright denial as well. Atropine is a drug that is necessary in any surgery where the patient is put under a general anesthetic, and denial or delay would significantly compromise Iraqi health care. Nevertheless, the United States objected to it, on the grounds that it can also be used as an antidote to nerve gas. The rationale was that it might be used by Iraqi soldiers if they became affected while deploying nerve gas on enemies. Once a soldier had inhaled nerve gas, he would have about two minutes, in the midst of battle, to self-inject the atropine correctly before dying of respiratory paralysis. (In discussions with UN staff, it was pointed out that if the Iraqi military wanted to use nerve gas, it would be much easier and more reliable for the Iraqi army to use the gas masks that were already provided to the soldiers.)

In the face of U.S. objections, UN staff presented the United States with extensive data on Iraq's needs for gentamicin, a widely used antibacterial agent that was used to treat meningitis, among other things;[109] streptomycin, an antibiotic used to treat tuberculosis;[110] doxycycline, which was used to treat cholera and malaria; and ciprofloxacin, which was used to treat typhoid and dysentery.[111] UN staff argued that antibiotics were among the most effective ways of addressing a variety of diseases in food animals.[112] UN staff provided the United States with documentation of the need for a number of antibiotics to be used with poultry, sheep, goats, and cattle, including ciprofloxacin, doxycycline, gentamycin, and streptomycin.[113] In regard to all of these medicines, the United States did not claim that the drugs themselves could be used as biological weapons. The rationale was rather that they could be used as an antidote to anthrax, if taken immediately and in large doses. Consequently, the argument went, allowing Iraq to import these antibiotics could indirectly facilitate the use of anthrax, if they were available to Iraqi soldiers deploying anthrax, in the event that the soldiers themselves were indirectly affected.

Similarly, the United States objected to Iraq's import of pralidoxime mesylate, a drug used to treat emergencies involving accidental poisoning from pesticides,[114] on the same grounds—that the Iraqi military might use it as an antidote for soldiers who were accidentally poisoned while employing chemical weapons.

The United States also objected to a number of organophosphorous pesticides. These included phostoxin—a pesticide used on rodents, where grain was stored or transported—as well as other pesticides used on corn borers, termites, and insects infesting pomegranates, date palm, citrus, and vegetables. Phostoxin is used for killing rodents in the field after the seeds have been planted, and phostoxin fumigants are used to protect grain, dried vegetables, and seeds in storage from insects, pests, and rodents.[115] All of these were critical in Iraq's agricultural production. The United States objected on the grounds that it was possible that Iraq might extract chemical components of the pesticides to make chemical weapons.

The United States also objected to the import of growth media to cultivate bacteria. These were in fact included on the 1051 list but UN staff argued that they were also necessary for veterinary diagnostic laboratories as well as for medical diagnostic laboratories for the human population. Growth media was also required to test water at water treatment facilities, in distribution networks, and at the level of household consumption. To obtain U.S. approval, UN personnel documented the need in considerable detail: there were 218 water treatment plants, 1,200 water compact units, and 90 wells. To determine if the water was fit for human consumption, all of these had to be routinely examined for bacteriogical content.[116]

Growth media was also used to test food in microbiology labs to ensure it was safe for human consumption. Again, to persuade the United States, UN staff documented the urgent and legitimate needs: there were dairy laboratories, a silo quality control laboratory, a foodstuff company laboratory, and vegetable oil factories,[117] and all of these needed growth media for their work. There was one occasion, when there was a cholera outbreak in the northern governorates, when the UN successfully appealed to the Security Council Committee to release one particular type.[118] However, the United States still objected to most of the growth media ordered, citing the 1051 list.

In the face of the urgency and the irreplaceability of these goods, UN personnel advocated, sometimes for months, to try to persuade the United States to change its position. In some cases, after going to great lengths to develop procedures to address U.S. demands, UN personnel were successful. In response to the United States' very speculative concern that Iraqi soldiers might deploy nerve gas—*and* would not use a gas mask while doing so, *and* would then be in a position, in the middle of battle, to self-inject atropine within seconds—UN staff ultimately persuaded the United States to permit atropine by proposing that Iraq could only import it in ampules too small to serve as antidotes.[119]

In some cases, UN staff were able to persuade the United States to approve goods by supplying extensive information documenting the exact amounts and locations needed and then providing monitoring for the actual use of the drugs. Once UN personnel calculated the quantities of these goods that would be necessary for legitimate uses, it would then be possible to gauge whether the Iraqi government was ordering excessive amounts that might then be stockpiled for military purposes. But this required a massive investment of labor on the part of UN agencies and the Iraqi government. The Iraqi Ministry of Health and WHO had to estimate the likely use of each of these medicines for every public and private hospital and clinic in Iraq, of which there were a total of 2,128; and every public and private pharmacy in Iraq, of which there were 4,229. The same process was followed for growth media. WHO and the Ministry of Health estimated the use of growth media in each of the 115 laboratories for public health, medical research, medical colleges, nursing schools, and environmental medicine, as well as the eight drug production facilities.[120] UN staff then had to estimate the number of sheep, goats, and cattle in Iraq (21 million as of November 2002) and the number of chickens in Iraq (234 million broiler chicks and 5.9 million layer chicks), and on that basis calculated the amount of antibiotics and growth media needed.[121] After weeks of advocacy, research, and documentation involving dozens of UN personnel, the United States in these cases finally relented and permitted Iraq to import those goods, subject to close monitoring.

The holds were a continual source of tension between the Security Council and the Secretariat, including OIP. By August 1999 the press had focused on the U.S. holds on humanitarian goods, particularly concerning water and sanitation, given the drought that had occurred in Iraq. The director of OIP, Benon Sevan, asked the committee to address the growing number of holds.[122] The U.S. delegate said that the United States had sped up its review of drought-related contracts and had released the holds on some of them.[123] But this was a minor concession: three-quarters of all contracts for the electricity sector remained on hold. The next year Sevan again spoke to the 661 Committee quite bluntly about the human damage done as a result of the holds:

As at 14 April [2000], the total number of holds was 1,180 with a total value of $1,726,891,635. As stated by the Secretary-General at the meeting of the Security Council on 24 March, many of the holds on contract applications do have a direct negative impact on the humanitarian programme, and on efforts to rehabilitate Iraq's infrastructure, most of which is in appalling disrepair . . .

I should like to reiterate the Secretary-General's appeal for a further review and reconsideration of positions taken with regard to applications placed on hold, many of which have a direct negative impact on the implementation of the programme and of our efforts to rehabilitate Iraq's infrastructure, most of which is in appalling disrepair. Otherwise, I am afraid, we will continue to sink further in to the present untenable quagmire.[124]

The holds illustrated many of the basic issues of the sanctions regime in general. As with the reverse veto, the U.S. positions came to be determinative of Security Council policy, even where U.S. positions were unsupported or directly opposed by literally every other nation on the Security Council; were directly challenged by the entire array of UN humanitarian agencies as well as the Secretariat; and at times were disputed even by the UN weapons inspectors themselves. Acting unilaterally—in this case without even the company of the British—the United States succeeded in shaping one of the fundamental policies of the UN as an organization: the question of how to resolve the conflicts between humanitarian interests and security concerns. At the same time there were serious questions about the credibility of U.S. judgments regarding security risks: How plausible were U.S. claims that antibiotics or water tankers could be used for weapons of mass destruction, or that particular goods were unacceptably dangerous, even when these claims were disputed by the weapons inspectors themselves?

At a meeting of the 661 Committee in April 2000, the U.S. delegate, Eugene Young, defended the U.S. policies, arguing that there was a need to ensure that the goods were not misused.[125] But at the same time it was also clear that the U.S. holds were, in part, quite unrelated to security concerns. Young noted that the United States had released holds on humanitarian contracts totaling $275 million in the prior two months. This did not represent a policy change, he said; rather, the United States had allocated more financial resources and personnel to the process of reviewing contracts.[126] Thus the United States had delayed these humanitarian contracts not because of security concerns but simply because it had been unwilling to provide sufficient personnel to review them, and placed contracts on hold by default.

If the United States wanted credibility for its much-vaunted security concerns, this was undermined every time the United States lifted holds on supposedly dangerous items in exchange for votes, or imposed holds as punishment for countries that did not do its bidding on political matters. This took place, for example, with the "smart sanctions" proposal.

In the winter of 2001 the United States blocked Iraq from importing child vaccines on the grounds that they might be used to produce biological weapons. The incident was leaked to the press, and there was an embarrassing series of articles publicizing the U.S. action. [127] The United States responded by pursuing a "smart sanctions" proposal that would ostensibly focus the sanctions on military goods while easing up restrictions on civilian goods. In reality, the plan would have effectively codified many U.S. practices and incorporated them as standard guidelines issued under the authority of the 661 Committee as a whole. If adopted, it would have potentially blocked the same array of goods that the United States had been stopping unilaterally, but without the political costs for the United States. In the aftermath of the debacle over child vaccines, the United States aggressively sought support for this new proposal. To secure China's vote, the United States agreed to lift $80 million worth of holds on Chinese contracts, including $60 million in telecommunications contracts for products such as fiber-optic cables. Yet these were contracts that the United States had blocked, claiming that they had military applications. Indeed, the United States had bombed Iraqi radar and antiaircraft installations earlier on the grounds that they had upgraded using fiber-optic cables; and the United States had then frozen Chinese contracts for these goods.[128] But for the sake of its political agenda at the time, the United States put aside its security concerns; it approved the Chinese contracts and China voted for the "smart sanctions" proposal.

Russia, by contrast, opposed the U.S. proposal. The United States responded by placing holds on all contracts with Russian companies. In May 2002, when a version of the U.S. proposal was finally passed, with Russia's support, the United States lifted holds on $740 million worth of Russian contracts, even though the United States had claimed earlier that those holds had been "necessary to prevent any military exports." Diplomats called it "the boldest move yet by the US to use the holds to buy political agreement."[129]

But the most stunning demonstration of how dubious U.S. "security concerns" were came at the end of the program.

In May 2002, in the face of widespread international pressure, a new version of "smart sanctions" was implemented. It was the Goods Review List, spelling out precisely which goods were clearly prohibited, what needed approval by the 661 Committee, and what was clearly allowed.

Whereas the United States had insisted for over a decade on an arbitrary right to interpret "dual use" and "potential WMD" as it saw fit, this new arrangement provided an explicit, transparent set of criteria. In addition, many of the goods that the United States had claimed for years presented a grave security risk were now—in the face of mounting political pressure–suddenly agreeable to the United States. There was another critical change as well. From the beginning of the program until summer of 2002, all contracts were circulated to all members of the 661 Committee, except for the few that were on the "green list," which bypassed the committee. Consequently, the United States had had the opportunity to review nearly every contract. But under the new system, the UN weapons inspectors first determined whether the goods were on the GRL, and if they were, the contract was then forwarded to the 661 Committee. If UNMOVIC determined that they were not on the list, then the United States had no opportunity to prevent their approval.

Once there were clear criteria, with holds requiring clear and credible reasons, it was immediately obvious that very few of the U.S. holds could be justified. And once the threshold determinations were made by UN weapons experts—not the United States—the approval rates skyrocketed.

As of June 2002 there were holds on 2,202 applications valued at over $5.4 billion. But once the GRL process began, UNMOVIC and IAEA found that only about 10 percent presented a security risk in any form.[130] Not surprisingly, the goods that were immediately approved, which had been blocked by the United States, included medicines and medical equipment, water treatment equipment, electrical generators, water pumps, and vehicles[131]—all of them basic and necessary goods for any modern society to function.

As new applications came in for review in fall 2002, it was clear that when UNMOVIC and IAEA were reviewing the contracts instead of the United States, under the explicit standards of the GRL instead of the overbroad and inconsistent criteria employed by the United States, the same patterns held: UNMOVIC and IAEA found that only about 5 percent of the contracts contained GRL items.[132] But the damage was already done. For six years the United States had successfully prevented over $5 billion in urgent humanitarian goods from entering Iraq.

Opposition to U.S. Practices

The extreme and arbitrary practices of the United States with regard to holds were met with open skepticism and considerable opposition.

There were frequent, direct challenges to U.S. practices from many of the delegates during 661 Committee meetings. At one point Turkey complained that requests were sometimes denied when only one item on a list of dozens was unacceptable.[133] In February and March 1999, Iraq asked the committee to address U.S. holds on medical equipment as well as on urgent contracts relating to electrical power and water supply. The U.S. delegate claimed that the water and electricity contracts could not be approved without "careful study" and that the medical equipment was dual use and therefore presented security concerns.[134] But the Bahrain delegate was skeptical since, he noted, this was exactly the same equipment included in the distribution plan that had been endorsed by the Security Council and approved by the Secretary-General.[135]

In October 1999 the committee again addressed the number of holds, which still continued to grow, and began to demand more accountability. There was opposition to the United States on many fronts. The Malaysian delegate spoke of how detrimental the holds were to the humanitarian program;[136] the delegate from Bahrain pointed out that the original objective of the embargo against Iraq had been very specifically to monitor Iraq's military forces, not to create a humanitarian crisis.[137] The Brazilian delegate described the holds as excessive and demanded better justifications as well as greater transparency.[138] The delegates from China, Russia, and France spoke out as well, endorsing these concerns.

Other delegates were deeply critical of the scale on which the United States had prevented humanitarian contracts from being implemented. The problem had reached "a critical point," said the Russian delegate;[139] the number of holds was excessive, said the Canadian delegate;[140] according to the Tunisian delegate, his delegation had often expressed its concern about the scale of the holds. The British and American delegates said they needed more monitoring for dual-use goods as well as more technical information. But the French delegate, Fabrice Mauriès, challenged this explanation: there was an elaborate monitoring mechanism for telecommunications equipment, and the ITU had been involved in assessing projects. Yet, he said, there were holds on almost 90 percent of telecommunications contracts. Similarly, there was already an effective monitoring mechanism for oil equipment that had existed for some time; yet the holds on oil contracts remained high. Nor was it the case, he suggested, that providing prompt, detailed technical information was sufficient to get holds released: a French contract for the supply of ventilators for intensive care units, a contract with an "obvious humanitarian character," had been on hold for more than five months, even though his government had provided a prompt and detailed response to the requests for information.[141]

The Russian delegate objected to the number of contracts for medical equipment blocked by the United States. The French delegate pointed out that the distribution plans, submitted by Iraq listing every item it might order in the coming six months, were first examined by experts, who verified the need for the items listed. In addition, he noted that while both the United States and Britain examined all contracts, the United States blocked ten times more contracts than Britain. China objected that the United States was slow to approve contracts, even after it had received all the information requested, and argued as well that the United States had a double standard—approving contracts based upon the nationality of the vendor, not the security risk posed by the item.[142] Opposition to the U.S. arbitrariness continued up through the end of the sanctions regime. In late January 2003 the Russian delegate asked for a list of the goods approved and rejected, and the reasons for the holds; the U.S. delegate replied that he did not remember any requirement to provide reasons for U.S. decisions.[143]

In the end, despite the persistent criticism and ongoing reports of the humanitarian crisis in Iraq within the Security Council, from UN relief and development agencies, from the Secretariat, and from international humanitarian organizations, the United States reduced the quantity of holds significantly on only three occasions during the Oil-for-Food Programme (see Figure 1). The first time was after Benon Sevan's detailed briefing in April 2000 regarding the damage being done by the holds.[144] The following month the United States reduced its holds from $1.95 billion to $1.34 billion. But in June they began climbing again. The second occasion was in June 2001, when holds went from $3.67 billion to $2.96 billion. That was in the midst of the attempt by the United States and Britain to persuade the Security Council to adopt the "smart sanctions" plan.

The number of holds did not go down again until the summer of 2002, under the new GRL system. Once the UN weapons inspectors, and not the United States, were judging the security risks of the contracts, the large majority of the contracts were immediately approved. Between July 2002 and October 2002—the first time that the United States no longer had the power to block goods unilaterally—the contracts on hold plummeted from $5.5 billion to less than $1 billion.

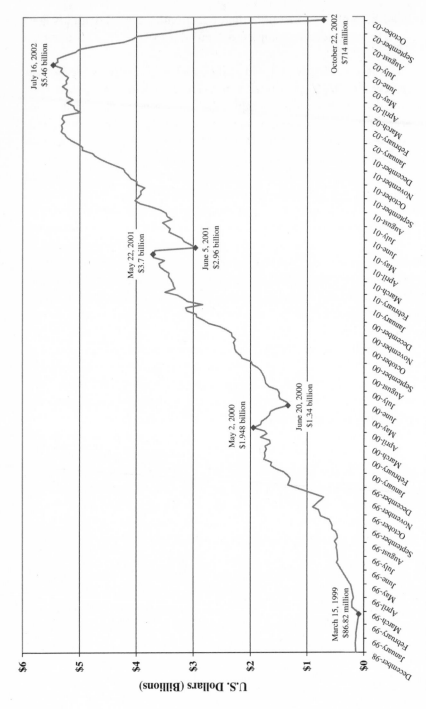

Figure 1. Total holds (humanitarian goods and oil spares). *Source:* Office of the Iraq Programme.

In the end, the United States was quite successful at using the consensus rule within the 661 Committee to prevent huge quantities of urgent and legitimate humanitarian goods from entering Iraq. Invoking "dual-use" claims, the United States was successful at preventing Iraq from importing nearly everything it needed to provide for its infrastructure: to pump water, to generate electricity, to deliver food, to operate hospitals, to have a functioning telephone system. While those within the U.S. administrations who were responsible for these practices may have believed they were justified, it was clear that these policies were brutal and indiscriminate in their impact on Iraq's civilian population. While the United States insisted that its policy was driven by security concerns, its determinations of what constituted a "security concern" were often ridiculed by other committee members and openly disputed by UN weapons inspectors. On many occasions it became apparent that the United States did not seriously believe its own claims regarding security concerns, particularly when U.S. objections simply disappeared in the face of embarrassing press coverage or were bartered away for votes. The story of the holds offers a stark illustration of the United States' willingness to go to extraordinary lengths to prevent urgent humanitarian goods from entering Iraq, even when its justifications were patently implausible and bitterly disputed by the international community, or when there was simply no justification at all.

5

THE MAGNITUDE OF THE CATASTROPHE

As the social and economic structure of Iraq deteriorated throughout the 1990s, there was a growing dispute over who was to blame. By all accounts, Saddam Hussein's political enemies were tortured and killed, the Kurds were badly mistreated, there was extensive suppression of speech and press, and the Shi'a majority were disenfranchised and persecuted. The perversity and irony of the sanctions regime, imposed under the auspices of international law, is that it may have done more human damage than Saddam Hussein's persecution of ethnic groups and human rights violations combined.

The United States consistently maintained that the harm done to the Iraqi population was entirely due to the policies of the Iraqi government. Some of the claims are true: there were kickbacks on contracts for the importation of goods, and for a short time on oil sales. There was ongoing smuggling, as trucks with oil and goods flowed between Iraq and its neighbors. Certainly the Iraqi government wasted money on prestige projects, such as palaces. It is also true that the government of Iraq had policies that were cynical and manipulative, such as using child deaths for propaganda purposes. At the same, it is also true that the United States, sometimes joined by Britain, imposed strictures on imports that were far more harsh than security concerns warranted, blocking goods such as shoe leather and plastic juice bottles on the grounds that these could contribute to Iraq's industrial capacity, military capacity, or production of weapons of mass destruction.

It is tempting to say simply that everyone contributed to the humanitarian catastrophe in Iraq, and leave it at that. But it is possible to go further than just listing all of these things. In this chapter I am not interested in those measures that were particularly petty or ridiculous, or those that caused inconvenience or discomfort, or marginally worsened the poverty and hardship, or caused illness, or even caused tens or hundreds of deaths. What I want to explore now is the question of how a human catastrophe *of this magnitude* came about: what the policies and practices were that caused hundreds of thousands of deaths; decimated the health of several million children; destroyed a whole economy; made a shambles of a nation's education and health care systems; reduced a sophisticated country, in which much of the population lived as the middle class in a First World country, to the status of Fourth World countries— the poorest of the poor, such as Rwanda, Somalia, Haiti; and in a society notable for its scientists, engineers, and doctors, established an economy dominated by beggars, criminals, and black marketeers. These things do not come from blocking shipments of glue and laundry detergent, or even from building useless palaces. They are the result of measures that compromised the economy as a whole by broadly restricting imports in a society that was heavily dependent on imports; by restricting or undermining oil sales in an economy that was heavily dependent on oil sales for its gross domestic product (GDP); and by undermining the infrastructure— electricity production, telecommunications, transport, and water and sewage treatment—in an advanced industrialized society that was highly dependent on modern infrastructure.

Consider the rate of child mortality. According to most of the studies undertaken by researchers, at least 500,000 children under age five who died during the sanctions period would not have died under the Iraqi regime prior to sanctions. Prior to the 2003 war on Iraq, UN agencies warned that 25 percent of Iraqi children were so severely malnourished that interruption of food access would put their lives at risk. What does this signify?

Child mortality will be low if there is an effective system for treating sewage, purifying drinking water, providing nutritious food, and providing health care to families. But all of these in turn assume a great deal: that there is enough electricity to fuel sewage and water treatment plants; that there is equipment to install water pipes and electricity for the pumps to send water through the system; that the education system trains enough doctors and health care workers to meet the population's needs; that there is electricity to fuel irrigation for crops; that there is an industrial capacity to produce fertilizer, pesticides, construction materials, and pharmaceuticals; that there are replacement parts and regular maintenance for medical equipment, electrical generators, and industrial facilities; that the education system has the capacity to train the agronomists, engineers, computer scientists, and meteorologists needed to support the infrastructure, agriculture, and industry; that there are enough equipment and materials to build hospitals, to maintain chlorination systems, to transport food, to refrigerate food and medicines, to operate warehouses, to maintain telephone systems, to run city buses, and to repair highways; and that there is a functioning economy that can privately or publicly pay those necessary to do all these things—construction workers, truck drivers, electrical engineers, farmers, and civil servants.

In the face of economic failure, war, or natural disaster, there would ordinarily be emergency measures taken at the time of crisis, followed by structural changes over time to rebuild or adapt to the new conditions. Iraq was particularly vulnerable because of its heavy dependence on imports and because of its reliance on oil as its major source of revenue. However, in addition to its oil wealth, it had extensive human capital and a good deal of fertile land for agriculture. Sanctions alone, even if they were long term, could not have brought about the collapse of so many systems; any sector of the infrastructure that became incapacitated could have been rebuilt if Iraq's other capabilities had remained intact. On the other hand, no temporary measure, however devastating, could in itself have brought about this degree of damage; even if the entire infrastructure were compromised, Iraq's oil wealth in combination with its engineers and civil servants would have made it possible for it to rebuild. However, in fourteen years, Iraq's economy and society never came close to achieving the level they had reached in 1990. Of all the acts that contributed to the problems in Iraq, what exactly were the measures that resulted in the *magnitude* of the humanitarian catastrophe?

One of these was the basic sanctions regime itself, which blocked nearly all imports for a country that had imported 70 percent of its food and was dependent on imports for nearly every aspect of its economy and public services. When there were humanitarian exemptions that theoretically permitted Iraq to purchase critical goods, the systematic, large-scale holds prevented many of these goods from ever arriving in Iraq. These in turn prevented the repair and reconstruction of the nation's infrastructure. The other major factors were: (1) the initial destruction of the infrastructure in the 1991 bombing during the Persian Gulf War, followed by the imposition of nearly comprehensive sanctions; (2) the collapse in Iraq's GDP and the economy as a whole; and (3) measures that prohibited, limited, or undermined income from oil sales. Not all of these measures were in place throughout the entire sanctions period, and not all of them affected every aspect of the economy and social systems. But these are the factors that were jointly responsible for the magnitude of the social, economic, and cultural catastrophe in Iraq from 1990 to 2003. For all of these measures, the United States held primary responsibility; Britain was often but not always a participant in their imposition. The Security Council measures, made far more draconian by the interpretations and agenda of the United States, simply overwhelmed every effort that Iraq made, and every effort it could have made. If Iraq had used every cent of its resources prudently and efficiently, if there had been no corruption or abuse at all, the magnitude of the human destruction inflicted by these measures would not have been substantially different.

The 1991 Bombing and Sanctions

The military coalition that attacked Iraq was a massive effort, in which the U.S. had a primary role. It took place under the command of U.S. general Norman Schwarzkopf and involved over a half million U.S. military personnel. In all, 130,000 tons of ordnance dropped on Iraq during forty-three days of intensive bombing in 1991 caused infrastructure damage estimated at $232 billion.[1] By all accounts the bombing was massive, and targeted not only military facilities but all infrastructure as well, presumably on the rationale that electricity, roads, and water treatment plants could be used by the military as well as civilians.

> The bombing of Iraq was aimed not only at military targets but also at such assets as civilian infrastructure, power stations, transport and telecommunications networks, fertiliser plants, oil facilities, iron and steel plants, bridges, schools, hospitals, storage facilities, industrial plants and civilian buildings. And the assets that were not bombed were rendered dysfunctional because of the destruction of power generating facilities.[2]

Prior to the war, the U.S. Defense Department anticipated that the damage from such a bombing campaign would be devastating to critical public services, which were already precarious. In January 1991, shortly before the bombing began, a memo from the Defense Intelligence Agency to Central Command described the vulnerability of Iraq's water system. The memo noted that Iraq depended on imported and specialized equipment, as well as imported chemicals for water treatment. Iraq had no domestic means of producing the equipment and materials for water and sewage treatment, and no significant alternative sources.[3] Reports indicated that the chlorine supply was already critically low, that the importation of chlorine was blocked by UN sanctions, and that Iraq's main production plants had been shut down for lack of materials and parts.[4] Without chlorine, the memo said, there would be an increase in waterborne diseases, and possibly epidemics of cholera, hepatitis, and typhoid.[5] In addition, a number of critical industries required pure water for production, including food processing, pharmaceuticals, and thermal power plants, and these were likely to become incapacitated.[6] If the situation continued, the memo noted, it would probably take at least another six months for the "full degradation" of the water treatment system.[7]

The bombing campaign that followed brought that about immediately, and much more besides. A World Health Organization (WHO) report noted that "most of the local pharmaceutical production facilities closed down (following the damage caused by the war such as the Samara Drug Industries (SDI) plant for syringes in Babylon Governorate)."[8] A mission from WHO and UNICEF, visiting Iraq after the war, noted that "all significant electrical power generating plants in Iraq have now been destroyed"[9] and that the plants that had produced the main elements for water treatment, aluminum sulphate and chlorine, were destroyed by bombing.[10] Even where water treatment plants themselves had not been bombed, they were only operating for a few hours per day, using emergency generators, because the power grid was incapacitated.[11]

One scholar noted that this vast scale of destruction, which must have set the economy back fifty years, should not be surprising in light of the fact that the initial plan of bombing had focused on 84 targets but had been expanded during the course of the war to include 723 targets.[12] In February 1991 a team sent by UNICEF and WHO surveyed the damage from the bombing throughout Iraq. They reported that, throughout the country, in urban as well as rural areas, the destruction to power plants and refineries was so extensive that "this necessitates a careful rationing of the system's remaining fuel supply, which will not last more than five weeks."[13] Iraq's infrastructure was so devastated that "Baghdad has no public electricity, no telephones, no gasoline for civilian vehicles, and less than 5% of its normal water supply."[14]

The damage to Iraq's electrical facilities was so extreme that the electrical output after the war was 4 percent of the prewar level, and four months later it was still only 20–25 percent of the prewar level.[15] A UN envoy sent to Iraq wrote that "nothing that we had seen or read had quite prepared us for the particular form of devastation which has now befallen the country. [Iraq] . . . had been, until January 1991, a rather highly urbanized and mechanized society . . . Iraq has, for some time to come, been relegated to a pre-industrial age."[16]

This was at the core of the devastation of Iraq's economy and society. On one hand, the bombing of infrastructure alone could have had only short-term consequences because Iraq had the human resources and the wealth to rebuild. On the other hand, if comprehensive sanctions had been imposed on Iraq without war, Iraq's industrial capacity and human resources were so extensive that it could well have been able to increase domestic industry and agriculture enough to compensate for the losses resulting from the sanctions, at least to some degree. However, the two in combination meant that the basic infrastructure necessary to run a modern, industrialized society was fundamentally compromised, and the sanctions then prevented rebuilding.

The Collapse of GDP and the Economy

The comprehensive sanctions imposed by the Security Council crippled Iraq's entire economy. According to 1990 testimony before Congress, the sanctions eliminated 90 percent of Iraq's imports and 97 percent of its exports.[17] As a result, per capita income went from $3,510 in 1989 to $450 in 1996.[18] In 1989 Iraq's GDP was $66.2 billion; in 1996 it was $10.8 billion. With the Oil-for-Food Programme the economy recovered to some degree, reaching a GDP of $31.8 billion in 2000.[19] Lost income and productivity for the period from 1990 to 1995 was estimated at $265.3 billion.[20] Iraq's illicit trade and other economic resources had little impact on the economy. Before the Gulf War, Iraq's annual oil sales were more than $10 billion, representing 61 percent of the GDP. After the war, Iraq could generate only $800 million per year from smuggling small quantities to Turkey and Jordan, liquidation of hidden assets, and government gold reserves.[21]

The economic collapse deprived Iraq of the foreign currency needed to operate industry and economic production.[22] To the extent that the Security Council permitted Iraq to import food and medicine, particularly before the Oil-for-Food Programme, the lack of cash prevented sufficient imports of food and medicine.[23] From 1990 to 1996, Iraq was explicitly blocked from importing any goods that constituted "industrial input," interpreted very broadly, and this restriction helped prevent Iraq from restarting its economy. As of 1997, the Economist Intelligence Unit reported that real GDP was estimated to have fallen by nearly two-thirds in 1991, and that "agricultural growth has since been low and erratic, and manufacturing output has all but vanished."[24] The Oil-for-Food Programme only brought goods into the country, without providing jobs or stimulating economic productivity. This never changed significantly during the course of the economic sanctions.

The situation for individuals mirrored that of the Iraqi economy as a whole: even when goods were available, few people had enough income to buy them.[25] This was due in large measure to the collapse in purchasing power of the Iraqi dinar, which depreciated by over 5,000 percent.[26] "In 1995, food prices were 4,000 to 5,000 times their August 1990 levels, while average monthly salaries were only 3,000 to 5,000 dinars. Consequently, families' real earnings have fallen to less than 5% of their presanctions level, as measured by their food-purchasing power."[27] Government employees earned on average from 4,000 to 6,000 dinars monthly (approximately $2 to $3) from 1993 to 1999.[28] As of 1999, average salaries were still on the order of $3 to $6 per month.[29]

By 1993 Iraq's GDP had fallen to 1960 levels, bringing about the "nullification of nearly half a century of growth and improvement in the living standards of the population."[30] The impact of the collapse of Iraq's economy was immediate, and affected every aspect of the daily life of the Iraqi population, including "exorbitant prices, collapse of private incomes, soaring unemployment, drastically reduced food intakes, large scale depletion of personal assets, high morbidity levels, escalating crime rates and rapidly increasing numbers of destitute people."[31]

A related factor was the impoverishment of the state itself and the state's lack of funds to pay civil servants. In a centralized economy where the state provided critical public services such as electricity and health care, the bankrupting of the state, which was the deliberate goal of the sanctions, had an enormous impact on the humanitarian situation. This did not improve significantly under the Oil-for-Food Programme, since the program (at least by design) did not allow any funds to go to the state.

In 2000 a review of the first decade of sanctions noted that one significant lesson learned was the need for a cash component: "Whereas under the OFFP, funds have been made available for purchase of supplies, no corresponding funds have to-date been realised for meeting such costs as transport, training, supervision and monitoring, etc. This has had a negative impact on the efficiency and effectiveness of the programme."[32]

This issue was raised repeatedly over the course of the Oil-for-Food Programme. A 2001 WHO report noted that implementing the humanitarian program in the health sector was "constrained by the fact that there is no cash component for labour, installation of heavy hospital equipment/systems," training of medical personnel, engineers, and technicians, or operation of epidemiological reporting systems.[33]

In 2002 a UNICEF report noted that

> the lack of a cash component for the south and centre of Iraq imposed serious constraints on national ability to use the supplies in an effective and efficient manner. Local costs such as transportation, storage and inventory, installation of equipment, and training to ensure proper operation and maintenance of equipment, could not be covered through the programme . . . [In addition,] funds from oil sales . . . could not be used to purchase locally produced supplies, which would have helped move the weak domestic economy.[34]

The same problems were visible in every sector. A water and sanitation consultant noted:

> It is clear from the very serious staffing shortage that the Iraqi authorities have insufficient local funds to implement their water and sanitation projects in an effective manner. Although the use of a cash component would not in itself resolve all constraints on effective implementation, it is essential to improve the operational capabilities of the relevant authorities. For example, in regard to planning and tracking of materials, computers and software are readily available on the local market in Baghdad but neither [of the water and sanitation agencies] can afford to purchase these in order to operate more effectively.[35]

Hans von Sponeck, the former UN humanitarian coordinator in Iraq, noted that the

> lack of cash prevented the implementation of a number of important projects included in the health, water, sanitation and education sectors. To give one example: in 1999, the municipality of Baghdad was facing a serious breakdown of the sewerage system in one

part of the city. It had to cancel orders for equipment because of a lack of cash for transport and installation.[36]

Limits on Oil Income

Given that oil sales were interrupted for six years and were then permitted on only a limited basis, the collapse of Iraq's economy was inevitable. In 1989 the contribution of oil to the GDP was 61.3 percent, while agriculture was 5 percent. The Persian Gulf War and the sanctions that followed meant an 85 percent decline in oil production.[37] Because of Iraq's heavy reliance on oil, the measures prohibiting, limiting, or undermining oil sales would have been sufficient in themselves to prevent Iraq's recovery, even without the restrictions on imports. These measures took several forms.

Ceilings on Oil Sales

The sanctions imposed on Iraq initially in August 1990 prohibited all UN member states from engaging in trade with Iraq, including oil purchases.[38] In the summer of 1991 the Secretary-General's envoy estimated that it would take about $20 billion to restore Iraq's basic services, including electricity, health care, water treatment, and food.[39] The cost of running minimal services for a one-year period was estimated to be $6.8 billion.[40] In light of this estimate, the Security Council offered an oil-for-food program,[41] but it was one in which the amount of funding was severely limited: the arrangement permitted Iraq emergency oil sales of $1.6 billion over a six-month period. However, of that amount, about one-third would go to Kuwait and to the UN for administrative expenses, leaving Iraq $930 million over six months. This was far less than what was needed just for food imports, much less even minimal costs to provide electricity, water and sewage treatment, or medical supplies.

When the Security Council authorized a second oil-for-food arrangement in 1995,[42] Iraq was permitted to sell $2 billion every six months, of which 30 percent was deducted for payments to Kuwait, as well as other deductions to pay for the United Nations Special Commission and UN administrative costs,[43] leaving slightly over $1 billion every six months for the bulk of Iraq's population in the south/center. In February 1998 the Security Council raised the ceiling on oil sales to $5.265 billion each six-month period, which (after deductions for the Kuwait compensation fund and UN costs) meant that $3.4 billion was available for humanitarian purposes. Finally, in December 1999, the ceiling was lifted altogether.[44] The ceilings on oil sales for the two oil for food programs up to December 1999 were so low that, under the best of circumstances, they did not come close to funding even the most urgent and basic needs identified by Aga Kahn's delegation in 1991; much less could they compensate for the additional deterioration that had taken place since 1991. Given that Iraq's GDP had gone from $66 billion to $10.8 billion, the oil income under the Oil-for-Food Programme could not have restored Iraq's economy in any significant way.

Deductions for the Kuwait Compensation Fund

While the ceilings on oil sales were set so low as to preclude significant improvement of the economy, that amount in turn was reduced substantially by amounts directed toward the Kuwait compensation fund that had been established. In 1991 in conjunction with the first oil-for-food program, the Security Council determined that up to 30 percent of any proceeds from oil sales should be directed to compensate losses suffered by Kuwaitis and others as a result of Iraq's invasion of Kuwait. That was reduced to 25 percent in December 2000.[45]

By late 2002, the Oil-for-Food Programme had transferred over $16 billion to the United Nations Compensation Commission (UNCC).[46] The magnitude of payments to the UNCC, while the humanitarian crisis in Iraq continued, was criticized by many involved in the humanitarian efforts. Von Sponeck noted:

> The fact that payments were made at a time when mortality and destitution rates were steeply increasing . . . remains one of the lesser known scandals involving the United Nations Security Council. Justified claims for well-endowed firms and governments could have been deferred without difficulty or injustice to the claimants to a date when the human condition in Iraq was less desperate.[47]

The problem was not only that an enormous amount of funds were earmarked for economic losses abroad at the expense of the humanitarian crisis in Iraq. It was also that there was considerable question as to whether all the compensation paid was legitimate. In June 2000, for example, the commission awarded the Kuwait Petroleum Company $15.9 billion as compensation for its losses. Critics argued that the amount was "implausibly large," and that the grounds for the projected losses were so speculative as to be unsound. According to one analysis, of the $15.9

billion awarded, "actual damages to Kuwait are overstated by at least $12 billion."[48] Even though $16.3 billion of Iraq's revenues generated under the Oil-for-Food Programme had gone into the compensation fund by October 2002,[49] Iraq had had little opportunity to question the accuracy of the claims made by the Kuwait Petroleum Company and others—because Iraq was not treated as a direct party to the process and did not have the right to be heard as a defendant.

Iraq also charged the commission with granting compensation that went beyond even the amounts sought by the claimants. In a Security Council meeting in December 1999, the Iraqi representative noted that the commission granted compensation of $153.4 million to the committee on missing persons, even though the committee had only submitted a claim for $58.5 million. The Iraqi delegate also maintained that in 575 cases the commission compensated claimants twice for the same claim.[50]

According to Iraq's legal counsel, under the UNCC procedure Iraq had no right to be informed of the claims against it; in some cases Iraq still had not been notified, years after claims were filed.[51] Iraq was not given the right to challenge the claimant's case and argue its own case. It was permitted only to comment, one time, on the Secretariat's explanation for its position.[52] Iraq was not entitled to see or address the evidence presented regarding the claims.[53] It was, however, required to pay not only for its own legal costs but for all of the administrative costs and legal fees for the UN and the claimants. As of October 2002 that amount came to $278 million.[54] But Iraq was also prohibited from using funds from oil sales to pay for these costs.[55]

Thus the severe limits on oil imports were made substantially harsher by the deductions for compensation to Kuwait, and these deductions were made even where that compensation was based upon questionable claims, which were not open to scrutiny or challenge by Iraq.

The "Lamentable State" of the Oil Industry

The condition of the oil industry was so poor that Iraq's ability to generate oil income was compromised, even when oil sales were permitted. In 1998 the ceiling on oil sales was increased to $5.3 billion, but by the end of the year it was clear that its production capacity could not keep up.[56] By 2000 the situation had not improved much.[57] The consultants hired by the UN to evaluate Iraq's oil production did not mince words. Their report of March 2000 stated bluntly that "the lamentable state of the Iraqi Oil Industry has not improved. The level of oil exports during phase 7 will decline from the level of 2.2 million barrels per day achieved in phase 6, to a level of between 1.8 to 1.9 million barrels per day."[58]

The primary reason that oil production continued to flounder was the lack of spare parts and necessary equipment.

> As reported in March 1998 "a sharp increase in production without concurrent expenditure on spare parts and equipment would severely damage oil-containing rocks, and pipeline systems." This has now occurred. The reasons for the lack of effectiveness of the spare parts and equipment program are many and the situation can be summarised as "too little, too late."[59]

The ongoing deterioration of Iraq's oil industry during the Oil-for-Food Programme was not new information. One member of the Security Council observed that six months earlier the Secretary-General had already stressed the need to allocate more funds for oil spares and equipment: "The state of the Iraqi oil industry was known to us even before the findings of the oil experts."[60]

Even though Iraq was permitted to allocate $400 million of the proceeds from oil sales to buy spare parts and equipment, a substantial portion of the equipment it contracted for was blocked or put on hold. As of October 1998, for example, there were contracts totaling $133 million for oil spares circulated to the committee; of those, $38 million in contracts were put on hold.[61] As of January 1999 Iraq had submitted $269 million in oil contracts for that six-month period; holds were placed on $51 million worth of those.[62] When one set of holds was lifted, another set of contracts would be blocked.[63] As with the holds on humanitarian imports, the United States alone was responsible for the overwhelming majority of these blocks; a few were blocked by Britain and a few were blocked by both countries. In March 2000, for example, the United States imposed 97 percent of the holds.[64] In August 2002 there were over 600 oil equipment contracts blocked; of those, the United States had placed holds on over 99 percent.[65]

While the United States justified its extreme and unilateral measures by invoking security concerns, the oil consultants questioned the legitimacy of these claims. The United States gave reasons for blocking particular contracts that were so vague neither the manufacturer nor the oil consultants could figure out what information to provide in response. Some equipment would be approved at one point, then rejected at another, with no apparent reason. Equipment was rejected as "dual use," although it was standard industrial equipment that was necessary for oil extraction. Once the United States had been provided with all the information it sought, it often continued to keep the holds in place without explanation. It would sometimes delay approval for a year or more, and by then the pricing of goods had changed so much that the contract had to be renegotiated altogether.[66]

An April 2002 report noted that there were contracts that remained "on hold for no specific reason," even though they were "an absolute priority" for oil production. The United States had blocked all of them, giving as reasons only that they were "pending further evaluation."[67] For over a dozen others, all information that the United States had requested was provided to it, but the United States simply provided no response—no further request for information, no approval, and no explicit disapproval.[68]

The U.S. holds were so extensive that when the Secretary-General proposed increasing the amount of funds that Iraq could spend on oil spares in order to increase its oil production capacity, members of the Security Council pointed out that doing so would be futile given the likelihood that those contracts would be blocked.[69] At the same time, for part of the period of the program, the revenues from the Oil-for-Food Programme were so low that there was not enough money to both pay for oil parts and meet the critical humanitarian needs.[70]

The Cash Component

In October 2000 Iraq approached the 661 Committee with a request for reimbursement of 50 cents per barrel for the costs of oil engineers, maintenance, and equipment. This was rejected. But in December 2000 the Security Council passed a resolution allowing for a cash component of 600 million euros for each six-month phase to pay for maintenance and operations within the oil industry.[71] UN officials viewed this as necessary to prevent the collapse of the oil industry.[72] The Council agreed that it was necessary for Iraq to be able to pay for the cash costs of maintenance and labor. In working out the mechanics of this procedure, Iraq agreed that all cash would be handled in such a way that the government of Iraq had no control over the funds, which was the primary concern of the United States and Britain. However, the United States and Britain objected to the proposed exchange rate of euros to dinars, and objected as well to operating the program through the central bank of Iraq or a Jordanian bank, which were the only possibilities. The oil cash component was never implemented.

Retroactive Oil Pricing

Shortly after the stalemate involving the cash component, reports began coming in that Iraq was charging kickbacks on oil sales: purchasers were paying Iraq generally 15 to 25 cents per barrel, under the table. The United States and Britain were indignant, claiming that the government of Iraq was using these kickbacks to buy weapons or luxuries for the elite. It seems that this is unlikely. As the Security Council noted, Iraq needed about $1 billion annually (1.2 billion euros) for costs of oil production. Because the illicit surcharges on the oil contracts amounted to only $229 million, it would seem that these funds would have been entirely consumed by the costs of oil production.

Nevertheless, in 2001 the United States and Britain instituted a "retroactive pricing" policy in response. Ordinarily, oil prices were set in advance for the coming month; Iraq and the UN's oil overseers would discuss the price, the 661 Committee would approve it, and that price would then be in effect for all purchases in the following month. But the 661 Committee operated by consensus, with the result that any member could veto any proposal, for any reason or for no reason. In retaliation for Iraq's surcharges, the United States and Britain simply began withholding their approval for each month's price, until the month had passed. The price was then set retroactively, using a formula based on the average market prices during the previous month.[73] Consequently, under this arrangement, the oil purchasers were required to sign blind contracts, in which they committed to purchases without knowing the price which they were obligated to pay until well afterwards. The United States and Britain claimed that this allowed the committee to determine retroactively what the fair market value of the oil had been the previous month and charge buyers accordingly.[74] Thus, the argument went, Iraq was receiving no more and no less than fair market value; that eliminated the premia that went to middlemen and consequently eliminated the possibility that the middlemen would pay Iraq illicit surcharges. However, it also meant that the commercial feasibility of Iraqi oil sales was substantially compromised. The chief economist at the American Petroleum Institute asked, "How can you do business if you don't know what the price is?"[75] As the oil overseers noted, "the more effective the measures taken by the Committee are, the more export levels will then be reduced."[76]

Thus it was not surprising when oil sales collapsed, triggering a financial crisis in the Oil-for-Food Programme. In February 2002 the oil overseers estimated that an additional 200 million barrels of oil, which were lost due to the pricing dispute, could have been lifted from December 2000 to January 2002.[77]

Iraq contributed to the financial crisis when it stopped selling oil for short periods of time. In June 2001, to protest the "smart sanctions" proposal, Iraq stopped selling oil, with a loss of income of $1 billion; and in April 2002, as a protest against Israel's actions against the Palestinians, Iraq again stopped lifting oil, with a loss of income of $1.2 billion. Even so, the collapse of income to the Oil-for-Food Programme was primarily due to retroactive pricing. One diplomat on the 661 Committee estimated that the retroactive oil pricing had resulted in a loss of $4.4 billion in sales for the period it was in place—a 40 percent reduction in income to the Oil-for-Food Programme.[78]

The impact on the program was severe. As of February 2002 there were 699 applications for humanitarian supplies, worth $1.6 billion, which had been approved but could not be purchased due to the drop in revenue from oil sales. In addition, there was another $5.32 billion in contracts that were on hold. If the United States and Britain had lifted the holds, there would have been no funds to pay for the goods; there would have been a total shortfall of $6.9 billion.[79]

As the financial crisis continued, the number of fully approved but unfunded contracts began to grow. In September 2002 the head of the Office of the Iraq Programme estimated that, combined with shortfalls from earlier in the program, there were now $2.3 billion in approved contracts for which there were no funds.[80] Two months later, in November 2002, the funding shortfall for fully approved contracts came to $3.3 billion; and if the contracts on hold had been approved, the shortfall would amount to over $10 billion.[81] As of February 2003 there were over 2,500 applications that had been fully approved but lacked funding, totaling nearly $5 billion. These included $770 million in materials and equipment for agriculture, $396 million for education, $561 million for electricity, $374 million for health care, and $628 million for housing.[82]

For example, as of November 2002, contracts for $3.36 million in medicine for leukemia had been approved but could not be purchased because of shortage of funds.[83] As pharmaceutical production was expanding, it was undermined by the lack of equipment and supplies, such as filters for "clean rooms." There were no filters because, while the contracts for them had been approved, there was no funding.[84] The need for medical oxygen was 8 million liters per year, of which less than 10 percent was produced in Iraq. A contract for oxygen plants, totaling $58 million, had recently been approved but could not be purchased because of lack of funds.[85]

By 2001 the prices were so low that it was clear that illicit surcharges were no longer possible. Even so, the United States and Britain refused to end the retroactive pricing. The practice continued until the end of the Oil-for-Food Programme, despite intense public criticism over the worsening humanitarian situation and internal criticism as billions of dollars of critical humanitarian contracts went unfunded. In the end, the policy continued until the war against Iraq in 2003.

Even if Saddam Hussein siphoned off millions of dollars, or for that matter hundreds of millions, or built $2 billion worth of palaces over a decade, as the United States often claimed, those were not what caused the magnitude of the humanitarian crisis in Iraq. What caused a catastrophic collapse of every system needed to sustain human life, and what maintained that state of crisis for over a decade, were the massive destruction from bombing in 1991; the inability of Iraq to import goods that might have allowed Iraq to rebuild its devastated infrastructure; the collapse of the economy overall; and once Iraq was permitted in principle to purchase imports, the measures that crippled Iraq's capacity to produce oil and generate income.

What is startling is that these measures were redundant: if some had not caused extensive damage, the others would have; if Iraq had been able to resolve one set of problems, the others would have ensured that the crisis continued. For example, by 2002 the quantity of goods on hold had grown to $5 billion. But during the same period, even if the holds had somehow been lifted, the retroactive oil pricing meant that the Oil-for-Food Programme was bankrupted and there were no funds to pay for the goods. Or take, for example, the ceiling on oil exports: once the ceiling on oil sales was lifted, Iraq was blocked from obtaining the equipment necessary to increase its oil production. Or consider the blocked contracts for electrical equipment: even if Iraq had been allowed to buy the equipment and chemicals for water and sewage treatment, there was not sufficient electricity to power the plants. There were multiple systems in place that prevented Iraq's economy and humanitarian systems from functioning; if Iraq had somehow found a way to work around any one of them, through greater efficiency or use of hidden resources or any-thing else, the other systems in place would still have ensured that there would be devastation affecting the totality of Iraqi society.

In the end, the result was far greater than the physical damage that could have been done by simply bombing, and the human losses were greater than those from a genocidal campaign conducted all at one time. Not only were infrastructure destroyed and lives lost, but the measures that prevented Iraq from rebuilding meant that the losses would not come to an end; the massive losses would continue year after year. It is not ex-cessive to say that these measures had the sort of impact on Iraq's popu-lation as a whole as do events such as war, famine, disease, and natural disaster—or more specifically, a war or natural disaster that continued nonstop for fifteen years. We might say that these measures, determined at every juncture by the United States and Britain and imposed in the name of international governance, were the horsemen of Iraq's apocalypse.

6

TENSIONS AT THE UNITED NATIONS

The Iraq sanctions created considerable tension within the UN, in part because it was a policy that stood in direct opposition to the normal mandates of the World Food Programme (WFP), the Food and Agriculture Organization (FAO), the United Nations Development Programme (UNDP), and other UN agencies. There were also deep schisms within the UN over the legality of the sanctions as the humanitarian cost continued to mount. The General Assembly, the Economic and Social Council (ECOSOC), and other organs within the UN challenged the sanctions as themselves constituting human rights violations, in violation of international law.

The pressure for measures that addressed the humanitarian crisis, and for sanctions reform, resulted in a series of formal changes in various policies and procedures. But these reforms were in turn compromised in a variety of ways. The United States consistently resisted attempts to document the humanitarian crisis, objected to attempts at reform, and, when reforms were eventually put in place, undermined their implementation.

Opposition within the Security Council

Although the Security Council passed numerous resolutions condemning Iraq for its failure to disarm or for other reasons, within the 661 Committee it was clear that the broad support of the Council for the sanctions regime began to erode once the humanitarian cost became apparent, shortly after the Gulf War of 1991. The United States often claimed that objections to the sanctions came from countries with economic interests in Iraq—Russia, France, and China; or those with political alliances, such as the Arab countries. In fact, the opposition to the sanctions within the Security Council was quite different. It is true that, beginning in the mid-1990s, France and Russia, sometimes joined by China, were vocal opponents of U.S. policies, including the no-fly zones and the sanctions, and challenged the United States on the question of whether Iraq had met its disarmament obligations. However, prior to that, France had joined the United States in conducting over-flights pursuant to the no-fly zones (and continued until 1998). Also, in the first half of the 1990s, France often joined the United States and Britain in blocking Iraq's import of goods. During this period there was very little opposition from Russia or China; in fact, both countries were almost entirely silent in the first five years of 661 meetings, neither blocking goods nor objecting to U.S. blocks, nor contesting the United States and Britain on other measures.

The most consistent opposition throughout the sanctions period came from elected members, particularly those from developing countries, even though they had no economic or political ties with Iraq and stood to gain nothing by challenging the United States on an issue where it had little tolerance for opposition. It was elected members—Canada and Brazil—that used their presidencies on the Security Council to implement major reform attempts: in 1999 Brazil's Celso Amorim successfully established the "Amorim panels" to investigate the humanitarian impact and recommend changes to the sanctions regime; and in 2000, Canada led a major reform effort as well.

Occasionally there were elected members, such as Austria and Japan, who joined the United States in blocking goods or condemning Iraq. In 1990 the delegate from Canada often sided with the United States and Britain in the disputes over whether there were "humanitarian circumstances" that warranted allowing Iraq to import food.[1] Those countries that sided with the United States were almost exclusively First World nations. But for the most part, the elected members provided the most consistent and vocal opposition to the arbitrary and harsh nature of the sanctions. In 1990, when India, the Philippines, and Sri Lanka sought permission to deliver food to their nationals in Iraq and Kuwait, the "non-aligned caucus" of the Security Council—including Zaire, Cuba, and Colombia—put forward a proposal to respond immediately to the urgent situation, in contrast to a P5 proposal to delay those efforts.[2] In the early 1990s it was the elected members who sought to establish clear criteria for approval of goods. When that effort failed, the delegates from Ecuador, Zimbabwe, and Cape Verde repeatedly insisted that the United States and others abide by the informal "gentlemen's agreement," which held that countries blocking goods should at least state their reasons rather than simply blocking goods arbitrarily and without justification.[3]

Despite the risk to their own relations with the United States, a number of Third World countries regularly challenged the harshness and the inconsistency of the United States, Britain, and France. During its time on the Council, Ecuador periodically reminded the committee that while Security Council resolutions imposed penalties on Iraq, it was not in fact a colony but rather a sovereign state.[4] In 1992 India challenged the United States, Britain, and France, who were blocking goods such as tires and fabric on the grounds that Iraq might use them for military purposes: "It [is] clearly not practical for Iraq to convert everyday articles to military uses given the high cost and high level of technology required. The Committee's decisions should therefore not be influenced by that unlikely possibility."[5] On one occasion, Morocco objected to the long list of goods blocked by the United States, including agricultural equipment, burial shrouds, and electric irons for household use. (The United States finally agreed to permit one of the items: shroud material for burials.[6]) On another occasion, Iraq wanted to purchase drugs for cancer treatment using funds in frozen accounts. The United States and Britain refused; Morocco and Brazil took issue, arguing that this was a clear case of humanitarian need.[7]

At one meeting, the Moroccan delegate articulated a lengthy critique of the arbitrariness and inconsistency of the holds in general. He questioned why members of the committee had blocked a contract for caustic soda, when this had been approved in the past. He challenged Britain's refusal to allow tractor brakes, since tractors were critical to agriculture. He then questioned the holds on equipment for water purification and refrigeration, as well as holds on women's clothing, brake fluid, fertilizer, and water treatment chemicals. He challenged the hold on a contract to buy paper from Jordan, noting that "paper did not seem to be a dangerous product." He argued for lifting the holds on insecticide and cement and remarked that the humanitarian value of tires for tractors and ambulances was obvious.[8]

The criticism from elected members continued throughout the sanctions regime. At a public Security Council meeting in 2001, the delegate from the Ukraine cited the Secretary-General's statement about how the number of contracts on hold had compromised the goals of the Oil-for-Food Programme.[9] At the same meeting, the delegate from Tunisia criticized the severity of the sanctions, "the most extensive and the harshest ever imposed by the United Nations on a country," as a result of which "Iraq's economy is devastated, its society is crumbling, and the humanitarian situation of the Iraqi people is on the brink of utter collapse."[10] The delegate from Bangladesh criticized the effects of the sanctions on the Iraqi people,[11] as did the delegate from Malaysia, who cited the Bossuyt report, issued by the UN's Commission on Human Rights, arguing that sanctions impacting the civilian population violated international law.[12]

Elected members often objected to the claims of security concerns invoked by the United States. On one occasion, when the United States sought to block fans, Zimbabwe and Ecuador argued that there was no credible claim that these were "dual use," but were just goods used to alleviate heat in tropical countries.[13] When France, Japan, and Austria sought to prevent Iraq from importing 2,000 tractors, requiring end-use information, the schedule of shipments, and distribution plan, the delegate from Morocco argued against these delays, pointing out a tractor could only be used for agricultural purposes; and the large number was required because the Iraqi countryside had been devastated.[14] On another occasion, where the United States and Britain blocked ambulance tires and tractors, they were challenged by the delegates from Oman, Djibouti, and Nigeria.[15]

At one meeting, the United States and Britain had blocked fabric, glue for making shoes, spare parts for refrigerators, tires, and aluminum foil, insisting that they first be provided with information about who exactly would be using the goods. The delegate from Zimbabwe was openly skeptical, maintaining that information "should be considered in good faith, and not with a view to finding hidden circumstances or inappropriate use."[16] On one occasion, the Malaysian ambassador commented to the Security Council that it was "ironic ... that the same policy that is supposed to disarm Iraq of its weapons of mass destruction has itself become a weapon of mass destruction."[17]

Thus, from the beginning, the U.S. positions within the Security Council were openly challenged as being both absurd and inhumane. These challenges did not necessarily come from nations that stood to benefit economically from trade with Iraq or from Arab countries that sided with Iraq for political reasons. The consistent criticisms against the United States and its allies were equally from those nations with nothing to gain and much to lose by alienating the United States—primarily poor countries who spoke out against the harshness of measures that deliberately worsened Iraq's impoverishment.

Conflicts within the UN: The UN Humanitarian Agencies

In addition to the ongoing conflict within the Security Council concerning the humanitarian impact of the sanctions, at the same time and for the same reason the Council found itself in opposition to almost every other part of the UN system. The conflicting mandates within the UN system—of enforcement of the sanctions regime on one hand, and economic development on the other—created a kind of institutional "Jekyll and Hyde situation."[18] The 661 Committee embodied this in that its mandate involved two tasks that were not only unrelated but in many ways inconsistent: enforcement of a trade control regime and mitigation of that regime for humanitarian purposes. These contradictions in the operations of the 661 Committee were reiterated at the level of the UN itself, in many forms. Within the 661 Committee, the UN's institutional ambivalence was reflected in incoherent policies, secrecy, lack of transparency, and lack of accountability. Outside the committee, the tension was articulated in the discrepancies between the agendas of the Security Council and the UN humanitarian agencies, in the struggle between the Council and the Secretariat, in the Office of the Iraq Programme's (OIP) protests regarding holds by 661 members, in the criticisms by ECOSOC, and in the attempts at reform directed toward the Security Council. It was also apparent in the relations of the UN to the nongovernmental organization (NGO) community.

A 1992 report described an "ongoing tension between the Security Council and the UN's humanitarian machinery."[19] That tension continued on almost every level throughout the history of the Iraq sanctions. At the same time that the Security Council was enforcing a highly restrictive policy on the importation of humanitarian goods into Iraq, the UN's Secretariat and humanitarian agencies were raising again and again the problem of the human damage done by these restrictions.

It began with the Ahtisaari and Aga Khan reports, which described the catastrophic circumstances in 1991 and anticipated that they would continue or worsen without intervention. UN documentation of this was extensive and continuous. For example, in March 1993 the UN Inter-Agency Needs Assessment Mission visited Iraq and found that the condition of the vulnerable groups had worsened.[20] In July 1993 WFP and FAO reported that

> notwithstanding the justification for their imposition, the sanctions
> have caused persistent deprivation, severe hunger and malnutrition

for a vast majority of the Iraqi population, particularly the vulnerable groups—children under five, expectant/nursing women, widows, orphans, the sick, the elderly and disabled. The [FAO/WFP] Mission believes that it would be impossible to continue the sanctions in their present form, without further aggravating the already grave food supply situation in Iraq. The lasting solution to the current food crisis would lie in the regeneration of the Iraqi economy which cannot be achieved without a resumption of international trade by the country.[21]

Iraq was one of a handful of countries that were included regularly in WFP's weekly emergency reports. WFP provided weekly updates on the alarming state of malnutrition in Iraq; the shortfalls in funding and food deliveries; the impact of the food shortages on women, young children, and other vulnerable groups; and the lack of household incomes with which to purchase supplements to the government rations.[22]

In 1995 the Department of Humanitarian Affairs (DHA), in conjunction with the Inter-Agency Standing Committee (IASC), commissioned a study, "The Impact of UN Sanctions on Humanitarian Assistance Activities."[23] The study showed that there was considerable awareness of the problem and pressure for reform, both within the UN and in the larger NGO community;[24] and diplomats and scholars had begun insisting on ground rules for UN sanctions.[25] The study drew on some forty-seven UN and NGO reports on Iraq produced since the sanctions were imposed in 1990,[26] as well as numerous other studies. The authors noted "the amount of information available today on the devastating economic, social and humanitarian impact of sanctions no longer permits [one] to entertain the notion of 'unintended effects.' "[27]

In 1996 the World Health Organization (WHO) wrote that the sanctions imposed on Iraq "have contributed to delays or, in some cases, even [caused the cessation of] attempts by the Government to repair vital damaged facilities and programmes. As a result, the quality of life of the average Iraqi citizen has been adversely affected."[28] The report describes "severe economic hardship, a semi-starvation diet, high levels of disease, scarcity of essential drugs," and severe social and psychological damage.[29]

In February 1997, at the beginning of the Oil-for-Food Programme, the Director-General of WHO visited Iraq and upon his return described the Iraqi health system as "close to collapse."[30] In October 1997 a joint FAO/WFP mission identified the prohibition on oil sales as a major cause of food shortages and malnutrition: "The imposition of UN sanctions in August 1990 have ... significantly constrained Iraq's ability to earn foreign currency needed to import sufficient quantities of food to meet needs. As a consequence, food shortages and malnutrition became progressively severe and chronic in the 1990s."[31] The FAO/WFP report stressed the need for rehabilitation of the agriculture sector, and the economy as a whole: even with the anticipated improvement in food rations under the Oil-for-Food Programme, the nutritional problems could not effectively be addressed without increased purchasing power and considerably more investment in agriculture and in every form of water availability.[32]

An overview report in 1999 by the UN system[33] to a Security Council panel documented the continued severity of Iraq's economic collapse, affecting every aspect of life: unemployment and underemployment, skyrocketing crime and juvenile delinquency, the disappearance of the Iraqi middle class, enormous increases in mental illness, deterioration of the education system, collapse of family incomes, increasing illiteracy, electricity shortages, tens of thousands of refugees, and so on.

The conflict between the Security Council and the UN agencies went beyond the agencies' documentation of the impact of the Council's sanctions regime. DHA, which coordinated the work of the UN humanitarian agencies in Iraq from 1992 to 1997, had no formal relation with the 661 Committee, even though the committee had tremendous control over the ability of all the UN humanitarian agencies to accomplish their work in Iraq. Until 1995, DHA officials never appeared before the committee or attended its meetings, and were not ordinarily even notified of its decisions.[34] The humanitarian agencies that were involved in DHA— such as UNICEF, UNESCO, WHO, and WFP—were "part of the broader institutional culture within the UN, whose humanitarian and economic organisations usually work with governments, rather than replacing or overriding them."[35] As a result, DHA was initially viewed as "siding with" the Iraqi government.[36]

The tension was also apparent when the Security Council prevented the UN agencies from carrying out their programs. While goods imported by the Iraqi government might be misused by the regime, there was little likelihood that UN agencies would use program materials in Iraq to produce weapons of mass destruction. Even so, the United States often took extreme and restrictive positions regarding UN humanitarian agencies. In 1996, for example, UNDP sought permission to introduce an agricultural program in Iraq to strengthen the quality of seeds, given that Iraq was now highly dependent on domestic agriculture to reduce malnutrition.[37] The United States repeatedly vetoed the project.[38] In 1998 the United States was still denying UNDP permission for this project, even though malnutrition was widespread, with the U.S. delegate saying that she doubted that the program was urgent.[39] UNESCO sought permission to bring photographic equipment to Iraq in order to document missing artifacts. The United States denied UNESCO's request on the grounds that it was not an essential need.[40] When FAO asked permission for a project to increase land under cultivation in order to increase vegetable production the United States blocked it on the grounds that it was a long-term development project rather than a relief effort.[41] FAO repeatedly asked for permission to bring spare parts to Iraq for repairs of helicopters spraying pesticides, offering to supervise their use and document that the parts would not end up contributing to the Iraqi military. Again and again, the United States delayed or blocked these requests.[42]

When WHO asked permission to organize regular evacuation flights for Iraqi nationals with urgent medical needs, the United States insisted that WHO first provide detailed information about these flights. They did; and the United States still refused to permit the flights.[43] When UNDP asked permission to use $1 million to build primary care health facilities, the United States delayed for months before finally approving them.[44] Even for food imports sponsored by UN agencies, the United States found reasons to refuse or to create impediments. When WFP asked for a general exemption to bring food into Iraq, the United States (joined by France and South Korea) refused on the grounds that they objected to giving a blanket authorization to one UN agency and not others,[45] even though foodstuffs in general had been authorized since 1991. At one point the 661 Committee permitted the Iraqi government to use cargo flights to ship in meat. While the flights were supposed to have been limited to cargo, it was discovered on one of the flights that there were some passengers as well. The United States from that point on blocked all air shipments of meat, even though the alternative—driving twelve hours through the desert, in temperatures of up to 120 degrees, with limited access to refrigerator trucks—made meat imports prohibitively difficult. DHA asked the committee to reconsider;[46] the United States refused.[47]

The conflict between the United States and the UN agencies was demonstrated graphically in a story told by Paul Conlon, an administrator for the 661 Committee. In 1991 the bombing during air attacks by the United States and Britain had destroyed the glass windows in a Baghdad building that housed a UN agency, the Economic and Social Commission for Western Asia.[48] The cost of replacing the glass was $56,000. As summer approached, air conditioning was not going to be possible without replacing the glass, and Iraq's hot summer temperatures would ruin the $4 million worth of UN computer equipment in the building. The UN itself applied for a waiver (all UN agencies, as well as international humanitarian organizations, were required to seek humanitarian waivers from the committee for their own economic transactions or transport of agency goods to Iraq). The United States vetoed the application on the grounds that the repairs would involve the purchase of $56,000 of glass and services from Iraqi glaziers, and this would constitute an impermissible input to Iraqi industry. "During acrimonious debate," Conlon writes, "no delegate [was] impolite enough to bring up the fact that the government taking the hard line in this matter had caused the damage in the first place."[49] The UN Secretariat intervened, and the matter was ultimately resolved diplomatically.

As UN humanitarian agencies struggled to respond to the worsening crisis, delays by the 661 Committee, along with its refusal to permit anything that it interpreted as long-term development, exacerbated both the humanitarian situation and the frustration of the agencies responding to it. Meanwhile, the aid agencies were put in the position of having to enforce the sanctions in various ways; UNICEF, for example, distributed and monitored the use of chlorine gas for water purification from the beginning of the sanctions regime. The multiple roles of the UN humanitarian agencies in turn hampered their work within Iraq. The Iraqi government was openly distrustful of the UN, given that the UN's Security Council had authorized massive devastation to be inflicted on the country through the bombing campaign of the Gulf War, and had then maintained much of that devastation through the vehicle of economic sanctions. Thereafter, the Iraqi government sought in various ways to restrict the movement of the UN humanitarian agencies, making their work considerably more difficult. Iraq had denied the UN permission to do nationwide surveys on the food situation in September 1990.[50] It permitted the Ahtisaari and Aga Khan surveys in 1991, but from 1992 to 1996 permitted only limited studies.[51] After the 1998 bombing by the United States and Britain, Iraq denied visas to all humanitarian aid workers of U.S. nationality.

111

Conflicts within the UN: The Secretary-General
and the General Assembly

There was tension not only between the Security Council and the UN agencies, but also between the Security Council and the UN Secretaries-General over the course of the Iraq sanctions regime. In 1995 Boutros Boutros-Ghali, in his "Supplement to an Agenda for Peace," described economic sanctions as a "blunt instrument" which raised ethical questions about the legitimacy of inflicting suffering on vulnerable groups, complicated the work of humanitarian agencies by imposing arduous bureaucratic requirements on them, and conflicted with the development objectives of the UN by doing long-term damage to the productive capacity of the country.[52] The Secretary-General's periodic reports on the Oil-for-Food Programme repeatedly stressed that the program was not at all adequate to remedy the humanitarian damage being done by the sanctions, given the burdensome procedures, the limited funding, the restrictions on infrastructure, and the holds on humanitarian contracts. Kofi Annan commented consistently on the failure of the program to meet the adequacy standard. In November 1997 he noted that 31 percent of children under five suffered from malnutrition,[53] that safe water and medicine were "grossly inadequate"[54] and that the health infrastructure suffered from "exceptionally serious deterioration," including unreliable electricity, inadequate storage conditions, interrupted water supplies, and nonfunctioning hospital waste disposal systems.[55] In his report of February 1998, Annan reiterated that deliveries of food were not adequate to address the urgent needs of the population, since "genuine nutritional security cannot depend on food alone, but . . . is affected by the prevalence and extent of coexisting disease, the deterioration in water and sanitation infrastructure, dilapidated health facilities, and reduced agricultural production."[56]

In a March 1998 report, Annan indicated that medical supplies that had arrived covered only 20 percent of what was required. He noted that health care providers were forced to reuse intravenous disposable equipment, which created a high risk of transmitting communicable diseases,[57] and that a number of hospitals were unable to function normally in the winter for lack of heaters, heating fuel, and blankets.[58] With the situation still quite dire, Annan reiterated in his March 2000 statement to the Security Council that "the humanitarian situation in Iraq poses a serious moral dilemma for this Organisation. The United Nations has always been on the side of the vulnerable and weak, and has always sought to relieve suffering, yet here we are accused of *causing* suffering to an entire population."[59]

Outside of the Security Council, this was the predominant view throughout the UN. Max van der Stoel, the Special Rapporteur of the Commission on Human Rights on the situation of human rights in Iraq from 1991 to 1999, was one of the few exceptions. Van der Stoel consistently blamed the Iraqi government alone for the decline in food and health care, on a variety of grounds.[60] He concluded that "there can be no doubt that the policy of the Government of Iraq is directly responsible for the physical and mental pain . . . of millions of people and the death of many thousands more."[61] However, his successor, Andreas Mavrommatis, reflected the view held more broadly in the UN, that while the Iraqi government was committing a number of human rights violations, the sanctions themselves also constituted human rights violations. He referred to "the long-term adverse effects of the embargo, which the Special Rapporteur deems to be the most serious problem that innocent people would continue to face for many years, if not generations."[62] Mavrommatis also raised the issues of the Security Council's holds on contracts, and the basic adequacy of the Oil-for-Food Programme.[63]

The General Assembly shifted views considerably over time. Although the Economic and Social Council of the General Assembly was deeply critical of the economic sanctions, the General Assembly itself passed a series of annual resolutions initially adopting the language of the van der Stoel reports, condemning Iraq for its human rights violations and blaming Iraq for the impact of the sanctions. In a 1996 resolution, for example, the General Assembly expressed

> its special alarm at the policies of the Government of Iraq . . . which prevent the equitable enjoyment of basic foodstuffs and medical supplies, and calls upon Iraq, *which has sole responsibility in this regard,* to take steps to cooperate with international humanitarian agencies in the provision of relief to those in need throughout Iraq.[64]

However, by 1999 the language of the resolutions had shifted considerably. Rather than condemning the Iraqi government for its failure to cooperate, and explicitly blaming the Iraqi government entirely for the humanitarian catastrophe, the February 1999 resolution called upon the government of Iraq "to *increase* its cooperation with international aid agencies,"[65] "to *continue* to cooperate in the implementation of [the Oil for Food Programme],"[66] and "to *continue to facilitate* the work of United Nations humanitarian personnel in Iraq."[67] Later resolutions adopted a similar tone.[68]

In 1997, and several times thereafter, the Sub-Commission on the Promotion and Protection of Human Rights (of the UN Commission on Human Rights) noted the humanitarian damage from economic sanctions and stressed the need for the sanctions to comply with international law, citing the UN Charter, the Universal Declaration of Human Rights, and the Geneva Conventions.[69] There were a number of similar reports and resolutions from other venues within the UN during the latter part of the 1990s: in 1997, the Committee on Economic, Social and Cultural Rights;[70] in 1998, the Committee on the Rights of the Child;[71] and in 1999, the Committee on the Elimination of Racial Discrimination.[72]

In 2000 the Commission on Human Rights commissioned a working paper by Marc Bossuyt, an expert in international human rights law, to assess the legality of economic sanctions. The working paper asserted that under Article 24 of the UN Charter, the Security Council is required to "act in accordance with the Purposes and Principles of the United Nations," and thus is not exempt from scrutiny.[73] Based on the Geneva Conventions, the Hague Convention, and other human rights instruments such as the Convention on the Rights of the Child, Bossuyt articulated a six-prong test for determining when sanctions conform to international law: the sanctions must be imposed for valid reasons; they must target the proper parties; they must target proper goods or objects; they must be reasonably time-limited; they must be effective; and they must be free from the protests that occur in regard to violations of "principles of humanity and the dictates of the public conscience."[74] He maintained that the sanctions against Iraq failed to meet these tests. On the basis of this working paper, the Sub-Commission passed a resolution appealing to states to reconsider their support for sanctions when the goals had not been met in a reasonable time, and to terminate sanctions regimes that adversely affect human rights.[75] In a second resolution in the same session, the Sub-Commission in strong language addressed the inadequacy of the humanitarian measures on Iraq, "considering any embargo that condemns an innocent people to hunger, disease, ignorance and even death to be a flagrant violation of the economic, social and cultural rights and the right to life of the people concerned," and appealed to the international community to lift the embargo provisions affecting the humanitarian situation and to facilitate delivery of basic humanitarian goods.[76]

The agencies and organizations within the UN system were not the only ones that were profoundly uneasy with their roles. In 1994 the president of the International Committee of the Red Cross addressed the General Assembly,

> inviting political leaders to take greater account of humanitarian criteria when taking decisions to impose economic and financial sanctions. Perhaps we should give special thought here to the grave public-health effects of the paralysis of water-purification and pumping installations. Is it not incongruous to apply the iron fist and then apply the velvet glove of humanitarian aid to restore supplies vital to the population's survival?[77]

There was a sense not only that the situation was characterized by the ugly irony of fixing the damage done by an institution ostensibly concerned with peace and security; but also that the aid work was itself making the damage politically acceptable. Many felt that the International Committee of the Red Cross (ICRC), UNICEF, and NGOs "were furthering the foreign policy of the great powers by making sanctions more palatable to the international community."[78]

Not only was there considerable awareness within the UN of the human damage done by the sanctions—accompanied by extensive documentation and statements of concern—but for nearly a decade there were numerous proposals for reform, identifying what needed to be changed within the sanctions regime to alleviate that damage.

Attempts at Reform

Throughout the sanctions period there were attempts to reform the system in several ways: acquiring reliable information about the humanitarian impact; making the humanitarian exemptions process more consistent and less arbitrary; increasing the transparency of the 661 Committee's work; and reducing the holds on humanitarian goods. The United States resisted each of these in turn and successfully undermined many of them.

From the beginning, several members of the 661 Committee pressed for transparency and consistency on the part of the United States because it was clear that the inconsistency and unpredictability of the U.S.

decisions compromised Iraq's ability to purchase even legitimate humanitarian goods. Many delegates on the committee suggested that there be criteria for identifying what items would be approved and what would be rejected. The United States opposed this, insisting that each item be reviewed on a case-by-case basis, even though this would delay the process, and created uncertainty that made the process more opaque and unpredictable for all the parties. When delegates criticized the arbitrariness of the U.S. and British positions, the U.S. delegate insisted that the United States was under no obligation to provide justification for its objections.[79]

The first significant attempt to bring consistency and accountability to the approval process was introduced in late 1991 by several elected members of the Council from the Non-Aligned Movement—India, Zimbabwe, Ecuador, Cape Verde, and Morocco. Based on the needs identified in the Ahtisaari report, they initially sought to establish a list of goods that would be automatically approved, upon notification to the committee. The United States, Britain, and France refused. What emerged instead was an informal "gentlemen's agreement" that the committee members would, on a case-by-case basis, "look favorably" on such goods as materials for agriculture and food production, water treatment, goods for children and infants, primary and secondary education, medical equipment, and civilian clothing.[80] But within a few months there were objections from Ecuador, Zimbabwe, Cape Verde, Austria, and other delegations to the violations of the "gentlemen's agreement" on the part of the United States and Britain.[81]

Even with the agreement in place, and despite the frequent protests of the other committee members, the United States blocked salt,[82] water pipes,[83] children's bikes,[84] materials for the production of diapers,[85] equipment to process powdered milk,[86] and fabric for civilian clothing.[87]

Beginning in the mid-1990s, there were more formal attempts to formulate and implement reforms. In 1995 DHA commissioned a study by two consultants, Claudia von Braunmühl and Manfred Kulessa, regarding the Iraq sanctions regime.[88] The consultants recommended the replacement of the case-by-case analysis of each item—which had created a logjam involving thousands of applications each year—with clear categories defining what goods were permissible, and what information was needed for each application.[89] While this eventually happened in 2002, it was never done by the 661 Committee in regard to its own humanitarian exemptions procedure. The consultants noted that impact assessment and monitoring of "unintended effects" was urgently needed,[90] and that the work of the UN humanitarian agencies (along with established international NGOs) should generally be exempt from the need to obtain approval for delivery of goods.[91] While UN agencies were eventually permitted to bring more goods into Iraq without committee approval, they were never exempted altogether from the cumbersome processes and restrictions that applied, for example, to agricultural machinery, medical equipment, and water treatment equipment and chemicals. The United States was responsible for most of these denials. In 1995 the consultants recommended that humanitarian advocacy should be included into the deliberations of the sanctions committees. But it was not until the late 1990s that the 661 Committee invited these agencies to present their views.

The same proposals were introduced repeatedly throughout the 1990s. In 1995 and 1996 the Security Council agreed to increase the transparency of the sanctions committees by issuing reports and press releases, as well as lists of "no objection" items; by providing a list of all committee decisions to any nation upon request; by supplying more detailed annual reports; by providing access to the parties affected by the sanctions; and by giving oral briefings to other member states on the decisions of the committee.[92] The same proposals for reform were introduced again and again. Most were not implemented until years later, if at all.

In 1997 the UN Office for the Coordination of Humanitarian Affairs[93] commissioned a second study on the management of sanctions, conducted by an entirely different set of consultants.[94] The proposals for reform were quite similar: the report recommended a systematic methodology for measuring the impact of sanctions both prior to and throughout the sanctions regime. In addition, the report recommended that DHA or its successor act as an advocate for humanitarian concerns within the Security Council and the sanctions committees. It also recommended that the exemption process and the discussion formulating exemptions policies be transparent. In addition, the report stressed the importance of consistency in decision making.[95]

As it became clear that the humanitarian situation in Iraq was not improving significantly, even with the creation of the Oil-for-Food Programme, the pressure to reform the sanctions process grew. In January 1999, under the leadership of Celso Amorim, the Brazilian president of the Security Council, the Council adopted another series of measures intended to give greater weight to humanitarian concerns; to give other member states (including those affected by sanctions) greater input into the committee; to make the committee's work and its decisions more public; and to put in place standing exemptions for basic humanitarian goods. The Council agreed that the sanctions committees should monitor the humanitarian impact of the sanctions; that procedures be put in place to facilitate the work of UN and other humanitarian organizations; that foodstuffs, pharmaceuticals, and medical supplies should be exempted from UN sanctions regimes, as well as standard medical, agricultural, and educational items. It also decided that to accomplish greater transparency, the committee chairpersons should provide "substantive and detailed briefings," and that public information on the sanctions committees' work should be made available on the Internet.[96] The following day the Security Council established three panels to look into issues related to the sanctions on Iraq. The panels were to address disarmament issues, humanitarian issues, and issues related to prisoners of war and Kuwaiti property.[97]

In March 1999 the three panels issued their reports. The humanitarian panel observed that no amount of improvements in the Oil-for-Food Programme would be sufficient to resolve the humanitarian crisis; indeed, that nothing short of actually lifting the sanctions would make it possible for the humanitarian crisis to end:

> The humanitarian programme implemented pursuant to resolution 986 (1995) can admittedly only meet but a small fraction of the priority needs of the Iraqi people. Regardless of the improvements that might be brought about in the implementation of the current humanitarian programme—in terms of approval procedures, better performance by the Iraqi Government, or funding levels—the magnitude of the humanitarian needs is such that they cannot be met within the context of the parameters set forth in resolution 986 (1995) and succeeding resolutions.[98]

In the absence of a decision to lift the sanctions, the panel recommended lifting the ceiling on oil exports in order to raise more revenue, as well as permitting greater investment in oil spare parts and equipment to accommodate the exports. It also recommended reducing the amount of funds that went to Kuwait for compensation,[99] providing a cash component, utilizing Iraqi labor and expertise, reducing the isolation of Iraqis through media access and intellectual and cultural exchanges, and stimulating local agriculture.[100] Some of the concrete recommendations were implemented: the ceiling on oil sales was lifted and compensation to Kuwait was reduced from 30 percent to 25 percent. However, many of the reforms regarding transparency and accountability, which had been adopted by the Council, were not put into practice.[101] Others were implemented, but in some cases the U.S. practices undermined their effectiveness. For example, the humanitarian panel recommended that "green lists" be created to reduce the number of holds on food, medicine, and agricultural and educational supplies. These goods would be notified to the committee, rather than circulated for approval. However, the impact of the green lists was limited; using the same practices it had employed in reviewing individual contracts, the United States now objected to the inclusion of necessary or innocuous goods on the green lists. For example,

> in February 2001, the OIP circulated the draft green list of items for the housing sector . . . Even though the entire list had been approved by UNMOVIC, the United States without explanation vetoed the inclusion of 27 out of 53 of the items, including switches, sockets, window frames, ceramic tiles and paint.[102]

A State Department official who was the sanctions officer at the U.S. mission to the UN described the U.S. policy. As the Security Council expanded the areas in which the Iraqis were permitted to buy goods, such as housing and electricity, "the US consistently fought against this expansion." When the review time was shortened in order to streamline the approval process, the United States responded to the new procedures by simply placing more contracts on hold: "There was no outright denial of a contract. Contracts that were never approved were indefinitely placed on hold."[103]

In 1999 the president of the Security Council, Ambassador Chowdhury of Bangladesh, asked German ambassador Tono Eitel to conduct a confidential review of the Iraq sanctions. He found that because the meetings where most policies were set were informal and closed, Iraq was effectively deprived of the right to participate in meetings that affected it, although the Charter mandated that the Security Council facilitate public meetings for the participation of all interested members.[104]

In April 2000, during Canada's presidency of the Council, the Council held a rare public meeting on the issue of sanctions, including presentations by some twenty-five nations.[105] Virtually all the delegations, even those of the United States and Britain, spoke of the need to reform sanctions regimes in order to minimize the impact on vulnerable populations, to implement greater transparency, and to achieve greater effectiveness. However, some delegations also spoke specifically of the failure of the Council and sanctions committees to implement reforms that had been proposed, or even adopted, repeatedly. The French ambassador noted that

> The rule of consensus is paralysing. Nothing in the Charter or in resolutions of the Council requires committees to take their decisions by consensus. The adoption of decisions by simple majority, at least for non-essential questions, could suffice. Transparency is also a concept that sanctions committees too often ignore. Third States and targeted States are not invited to speak before the committees. Measures were planned to that end but have not been applied. Proposals have been made but have been rejected by certain members. Even briefings by representatives of United Nations agencies are often problematic. It is essential that the practice of hearing outside speakers be the norm.[106]

One outcome of the Council's meeting in April 2000 was the establishment of the "Working Group on General Issues of Sanctions."[107] As a member of the group, the United States sought first to limit the testimony available to the committee. The United States, together with Britain, blocked Denis Halliday and Hans von Sponeck, both of whom had served as humanitarian coordinators for Iraq, from testifying before the Working Group on Sanctions, claiming they were "not sanctions experts."[108]

In February 2001 Ambassador Chowdhury issued a draft report. He recommended that:

> Access to sanctions committees by States affected directly or indirectly be maximized; the sanctions committees also provide opportunities for representatives of relevant international . . . organizations, experts and UN agencies to brief them; . . . the sanctions committees seek reports . . . [on the] economic and humanitarian impact . . . the sanctions committees make the reports requested by them public unless there are reasons for confidentiality; sanctions committees consider majority voting for reaching decisions either of a procedural nature or related to humanitarian exceptions.[109]

The draft report also emphasized that sanctions regimes should "be imposed for limited periods of time . . . and renewed by decisions of the Security Council" in cases where the targeted regime has not complied.[110]

However, once the working group arrived at its recommendations, it was blocked from issuing a final report by the United States. Although it was clear that the "consensus" method of working, effectively giving each country veto power over every issue, had paralyzed the committee and served to severely reduce humanitarian exemptions, the United States successfully fought to prevent the group from recommending majority voting or time limits on sanctions.[111] For years the working group could not agree on its recommendations and issued no report. Finally in 2006—six years after it was established—it issued its report. The report contained no mention of majority voting or time limits on sanctions. The recommendations, if implemented, would do little to prevent the kinds of practices that had been employed by the United States and Britain.[112]

The United States consistently sought to undermine other reforms regarding transparency and accountability. Despite the explicit mandate from the Security Council to monitor the humanitarian situation in Iraq more effectively, the United States and Britain often sought to undermine the committee's efforts in this regard. In August 1999, for example, the French delegate, citing the recommendations of the Amorim panels, proposed that the head of UNICEF in Baghdad, Anupama Rao Singh, who had participated in the recent study on child mortality in Iraq, be invited to speak to the committee.[113] Nearly every member of the committee spoke in support of the invitation: the Russian and Chinese delegations, as well as those of Brazil, Malaysia, Argentina, Slovenia, Gambia, and Namibia. Even the British delegate agreed to invite her. But the U.S. delegate suggested that reporting to the 661 Committee in accordance with the Security Council mandate would interfere with UNICEF's work, saying "he did not feel it would be reasonable" to take her away from UNICEF's humanitarian work on the ground.[114] Six months later, when Mrs. Rao Singh was in New York, the French delegate again proposed inviting her to meet with the committee. But the U.S. delegate again objected, this time saying that the proposal "required a lot of study and preparation" and raising a barrage of objections.[115] In the end, the head of UNICEF in Iraq was invited to speak to the committee, six months after it was suggested at a committee meeting, and a year after the Amorim panels had stressed the urgency of better monitoring the humanitarian situation in Iraq. Similarly, the French delegation repeatedly tried to invite Hans von Sponeck, then the humanitarian coordinator in Iraq, to speak to the committee, despite the repeated objections from the United States.[116]

Commercial Protections

Some of the goods purchased under the Oil-for-Food Programme were substandard or defective. On many occasions, for example, manufactured goods were poorly made, medicines were delivered after their expiration dates, or rotten or moldy food shipments were delivered. The United States often claimed this was because the Iraqi government intentionally bought shoddy goods with funds from the Oil-for-Food Programme to obtain kickbacks, to give business to allies, or simply out of indifference to the welfare of the Iraqi population.

However, both Iraq and OIP repeatedly tried to introduce commercial protection measures into its contracts for humanitarian goods to address the problem of the unreliable quality of goods that were being delivered. One of these measures was a retention clause, where most of the contract would be paid upon delivery of the goods but a portion of the price would be withheld until independent inspection agents confirmed that the quality of the goods was satisfactory. Another measure was a performance bond, where a surety guarantees the vendor's performance and pays the amount of the bond if the vendor fails to provide the goods or services promised in the contract.[117]

In July 1999 OIP circulated a proposal to introduce standard commercial protections, including retention clauses and performance bonds, that would address the problem of the delivery of poor-quality goods or the failure of contractors to provide services after they had received payment.[118] The United States and Britain successfully prevented these measures from being implemented. Even though the French delegate pointed out that these provisions were in fact a "normal commercial practice" that served to guarantee the quality of the goods delivered,[119] the British delegate argued that performance bonds were prohibited by the Committee's procedures. In March 2000 France again pressed the committee to consider standard commercial protections for Iraq's imports.[120] Three years later, in 2002, OIP was still asking the Security Council to permit Iraq to include commercial protections in the import contracts.

Suppliers are paid immediately upon goods' arrival in Iraq, before they can even be tested, with the result that "there are numerous defective items sitting idle in warehouses, useless for any purpose." The prohibition on including performance bonds in contracts leads some suppliers not to ship goods when the prices are not in their favour, further disrupting the implementation of the "oil for food" programme.[121]

According to von Sponeck, it was clear that it was indeed standard international business practice to withhold 5 to 10 percent of the payment until goods were delivered and were inspected to ensure that the quality and quantity met the contractual specifications. When Iraq began to include these provisions and OIP sought approval, "US and UK representatives in the UN Sanctions Committee in New York refused to clear such contracts." They argued that these clauses would allow over-invoicing and would put cash in the hands of the Iraqi government. But according to von Sponeck this made no sense, since the commercial protection clauses would have had no relation to invoicing, nor would they have entailed any cash payments. The lack of commercial protections was problematic for the entire program: "Full payment for goods yet to be received has encouraged suppliers to neglect standards. Replacing sub-standard goods with goods meeting quality standards became cumbersome and further delayed the arrival of items needed by the civilian population. This unnecessarily intensified deprivation and suffering."[122]

In the end, at every juncture where UN agencies or other members of the Security Council raised concerns about the humanitarian impact of the sanctions or sought to increase transparency, streamline the approval process, and facilitate the work of UN agencies, the United States either prevented the reforms from being adopted or undermined their implementation after they had been adopted. Some have suggested that the Iraq sanctions were poorly designed or badly managed because the Security Council had never imposed a sanctions regime of such magnitude and complexity. Others have argued that there was no credible documentation of the humanitarian impact of the sanctions. But, in fact, there was a great deal of credible evidence presented in every possible venue within the UN. It was not from lack of information or lack of understanding that

123

the sanctions regime was as relentlessly damaging and indiscriminate as it was. Rather, it required an ongoing, concerted effort on the part of the United States and its allies to deflect the continued criticisms and undermine the many proposals for reform that came from throughout the UN system, as well as from within the Security Council itself.

7

THE ROLE OF THE IRAQI GOVERNMENT

All three U.S. administrations consistently maintained that the Iraqi regime was responsible for the harm done by the sanctions in several ways: that Saddam Hussein's regime wasted money on building palaces that could have gone to food; that by invading Kuwait, Iraq brought the sanctions on itself; that the sanctions would have been lifted if the regime had cooperated with weapons inspectors; that Saddam Hussein himself probably had billions of dollars and chose not to spend it on his people; that the Iraqi government was smuggling oil and getting kickbacks, and spent that money on arms or on luxuries for the elite; and similarly, that the Iraqi government was using illicit income from the Oil-for-Food Programme to buy arms and luxuries for the elite.[1]

The Clinton administration blamed the Iraq government for the sanctions in general. A State Department spokesman said, for example, "If they'd never invaded Kuwait to begin with; if they'd never engaged in this kind of bellicose dealing; if they had never backed out of oil-for-food for a period of time . . . It's Iraq's fault that Iraq is in the situation it's in."[2] The United States maintained that, consequently, there was no reason to remove the sanctions because any damage was done by Hussein's policies, not the sanctions. A State Department official said, "Let's put it this way: I mean, you say, 'Remove economic sanctions.' Here's what Saddam Hussein can order now: He can order virtually any food and medicine he wants. He can order infrastructure repair equipment for anything to do with the humanitarian well-being of the Iraqi people. He primarily cannot import weapons. What's the difference?"[3]

After the war against Iraq began in 2003, as the U.S.-led occupation authority struggled to control the social discontent from the lack of public services, U.S. officials insisted that the infrastructure of Iraq in the south/central governorates—electrical production, telecommunications, water and sewage treatment—were in such terrible disrepair because Saddam Hussein's regime neglected them unconscionably. A State Department official stated that reconstruction "will take time because this is not just reconstruction from a war, it's not even reconstruction from sanctions; this is the renewal of a country that was oppressed for over 20 years by a completely kleptocratic elite."[4] A top U.S. military commander in Iraq maintained that

> the infrastructure in Iraq has not been tended to since 1979. Saddam put all his money into castles and things he liked. But the water infrastructure, the power infrastructure, schools, hospitals, the port infrastructure—no money was put into that. The reason things are in the shape they are today is not because of the Iran-Iraq War, the Gulf War or the second Gulf War. It's because of Saddam not putting a nickel into infrastructure. Things were not taken care of. Probably 70 percent of the infrastructure problems were due to neglect over the last 30 years of Saddam's reign.[5]

Many of the U.S. claims were distorted. In light of the continual U.S. efforts to block Iraq's imports of materials and equipment for its infrastructure, U.S. accusations had little credibility among those familiar with the sanctions regime. To the extent that there was in fact corruption and waste, the impact on the Iraqi economy as a whole was marginal. The $2 billion in total illicit payments during the Oil-for-Food Programme and the $8 billion in illicit trade could not have significantly restored an economy reeling from $200 billion in damage from the 1991 war and a loss of GDP on the order of $40 billion per year.

But there were criticisms by UN agencies during the sanctions period that were more accurate and credible. At one point the Food and Agriculture Organization maintained that the amount Iraq was spending on agricultural inputs was inadequate, given the needs for rehabilitation of agricultural infrastructure.[6] On other occasions the government of Iraq was criticized by the UN for spending too much on food[7] or for submitting distribution plans without adequate prioritization.[8]

The Iraqi government was criticized at various points for being slow to submit contracts for goods. In November 2000 the World Health Organization (WHO) reported that the Iraqi government had been slow to contract for medicine and medical supplies.[9] Because Iraq preferred to contract with vendors from countries that were its political allies, the quality of medicines was sometimes inferior to those Iraq had previously imported from U.S., Swiss, and German companies.[10] According to one report, Iraq's preference for dealing with political allies meant that certain specialized pharmaceuticals were not available.[11] The Iraqi government was also criticized from time to time for failing to order particular items, or failing to submit the required paperwork.[12]

There were recurrent claims that food distribution was sometimes skewed to favor government supporters, or to punish individuals or ethnic groups in disfavor. One claim was that as many as a million rations were controlled by the Ba'ath party.[13] While UN agencies and others found that the ration system was generally equitable, opposition groups maintained that there were political restrictions: rations would not be given to families of deserters, those with criminal records, or those blacklisted by the Ba'ath Party.[14]

One criticism by UN staff was that Iraq would not permit UN monitors to travel without government escorts and sometimes restricted UN staff from going to particular locations.[15] On other occasions, the Iraqi government refused to cooperate with UN evaluations of the humanitarian situation, unless the evaluation concerned only the impact of the sanctions. It refused to cooperate with groups appointed to evaluate the humanitarian situation under Security Council Resolution 1302.[16] But it was not true that the Iraqi government was so callous and corrupt that it did nothing to help the Iraqi people.

Measures by the Iraqi Government to Mitigate the Effects of the Sanctions

Despite the claims of the United States and others, the Iraqi government undertook several important efforts to meet the needs of the Iraqi population. The most effective of these measures were in the areas of food, health care, and infrastructure repair.

Food

Once the economic sanctions were imposed, the Iraqi government introduced a number of measures to increase food production and meet basic nutritional needs for the population. Immediately after sanctions were imposed in 1990, the government of Iraq implemented a series of efforts to increase domestic food production. These included guaranteed prices for grain, low-interest loans, low-cost rentals of state land for farming, and fertilizer.[17] A 1995 UNICEF report noted that the government of

Iraq "has over the past five years accorded utmost attention and priority to the agricultural sector in search of food security and self-reliance."[18] There were significant results. For example, through the efforts of the Iraqi government, the number of date trees increased by about 2 million between 1991 and 1995.[19]

In addition to increasing agricultural production, a critical undertaking of the Iraqi government was the food rationing system. Famine would certainly have occurred were it not for the food distribution system put in place by the Iraqi government immediately after sanctions were imposed, as well as other measures by the government to increase food availability.[20] The state took over distribution of basic food commodities that had been available in the private sector; grains and other foodstuffs were shifted from market-based distribution to the ration system.[21] Some have suggested that the Iraqi government did so in order to maintain political control and stave off insurrection.[22] Whatever the motivation may have been, in September 1990, a few weeks after economic sanctions were imposed, the Iraqi government established food rations. According to the Red Cross, "Rations have kept the majority of people alive."[23]

> Aid agencies have praised the Iraqi government's achievements in creating a well-run national rationing system, which has helped ensure that, despite delays and shortfalls, the vast majority of the Iraqi population has had access to at least a portion of the [minimum family food allotment] since sanctions were imposed.[24]

The ration system was "comprehensive and nontargeted: everyone is entitled to the ration regardless of means and the ration and its price are uniform across the country."[25] Although the amount of food available was well below nutritional requirements for several years, by many accounts the rationing was implemented with a relatively high degree of fairness and equity. There were some accusations that the food ration was used by the state as rewards, and were denied as a form of punishment. But several studies in the early 1990s found that such abuses were marginal.[26] Once the Oil-for-Food Programme began, UN staff conducted systematic studies throughout the country to monitor equitable distribution.

To compensate for nutritional deficiencies, the Iraqi Ministry of Health in conjunction with UN agencies established programs to fortify wheat flour with iron,[27] as well as to provide iodized salt.[28] Under the Oil-for-Food Programme, the Iraqi government began including therapeutic milk and high-protein biscuits as part of its imports.[29] When there were delays in deliveries of the program's foodstuffs, the government of Iraq on many occasions loaned the program supplies from the national stock to meet the requirements of the "food basket," the minimum family food allotment.[30]

Just prior to the war in 2003, the Iraqi government distributed a four-month supply of food to each household to provide a buffer during the war. As a result, there were no major food shortages for the next three months, when the rations were reestablished.[31] Once the war was over, Iraq's Ministry of Trade worked with the UN's World Food Programme to restore the food rations, and did so in much of Iraq.[32]

Health Care

Although much of the health care system collapsed during the sanctions, the state nevertheless implemented several vaccination campaigns targeted at children. In the face of a measles epidemic, the Iraqi government implemented an intensive national vaccination campaign in late 1992, and as a result measles declined in 1993.[33] By 1995 cases of measles were reduced by 57 percent, and mortality from measles was reduced by 65 percent.[34] Working with UNICEF and WHO, the Iraqi government also strengthened its polio immunization process. By 1994 the number of polio cases was less than half of what it had been in 1992. In 1995 the campaign immunized 4 million children under age five against polio.[35] Another campaign against polio, which UNICEF reported to be thorough and well planned, took place in 1999.[36] As of February 2003 the country had remained polio-free for thirty-seven months. This was the result of the vaccination program, in which 95 percent of the 4.3 million children targeted were reached through house-to-house visits.[37]

The state also permitted the expansion of the private sector in health care, to compensate for the state's inability to meet health care needs.[38] The number of private hospitals and clinics increased and public hospitals were permitted to charge fees for some services. Physicians working for public hospitals and clinics were permitted to open private practices on the side, which made it possible to retain them to work part-time in public facilities.[39]

Post–Gulf War Reconstruction

After the extensive bombing campaign of the Persian Gulf War in 1991, Iraq responded very quickly to restore basic services to the extent possible, in light of the massive damage. The Iraqi government began a three-month emergency reconstruction campaign, which had the immediate effect of restoring electricity, telephone communications, water treatment, and roads and bridges, some only partially, some temporarily. The restoration activities were "accomplished through such methods as cannibalizing parts from damaged units, making risky makeshift repairs and operating the remaining plants without the normal breaks for maintenance and repairs."[40] One observer noted that "every civil engineer and nuclear physicist was out rebuilding bridges." As a result of these efforts, by July 1991 electricity generation had been restored for the short term to 40 percent of the 1990 level.[41] Domestic telephone service had been restored to 30 percent of the prewar level, but international lines were still not functioning. By the end of 1992, much of the telecommunication system was repaired. Two of the three main arteries in Baghdad were functioning again. Many of the roads and bridges had been repaired, although not to the original standards.[42]

Although there had been considerable damage to oil pumping facilities and pipelines, a year after the war ended the Iraqis had restored enough oil capacity to fuel transportation. Many factories were operating, although they were limited by the lack of spare parts, and there was considerable construction taking place.[43] An American anthropologist observed that

> when we there one year after the war started, everyone was talking about the "Iraqi Miracle." Indeed, one would pass bombed out power plants with smoke coming out of them, busy generating electricity, and there was evidence everywhere of people coming together and using some combination of duct tape, bailing wire, chewing gum or whatever to put the place back together again.[44]

While the initial reconstruction happened very quickly, there was considerable strain on electrical generators and other infrastructure from operating with makeshift repairs, and from operating continuously to compensate for the plants that were completely disabled. For this reason, the report of the Secretary-General's envoy (the Aga Khan report of July 1991) had anticipated that "little more can be done to increase power generation further unless major imports of new parts are allowed."[45] This in fact was what happened, as similar problems affected all areas of infrastructure over the mid and long term.

130

By 1994, aid agencies and the United Nations were reporting increased electricity outages, in addition to problems with spare parts
and parts for vehicles, thereby affecting hospitals, water and sanitation facilities. Shortages of spare parts likewise adversely affected
agriculture, for which basic inputs of good quality seed, fertilizers
and pesticides were also inadequate.[46]

Infrastructure and Public Services during the Oil-for-Food Programme

Under the Oil-for-Food Programme, the Iraqi government, working in
conjunction with UN agencies, implemented a number of measures that
directly resulted in humanitarian improvements. The government adopted
a policy of heavily subsidizing inputs to agriculture, providing up to 80
percent of fertilizer and seeds used in Iraqi agriculture.[47] Although the
amount of agricultural machinery imported was still quite inadequate,
according to the assessment of the UN's agricultural program in Iraq, the
government was delivering the available machinery quickly and efficiently, and did so on an equitable basis.[48] The UN's Agriculture Sectoral
Working Group also assessed the government's attempts to rehabilitate
the cold chain to preserve veterinary medicines and vaccines. They found
that the supply of refrigerators and generators had been well used, along
with refrigerated trucks to transport vaccines and medicines, and had
had a significant impact on maintaining the cold chain.[49] The government of Iraq effectively used imports from the program in the irrigation
infrastructure for agriculture, drilling deepwater wells, and clearing drains
and streams.[50]

In all sectors there were indicators that the government of Iraq had
put Oil-for-Food imports to good use. Between 1998 and February 2003,
egg and chicken production increased sevenfold.[51] In the area of education, 150,000 school desks were repaired at vocational school work-
shops.[52] Similarly, housing construction increased substantially. There
was a targeted housing program to address the population most in need.
By May 2000 there was significant progress in this. Building permits
increased as the government streamlined the procedures to facilitate the
distribution of construction materials.[53] Between 2001 and February
2003, cement production increased by 30 percent.[54] In the area of telecommunications, a UN report found that the government had used imports
from the Oil-for-Food Programme to replace cables and add facilities to

131

improve the network. It also established a network of card-operated pay phones in public places.[55]

In the areas of water and sanitation, the government responded to the needs of a growing population and expanded the water distribution network. A UN water and sanitation consultant noted in 2000 that the "clear priority" of the Iraqi government in this sector was "to maintain the volume of treated water available to domestic consumers."[56] By October 2000 the Iraqi government had installed over 250 centrifugal pump sets, which resulted in a 30 percent increase in water supply to farmers for agriculture and livestock and guaranteed a water supply for some water treatment plants.[57] The Iraqi government installed water pumps, aluminum sulphate dosing pumps, chlorinators, and other equipment to process water for human consumption.[58] As a result, there was continuous improvement in the production of potable water. In Baghdad there was significant improvement, bringing water to 8,000 beneficiaries who had had no access to potable water.[59] In the other governorates, the average plant performance increased from 33 percent to 45 percent.[60] In 2002 about 120 kilometers of new piping was laid, affecting some 1 million beneficiaries.[61]

The Failures of the Iraqi Government

While the anecdotes of corruption and luxuries for the elite are familiar, in fact that was not the primary reason for the Iraqi government's failure to respond effectively to the humanitarian situation. The more serious failings concerned the basic structure and policies of the Iraqi government itself: the centralization, the reliance on oil income, reliance on imports and on foreign professionals, and the reliance on advanced technology. These criticisms, however, paint a very different picture than the criticisms of U.S. officials. The structural criticisms were not so much of a government whose basic functions were distorted by callousness and corruption, but rather of a state unable to bring about the massive reorientation needed to respond effectively to the changed circumstances; a state unable to introduce effective coping mechanisms that might have made better use of the limited resources available.

The Iraqi government resisted reorganizing services and administration, hoping that sanctions would end soon with a return to prosperity. The Iraqi national consciousness of "sitting on a sea of oil" also mitigated a culture of adaptation to what became a severe and sustained capital shortage. Additionally, the highly centralized, one-party political system simply did not permit the Iraqi people to demand a more effective response by the government.[62]

One Iraqi government policy that was a significant factor in worsening the humanitarian impact, or failing to mitigate it effectively, was the reliance on centralized high-technology systems for public services, modeled on those of First World countries. As UNICEF noted,

> The Iraqi health system was developed throughout the 1970s and 1980s according to a highly centralized, hospital based, capital-intensive model of curative care. It required continuous large-scale imports of medicines, medical equipment and even service workers like nurses. It focused mainly on sophisticated hospitals for advanced medical procedures, provided by specialist physicians, rather than population based care through primary care practitioners.[63]

There were clearly some benefits of highly centralized systems. In education, such a system was fairly efficient.[64] The centralized welfare state was able to respond quickly to restart critical public services after the 1991 Gulf War.[65] However, while the government functions were highly centralized, they were not always well-coordinated. The various ministries often functioned independently of each other, even when there were issues or problems that needed to be addressed by several different sectors. "For example whilst the Ministry of Interior was responsible for water supply, the Ministry of Health was responsible for water quality and there [was] inadequate coordination between the two to ensure that both dimensions of water supply were addressed."[66] Likewise,

> the Ministries of Agriculture and Irrigation are responsible for delivering bulk raw water, whilst the responsibility of delivering safe drinking water to rural communities is that of the Ministry of Interior who obtains the raw water primarily from irrigation canals and then treats it. Weak coordination, communication and collaboration have often left rural water treatment plants without bulk raw water deliveries for several hours and often days.[67]

Iraq's social services relied heavily on equipment and expertise, but were not supported by strong planning.

133

Limited expertise in health planning existed, as the state focused heavily on training clinical specialists and was virtually without staff trained in health administration or public health. The country had no food and nutrition policy, and management expertise for monitoring, supervision, or assessment of the quality of care was limited.[68]

For the first few years after the 1991 Gulf War, in planning for the operation of the infrastructure the managers of public services (health, water and sanitation, and electricity) simply did not consider the possibility that the embargo could remain in place.[69] The resistance to acknowledging and adapting to Iraq's reduced circumstances was combined with gaps in their training. According to one researcher, in 1996 Iraqi doctors said that "they were not trained to practice medicine in such primitive conditions."[70] As late as 2000, a UN water and sanitation consultant noted that Iraq was

> not making optimal use of the resources available [under the Oil-for-Food Programme] because the strategy of emergency response and the severely limited resources to undertake any other response, is inherently potentially wasteful. The same level of resources properly planned and implemented, could . . . achieve as much as 50 per cent more value.[71]

The Oil-for-Food Programme, which permitted the parts of Iraq under government control to use oil income only for imports, reproduced this problem. For example, the program "created an imbalance in the health system making it commodity rich but poor in human resources and service quality."[72] As a result, "the large dollar value of the program fed the continuing goal of re-establishing an import-based, capital-intensive service model similar to those in developed countries."[73]

Factors Undermining the Iraqi Government's Capacity to Respond

The Iraqi government can legitimately be criticized for certain measures that significantly worsened the situation for the Iraqi population, or failed to mitigate the effects of the sanctions for the population as a whole: the excessive centralization, the failure to adopt low-tech measures in health care and other systems, inefficiencies in contracting for imports and in distribution of goods. At the same time, however, the Iraqi government's capacity to respond to the ongoing crisis, and to mitigate the effects of the sanctions, was crippled by the government's lack of cash and the "brain drain" that happened on many levels.

The Impoverishment of the State

One of the central goals of the sanctions was to deprive the Iraqi state of income by blocking oil exports. While Iraq was permitted to import humanitarian goods from 1991 to 1996, it could not export oil to generate funds to pay for them. Once the Oil-for-Food Programme began, the Iraqi government still could not legally receive any funds; all legal income from oil sales went into a UN-controlled escrow account, which was then used to pay for imports. Outside of the northern governorates administered by the UN, the Oil-for-Food Programme was purely an import program, with no provisions for paying labor or the other costs borne by the state, such as the transport of goods, installation, repair and maintenance, or the purchase of local goods. Because the overall economy had collapsed, the state could not generate significant income through increased taxation. When the state generated cash in the early 1990s by simply printing more money, this triggered hyperinflation and a collapse in the value of the currency. The income from Iraq's illicit trade, which averaged less than $1 billion per year, was not nearly enough to compensate for Iraq's loss of revenue from oil sales.

And indeed, the government of Iraq was nearly bankrupt. While this prevented the state from rebuilding the military, it also undermined the state's ability to provide governmental functions. Because Iraq's social services and infrastructure were operated by the state, its impoverishment impacted all of Iraq's economy and public services. It also contributed to a massive increase in unemployment, since nearly a quarter of all Iraqi workers were employed by the government.[74]

According to estimates by UN agencies, nongovernmental organizations (NGOs), and other sources, government budgets in most areas were cut by 90 percent.[75] The Iraqi government prioritized the ration system, although at the expense of other government expenditures.[76] Still, by 1995 the basic food rations had been reduced by a third due to the state's lack of cash, and there were indicators that famine was imminent.[77] In the 1980s the Iraqi government had invested an average of $100 million per year in water and sanitation, primarily for staff salaries, operations, and maintenance costs. There were over 5,000 staff, including 1,100 administrators, 350 engineers, 1,400 operators, 500 technicians, and 1,700 unskilled laborers.[78] After 1990, the annual budget for maintenance of water treatment plants went from $100 million to $8.5 million.[79] The lack of funds meant that the Iraqi government could not buy equipment and spare parts, even if the UN sanctions committee had permitted it.[80] The inability to fund repairs and maintenance, pay staff, and purchase spare parts for pumps and equipment in turn had a considerable effect on infant and child mortality.[81]

Health sector imports in Iraq went from $500 million in 1989 to $50 million in 1991.[82] In education, Iraqi government reports indicated that $230 million was allocated for education in the 1988–1989 school year. By contrast, in the first two years of the Oil-for-Food Programme the government averaged $23 million annually in expenditures for education.[83]

Because of financial shortages, a number of programs that had been in place prior to 1990 were compromised. In 1993 the state eliminated subsidies that had been distributed to low-income households and households headed by women, as well as subsidies to orphans and the disabled.[84] Because of financial constraints the government cut back on teacher training; the state did not have the resources to print textbooks; and as teachers' salaries declined precipitously from inflation, many left the profession.[85]

Even though the Oil-for-Food Programme grew considerably, the lack of a cash component alongside the impoverishment of the Iraqi state had consequences throughout the length of the program. UN agencies repeatedly documented problems that resulted because neither the Iraqi government nor the Oil-for-Food Programme had cash to pay for salaries and to buy locally produced goods. A 1998 WHO report noted that delivery of health care goods to local distribution centers was undermined by a lack of transportation, communication, and manpower.[86] A 1998 UNICEF report on education noted that of the materials that had arrived in the first three phases, only about 6 percent had been delivered to end users, due in part to a lack of transport and to the Ministry of Education's lack of cash for implementation.[87] In education, the lack of a cash component meant that the Oil-for-Food Programme could not contribute to expenses such as teachers' salaries, even though during the sanctions period those dropped from US$500 per month to US$5–US$30 per month and many teachers left the profession.[88] It also meant that program funds could not be used to purchase school furniture within Iraq and could not be used to install wiring for computers or provide necessary support, such as air conditioning for computer rooms.[89] Even plain wooden school desks had to be imported because there was no cash to hire Iraqi labor.[90]

The Brain Drain

During the sanctions period, when Iraq most needed functioning ministries and experienced personnel—to manage the distribution of food rations, to support increased agricultural production, to maintain the precarious and deteriorating infrastructure, to implement new strategies involving appropriate technology, and for public health campaigns—the Iraqi government lost much of its labor and intellectual resources.

Following the Gulf War in 1991, some 663,000 people died or left the country. Many of these were foreigners who worked in agriculture, which impacted Iraq's domestic food production at a time when its imports of food had been interrupted since August 1990.[91] In the face of the severe shortages, after the Gulf War of 1991, many Iraqi professionals left the country, as did foreign professionals. As the economic crisis took hold and the dinar was devalued, civil servants left their jobs because their salaries were no longer sufficient to support their families. At the same time, the travel restrictions and the crippled communications network isolated Iraqi professionals from normal professional interaction with those outside the country.

When UN agencies tried to provide training or technical assistance to Iraq, these efforts were often blocked by the United States and its allies. On one occasion, the UN Development Programme wanted to train Iraqis in essential humanitarian sectors so that they would be better able to evaluate problems and recommend effective solutions. The United States vetoed this on the grounds that it was providing long-term development, not vital humanitarian aid.[92]

Those who remained employed by the state saw their salaries deteriorate, as hyperinflation set in and the state was not able to raise salaries enough to keep up. Prior to sanctions, the salaries of civil servants had been $150–$200 per month. By 1996 the income for most Iraqi government employees ranged from 5,000 to 10,000 Iraqi dinar per month, or between $3 and $5, while the minimum amount needed to support a family of five was $100 per month.[93] To retain employees, the state reduced working hours, which permitted employees to supplement their income with other jobs.[94] Of those who remained, many reduced their work time at their state jobs in order to work at other forms of employment to support their families. One observer noted that "there has been considerable migration of employment from the formal sector (professional or skilled) to the informal, unskilled sector. Engineers and technicians, for example, can be seen underemploying themselves by selling vegetables and cigarettes on street corners and in markets."[95] Government planning and coordination deteriorated so badly that "after 1990, estimates were not available on government allocations to the different social sectors. In fact, the whole budgetary and planning process began to break down."[96] There was a collapse not only in budgeting and planning, but also in simply managing day-to-day operations. Health services declined not only because of shortages of medicine and equipment but also because of a "general breakdown in the organisational capacity of the Ministry of Health."[97]

In water and sanitation, there was a loss of over 50 percent of key technical and managerial staff.[98] The water and sewage treatment plants, which were all imported, state-of-the-art equipment, had relied heavily on foreign technical experts for their operation. About 20 percent of the labor in the water and sanitation sector, especially in key technical positions, had been foreigners.[99] Maintenance and repairs were primarily done by foreign companies.[100] When they left, the Iraqi staff who remained were ill trained and poorly equipped to run the plants. Because the instruments for water and sanitation systems had been damaged, they had to be operated manually, which was difficult and time consuming. At the same time, there were no opportunities for local staff to receive training, so they learned on the job as best they could.[101] Even after Iraqi personnel took over, there were still severe shortages of staffing at every level. The number of vacancies in every position were extremely high. In 1996, 70 percent of the positions for administrators and engineers were vacant, as were almost 80 percent of the positions for technicians and more than 70 percent of the positions for unskilled labor.[102] The total personnel working for the water and sanitation sector went from 20,000 to 11,000, and the average years of experience went from twenty years to nine.[103] A UN consultant noted the level of understaffing was so serious that, for example, the Daura water treatment plant, which needed a staff of fifty technical personnel, was operating with only two.[104]

According to a 1995 UN study, some of Iraq's hospitals had lost as much as 75 percent of their staff.[105] In the area of health care, the staffing shortages meant that even when equipment finally arrived there was often no longer adequate personnel with the experience to use it effectively, or to perform repairs.[106] The loss in health care staffing contributed to the collapse in primary health care—from 1,800 health care centers before the Gulf War to just over 900.[107] Those doctors who remained in Iraq had little training or experience in the kinds of medical problems that were suddenly present in huge numbers across the country, such as those from nutritional deficiencies like marasmus and kwashkior.

In education, 40,000 teachers left their jobs over the course of the 1990s. The state filled in the gaps by hiring less-qualified teachers. Prior to 1990, teachers had three to five years of training after secondary school; by the end of the 1990s, 20 percent had only one year of training before starting to teach.[108] At the same time, the expertise to manage the educational system eroded as well: 15 percent of planning personnel at the national level left their jobs; 22 percent at the regional level left. As a result, the Ministry of Education used schoolteachers with no training in management to plan and direct educational operations.[109]

Technical Isolation

The inability to travel or to obtain materials in their fields resulted in intellectual isolation for Iraqi professionals. "Certain external constraints such as restrictions of foreign travel by Iraqis and its isolation from the world for thirteen long years also prevented new ideas from flowing in and improving quality parameters in education."[110] In education, for example, Iraq was isolated from global trends in education that were being promoted by international agencies.[111] Secondary education was undermined in several ways: "the failure to upgrade curricula, severe shortage of books, equipment and science labs, [Iraq's] isolation from the rest of the world, and inability to upgrade and modernise its overall education quality to incorporate new subjects like IT and computer applications."[112] In health care, the lack of access to professional communication and training from experts outside Iraq meant that it was difficult to bring in adequate expertise in low-cost appropriate technologies, which was particularly urgent since the imported high-tech systems that were in place could not function under sanctions.[113] Scientific activity in Iraq was crippled from the lack of journals and textbooks.[114]

From the time the sanctions were imposed on Iraq by the Security Council, the United States consistently held that the suffering that took place in Iraq under sanctions was attributable primarily to the Iraqi government's neglect and corruption. However, the reality was much more complex. While the Hussein government was repressive and corrupt in many regards, its history was one of substantial investment in social welfare. During the sanctions period, there were instances of effective and immediate policies to address critical needs. But more generally there was a failure on the part of the state to adapt effectively and to use the available resources well. At the same time, however, the impoverishment of the state and the lack of funds to support the expertise and personnel needed to operate the country's infrastructure and public services was devastating. No matter what the intent of the government, there simply were not sufficient resources, by any stretch of the imagination, to meet the country's needs, even on the most minimal level. And the collapse of Iraq's human resources meant that Iraq's efforts to adapt and make better use of the resources that were available were compromised at every level.

8

CONGRESS AND THE SANCTIONS

The U.S. policies regarding the Iraq sanctions were shaped almost exclusively by the various U.S. administrations, with little involvement or interest from Congress. After the sanctions were lifted and there were accusations of corruption in 2004, there was something of a feeding frenzy as members of Congress from both parties and multiple committees vied with each other to denounce the Oil-for-Food Programme and the UN in general. But for the preceding fourteen years, the majority in Congress had no interest in the humanitarian impact of the Iraq sanctions and little knowledge of how the U.S. sanctions policy actually worked. To some extent this was because the State Department regularly repeated statements that were inaccurate or misleading, such as the claim that the sanctions had never prevented Iraq from importing food or that the administration was doing its best to maximize the importation of humanitarian goods into Iraq. Any congressional efforts to reform sanctions were also stymied because the sanctions, on their face, were a Security Council measure, not a U.S. policy. It was almost ten years before it was apparent to anyone in Congress, even the most vocal critics, that the Security Council sanctions were fundamentally shaped by unilateral U.S. policies.

To the extent that members of Congress were interested in Iraq, they were almost exclusively concerned with the security threat posed by Iraq and with punishing and removing Saddam Hussein. Numerous bills were introduced and several dozen congressional hearings were held between 1990 and 2003 concerning weapons of mass destruction, no-fly zones, and regime change, and the Iraq Liberation Act (ILA) was passed in 1998. Congress showed far less interest in the humanitarian situation. In that fourteen-year period there were three actual hearings on the humanitarian situation, a few unsuccessful attempts to pass legislation allowing U.S. companies to sell food and medicine to Iraq, and a number of letters sent to the administration asking that sanctions on nonmilitary goods be lifted. Throughout the 1990s there were only a handful of senators and members of Congress who were vocal on the issue of the humanitarian situation in Iraq. To the extent that there were members of Congress who *were* concerned, the party leadership in both parties undermined their efforts to bring visibility to the issue. By the late 1990s, as public pressure grew and the humanitarian crisis was documented by national and international bodies, there were several dozen members of Congress who expressed their concern, primarily by cosigning letters to the administration.

But for the entirety of the sanctions period, most of Congress simply did not ask about the humanitarian impact of the sanctions on Iraq or about the role of the United States in determining their severity; and when they were told, they simply did not care. This was the case even though information about the humanitarian crisis was provided by the Congressional Research Service (CRS) or by highly credible witnesses at committee hearings ranging from the director of intelligence for the Joint Chiefs of Staff to William Webster, director of the Central Intelligence Agency (CIA). In the late 1990s, as the movement for sanctions reform grew, there was even active opposition on the part of some conservatives to measures that streamlined the delivery of humanitarian goods. There were also hearings where committee members and witnesses flatly opposed the Oil-for-Food Programme, along with criticisms that the administration had made too many concessions on humanitarian imports, and complaints that "Saddam was getting away with too much."

It did not help matters that all three administrations, whether Republican or Democrat, denied the severity of the situation and denied U.S. responsibility for any part of it, even when pressed by members of Congress. But in the end it made little difference: Congress was, overwhelmingly, simply indifferent to the suffering caused by the sanctions in Iraq, regardless of the role of the United States. This was true during the first half of the 1990s, when the humanitarian crisis was most severe, and it was also true in the later years of the sanctions, when the crisis received a great deal of public attention. It was true regardless of which party controlled Congress, and it was true regardless of who was in the White House.

The situation changed dramatically in 2004 when there were accusations against the Oil-for-Food Programme alleging mismanagement and corruption on the part of the UN. Congressional interest suddenly skyrocketed; there were nearly two dozen hearings with eager participation of dozens of members of Congress, all highly publicized. The same members of Congress who for years could say nothing more about the sanctions than "It's all Saddam's fault" quite suddenly became expert in the most arcane details of how pricing was determined for infrastructure contracts. Those who had never asked about the humanitarian situation in Iraq, and ignored those who had, now expressed frequent outrage that the humanitarian needs of the Iraqi people had been of so little concern to the UN and to the Iraqi government.

Immediately after the Security Council imposed the sanctions on Iraq, Congress passed the Iraq Sanctions Act of 1990, which, along with the president's executive orders, prohibited U.S. nationals from trading with Iraq.[1] Some weeks into the sanctions regime, Senator Daniel Patrick Moynihan pointed out that embargoes presented moral issues. Ethical questions, he said, "inevitably arise in connection with economic sanctions, and it would seem to this Senator that we would do well to think about them a bit now, at the outset, rather than wait for them to crash in upon us further down the line."[2]

Moynihan observed that this was particularly true if the sanctions affected Iraq's food supply: "Food present[s] a special case. Nothing works like famine."[3] He noted that "the punishment would bear most cruelly upon the non-combatants, especially upon children. To many, a hunger blockade would seem nothing short of war of the most savage kind."[4] And Moynihan quoted a U.S. military officer after World War I regarding food embargoes:

> We must in all honesty admit that food embargoes, placed against a country which really needs the food, are not persuasive measures, but the most savage of war measures. They are particularly difficult to uphold on merely moral grounds, since they bear more heavily on the civilian population than on the army, and more heavily on women and children than on the men. For effectiveness, and for moral standing, a really successful food embargo ranks well in advance of torpedoing hospital ships and is somewhere near the class of gassing maternity hospitals. So if a food embargo be considered an act of war, well and good. If it be considered a

means of moral suasion, there seems to be some weakness in the argument.[5]

Days after Moynihan's comments, the CRS was reporting that the sanctions had already taken a toll on the Iraqi population. Citing economists from the U.S. Department of Agriculture (USDA), CRS researchers said to "expect drastic shortages by November or December 1990. Extreme hardship will likely be apparent by the end of the year."[6] Including that year's harvest, the USDA gave the following estimates of Iraq's food supply:

> 4 to 5 months for wheat; 4 to 5 months for rice; immediate impact for sugar; immediate impact for vegetable oils; 6 months for barley; immediate impact for corn and soybean meal that will have an impact on Iraqi poultry sector which provides more than one-half the total meat consumed in Iraq.[7]

CRS also reported on the measures taken by the Iraqi government to mitigate the humanitarian crisis through food rationing, stimulating agricultural production, and illicit trade with neighboring countries. A CRS report from September 1990 noted that "Effective rationing [by the government of Iraq] and embargo leaks appear to be essential in enabling Iraq to survive the next six months."[8] At the same time, CRS reported, while the Iraqi government's measures could be expected to produce greater grain harvests ten months down the road, there would still be extreme shortages of meat and animal protein.[9]

> Iraq plants its barley and wheat crops in October or November ... and harvests the grains in May or June. So even though Hussein has offered free fertilizer and other farm subsidies to farmers to increase domestic production, they won't be able to increase grain production there until spring 1991 at the earliest.[10]

But other than Senator Moynihan's comments, there was little further discussion in Congress that fall concerning the ethical problems presented by the sanctions. On the contrary, in late fall of 1990, as the first Bush administration was gearing up for war, there was intensive discussion in Congress about whether the sanctions were effective and whether military intervention was warranted, with many arguing that sanctions were an important and humane measure that should remain in place.

From late November through early January 1991 there were more than a dozen hearings held by the Senate Armed Services Committee, the Senate Foreign Relations Committee, and the House Armed Services Committee. There were advocates for a broad array of positions, with witnesses including Henry Kissinger, Robert McNamara, Arthur Schlesinger, Cyrus Vance, Alexander Haig, Jesse Jackson and George McGovern, as well as scholars, military analysts, and administration officials.[11] There was considerable testimony concerning the sanctions regime that had been in place for four months, as members of Congress questioned the administration's claim that the sanctions had definitively failed and that military intervention was now required. Some witnesses, such as Richard Perle,[12] maintained that sanctions were inadequate and military intervention was warranted. Others, such as sanctions specialist Gary Hufbauer, argued that it was likely that the sanctions would be successful in inducing Saddam Hussein to withdraw from Kuwait.[13] William Webster, director of the CIA, testified that the sanctions had severely compromised Iraq's economy and industrial production.[14]

In the Senate debate on whether to use military force against Iraq, Senators Paul Wellstone, Claiborne Pell, and Paul Sarbanes argued that sanctions successfully provided an alternative to "the slaughter that modern-day warfare brings";[15] that Iraq's gross national product had fallen by 40–50 percent and its infrastructure and military potential were compromised;[16] and that Iraq had been "deterred, ostracized, and punished."[17] In the House of Representatives, Representative Kweisi Mfume noted that CIA director William Webster had said sanctions were working[18] and maintained that President Bush had "upped the ante with his steadfast promotion of the military option before we could determine whether sanctions and other international initiatives had a chance to take root."[19]

At the same time, conservative Republicans such as Senator Strom Thurmond maintained that sanctions "have not had the effect we sought and may not for some time."[20] Senator Orrin Hatch likewise argued that "after 6 months, sanctions have had their day in court. But it is time to recognize the fact that economic sanctions alone will not force Saddam Hussein to withdraw from Kuwait. They can impoverish Iraq, but they cannot break Hussein's will."[21] In the House the same arguments were made by Republicans such as Representatives Dennis Hastert, Sidney Morrison, and Joe McDade.[22]

Regardless of its misgivings, in January 1991 Congress voted over-whelmingly to authorize the president to use armed force against Iraq.[23] The war itself, which lasted a matter of weeks, was seen in Congress as a tremendous success.

From the end of the 1991 war until 2003, under both Democratic and Republican control, the overriding concern regarding Iraq for congres-sional leadership and for most members was the potential military threat presented by Iraq and the removal of Saddam Hussein from power. Throughout this period there were numerous hearings held by the House Foreign Affairs Committee, the Senate Foreign Relations Committee, and the Senate and House Armed Services Committees, as well as occasional hearings by other committees addressing the military threat presented by Iraq and the issue of containment.[24] There were hearings specifically fo-cused on Iraq's purported weapons of mass destruction[25] and numerous others that included testimony regarding Iraq's weapons of mass de-struction.[26] There were some hearings devoted entirely to monitoring and weapons inspections,[27] and numerous other hearings that included testimony on disarmament and inspections.[28] The no-fly zones were dis-cussed in a half dozen hearings.[29]

In addition to containment, the other concern of the majority of the Congress and the congressional leadership was regime change, accompa-nied by frustration that it had not yet taken place. This culminated in the ILA, which formalized the U.S. policy of regime change in Iraq, and, in turn, in the frustration that the ILA was not being implemented aggres-sively enough. There was a staff report to the Senate Foreign Relations Committee in May 1991 regarding the near-overthrow of the Hussein regime and the collapse of the Iraqi uprising in the face of U.S. abandon-ment.[30] There were several hearings devoted entirely to this topic, such as "Iraq: Can Saddam Be Overthrown?"[31] "U.S. Policy toward Iraq: Mobi-lizing the Opposition,"[32] and "The Liberation of Iraq: A Progress Re-port."[33] There was also a great deal of discussion about regime change in hearings more broadly concerned with the situation in Iraq,[34] and funds were authorized by Congress that went toward support for oppo-sition groups.[35]

In addition to containment and regime change, Congress occasionally addressed other issues related to Iraq. The situation of the Kurds and Kurdish refugees received attention in Congress, first in response to the refugee crisis of 1991, but there was also ongoing sympathy over the course of the next decade. In response to the failed uprisings against the Hussein government and the ensuing refugee crisis, there was a sense of obligation to provide assistance to the Kurds as well as commendations for U.S. relief efforts that had taken place.

> If one thing loomed large with members of Congress, it was the situation of the Kurds and the refugee crisis in the north. The military had mobilized resources in what was seen as one of the most effective refugee assistance programs ever. At the same time, there was a sense of guilt about the violent suppression of the 1991 uprisings which the U.S. had encouraged. Individuals who had been working at the CIA had been in touch with opposition groups. They had gotten reports from the field, and they felt a burden of responsibility: we encouraged the Iraqis to rise up; they did; then they were crushed, and we just stood by.[36]

There was one committee report, in May 1991, for the Senate Foreign Relations Committee, which described the uprisings in Iraq and their aftermath.[37] However, there was little acknowledgment that the Bush administration's overt statements of encouragement had played any role in the uprisings by Kurds and Shi'a in 1991, or that the U.S. failure to act on these assurances had been a factor in the uprisings being crushed by Saddam Hussein or the ensuing refugee crisis. Even so, the Senate passed a resolution recognizing that the United States had a "moral obligation" to provide humanitarian relief for the Kurds.[38] In May 1991 there were proposals to provide humanitarian relief for refugees,[39] and in June a bill passed to provide $500 million for humanitarian relief for the Kurds and other refugees.[40] There was a hearing by a Senate committee on the refugee crisis, a report that the U.S. relief effort had saved 20,000 lives,[41] and a Senate resolution commending U.S.-led relief efforts for refugees.[42]

In 1992 there were proposals to extend the UN presence in the north and to provide additional humanitarian help to the Kurds.[43] In 1993 there were proposals to lift the sanctions in the areas where the Kurds were affected.[44] In 1993 and 1994 there were hearings on the situation of the Kurds and their treatment by the Iraqi government.[45] In 1994, in support of the Kurds, Congress passed a bill proposing that the sanctions in northern Iraq be relaxed.[46] There were hearings that included discussion of the Iraqi government's abuses of the Kurds.[47]

There were several occasions on which proposals were introduced in Congress to establish a war crimes tribunal for Saddam Hussein. In October 1991, in the Foreign Relations Authorization Act, Congress included a provision that the president should propose that the UN Security Council establish such a tribunal.[48] In 1994 Representative Gerald Solomon, a conservative Republican from New York, introduced similar legislation.[49] Proposals for war crimes tribunals were introduced later as well; one was passed by the House in 1997, another by the Senate in 1998, and language regarding the establishment of a war crimes tribunal was included in the ILA, which was signed into law in late 1998.[50]

In addition, there were hearings and proposed legislation regarding reparations and compensation to Americans with claims arising from the Iraqi invasion of Kuwait that would not be covered by the UN Compensation Commission.[51] There were proposals to give American claimants access to frozen Iraqi funds to obtain compensation.[52] Congress also occasionally addressed other issues; for example, a Senate committee held a hearing on whether U.S. exports of biological and chemical weapons materials to Iraq in the 1980s had been used in the Gulf War and had damaged U.S. soldiers in that conflict.[53]

Although the Democrats controlled both houses of Congress until 1995, for the most part they had little interest in the humanitarian situation. In the early 1990s the Democrats wanted little to do with Iraq. They had been skeptical of the Bush administration's drive in the fall of 1990 for a military invasion, and some Democrats had voted against its authorization; but in the end it received overwhelming support from both houses. The Bush administration had built a broad international coalition, the war was brief and there was little loss of American lives. The broad perception was that the war had been successful and that the Democrats, to the extent that they had opposed it, had been on the wrong side.

In 1991 and early 1992, in response to the highly publicized UN reports of the devastation in Iraq, there were a few hearings on the humanitarian situation and there was some discussion of unfreezing Iraqi assets for use by UN agencies in Iraq. But these efforts dropped off quickly. From then on, for the most part the Democratic leadership wanted to distance itself from Iraq issues as much as possible, and certainly did not want to be seen as arguing that sympathy should now be shown to "Saddam's Iraq." After 1995, under Republican control of the Congress there were no hearings on the humanitarian situation by the Republican-chaired committees and there were rarely any witnesses invited to other hearings on Iraq who could speak knowledgeably about the humanitarian crisis. When the Democrats lost control of Congress, a former congressional aide said, "It was like a tidal wave." The range of views that had been present in the

1990 hearings was no longer visible. "In 1990, prior to the Gulf War, there were people advocating each position—sanctions, diplomacy, and war. When the Democrats lost Congress, all of that just disappeared."[54]

The Democratic leadership had no interest in part because President Clinton was vulnerable to attacks by hawks—Jesse Helms famously said that Clinton was unfit to be commander-in-chief—and any concern with the humanitarian situation would have been seen as a further sign of weakness on his part. According to one congressional staffer, in regard to humanitarian concerns, "No one wanted to touch Iraq, especially the Democrats."[55] In addition, the Democratic leadership saw sanctions as a kind of a buffer: Senator Joseph Biden privately told congressional critics that if sanctions were removed as an option the Democrats would be painted into a corner where the only remaining alternatives for dealing with Iraq would be military ones.

Congressional Interest in the Humanitarian Situation: 1991–1996

In March 1991 the UN Secretary-General's envoy, Martti Ahtisaari, issued his report of the conditions in Iraq, with projections that the situation would worsen. The impending humanitarian crisis came up in an April 1991 hearing before the Subcommittee on Immigration and Refugee Affairs, of the Senate Judiciary Committee, along with a staff report in May. The report included findings on the Kurdish refugees in Iran regarding the imminent health crisis and increasing mortality rates.[56] There were findings as well about the coming health crisis among the Kurds; it was expected that sources of water available to the Kurdish refugees would dry up within three weeks.[57] There was also information on the refugee crisis and displaced persons within the southern and central governorates. The Harvard Study Team (HST), a twelve-member group of experts that had reviewed the humanitarian situation in April, projected that 170,000 children would die of malnutrition and disease if international emergency aid was not provided right away.[58] In May 1991 Representative Henry Gonzalez of Texas wrote the president, asking that the administration "initiate an immediate and massive international effort" to provide food and medical relief for the situation resulting from the embargo.[59] In June 1991 Gonzalez spoke about the urgency of the humanitarian situation[60] and introduced a resolution to lift the embargo altogether, citing reports by the UN, the HST and nongovernmental organizations (NGOs) documenting the collapse of Iraq's infrastructure and the crisis of public health and child mortality.[61]

In July 1991 UN Secretary-General envoy Sadruddin Aga Khan visited Iraq. He reported on the collapse of infrastructure and stated that epidemics were imminent. Senators Dodd, Wellstone, Pell, and others, citing the "public health catastrophe," introduced a resolution in the Senate to use frozen Iraqi assets to fund humanitarian needs in Iraq, noting that there were $3.75 billion of frozen assets of the Iraqi state, of which about 40 percent was in the United States.[62] In November, Representative Timothy Penny, a Democrat from Minnesota, introduced a similar resolution, proposing to release Iraq's frozen assets to UNICEF.[63]

As the humanitarian crisis set in in the summer of 1991, there was also a series of hearings held by the House Select Committee on Hunger, in August 1991, November 1991, and March 1992, with testimony from NGOs, UN agencies, public health experts, and Congressman Jim McDermott, who had visited Iraq. All reiterated the findings of the UN Secretary-General's envoy regarding the extent of the crisis and the critical role of restoring infrastructure. These were chaired by Byron Dorgan, a Democrat from North Dakota, with the active participation of Congressman Penny. In two of the hearings, David Bonior, a Democrat from Michigan, was invited to participate[64] and gave statements strongly critical of the humanitarian impact. The witnesses invited by the committee represented highly credible relief agencies that were working in Iraq, such as UNICEF, Catholic Relief Services, and the International Rescue Committee. In addition, there were well-respected scholars such as John Osgood Field of the Tufts study team in Iraq and Julia Devin, coordinator of the HST and the International Study Team (IST), a group of eighty-seven researchers from multiple disciplines who went to Iraq in August.[65] Jim McDermott, a member of the House from Washington State and a physician, visited Iraq in August 1991 with a relief agency and testified about what he described as the "public health crisis" in Iraq at the November 1991 hearing.[66]

All of these witnesses described the situation in the same terms as the Aga Khan and Ahtisaari reports: that the destruction of the infrastructure meant that bringing in food and medicine was not enough and that equipment and spare parts were equally urgent,[67] and that the crisis was not due only to shortages of goods for consumption but also to the economic situation, particularly the collapse in purchasing power. A representative from UNICEF testified that this is not the kind of thing I have seen before at this magnitude in the quarter of a century that I have spent overseas, working in nine different countries in situations similar to this . . . Right now a five pound bag of flour costs $80, and to buy 12 eggs, a dozen eggs, it will cost you over $50.[68]

Witnesses stressed the particular need to support electricity generation, since everything else in turn depended upon that: "The causes [of the crisis] have to do with the end of electricity in a country that is very high tech dependent . . . The generators that are supposed to be rested 12 hours a day are running 24 hours a day, and something is going to snap."[69] Another witness noted that "power provided by electrical power plants is sporadic and intermittent at best. Hospitals, water purification and sewage treatment plants throughout Iraq lack sufficient and constant electrical power to operate properly."[70]

Committee members as well as witnesses referred frequently to the reports of the HST and the IST. Witnesses noted that the IST found that the mortality rate for children under five had increased drastically;[71] that both missions had gone to all eighteen governorates and visited the thirty largest cities in Iraq;[72] and that the IST surveyed over 9,000 households, one of the most extensive surveys ever done in Iraq.[73] Congressman McDermott noted that he saw evidence of everything reported by the HST and the IST: "I think everything that they report in that summary I saw . . . I visited water plants. I saw hospitals. I saw drug stores. I saw the kinds of things that they are talking about."[74]

The witnesses also reported that the Iraqi government was not as unrelentingly cruel to the population as the administration and most of Congress maintained. One of the lead researchers noted that the Iraqi government had taken immediate measures to restore water, sanitation, and health services as well as an aggressive infant immunization program.[75] The witness from UNICEF noted that his staff had monitored the arrival and distribution of goods without interference from the Iraqi government.[76] The IST report noted that the Iraqi government had used salvaged parts and improvised methods to restore electricity in the absence of proper equipment and spare parts.[77] The witness from Catholic Relief Services noted that the Iraqi government had been fairly cooperative with his agency's staff.[78] The witness from UNICEF noted that the government's rationing worked well, as had the immunization program, until the disruption of electricity and the breakdown of the cold chain.[79]

At these hearings the State Department witnesses consistently sought to minimize the humanitarian harm, insisting that the situation was not as bad as others suggested. At the August hearings the State Department representative maintained that there were over 200 trucks per day coming into Iraq.[80] In the November hearing the State Department representative said that trucks were "streaming across the border" from Jordan, Turkey, Syria, and Iran;[81] that there were "vast quantities" of goods in the pipeline;[82] and that shortages were due to the Iraqi government diverting goods for its own purposes.[83] But as the State Department witnesses sought to minimize the shortages, others challenged this position. When the State Department witness said that over 6,000 tons of food arrived in Iraq each day,[84] the UNICEF witness noted that Iraq's food import needs were about ten times that amount.[85]

In November, in introducing a resolution to release frozen assets to UNICEF, Congressman Penny spoke at length about the humanitarian crisis in Iraq.

> Mr. Speaker, this resolution has gone through a variety of changes in the last several days and hours, and I appreciate the work of the many, many Members who have participated in assisting in the development of this legislation.
>
> Mr. Speaker, for 6 long months we have watched as the death toll among young children in Iraq mounts. For the children of Iraq are in peril—not from bombs or bullets but from the effects of malnutrition and disease. This Thanksgiving while thousands of American children are feasting on roast turkey and all the trimmings, one thousand Iraqi children will likely die from starvation or illness.[86]

He referred as well to the extensive documentation of the crisis by UNICEF, the Secretary-General's envoy, public health experts, and medical groups.

> Since May, study teams from a variety of institutions have been to Iraq and have reported on the troubling situation there . . . Nearly concurrent with the Harvard study, a group of Arab-American doctors of the Arab-American Medical Association visited Iraq and publicized their findings with a report and videotape that was shared with every Member of Congress.[87]

152

While Congressman Penny placed blame on Saddam Hussein for his "continued intransigence" in rejecting Security Council Resolution 706 (the first oil-for-food program), Penny also took the view that this did not release the United States from an obligation to take other steps within its power to remedy the situation.

> With yet another study before us confirming what we had already known and with Saddam Hussein's continued intransigence in refusing to accept the U.N. mechanism that would bring help and health to the Iraqi people, it left me and others concerned with this situation still asking the question: What can we do? . . .
>
> It appears that we are at a stalemate on this issue. All the while, time is running out for the children of Iraq. Hundreds more children are dying or having their futures put at risk by lack of proper nutrition and medical care during critical developmental stages in their lives.[88]

But these attempts all failed. In 1994 there was another proposal, this time by Representative David Bonior, that Iraq's frozen assets be used for humanitarian goods,[89] arguing that in the face of the stalemate there was still an obligation to act.

> At this point, Mr. Speaker, we must ask ourselves one simple question: Do these two U.N. resolutions let us off the hook for the continued suffering of the people of Iraq?
>
> Do they allow us to throw up our hands, turn a blind eye, point a finger at Saddam, and say we tried?
>
> Or do we have a continuing responsibility as a compassionate nation to do all we can to provide humanitarian relief to the mothers and children who are starving and dying? . . .
>
> Mr. Speaker, as a first step, if we use just some of those frozen assets to provide medicine—or food—to the people of Iraq, it will make a world of difference.[90]

He noted that the humanitarian situation had become much less visible in the United States, even though things had not improved in Iraq at all: "Ever since CNN and all the foreign correspondents left Baghdad 3 years ago, we haven't paid much attention to Iraq."[91] In addition, in the first half of the 1990s there were few grassroots organizations in the United States focusing on the humanitarian impact of the sanctions. In the United

153

States, those activists who did try to bring attention to the humanitarian situation in Iraq were often dismissed as lacking in credibility. Some maintained that child mortality rates had skyrocketed under sanctions—which was indeed true—but these advocates were accused of relying uncritically on Iraqi government data for their claims, and were often dismissed as defending the Hussein regime. One activist commented that:

> Unfortunately, some of the early visible opponents of sanctions were Ramsey Clark and his associates with the *Worker's World,* who were seen as flagrant apologists for Saddam Hussein's regime. Since there was virtually no media coverage of Iraq in this period, there were few voices speaking against sanctions, and some of those who were had little credibility.[92]

Overall, from 1992 to 1995, except for a few individual members, such as Representatives Bonior and John Conyers, congressional interest in the humanitarian situation disappeared entirely, even though the situation in Iraq was at its worst. Media interest evaporated in part, as Bonior noted, because the ongoing deterioration of the economy was not compelling news in the way that the war had been. But it was also because the Iraqi government allowed in few reporters from the Western media and most NGOs had pulled out of the central and southern governorates.

A congressional aide working on the issue described the information vacuum:

> In general, there was very little expertise in Washington on Iraq. There was a handful of knowledgeable individuals. At the policy level, there was nothing to draw on, because no one was on the ground in Iraq. At the academic level, Americans couldn't go to Iraq to do research, so there was no one for the administration to talk to.[93]

Even so, there were indications of the urgency of the situation. At a briefing in 1993 by the Joint Chiefs of Staff, Admiral Mike Cramer, Director of Current Intelligence, described to the Senate Armed Services Committee both the extent of the humanitarian crisis at that time and the measures that had been taken by the Iraqi government to address it.

> The embargo has resulted in a serious degradation of the Iraqi economy and the people's standard of living since July 1990. Prices of

some basic staples have increased almost 10,000 percent . . . Private sector industrial production is operating at less than 30 percent of capacity. Unemployment is high, savings are being exhausted, and the middle class is being destroyed. Malnutrition is increasing and health care, sewage, and water system are declining.

Essential needs and services are being met by drawing down stockpiles, cannibalization, and by importing relatively small amounts of critical raw materials . . . Rationing has prevented widespread starvation . . .

Total earnings have been cut from $16 billion to as little as $400 million.[94]

In 1996 Iraq specialist Phebe Marr from the National Defense University testified that the situation had not changed much. While it was difficult to gauge the extent of the damage, she said, the UN teams in Iraq reported serious malnutrition and deterioration of infrastructure.[95]

But while UN reports repeatedly documented the worsening crisis, on the rare occasions when the humanitarian situation was mentioned by members of Congress or by witnesses invited to testify at congressional hearings, it was usually to minimize the suffering from the economic deterioration, or to attribute it to Saddam Hussein's callousness. At a hearing in 1992 one witness stated that there simply was no humanitarian crisis. "Times are tough in Baghdad, but there is no public health crisis. I want to emphasize this point, because the war period formed in the public mind an image of Iraqi starvation and deprivation."[96] He maintained that "the image of an imminent public health catastrophe has persisted long after its reality has faded."[97] At a hearing in 1993 a State Department official, Edward Djerejian, acknowledged that "the economy is deteriorating. The effects of the sanctions are having a toll over the long term," but maintained that it was Hussein's refusal to accept the proposed oil-for-food program that had "caused economic disruption and scarcity and only exacerbate[d] the suffering of the Iraqi people." The subcommittee chairman pressed him: "Do you think there is real hardship there in terms of food, not only for the military but for the people as well? . . . it is an increasingly desperate, deteriorating situation, is that clear?" The State Department official acknowledged that was correct, but implied that this was Saddam Hussein's choice, saying that Hussein made sure that his security forces were well taken care of.[98]

155

Congress and the Oil-for-Food Programme

By 1995 the tension in the Security Council reflected the reality that the situation in Iraq was untenable. The United States had seen a considerable erosion of international support for the sanctions, and Hussein was still in power. Within Iraq, there was intense domestic pressure from the hyperinflation, the shortage of affordable critical goods and the deterioration in electricity and public services, as well as defections and coup attempts. For all the parties the situation was both volatile and intractable, and this made possible enough compromises to negotiate the Oil-for-Food Programme.

But in the mid-1990s, as the Oil-for-Food Programme was being negotiated and began operating, there was little sense in Congress that it was a response to an increasingly desperate and irresolvable situation in every regard. In fact, there was indignation that the sanctions hadn't done more harm. Indeed, there was a suggestion that the United States and the UN had not been sufficiently aggressive with Iraq—"We have pin-pricked Iraq," according to Senator Kay Bailey Hutchison, a Republican from Texas, in 1996;[99] another member of Congress referred to "our pinprick response to Saddam Hussein's aggression."[100]

While the UN and the international community saw the Oil-for-Food Programme as an urgent measure to address the worsening humanitarian situation, conservatives in Congress sought to undermine the program, proposing instead that the income from the oil sales be directed to reimburse U.S. costs rather than being spent on humanitarian goods for the Iraqi population. Some proposed that any funds generated by oil sales first go to the United States as reimbursement for its military costs in Iraq, or counted toward U.S. dues to the UN. Republican Trent Lott proposed a Senate resolution that the United States would "ensure that American taxpayers' interests are protected by rejecting any Iraq–United Nations oil sale agreement which does not reimburse the United States for the costs of Operations Southern Watch and Provide Comfort."[101]

But in 1996, even though some in Congress actively opposed measures that would improve Iraq's humanitarian situation, the critics of sanctions were also beginning to gain some traction.

Grassroots organizations began to build a more mainstream sanctions reform movement. There were groups like Voices in the Wilderness, the Center for Economic and Social Rights, Veterans for

Peace, the American Friends Service Committee, Physicians for Social Responsibility, and activists with Amnesty International taking up the issue. Most of these groups were for "de-linking"— lifting economic sanctions, while keeping military sanctions in place—and they received much broader support than those who simply wanted to lift all restrictions off the Iraqi government.[102]

In May 1996 Madeleine Albright was interviewed by Leslie Stahl for *60 Minutes*, and Stahl asked her about the sanctions: "We have heard that a half million children have died. I mean, that's more children than died in Hiroshima. And, you know, is the price worth it?" Albright famously replied, "We think the price is worth it." According to one activist,

> this was very influential. People started to see that "the war hadn't ended" in Iraq—it had simply moved from the battlefield into people's homes and communities. The casualties were no longer soldiers. Instead the war dead were primarily the elderly, children, women, and other vulnerable Iraqis. Groups like VITW and Veterans for Peace cranked out copies of the "60 Minutes" interview, and circulated it everywhere, as together we started to build a more mainstream sanctions reform movement. After May 1996, thanks in part to constituent pressure, we started to suddenly see members of Congress show more of an active interest in the issue.[103]

By 1996 there was also better information available from within Iraq. In 1996 Congressman Conyers issued a statement criticizing the Clinton administration for holding up the Oil-for-Food Programme and citing a report by the UN's Food and Agriculture Organization (FAO) that estimated how many children in Iraq had died as a result of the sanctions.[104] At the same time, "groups like Voices in the Wilderness were sending delegations to Iraq, and those people were then reporting on what they had seen."[105] Among activist groups there was a "hope to establish some momentum, establish some idea of the spirit of the United States as a nation that responded to suffering, and establish that as a new priority, beyond just containment and regime change.[106]"

The Late 1990s

By late 1997 there was considerable frustration in Congress over the stalemate in Iraq—not with the humanitarian deterioration but rather in regard to the continuation of Saddam Hussein's regime. In November 1997 the House passed a resolution which authorized unilateral U.S. military action in Iraq as a last resort. The Senate considered a similar resolution, but there were objections from those in the Senate who wanted the resolution to explicitly call for the overthrow of Hussein.[107]

In 1998 there was a series of standoffs between Iraq and the United Nations Special Commission (UNSCOM). The hawks in Congress viewed this as evidence that the Oil-for-Food Programme had undermined the sanctions, and that since Iraq had been "rewarded" for its uncooperative behavior, it was now encouraged to flaunt the disarmament regime further.

In February 1998, in the face of a confrontation between the Iraqi government and UNSCOM, congressional hawks began pushing for a military response. But Secretary-General Kofi Annan went to Baghdad and was able to negotiate a solution to the crisis. While some, such as Democratic representative Sheila Jackson-Lee, applauded his work,[108] others, such as Senator John Ashcroft, denounced Annan's successful efforts. Ashcroft responded with open contempt: "At the moment of truth, America's acting Secretary of State—Kofi Annan—cut a deal with the devil and, tragically, a weakened, uncertain President endorsed the settlement before the ink had even dried."[109]

Within Congress, new energy went into bringing about regime change. In May 1998 Congress provided $5 million for regime opposition. In July 1998 Senator Slade Gorton proposed a resolution finding that Iraq was in "unacceptable and material breach" of Security Council resolutions and urging the president "to act accordingly."[110] In August 1998 Congress declared that Iraq was not in compliance with its international obligations.[111] In October 1998 Congress passed the ILA with overwhelming support from the House of Representatives and unanimous support from the Senate. The ILA provided $97 million to support democratic opposition groups within Iraq, opposition broadcasting within Iraq, and military supplies and training for opposition groups. The statute called upon the UN to establish a war crimes tribunal for Saddam Hussein and sketched out a post-Hussein transition for Iraq.

Meanwhile, as the Oil-for-Food Programme was expanded or reformed in response to broad international criticism—and as the movement for sanctions reform gained ground—conservative groups and think tanks, including Patrick Clawson and others from the Washington Institute for Near East Policy, as well as the American Israel Public Affairs

Committee (AIPAC) and Gary Milholland of the Wisconsin Project, were lobbying to maintain or tighten the sanctions.[112] There was virulent opposition to reform efforts from hawks in Congress, especially those from oil-producing states.

In the Senate, Republican Frank Murkowski of Alaska was perhaps the most vocal opponent of every aspect of the Oil-for-Food Programme, presumably because Iraqi oil sales would compete with Alaska's oil interests.

> The teeth in Resolution 687 have effectively been removed with the expansion of the so-called "oil-for-food" exception to the sanctions. The first loosening of the sanctions occurred in 1995, when Security Council Resolution 986 allowed Iraq to export $1 billion in oil every 90 days—$4 billion over one year.
>
> And most recently, during the period when Saddam was again violating Security Council resolution[s] by refusing to allow international inspectors to conduct their work, the United Nations voted to more than double the amount of oil Iraq can export per year.[113]

In 1998 and 1999 Murkowski repeatedly criticized the Oil-for-Food Programme, especially the expansion of its humanitarian programs.[114] While UN officials had for years stressed the urgency of restoring Iraq's infrastructure and public services, Murkowski objected vehemently when the UN program allowed proceeds from oil sales to be used for electricity and sewers,[115] and he introduced a Senate resolution opposing any expansion of the Oil-for-Food Programme.[116] When the administration supported a Security Council resolution to lift the ceiling on oil sales, Murkowski described the Oil-for-Food Programme as "really a wolf in the humanitarian clothing . . . of a sheep."[117] Senator Don Nickles of Oklahoma likewise wanted to tighten the embargo further,[118] and complained that the amount of oil sold under the program had more than doubled.[119]

Senator Jesse Helms chaired hearings in 1998 and 1999 in which many of the witnesses, as well as committee members, criticized the expansion of the Oil-for-Food Programme and the measures to streamline the program, and maintained that these efforts constituted a policy of appeasement by the Clinton administration. Helms was critical that the Oil-for-Food Programme existed at all; he objected to "how the Iraq sanctions have been watered down since the end of the Gulf War"[120] and to the "so-called streamlining of the contract approval process . . . [which would] be tantamount to lifting the sanctions altogether."[121] Senator Nickles was openly contemptuous of the Clinton administration for supporting the Oil-for-Food Programme: "This administration's policy has been appeasement. This administration's policy has been to reward [Iraq's] noncompliance."[122]

In 1999 Representative Bill Archer, the Republican chairman of the Ways and Means Committee, lobbied the Clinton administration to reduce the Oil-for-Food Programme back to pre-1998 levels.[123] A dozen members of Congress signed on to a resolution sponsored by Representative Wes Watkins urging the president to oppose expansion of the program.[124] In 2001 Murkowski repeatedly attacked the Oil-for-Food Programme, making numerous statements in the *Congressional Record* and publishing an op-ed article in the *Washington Post*. He accused Iraq of spending "only a fraction" of the funds available on humanitarian needs while spending "that money on items of questionable, and often highly suspicious purposes,"[125] and he introduced legislation that would prohibit U.S. purchasers from buying Iraqi oil on the grounds that importing Iraqi oil was inconsistent with national security.[126]

Attempts at Sanctions Reform within Congress

In the late 1990s liberal Democrats and other critics of the sanctions had limited venues in which to raise their issues, given the Republican control of Congress and the dominant concern, in both parties, with containment and regime change. Even so, by the late 1990s a sanctions reform movement was gaining ground. There was no support within Congress for lifting sanctions altogether; no one would have argued for allowing Iraq to rearm. The central strategy that emerged was "de-linking"— lifting the sanctions that affected the civilian population while leaving in place the sanctions on military goods. There was broad support for this among religious and grassroots organizations.[127]

When the Republican committee chairs would not hold hearings on the humanitarian issues in Iraq, the critics of sanctions held briefings of their own. In February 1998 Representative Conyers sponsored a "teach-in" for members of Congress on the humanitarian issues, with presentations by Raymond Zilinskas, a former UN weapons inspector; Michael Ratner and Jules Lobel from the Center for Constitutional Rights; Clovis Maksoud, a former Arab League ambassador to the United States and the UN;

Peter Pellett, a nutrition expert who conducted studies for FAO in Iraq; Phyllis Bennis of the Institute for Policy Studies; and Zainab Salbi, an Iraqi American active in the exile community.[128] Representatives Conyers and Carolyn Kilpatrick sponsored a briefing for members of Congress and their staff in July 1998 on the humanitarian impact of sanctions on Iraq, with presentations by Phyllis Bennis; Khaled Elgindy of the Arab-American Institute; and Carl LeVan, Conyers's legislative director.[129] In October 1998 Conyers and Kilpatrick, joined by Representatives Tom Campbell and David Bonior, held another briefing, on "The Poverty of Civilian Sanctions: The Humanitarian Crisis in Iraq," with presentations by Denis Halliday, the former UN humanitarian coordinator in Iraq; Peter Pellett; and Phyllis Bennis.[130] Carolyn Kilpatrick held a briefing for her constituents, with several speakers, and Representative Dennis Kucinich, a liberal Democrat from Ohio, also held briefings. At the height of the anti-sanctions movement, there were three or four such briefings each year.[131]

Although there was little support in the late 1990s for lifting the Iraq sanctions altogether, there was growing criticism of sanctions in general. In 1997 legislation was introduced that sought to establish restrictions on the president's ability to impose economic sanctions, requiring the president to submit a report to Congress on the likely impact of sanctions on U.S. interests and the U.S. economy before putting sanctions in place.[132] It was supported by manufacturing and agricultural interests such as the National Association of Manufacturers, the Missouri Farm Bureau, and the U.S. Rice Federation.[133] In 1999 there were also bills introduced to build in greater exemptions or to make it more difficult to impose sanctions in general, such as the "Economic Sanctions Reform Act," which required both the executive and legislative branches to review any unilateral sanctions imposed by the United States.[134]

Much of the criticism of sanctions came from farm states. In 1998 Senator Conrad Burns of Montana noted that wheat imports to Iraq, Cuba, and other embargoed nations had doubled since 1995, accounting for 11 percent of the world's trade, and U.S. producers were excluded from that market.[135] Senator Chuck Hagel of Nebraska echoed this view.[136] Senator Richard Lugar, from Indiana, proposed legislation to require a cost-benefit analysis before the executive branch could unilaterally impose sanctions. Criticizing economic sanctions, Senator Pat Roberts of Kansas said, "They do not achieve their policy goals. They are very counterproductive, and as has been indicated by some across the aisle, and others, we shoot ourselves in the foot."[137] Senator Hagel argued that the United States had imposed sanctions on thirty-five nations, constituting almost half the world's population, and that the United States had lost $20 billion in exports, along with 200,000 jobs, as a result of unilateral sanctions.[138]

Senator Dorgan of North Dakota argued similarly:

I represent one of the most agricultural States in the Nation. And nearly 10 percent of the market for wheat is out of limits or off limits to our family farmers because we have decided to impose sanctions and therefore take those markets off limits to our farmers.[139]

He then tied this to humanitarian concerns:

Halfway around the world there are people in Sudan, we are told, old women, climbing trees to forage for leaves to eat, leaves because they are on the abyss of starvation . . . Turn the globe another halfway around and you will find America's farmers, who are the economic all-stars, produce food in abundant quantity, and they are told in our system . . . that their product doesn't have value, doesn't have worth.[140]

Congressman Ron Paul also argued that U.S. business interests overlapped with humanitarian concerns.

Our sanctions policies undermine America's position as a humane nation, bolstering the common criticism that we are a bully with no respect for people outside our borders. Economic common sense, self-interested foreign policy goals, and humanitarian ideals all point to the same conclusion: Congress should work to end economic sanctions against all nations immediately.[141]

There were also attempts at legislation that focused specifically on exempting food and medicine from any sanctions regime, again citing both humanitarian concerns and U.S. business interests. Led by senators from farm states, these included the Food and Medicine for the World Act in 1999[142] and the Food and Medicine Sanctions Relief Act of 1999.[143] In 2000 Senator Dorgan supported a proposal to end all U.S. sanctions on food and medicine, arguing that "it is fundamentally immoral for our country to decide what they will withhold and prohibit the shipment of food and medicine to any country in the world. It doesn't make any sense," while noting again that it concerned him that "11 percent of the international wheat market is off limits to our family farmers."[144]

The most significant legislative attempt that specifically addressed the Iraq sanctions was the Humanitarian Exports Leading to Peace (HELP) Act, which was introduced by Congressman John Conyers in 2000 and 2001.[145] It cited the hardships of the Iraqi population while noting that Iraq represented a potential market of $1 billion in U.S. agricultural products, and sought to lift U.S. restrictions on U.S. companies that had effectively precluded them from selling food and medical supplies to Iraq, even within the context of the Oil-for-Food Programme. There was broad grassroots support from the Arab-American Antidiscrimination League, Voices in the Wilderness, and other organizations. Although it would not have directly increased the flow of goods into Iraq, its supporters hoped it would bring in new allies from U.S. agriculture and other business interests in opposing the Iraq sanctions. It had a number of cosponsors, and there was enough support to sponsor a companion bill in the Senate as well.

In addition to these legislative efforts there were several individuals in Congress who were very vocal in opposing the sanctions, in hearings and in letters to the president and the State Department. These letters were significant in part because they included signatures from a number of Republicans, despite their party's singular interest in regime change and security issues. But for Democrats as well it was an important statement: signing on to the letter meant going against the party leadership and their own administration by bringing attention to an issue that was embarrassing for the White House. While the Clinton administration and the Democratic leadership did not want to address humanitarian issues in Iraq for fear that President Clinton would be painted as "soft on Saddam," the critics of sanctions circulated letters to the White House and the State Department, some of which received scores of signatures, challenging the sanctions and demanding explanations.

In September 1996 Representative Conyers sent a letter to President Clinton asking that the United States not block the proposed Oil-for-Food Programme.[146] In October 1998 Conyers, Bonior, and Kilpatrick sent President Clinton a letter signed by forty-eight members of the House of Representatives. It called for a de-linking of the economic sanctions from the military sanctions, in light of the humanitarian crisis.[147] In a letter to the president, Representative Kilpatrick maintained that "History is proof that it is in the United States' best long-term interests to shape a policy that embraces humanitarian concerns and allows new ways to address the legitimate security concerns of the United States."[148] The following March, in the *Congressional Record*, Representative Conyers again urged a solution that would tighten the military embargo while easing the humanitarian restrictions,[149] arguing that "it has often been said that you cannot achieve democracy by undemocratic means. I would add as a corollary that you also cannot inspire respect for human rights by undermining them."[150]

In addition, while critics of the sanctions could not sponsor hearings on the humanitarian impact, when there were hearings on disarmament issues in Iraq or regime change, a number of individuals used these opportunities to raise humanitarian issues, either as witnesses or committee members.

In the summer of 1999, at a hearing held by the Senate Foreign Relations Committee on the topic of mobilizing the opposition toward regime change, Senator Wellstone raised the humanitarian issues in Iraq:

> The reports we receive are still very disturbing. As many as 30% of Iraq's children are malnourished; infant mortality rates are soaring; much of the population lacks access to clean water and sanitation . . . We may inadvertently contribute to such an outcome if we do not take steps to tangibly improve the lives of ordinary Iraqis.[151]

Wellstone then pressed a State Department witness at length to justify the humanitarian situation. A few months later, Wellstone reiterated his concerns again at another Foreign Relations Committee hearing, citing the UNICEF report, the child mortality rate, and the overall humanitarian impact of the sanctions.[152]

In August 1999 aides from five members of the House traveled to Iraq to look at the effect of the economic sanctions on the civilian population. They met with the senior UN officials from the World Health Organization, UNICEF, FAO, the World Food Programme, the de-mining program, and the housing construction program, as well as the humanitarian coordinator. They wrote a report documenting the severe impact of the sanctions, and circulated it widely in Congress.[153]

In February 2000 another letter was sent to President Clinton by members of the House, questioning the viability of the Iraq sanctions. Circulated by Representatives Tom Campbell and John Conyers, it was signed by some seventy members of the House.[154] By this time the criticism of the Iraq sanctions also became much more specific and well-informed, reflecting an awareness of the particular role of the United States, for example, in the imposition of holds. Republican representative Chris Smith, chair of the Foreign Affairs Subcommittee on International Operations and Human Rights, wrote to Secretary of State Albright asking for information on the institutional policies that contributed to the ongoing humanitarian crisis in Iraq.[155] The letter asked her whether UN staffing was adequate and whether the government of Iraq was cooperating. But Smith also asked for a list of contracts that the United States had placed on hold, whether U.S. Treasury Department restrictions impeded donations, and when the fast-track list of goods would be approved. The next month, at the hearing on Iraq policy in the House, Smith discussed the UNICEF report on child mortality, which he found troubling.[156]

Vocal opposition within Congress continued to grow, and was increasingly articulate and explicit in addressing U.S. practices within the Security Council and the 661 Committee. In March 2000 Wellstone and Senator Russell Feingold coauthored a letter to President Clinton, asking the administration to implement the recommendations made by the Security Council's humanitarian panel, which included allowing Iraq's infrastructure to be restored, implementing fast-tracking, and taking steps toward greater transparency of the 661 Committee.[157] At a March 2000 hearing, Conyers testified, citing the UNICEF report that 5,000 children per month were dying as a result of the sanctions, and referred to the resignations of Denis Halliday and Hans von Sponeck, who had served as humanitarian coordinators in Iraq.[158] Representative Sam Gejdenson noted that support for the sanctions regime had diminished both in the Security Council and within the international community.[159] In the parallel Senate hearing, Wellstone discussed the report issued by the humanitarian panel of the Security Council, which described the ongoing impact of the sanctions as "devastating." They also described the Red Cross and UNICEF reports, which "all made it clear that a public health emergency exists in . . . the country."[160]

The following month, in April 2000, Representative Dennis Kucinich sent a letter with twenty-five signatures to Secretary of State Albright asking to discuss Iraq policy, citing reports on public health and humanitarian impact.[161] Also in April 2000, Congressman Tony Hall visited Iraq. Upon his return, he wrote Secretary of State Albright asking that the United States support several of the critical changes that had been under discussion at the UN that "would improve the humanitarian situation without leading to increased military capacities for the Government of Iraq." These included U.S. support for a cash component in the south/center; that the United States should review its standard for "dual-use" review; and that the United States should explicitly say what information it required to expedite approval and remove holds.[162] At a hearing in September 2000, Representative Gejdenson raised concerns about the humanitarian impact of sanctions at a hearing of the International Relations Committee. The sanctions policy, he said, "is hurting the people. It is not hurting Saddam."[163] He was joined by Representative Barbara Lee, who suggested de-linking military sanctions from economic measures and asked, "Are we participating in a process that is creating more pain than would be the case had we not imposed sanctions?"[164] At a Foreign Relations Committee hearing in March 2001, Wellstone again raised the issues of the need for greater transparency, restoring the infrastructure, the preapproval of humanitarian items, and the need for a cash component for local Iraqi purchases.[165] In June 2001 another letter was sent to the secretary of state, signed by some forty members of the House, noting that the embargo was preventing Iraq from purchasing equipment for water treatment, electricity, agriculture, and other critical infrastructure.[166]

In the fall of 2002, others in Congress joined in the criticism of the sanctions. Representative Bobby Rush, a Democrat from Illinois, argued that

> despite the President's proclamation that America is a friend of the Iraqi people, we cannot insult the American people by ignoring the fact that U.S.-led sanctions have created a hotbed of disease and extreme poverty in Iraq, and war will only plunge the Iraqi people deeper into death and despair.[167]

He was joined by Representative Jesse Jackson: "President Clinton stated sanctions will be there until the end of time or as long as Hussein lasts. But economic sanctions are only hurting the people, making life miserable for the average Iraqi, causing an estimated 500,000 deaths, mainly women and children."[168]

The increasing support in Congress for sanctions reform was due in large measure to the growing visibility and advocacy of the activisim against sanctions, which brought political pressure to bear but also provided detailed information about the depth of the humanitarian crisis in Iraq, as well as the U.S. holds and other specific practices that directly contributed to the crisis. These efforts were supported by UN documents and reports by public health experts. Voices in the Wilderness, founded in 1996, was one of the most significant grassroots organizations opposing sanctions, sponsoring trips as well as material aid shipments and public education. In June 1998 the National Iraq Network, a coalition of about two dozen organizations, sent a letter to every member of Congress, which in turn cited the U.S. Catholic bishops' statement against the sanctions, signed by fifty-four bishops.[169] In April 2000 the Education for Peace in Iraq Center (EPIC) sent letters to senators, noting that according to the UN, all telecommunications contracts, two-thirds of electricity contracts, and over half of water contracts were on hold, and holds on oil spares were so extensive that Iraq's income from oil sales was expected to be $13 billion instead of $19 billion. The letter also asked support from the Senate in requesting the administration to implement the recommendations from the March 1999 Security Council humanitarian panel to streamline the approval process and implement measures for greater transparency and oversight.[170] By June 2000, EPIC's lobbying efforts included detailed information about U.S. holds on contracts, noting for example that as of May 2000, nearly 1,100 contracts worth $1.6 billion were on hold, including goods ranging from water pumps to kidney dialysis machines.[171]

By 2000 there were public demonstrations against the sanctions involving dozens of religious and political organizations. The National Mobilization to End the Sanctions Against Iraq held a march sponsored by nearly 100 organizations in August 2000.[172] In May 2001 a letter was sent to President Bush from over 100 religious leaders and faith-based organizations, citing the holds and asking that sanctions be lifted.[173] In June 2001 the Campaign of Conscience for the Iraqi People, representing 115 organizations and 2,000 individuals, sent a letter calling on members of Congress to lift the sanctions.[174] In March 2002 letters were sent again to everyone in the Senate, noting that $5 billion of humanitarian contracts were on hold and that the holds, "combined with declining oil revenues, have nearly brought the UN's contract review process to a standstill."[175]

In addition, EPIC coordinated lobbying efforts in which constituents and activists met with several dozen members of Congress or their aides, and did so every spring and summer, and sometimes in the fall as well, from 1998 to 2002. It was often the case that the aides or congressmen neither knew nor cared that there was a humanitarian crisis in Iraq, or that the United States had a role in it. The lobbyists wrote reports of each meeting, noting whether the representative, senator, or aide was familiar with the humanitarian crisis; held a position in regard to the sanctions; or had questions or concerns. EPIC lobbyists described the offices of Representative Judy Biggert,[176] Senator Blanche Lincoln,[177] Representative Paul Ryan,[178] and Representative John Lewis,[179] for example, as having no familiarity with the humanitarian crisis in Iraq. Those who were familiar with it, such as the offices of Senator Carl Levin,[180] Representative Cynthia McKinney,[181] Representative William Clay,[182] Senator Russell Feingold,[183] and Representative Anna Eshoo,[184] were often supportive of letters to the administration, proposals to de-link Iraq's military cooperation from civilian imports, or bills to allow food sales. In some cases the congressmen or aides believed that the humanitarian crisis was created because Saddam Hussein was deliberately starving Iraqis and that the United States had no role in it. Some, such as the offices of Representatives Ileana Ros-Lehtinen[185] and William Coyne,[186] had no knowledge of the humanitarian crisis and little concern. Some, such as the offices of Representatives Joseph Hoeffel,[187] Lee Terry,[188] and Robert Menendez,[189] were familiar with the crisis but were unsympathetic.

Yet even with lobbying, public protests, high-profile incidents such as the resignations of Halliday and von Sponeck, and highly publicized information such as the UNICEF report, and even when detailed information was provided on the U.S. role in the humanitarian crisis, it was still the case that the overwhelming majority in both houses simply showed no interest or concern about the humanitarian situation in Iraq, at any point in the entire course of the sanctions regime, regardless of how desperate the situation was or how clear it was that the United States bore a great deal of responsibility for it.

The Iraq War of 2003

In the run-up to the 2003 war, much of the congressional activity paralleled the debate of 1990. Hawks argued that the sanctions had failed—this time because they were so lax due to the expanded humanitarian exemptions—and that military intervention was the only solution. A few argued that the humanitarian effects of the sanctions were likely to compromise the justification or success of a military action. Senator Feingold asked whether the U.S. role in the humanitarian crisis might affect the reaction of the Iraqi people if the United States went to war.[190]

Representative Cynthia McKinney invoked the sanctions in challenging the administration's justification for the war.

> If our Nation really cared about Iraq's neighbors, we would never have supplied [Iraq] with the military arsenal that we did ... If we cared about the Iraqi people, we would have done something to lift the burdens imposed on them by the U.N. sanctions, which today have claimed in excess of an estimated 500,000 Iraqi children.
>
> But the truth is we didn't really care about any of that suffering.[191]

But for the most part the failure of the sanctions were invoked as a reason to go to war. One witness maintained that Iraq "has slipped out from under sanctions ... The stark facts are that inspections are dead, and sanctions are dead, and they cannot be resurrected."[192]

The secretary of defense, Donald Rumsfeld, argued that since Saddam Hussein was still in power, sanctions hadn't produced results and military action was needed.[193] Members of Congress echoed this: Senator Jean Carnahan maintained that "We have tried to contain Saddam Hussein with sanctions. But the world has been unwilling to enforce them."[194] Representative Grace Napolitano likewise held that previous efforts, including UN resolutions, sanctions, and inspections, had not produced results.[195] At the end of the debate, Congress supported the U.S. attack against Iraq even in the absence of Security Council authorization.

The Erosion of Support

Throughout the sanctions period, there was recurring concern in Congress that international support for the sanctions had eroded. Although there was certainly a good deal of posturing and rhetoric, there also seemed to be genuine puzzlement as to why the international community would be unwilling to support what appeared to be clearly a right and good measure against an evil government. Within Congress, the opposition from the international community was dismissed as self-interest or America-bashing, or was viewed as reflecting ignorance and confusion.

The erosion of support within the Security Council was certainly clear by early 1994, when Russia, France, China, and Brazil pressed to recognize Iraq's cooperation with UNSCOM, while the United States and Britain refused. A report from the CRS noted that while no one was arguing to lift sanctions altogether, "divisions within the Council may worsen as UNSCOM moves closer to indicating that Iraq has satisfied the [disarmament and inspection requirements]."[196] By 1996 none of the U.S. allies in the Gulf, except Kuwait, were willing to let the United States use their territory for retaliatory strikes against Iraq.[197]

Within Congress, this was consistently attributed to the international community's failure to understand that the humanitarian crisis "was Saddam's fault." At a hearing in 1998 military expert Richard Haass testified that "there is tremendous lack of sympathy for the economic sanctions. To the extent they have had adverse humanitarian consequences, it is Saddam's doing, but all the same, the political reality is that the sanctions are largely blamed for that."[198] Thomas Pickering, a State Department official, testified that after eight years of sanctions, "most states in the world either do not understand or do not care that the Iraqi Government is fully responsible for the Iraqi people's suffering—they just want that suffering to end."[199] Beginning in the late 1990s, these sentiments were repeated regularly at hearings on Iraq before the House and Senate, in particular at a 1999 hearing of the Senate Foreign Relations Committee entitled "Facing Saddam's Iraq: Disarray in the International Community."[200]

Outside of a handful of individuals, there seems to have been little sense in Congress that the lack of international support for the U.S. agenda might be grounded in the reality of how ineffectual and gratuitously damaging the policy actually was. Almost no one in Congress questioned the legitimacy or entitlement of the United States to demand the removal of a foreign government, beyond a few who voted against the ILA for this reason. Nor did anyone publicly note that regime change was not something contained in the Security Council resolutions and that seeking the overthrow of a foreign state constituted aggression under the UN Charter and in international law. Even the most vocal and liberal members of Congress only sought to alleviate the humanitarian crisis. The right of the United States to unilaterally insist upon the removal of a government and to approve its replacement was simply not questioned by almost anyone in Congress at any point.

For the most part, Congress had little role in shaping the U.S. policy regarding the Iraq sanctions. Few members of Congress had any substantial interest or knowledge of their humanitarian impact outside of a short-lived concern for the humanitarian situation in 1991 and 1992, and a limited number of very vocal legislators, although several dozen more began to express some concern after the sanctions had been in place for a decade. Throughout the sanctions regime, neither party's leadership wanted to bring visibility to the humanitarian situation in Iraq. To the extent that it was mentioned in hearings or in the *Congressional Record,* the humanitarian crisis was often minimized or dismissed or simply attributed to Saddam Hussein in some fashion.

For the first several years of the sanctions regime it seems to be the case that almost no one in Congress had any awareness of the entire body of UN and NGO reports documenting Iraq's humanitarian crisis. Although the UN Secretary-General and UN agencies had issued continual reports on the humanitarian crisis since 1991, it seems that the only ones of which there was any awareness in Congress were the highly publicized reports of the Secretary-General envoys in 1991 and the 1999 UNICEF report on child mortality, along with the high-level resignations of Denis Halliday and Hans von Sponeck.

Until the late 1990s there was no indication that anyone in either house of Congress had any actual knowledge of the U.S. role in the sanctions. There was certainly no sign that anyone in Congress knew that the United States was blocking everything from tractor tires to ambulances to women's clothing, or that there was even a process for humanitarian exemptions. This was in part because the State Department often presented a distorted picture of the humanitarian situation in Iraq and of the U.S. role, maintaining that the Iraqi government was exaggerating and that it was able to buy all the humanitarian goods that were needed. But even if the information coming from the administration was misleading, it was also the case that almost no one in Congress cared.

By the late 1990s there was no lack of credible information documenting the severity and causes of the crisis, or for that matter, the U.S. role. Those in Congress who *were* concerned about the humanitarian crisis in Iraq, primarily liberal Democrats joined by legislators from farm states, were very vocal and very knowledgeable. They wrote individual letters to the administration citing UN reports of the bottlenecks in the program as well as addressing in detail the issues regarding the administration's review of contracts, including the holds and the ambiguous "dual-use" standard. They also sponsored "Dear Colleague" letters, which were circulated widely in Congress, then sent to the administration with dozens of signatures. In addition, the report by congressional aides from their trip to Iraq was widely circulated.

But even when the humanitarian issues were raised, pointedly and repeatedly, by Senators Wellstone and Feingold, and Congressmen Conyers, Gejdenson, Campbell, Kilpatrick, Bonior, Smith, and others, and even when there was information that was deemed credible, particularly the UNICEF report of 1999, there was little interest. While the House and Senate committees on foreign relations held dozens of hearings on Iraq spanning more than a decade, almost none of them mentioned the humanitarian crisis. In general hearings on "the situation in Iraq," no witnesses gave testimony on the humanitarian situation, except to say that claims of a crisis were exaggerated or to bemoan the fact that somehow, inexplicably, Saddam had "won the propaganda war," successfully manipulating the world into believing that the sanctions had caused harm. The only committee that held actual hearings on the humanitarian impact of the sanctions was the Select Committee on Hunger in 1991 and 1992, but that interest was short-lived and was explicitly driven by farm states concerned with interference in potential markets for U.S. agricultural sales.

Legislation was introduced on numerous issues: establishing a tribunal to try Saddam Hussein for war crimes; compensation for U.S. nationals; and of course the ILA, which funded efforts at ousting Hussein. But in regard to legislation, the closest anything came to responding to the humanitarian situation were proposals to allow U.S. companies to sell agricultural and medical goods to Iraq under the Oil-for-Food Programme—goods that Iraq could already buy elsewhere—giving U.S. businesses a share of the market.

And just as there was little interest in the humanitarian situation in Iraq generally, the level of interest in the actual workings of the Oil-for-Food Programme was almost nonexistent until there were accusations of UN improprieties, and then interest skyrocketed.

9

THE OIL FOR FOOD SCANDAL

The sanctions on Iraq lasted for more than a decade and did terrible damage to a population and a nation. Yet there was no aspect of the sanctions themselves that received nearly as much attention as the accusations that were brought against the Oil-for-Food Programme beginning in 2004.

"A mountain of evidence has now accumulated to suggest the Iraqi people suffered from shortages of quality food and medicine not because international sanctions were too strict, but because lax or corrupt oversight at U.N. headquarters in New York allowed Saddam Hussein to exploit the system for his own purposes," read a *Wall Street Journal* editorial.[1] William Safire of the *New York Times* proclaimed it "the largest financial rip-off in history."[2] At a hearing he chaired, Congressman Ralph Hall stated: "By allowing such fraud and deception to continue, and for U.N. employees to participate in it, has probably resulted in the deaths of thousands of Iraqis through malnutrition and lack of appropriate medical supplies. We have a name for that in the United States, it is called murder."[3]

The UN was accused of allowing Saddam Hussein to manipulate the program, permitting him to acquire billions of dollars through smuggling and kickbacks. Some 2,000 companies apparently paid kickbacks to Iraq and about a dozen individuals were charged with criminal violations. The Secretariat was accused of failing to establish structures of accountability and transparency that would have prevented the improprieties from taking place. The accusations received enormous attention from the media, particularly in the United States, as well as from Congress. Secretary-General Kofi Annan himself was accused of improprieties, although in the end these claims were found to be without substance. Critics of the UN seized on the accusations regarding the Oil-for-Food

173

Programme as grounds for demanding Annan's resignation and for claiming that the UN was a failed institution. Over a dozen individuals were prosecuted, including some UN officials. Benon Sevan, the director of the Office of the Iraq Programme (OIP), was accused of improperly receiving $160,000. In the end, the view that was completely pervasive—in the press, in the U.S. government, and in the minds of the public—was the certainty that the Oil-for-Food Programme was deeply corrupt and that the UN itself was inept and untrustworthy.

Beginning in 2004, there were nearly two dozen congressional hearings regarding the claims of corruption, as well as a number of extensive, thorough investigations conducted by other bodies. The General Accounting Office (GAO)[4] published a series of reports beginning in April 2004.[5] Another major study was conducted by the Iraq Study Group, in affiliation with the Central Intelligence Agency (CIA). Headed by Charles Duelfer, its report was released in September 2004 and totaled approximately 1,000 pages.[6] The UN itself responded to the accusations by creating the Independent Inquiry Committee (IIC), headed by Paul Volcker, former chairman of the Federal Reserve Bank. He was joined by Swiss international law scholar Mark Pieth and South African supreme court justice Richard Goldstone. The IIC, which came to be known as the Volcker Committee, spent over $35 million, had a staff of sixty, and in the end issued reports totaling over 3,000 pages. The IIC reports were the most thorough and credible of the various investigations conducted. In September 2005 the IIC released its final report.[7] It discussed the Secretariat's overall administration of the Oil-for-Food Programme, the manipulation of the program to produce kickbacks and other forms of illicit income, the lobbying activities of two or three individuals on behalf of Iraq, and some of the elements of the program's design that made abuses possible.

In addition to investigating the accusations of improprieties, the Volcker Committee also commissioned a group of experts in public health and other fields to measure the effectiveness of the program as a humanitarian operation. Their findings were issued along with the final report of September 2005. This group found that the Oil-for-Food Programme had significantly reduced malnutrition among Iraqi children and significantly improved the health of the Iraqi population in several other regards.[8]

The were several types of accusations that were raised in the course of the many investigations. There were issues involving the basic design of the program, in particular that Iraq was permitted to choose its own trade partners, enabling Iraq to use trade opportunities to leverage political support. There were questions about the implementation of the program, particularly the approval of contracts with pricing irregularities. There were issues concerning accountability and oversight. These ranged from the assertion that "there was no accountability or transparency"—which was factually inaccurate but often repeated—to the more legitimate claim that the auditing process was inadequate. There were also issues involving individual claims of corruption on the part of particular UN officials. There was enormous attention devoted to improprieties concerning a handful of contracts involving relatively small amounts of money, and where no funds were missing or misused. These were the claims pertaining to the "2.2% account," for which the UN itself negotiated contracts for services related to the Oil-for-Food Programme's operations (banking, inspection of imported goods, and oil industry consultants).

All three of the major investigations—the Duelfer report, the GAO, and the IIC—found that the bulk of the illicit activities consisted of Iraq's trade with neighboring countries, unrelated to the Oil-for-Food Programme. The remainder concerned Oil-for-Food Programme contracts, in regard to both imports and oil exports. Prices on import contracts were set at 5–10 percent above the actual cost, such that vendors received payments from the Oil-for-Food Programme account in excess of the value of the goods and then illicitly returned the difference to the Iraqi government. It seems that this practice took place throughout the length of the Oil-for-Food Programme. In some cases the Iraqi government improperly charged "after sales service fees," which were then paid to the Iraqi government. In addition, the Iraqi government obtained some illicit income from oil sales. Prices on oil contracts were set low, and oil purchasers then paid the Iraqi government additional fees under the table. These practices took place for a period of a few months in late 2000.

The Volcker Committee estimated that overall there were oil surcharges that came to $229 million, and estimated improper fees on import contracts to be $1.55 billion, with all illicit funds involving the Oil-for-Food Programme totaling about $1.8 billion during the period from 1996 to 2003.[9] This came to about 1.5 percent of the $100 billion in transactions that took place. The majority of Iraq's illicit activities involved smuggling: over the thirteen-year history of the sanctions, Iraq had $6 billion in illicit trade with Jordan,[10] $800 million with Turkey,[11] and $3 billion with Syria.[12] The estimates from the GAO and the CIA's Iraq Study Group were similar.[13]

While much was made of the UN's failures of oversight, what was rarely mentioned was the role of the member states, particularly those in the Security Council, including the United States. Iraq was able to obtain kickbacks and surcharges because it had the power to choose its vendors and purchasers and could then demand illicit fees in exchange for doing business. While "the UN" was often blamed for allowing Saddam Hussein to choose Iraq's trade partners, in fact this was an explicit term of the Oil-for-Food Programme, to which the United States agreed, along with the rest of the Security Council. One diplomat noted, "Iraqi control over contractors was the crucial compromise that overcame Iraqi opposition and paved the way for OFF in the first place."[14] Everyone involved with the program understood what the consequences of this arrangement would be. According to a British official, "It was realized that a certain amount of misbehavior was going to happen on the Iraqi side if they were going to accept this [the Oil-for-Food Programme]."[15] Another diplomat commented that under Resolution 986, "Saddam Hussein exercised so much control over the program . . . that it was only to be expected that he would find ways of turning his wide discretionary powers into money."[16] One commentator noted, "Officials from the major countries understood the game in all its complexity and cynicism. It was ugly, but it worked."[17]

Smuggling

While the United States was one of the most vocal critics of the smuggling, within the 661 Committee the United States did not show any consistent concern about the ongoing smuggling. To the contrary, the U.S. government took elaborate measures to protect U.S. allies in the region who had ongoing illicit trade with Iraq.

By far the greater part of Iraq's illicit funds came from ongoing trade with Jordan, Turkey, and Syria. Of Iraq's illicit trade, the majority ($6 billion) was with Jordan. The Security Council was quite aware of Jordan's illicit trade with Iraq, which started from the time sanctions were first imposed on Iraq. While the United States had introduced the comprehensive sanctions on Iraq in August 1990 and lobbied aggressively for their adoption, it took a different posture with regard to Jordan, the United States' closest ally in the Arab world. The United States blocked any punitive action by the Council against either Jordan or Turkey, and neither the Secretariat nor the Security Council could have taken actions against Jordan, given the veto held by the United States. In May 1991 the Security Council sanctions committee "took note" of Jordan's illegal trade with Iraq—and did nothing to interfere, then or at any point in the next twelve years.[18] This occurred even though, according to the Duelfer report, "The [trade] Protocol with Jordan ensured the Regime's financial survival until the UN [Oil-for-Food Programme] began in December 1996."[19] Similarly, Turkey was one of Iraq's major illicit trade partners, with Iraq's earnings from that trade totaling $710 million.[20] But like Jordan, Turkey was a critical ally to the United States. Even though it was the responsibility of the Security Council to address sanctions violators, U.S. interests substantially compromised the Council's ability to take action against this major source of Iraq's illicit income.

Protecting Jordan and Turkey against any consequences for their illegal trade with Iraq was an explicit and public policy of the U.S. government. Under the U.S. Foreign Operations Assistance Act, any country that traded with Iraq in violation of the Security Council sanctions was not eligible to receive financial or military assistance from the United States. However, this penalty could be waived if the administration certified to Congress that it was "in the national interest" of the United States to do so. Not only did the United States turn a blind eye to Iraq's illegal trade with Jordan and Turkey, but each year—throughout all three administrations—the State Department provided Congress with a waiver ensuring that Jordan and Turkey would not lose any U.S. assistance as a result of their illicit trade with Iraq.[21]

When the information about the waivers and the U.S. positions within the Security Council regarding Jordan and Turkey came out in congressional hearings in 2005, the State Department insisted that Iraq's trade with Jordan and Turkey was not really illicit after all. One State Department official testified that the large-scale, ongoing illegal trade that Iraq maintained with Jordan and Turkey was "in no way comparable to the kind of corruption, bribery, or kick backs" that were under investigation by congressional committees.[22] In reality it was no different, except for the fact that it was supported and protected by the United States.

The Multinational Interception Force

While Iraq's illicit trade with Turkey and Jordan was overland, Iraq also smuggled oil out of the country by ship. Security Council Resolution

665, passed in 1990, called upon member states with naval forces in the area to intervene to enforce the sanctions. The result was the establishment of the Multinational Interception Force (MIF). The MIF involved some participation at various points from twenty or so different nations, but it was dominated by U.S. naval forces and was headed by U.S. naval officers. The commanders at every point in the MIF's operations were rear admirals or vice admirals from the U.S. Fifth Fleet,[23] while the deputy commanders were British. The force itself consisted overwhelmingly of U.S. ships. In 2000, for example, the United States contributed eighty-six vessels, Britain contributed seven vessels, Canada contributed one vessel for two months, and the Netherlands contributed one vessel for one month.[24]

According to its reports, the MIF was quite active, boarding hundreds of ships each year,[25] and there is no reason to suggest that the MIF was incompetent or poorly run. However, while the UN was criticized for allowing the smuggling to take place, it made little sense to blame the Secretariat, the Oil-for-Food Programme, or the UN as a whole for failing to stop Iraq's illicit oil smuggling. There was no authorization for any UN entity to take actions to intervene; Security Council Resolution 665 only invited member states to take these measures. To the extent that Iraq engaged in maritime smuggling, it was done on the watch of the U.S. Navy.

Import Contracts

In the summer of 2003 Iraqi ministry officials told interviewers from the Coalition Provisional Authority that they had been instructed to inflate contracts for the purchase of goods under the Oil-for-Food Programme by 10 percent.[26] The overage was then returned to the government of Iraq illicitly. A study of several hundred contracts by the Defense Contract Audit Agency found that about half were reasonably priced and about half were "potentially overpriced," meaning that the price exceeded the contract value by 5 percent or more.[27] While many criticized "the UN" for failing to prevent these illicit payments, it was more complicated than that: the Secretariat in fact did not have the authority to deny payments. Only the members of the 661 Committee had that power.

Over the course of the Oil-for-Food Programme, while U.S. representatives on the 661 Committee periodically accused Iraq of getting kickbacks, they offered little evidence of this to the committee or to UN staff.[28] At a meeting in January 2002, Britain circulated a number of newspaper articles about an oil pipeline that might be used for smuggling.[29] The United States and Britain later circulated another newspaper article about an illegal oil deal between Iraq and Lebanon. The delegates from Singapore, Russia, and China complained that internet articles citing no sources for their information were not sufficient to warrant a response by the committee.[30]

At the same time, when UN personnel provided documentation indicating financial improprieties on particular contracts, the United States took no action. Where there were obvious pricing irregularities, clearly allowing for kickbacks, OIP contacted the vendor for an explanation. If the explanation was not satisfactory, OIP then presented the documentation to the 661 Committee, giving all of its members the opportunity to block contracts where kickbacks were likely occurring. In over seventy cases OIP provided the committee with evidence of pricing irregularities indicating kickbacks. Yet neither the United States nor any other member of the 661 Committee blocked any of them.[31] Although the U.S. government employed some sixty technical experts to review the contracts, far more than any other nation on the Council, there was little U.S. interest in the pricing of the import contracts. Ambassador Patrick Kennedy testified that the preoccupation of the U.S. Mission to the UN was preventing any goods from entering Iraq that could be used for military purposes, particularly weapons of mass destruction.[32] John Ruggie, the Assistant Secretary-General of the UN charged with relations with the U.S. Mission, noted that the 661 Committee

> approved roughly 36,000 contracts over the life span of the program. Every member had the right to hold up contracts if they detected irregularities, and the US and Britain were by far most vigilant among them. Yet, as best as I can determine, of those 36,000 contracts not one—not a single solitary one—was ever held up by any member on the grounds of pricing.[33]

Oil Surcharges

All oil contracts, like the import contracts, required the approval of the 661 Committee. The 661 Committee approved a list of oil purchasers and any member of the committee could remove any purchaser from eligibility for any reason. The oil overseers—experts from the oil industry hired to monitor the process—were hired by the Secretariat, subject to the approval of the 661 Committee. For each contract period, the oil overseers recommended the price to be set and the 661 Committee had the power to approve or reject it. Thus, as with the import contracts, direct responsibility for all the terms of oil sales, as well as the approval of the purchasers, lay with the 661 Committee and its members.

In the latter part of 2000 Iraq began using a different structure in its contracts with oil purchasers. This became apparent when oil purchasers started to demand a "premia"[34] in contracts for oil sales (essentially the profit that goes to the contractor when he re-sells the oil to refiners) ranging from 5 cents per barrel to 50 cents per barrel.[35] The UN's oil overseers considered that to be above the industry standard and informed the 661 Committee that it was likely that the oil purchasers were then returning the income from this margin to Iraq under the table.

Within two months the oil overseers saw the high premia in the contracts; they investigated, and notified the 661 Committee that Iraq was likely to be receiving improper payments as a result of the margin. In response to the oil overseers' concern, the United States and Britain "made creative use of the consensus rule," in the words of a U.S. diplomat,[36] by implementing a "retroactive pricing policy." The normal practice in the industry, and for the Oil-for-Food Programme, was to set the price for the coming month. Under retroactive pricing, the United States and Britain withheld their approval for the price until the purchase period had passed. This meant that buyers literally were required to sign contracts for oil purchases without knowing what the price was until after they were committed to pay it.

The new pricing policies did eliminate any margin for surcharges. But it had another result as well—that oil sales were substantially compromised. Predictably, few buyers were prepared to purchase Iraqi oil without knowing the price. The result was a dramatic shortfall in funding for humanitarian contracts. In February 2002 OIP reported that there were nearly 700 contracts, with a value of $1.6 billion, waiting to be funded. If all holds were lifted—at that point totaling $5.3 billion—there would have been a shortfall of $6.9 billion.[37] In May 2002 OIP reported that the retroactive pricing, in combination with demands for high premia, had resulted in a loss to the program of $1.2 billion in the prior six months. OIP recommended canceling nearly $2 billion in contracts that had been approved more than a year earlier or were waiting for letters of credit, since it was unlikely that there would be funding to pay for them.[38] By 2002 the funds for a six-month period were spent before the period was half over. One member of the 661 Committee noted privately that "exports are now so low that the program is on the verge of collapsing."

Thus, while the Iraqi government illicitly obtained $229 million in oil surcharges that should have gone to the Oil-for-Food Programme, UN staff reported it quickly. But the measures taken by the United States and Britain in response to this action cost the Oil-for-Food Programme billions of dollars in lost income.

Accusations against UN Officials

Perhaps the most disturbing of the accusations was the claim that Benon Sevan, the director of OIP, accepted money from Iraq, for which he was eventually indicted. Even if this were true, it is not clear that the operation of the Oil-for-Food Programme was affected. While many suggested that the program's operations must have been corrupted as a result, in actuality Sevan's policies and actions did not indicate any particular favoritism toward Iraq. Sevan did not stand out as a particularly vocal advocate for Iraq. When he advocated reducing the holds on import contracts, his position was no different from that of all nine of the UN agencies working in Iraq or the majority of the Security Council. Indeed, he was often critical of the Iraqi government. He pressed the Iraqi government to reduce the delays on its end and also advocated for a monitoring mechanism that would meet the demands of the United States and Britain.[39] He urged the Iraqi government to be more selective in choosing its suppliers and to reduce the amount of defective goods arriving in Iraq, and on multiple occasions he pushed the Central Bank of Iraq to act more quickly to issue letters of credit.[40] He chastised the Iraqi government for delaying or canceling contracts after the holds were lifted and repeatedly criticized it for refusing to issue visas to UN staff for northern Iraq.[41] Sevan chastised the 661 Committee and the Iraqi government for their roles in the crisis resulting from the retroactive pricing impasse.[42]

In other areas, even where improprieties in the Oil-for-Food Programme occurred, it was not clear that there was any effect on the program's operations. One accusation was that Kofi Annan's son, Kojo, had had a role in arranging for an inspection contract to go to Cotecna, a company for which he had previously worked. The Volcker Committee report spent hundreds of pages describing phone calls and meetings to determine if this was true, and the issue was repeatedly raised in the press and in congressional hearings as being emblematic of the failure of the

Oil-for-Food Programme as a whole. But in the end, there was no finding that the contract or its terms had been affected by Kojo Annan's activities, given that Cotecna had submitted the lowest bid for the contract, and by all accounts fulfilled all of its contractual obligations.

Overall, the UN as a whole, and the Secretariat in particular, were excoriated not only for their own administrative lapses, but also for policies and decisions that in fact were the responsibility of the Security Council, or of member nations. Whatever improper acts were committed by individuals, the claims regarding corruption presented a distorted view of who was responsible for making the critical decisions regarding the Oil-for-Food Programme that allowed Iraq to obtain illicit funds.

There was another issue as well. In the course of the Oil-for-Food scandal it was commonplace to hear that "Saddam skimmed billions for luxuries for himself and his cronies." There was no suggestion that the kickbacks and smuggling could in part be a response to the impoverishment of the Iraqi state and the need for resources to perform legitimate government functions. Yet for the entire duration of the sanctions regime, including the Oil-for-Food Programme, there was no way for the Iraqi state to legally raise cash for critical government functions. While a cash component was authorized in principle in 2000, it was never implemented. Consequently, a significant portion of the funds from illicit trade would have to have been used to fund the costs of food, the medical system, salaries for civil servants, and other legitimate and necessary government functions.

One estimate puts the cost of the ration system, prior to the Oil-for-Food Programme, at $1.5–$2 billion annually.[43] By one estimate, the budget for health care in the 1990s was $22 million annually.[44] This was much reduced from the prewar expenditures on health care, but even so, there was no legal way to raise those funds. If indeed the government of Iraq obtained some $10 billion in kickbacks and illicit trade over the thirteen-year course of the sanctions regime, the level of state expenditures on food rations and the costs of operating electricity generation, water treatment, and other public services would have consumed nearly all of the income.

Hans von Sponeck, the former UN humanitarian coordinator in Iraq, suggested that there was a clear relation between the impoverishment of the state and the smuggling and kickbacks. He maintained that the illicit trade was at least in part the fall-out of the continued absence of licit cash. The Government of Iraq had no choice but to increase its clandestine efforts to obtain cash through illegal oil exports, surcharges on contracts and paybacks. It can not be argued that illegal income on the part of the Iraqi Government had nothing to do with Security Council policy. It had. An assessment of the motives for obtaining resources outside the oil-for-food programme had to go beyond the justified criticism of the Government of Iraq for its wasteful expenditures involving construction of palaces and other public buildings, the import of luxury goods and weapons research and development. The need to find resources to run the nation was . . . a major reason for seeking extra funds.[45]

Postwar Corruption

While much was made of the fact that the Iraqi government was able to skim funds from the Oil-for-Food Programme or circumvent the sanctions with illicit trade, these practices were far less extensive and did far less damage than the corruption and misuse of funds that occurred after the end of the Hussein regime, beginning with the postwar occupation.

Under the terms of Security Council Resolution 1483, adopted in May 2003, the Coalition Provisional Authority (CPA) was recognized as the governing power in Iraq, with control over Iraq's assets and revenues. It was predominantly managed by officials from the U.S. military, U.S. AID, and other U.S. government agencies. The chief executives were Americans, first retired general Jay Garner, then Paul Bremer. Resolution 1483 established the Development Fund of Iraq (DFI) to hold Iraq's assets and income from oil and other sources, to be controlled by the CPA. Resolution 1483 required that these funds be used "in a transparent manner to meet the humanitarian needs of the Iraqi people, for the economic reconstruction and repair of Iraq's infrastructure . . . and for other purposes benefiting the people of Iraq."[46]

However, while calling for transparency in the CPA's use of Iraq's assets, Resolution 1483 also removed the oversight mechanisms that had been in place. During the Oil-for-Food Programme, UN experts in health, education, nutrition, and infrastructure had reviewed all of Iraq's import contracts to see whether they were consistent with humanitarian priorities. Resolution 1483 eliminated that review process, placing decision making solely in the hands of the CPA. UN monitors in Iraq had conducted thousands of inspections and site visits to determine whether the food, medicine, and other goods that arrived had been distributed equitably and efficiently. Under Resolution 1483, these positions were eliminated. Under the Oil-for-Food Programme, there were oil overseers who had reviewed the pricing of oil contracts (and had quickly discovered the skimming from those transactions when they occurred). Those positions were also eliminated. Where the Secretary-General had reported quarterly on the situation in Iraq, providing considerable detail about the condition of the country, the CPA had no such obligation. Under Resolution 1483, the CPA was "encouraged" but not required to report to the Security Council on its activities. The 661 Committee, which broadly monitored the situation in Iraq and reported to the Security Council itself, was eliminated and replaced by a committee whose sole function was to locate Iraqi assets that could be turned over to the CPA.

While there were few mechanisms in place to provide accountability during the planning and decision making regarding Iraq's funds, Resolution 1483 did contain provisions for auditing the funds after they had been spent. There was a UN body, the International Advisory and Monitoring Board for Iraq (IAMB), which hired the firm KPMG to audit the DFI. In addition, there were also audits by U.S. agencies, most notably the Inspector General for the CPA (later the Special Inspector General for Iraq Reconstruction, SIGIR), which audited both the DFI and U.S. funds allocated to Iraq reconstruction.

The total funds in the DFI over the course of the occupation came to $20.6 billion. Of that, the CPA spent $13.1 billion and committed another $4.6 billion, leaving the successor interim Iraqi government a total of $2.9 billion in the national treasury.[47] Many of the funds were spent on contracts with U.S. companies. For example, a report by the CPA's Inspector General showed that of contracts with a value greater than $5 million, paid for with Iraqi funds, 74 percent went to U.S. companies. Only 2 percent of the contracts went to Iraqi companies.[48]

Over the course of the fourteen-month occupation there were instances where enormous amounts of money—over $8 billion on one occasion—simply disappeared. In addition, the auditors documented continual systemic failures by the CPA to provide an accurate account of Iraqi funds, to direct them toward projects that would benefit Iraq, or to execute those projects competently. On one occasion, the Inspector General

184

found that "approximately $1.5 billion in cash allocations were made to Iraqi banks between January and April 2004 for ministry operating expenses, yet spending plans supported only approximately $498 million in operating expenses," with over $1 billion that was simply transferred with no stated purpose.[49] In December 2004 a UN report noted that there were "hundreds of irregularities" in the CPA's contracting process. One of KPMG's audits for the first half of 2004 was typical. It found, for example, thirty-seven cases involving $185 million of contracts where contract files simply could not be located.[50] There were 111 cases where no documentation could be found for services performed under the contracts.[51] According to one report, the spreadsheets kept by the CPA were so poorly maintained that auditors could not locate thirteen of sixty-two contract files listed.[52] In one audit, of twenty-six paid receipts that were examined, twenty-five had no supporting invoices.[53] One audit report from the CPA Inspector General, which was not at all atypical, found that 67 percent of purchase contracts the auditors examined had incomplete or missing documentation. The auditors concluded that they were "unable to determine if the goods specified in the contract were ever received, the total amount of payments made to the contractor, or if the contractor fully complied with the requirements of the contract."[54]

One of the recurring critical problems was the absence of equipment to meter the oil being exported from Iraq. The lack of metering equipment meant that it was impossible to know how much oil was being misappropriated. This was critical, given how much Iraq's economy depended on oil income. In March 2004, shortly after it began operating, the IAMB pressed the CPA to install metering equipment. The auditors reported that "contrary to earlier representations by the CPA," the arrangements to have meters installed had been delayed, and it was therefore impossible to account for the Iraqi oil that had been sold to date.[55] Months later, as the occupation came to a close, another audit noted that a "priority finding" was the "weakness in controls over oil extraction,"[56] including lack of metering. In June 2004 the CPA informed the IAMB that it still had not concluded an oil metering contract and acknowledged to the IAMB that over the prior fourteen months "some of Iraq's oil resources were not accounted for and had been smuggled."[57]

A number of audits reviewed contracts with Kellogg, Brown and Root (KBR), a subsidiary of Halliburton. KBR alone received 60 percent of all the contracts paid for with Iraqi funds.[58] The CPA extended and expanded KBR's contracts repeatedly, even though KBR's history throughout the occupation and after the handover was marked by repeated criticisms for its failures to perform its work honestly and competently. An audit report from the Defense Contract Audit Agency (DCAA) for August 16, 2004, found that there were "significant unsupported costs" in KBR's contract proposals and recommended withholding further payment.[59] The report of the Inspector General for November 2004 stated that his office could not even complete its audit of KBR because KBR did not provide the Army with enough data to evaluate whether the project costs were legitimate. On another occasion, the auditors found thirty-four cases where advance payments totaling $1.5 billion were made to the Army Corps of Engineers to pay for fuel imports, although KBR was supposed to have been providing fuel under its contract.[60] KBR had a contract to manage government property in Kuwait, yet an audit found that KBR was unable to account for nearly half the property it was supposed to be managing.[61] For just one of Halliburton's contracts, an audit by the DCAA found that there were overcharges of more than $218 million.[62] A March 2004 DCAA audit found that KBR "significantly and systematically" violated U.S. federal contracting rules by providing false information about its costs.[63]

By 2005 the projects for which the CPA had signed contracts, using Iraqi funds, began to reach completion. As they were completed, in many cases inspections found that the projects were nearly worthless. For example, according to a SIGIR audit from July 2005, three of the water treatment plants that had been built or rehabilitated with reconstruction money were done so poorly that they literally produced no usable water. At the Al-Wahda plant, located in Baghdad, the contractor did not complete the work necessary for the water treatment facility to function.[64] As a result, the audits showed, the plant "did not and will not increase the quantity or quality of potable water." The contractor's design for the Al-Sumelat water plant not only was in violation of the contract's requirements but was inadequate for the project. The plant could produce no potable water because the pipeline was installed in three unusable segments, none of which were connected to the water main.[65]

In another case, a plant to convert high-voltage electricity to low-voltage electricity for consumption, the Shatt Al Arab Substation, was built in Basrah. According to the Inspector General's assessment, the contractor's quality control plan and the U.S. government's quality oversight were sound. There were maintenance manuals, training of employees to operate the plant, and spare parts for maintenance. However, the facility could not begin operation until distribution lines were installed to carry electricity to consumers. The Inspector General's office noted that there were no such plans, let alone any projects under way. "As a result, the value and benefit of the substation will not be realized until an end user distribution system is connected"—that is, the entire project was useless, and would remain so indefinitely.[66]

An audit from January 2006 describes a particularly striking case. The contract involved funds from the "Rapid Regional Response Program" (RRRP), a pool of funds that permitted highly discretionary decisions with less oversight than the main fund. The South-Central Region of the RRRP awarded a contract in March 2004 for $662,800 to renovate the Al Hillah General Hospital. The renovations were to include the installation of four new elevators. On June 10, 2004, a few weeks before the handover to the new Iraqi government, the U.S. project officer signed a certificate of completion, authorizing full, immediate payment even though the project was not yet completed. He noted that he was confident that the contractor would complete the work within the next twenty days. Three months later one of the "new" elevators crashed, killing three people. It turned out that the contractor had never installed the new elevators, only renovated the existing ones, and apparently not very well.[67]

As the occupation came to a close, the Iraqi funds under U.S. management were distributed almost frantically, with little regard for any standard of accountability or concern for the welfare of the Iraqi people. According to the staff of the House Committee on Oversight and Government Reform,

> Nearly half of the currency shipped into Iraq under U.S. direction—more than $5 billion—flowed into the country in the final six weeks before control of Iraqi funds was returned to the interim Iraqi government on June 28, 2004. In the week before the transition, CPA officials ordered urgent disbursements of more than $4 billion in U.S. currency from the Federal Reserve . . .
>
> One contractor received a $2 million payment in a duffel bag stuffed with shrink-wrapped bundles of currency . . . One official was given $6.75 million in cash, and was ordered to spend it one

week before the interim Iraqi government took control of Iraqi funds.

A summary of the minutes from a May 2004 CPA meeting show a single disbursement of $500 million in security funding labeled merely "TBD," meaning "to be determined."[68]

The single largest transaction was a transfer by the CPA of over $8.8 billion to Iraqi ministries, with no accountability or information about how those funds were used. A memo of the House Committee on Oversight and Government Reform describes an inquiry into these funds with retired admiral David Oliver, the principal deputy for financial matters for the CPA.

When asked what happened to the $8.8 billion in DFI funds, Admiral Oliver responded:

> *Oliver:* I have no idea, I can't tell you whether or not the money went to the right things or didn't—nor do I actually think it's important.
>
> *Question:* Not important?
>
> *Oliver:* No. The coalition—and I think it was between 300 and 600 people civilians—and you want to bring in 3,000 auditors to make sure money's being spent?
>
> *Question:* Yes, but the fact is billions of dollars have disappeared without a trace . . .
>
> *Oliver:* Of their money. Billions of dollars of their money, yeah I understand, I'm saying what difference does it make?[69]

Under the Oil-for-Food Programme, the Iraqi government skimmed about 10 percent from import contracts and for a brief time received illicit payments from oil sales. The two combined amounted to about $2 billion, from the beginning of the program's operation in 1996 to the war that deposed Saddam Hussein in 2003. From 1990 to 2003 Iraq averaged about half a billion dollars in illicit trade annually. By contrast, in fourteen months of occupation, the U.S.-led occupation authority depleted $18 billion in funds, a good deal of it on questionable contracts with little justification, but much of it just an outright giveaway of cash. In one transaction—the transfer of $8.8 billion—more funds disappeared than in thirteen years of Iraq's trade with Jordan, Turkey, Syria, and Egypt combined. The single disbursement in May 2004 of $500 million, whose purpose was "to be determined," was more than twice the total illicit oil surcharges in the Oil-for-Food Programme.

While the smuggling that occurred throughout the sanctions regime and the improprieties that took place during the Oil-for-Food Programme received enormous attention, and brought into question the credibility of the UN itself, by far the greater scandal was the misuse and disappearance of funds after the end of the Hussein regime, particularly during the fourteen-month period of the U.S.-led occupation, which was an order of magnitude greater and did incalculably more harm.

10

Over the course of the sanctions regime, throughout all three U.S. administrations the consistent goal up to the time of the U.S. invasion in 2003 was to keep Iraq from rearming by bankrupting the state, and to reduce Iraq's society and economy to the most primitive conditions possible and keep it in that state indefinitely. Throughout the sanctions regime, while all three U.S. administrations publicly professed concern for the Iraqi people, the actual internal decision-making process reflected no such concern. While there was no particular animosity toward the Iraqi population, neither was there any actual interest in their well-being. Internally, for all three administrations, the attitude was one of indifference to the humanitarian impact of the sanctions on the Iraqi population, except insofar as it created political pressure or embarrassment for the United States. As the humanitarian impact became known, all three U.S. administrations disparaged or dismissed those who criticized the United States for these policies or documented the human damage, including members of the Security Council, UN agencies, and international nongovernmental organizations. The U.S. response to their criticisms was a combination of outright lies, and indignation by U.S. officials that they would be accused of lying; along with absolute disinterest in the human damage came regular protestations of deep and abiding concern for the Iraqi people. Even as U.S. officials constructed implausibly thin rationales for their objections to antibiotics, pencils, or eggs, there was at the same time a level on which these same officials also accepted and believed the justifications they had created. While U.S. officials designed and implemented policies that literally excluded the humanitarian damage as a factor in their decision making, at the same time they seemed genuinely stung by the accusations of callousness.

On the face of it, there was a certain amount of ordinary hypocrisy; the State Department simply generated whatever sorts of statements would deflect criticism. But at a deeper level, within the U.S. agencies involved, the indifference to the humanitarian impact emerged from a culture that was dominated by a single-minded preoccupation with the potential military threat posed by Iraq. Within that culture, any security concern, however slight or speculative, overrode any humanitarian concern, however extensive and certain. Within that culture, nearly any speculation about Iraq's military uses of goods, however implausible, was given credence and served as the basis for decision making. This practice emerged from an internal process in which any concern with humanitarian issues was marginalized, or explicitly excluded from consideration; as one State Department official said, "It was not our job. It was not part of our skill set."[1]

On some occasions U.S. officials seemed quite sensitive to the public criticisms directed at the sanctions regime. A senior State Department official maintained, "We were very conscious of the humanitarian impact from the beginning, on its merits and for the political effect on the sanctions regime as a whole."[2] But if U.S. officials were aware of criticism, it was not reflected in the U.S. government policies. The sheer quantity of blocked goods told a different story: as of April 2002 there were over $5 billion in contracts on hold; a disturbing number given that only about $20 billion in goods had been delivered to Iraq, in total, since the Oil-for-Food Programme began in 1996. And since most of those goods were equipment for Iraq's electrical production, transportation, and infrastructure, if they had arrived in Iraq, Iraq's capacity for its own agricultural and industrial production, and the well-being of Iraqis, would have significantly increased.

The U.S. Decision-Making Process

The U.S. process for making decisions regarding Iraq's imports was one that maximized delays and denials. The actual decision to block a contract came out of an elaborate bureaucratic process in which responsibility was diffused among dozens of people at numerous agencies. Contracts were circulated to the Department of State's Bureau for Nonproliferation Affairs, Sanctions Office, and Bureau for Near Eastern Affairs, as well as to the Department of Defense's Threat Reduction

Agency, the Department of Energy, the Central Intelligence Agency (CIA), and other agencies.[3] The Department of State then compiled the responses, and its Bureau of International Organizations issued instructions to the U.S. representative on the 661 Committee. There were two or three people at the U.S. mission to the UN who distributed contracts for review among U.S. government agencies and about sixty people within the various agencies who reviewed the contracts for possible military uses.[4] For each contract there was a "technical input stage," where experts from various areas and agencies evaluated the contract for possible use in weapons; and there was also a policy review by the State Department's International Organizations Bureau and Bureau for Near Eastern Affairs.

Participants in the process noted that it was nearly always possible to find a potential military use for anything. Consequently, the overall process worked in such a way that contracts that were circulated were denied routinely, and approved only in rare or extreme circumstances. As one observer noted,

> Obviously, looking at the number of contracts blocked, that suggests that it was pretty easy to block them . . . There was no incentive to let goods through. There were not a lot of tears shed about what Saddam was not getting. There was the sense that Saddam needed to be pressured to the max, and there was no incentive to ease up.[5]

The various agencies involved in the process did not always hold identical positions. The State Department's Nonproliferation Bureau and the Defense Department tended consistently toward denial of goods, while the State Department's Sanctions Office and the U.S. Mission to the UN sometimes argued for approval. However, in general, any discussion about whether to block or permit a contract for humanitarian goods was overwhelmingly influenced by security concerns. A congressional analyst observed that

> meetings were dominated by proliferation experts. They knew the details of every little gadget and what it could be used for. If you had 30 people at a meeting, 25 or 28 were proliferation experts. The review process was not for the purpose of determining how the Iraqi people would be affected. The process was to determine if there was any potential for WMD use for goods sold to Iraq.[6]

Of the agencies involved in this process, the International Organizations Bureau and the U.S. Mission to the UN faced the most political pressure. When the weapons experts within the U.S. administration blocked child vaccines on the grounds that the order was "suspicious" and "could be used for nefarious purposes," the officers at the U.S. Mission to the UN were forced to defend this position.[7] State Department officials faced scathing criticism when the United States took a patently implausible position. This occurred, for example, when U.S. weapons experts sought to block Iraq from importing personal computers on the grounds that these would "help Saddam rearm," even though the same personal computers could be purchased on the streets of Baghdad.

On rare occasions there were internal disputes over the most extreme positions. For example, at one point Donald Rumsfeld complained to Colin Powell,

> Look at what they are buying . . . They are buying these dump trucks. They can take off the hydraulic cylinder that pushes the truck bed up and they can use it for a launcher for a rocket . . . For Christ's sake, Powell said, if somebody wants a cylinder to erect a rocket, they don't have to buy at $200,000 dump truck to get one![8]

The attitude toward humanitarian imports changed somewhat over time, in response to political or international pressure. Robert Einhorn, the assistant secretary of state for nonproliferation, stated that

> In the early days, there was no problem with holds, because no one was objecting to them. Anyone in any agency could put a hold on any contract. There was no cost—the attitude was "If there's any risk, put a hold on it." This led to huge lists of holds, and that then led to a backlash. Later, blocking contracts was more of an issue, and there was more of a debate. Often the State Department Nonproliferation Bureau and Department of Defense sided with each other, and the regional side, especially in the State Department, was concerned about running up high balances [of holds]. Then Secretary Powell decided that these huge balances of holds were a huge political liability for us.[9]

The analysis did not weigh the security risk presented by toothpaste or vaccines or dump trucks against the benefit of allowing them into Iraq and the harm done to the Iraqi population by their denial. Instead, as Ambassador Peter Burleigh noted,

The default was to denial; it was a risk analysis only. That view prevailed until 1999 or 2000. The committee's mentality was default to denial—if any doubt at all, the contract was denied. For example, an Iraqi university wanted chemicals; if there was any doubt, the answer was no. Certainly through 1999 the process was skewed deliberately and publicly to default mode of denial.[10]

But public criticism forced the U.S. administrations to make modest concessions. Former assistant secretary of state David Welch commented that "As pressure rose because of what people perceived as the humanitarian impact, there was much greater attention paid to risk/benefit. Truth be told, if we had administered the program as we did at the outset, there would only have been risk analysis."[11] But by 2000 and 2001, according to one State Department official, "the US was under tremendous pressure to lift holds. We were being blamed for ongoing humanitarian suffering because we weren't allowing certain types of valves, pipes, for irrigation, sanitation."[12] According to a congressional analyst,

> It was because of the holds crisis that the US and its partners agreed to the fast track program. Halliday and von Sponeck resigned, and there was so much outcry from UN people on the ground. Kofi Annan at one point spoke out on holds. Then the US and UK agreed to fast track.[13]

In very limited circumstances there were concessions where particular goods had potential military use but were also critical humanitarian goods for which there were no substitutes. According to Welch,

> There were a few instances where we agreed that the benefit overrode the risk—certain vaccines that some said could be used for biological warfare; chlorine—for that we did more rigorous study of what would be normal stock; pumps—could be used for flow processing for biological or chemical weapons, but also were used for irrigation and water control. In some cases we agreed on the condition that there was monitoring also.[14]

For the most part, however, the United States not only focused on risk; it also judged risk in a very extreme way. A State Department desk officer maintained that "To the extent possible, we tried to make use of . . . information, and imagine what was possible. When you say 'imagine what's possible,' it opens the door to expect that we would jump to the worst case scenario." But, he maintained, "that did not always happen. While I was working, we tried to apply some realism, look at what was likely."[15]

Yet it seems that the U.S. officials involved did not do that at all; rather, they speculated that some highly implausible scenario was theoretically possible, then concluded that a security concern was actually present.

> We blocked ambulances at one point, because there was intelligence, or a perception, that Saddam was misusing these goods. It was the same for tires, at one point. What would happen is that at a meeting the CIA would say "we have information that Saddam is misusing this." There was a major dispute about refrigeration equipment, that went on and on. Vaccines were degenerating, foods spoiling.[16]

But in fact there was very little information or evidence about how goods were being used in Iraq. By 1995, "the CIA didn't have a single source inside Iraq . . . Not only were there no human sources in country, the CIA didn't have any in the neighboring countries—Iran, Jordan, Turkey, and Saudi Arabia—who reported on Iraq."[17] The United States had relied almost exclusively on United Nations Special Commission (UNSCOM) inspectors for information from 1991 to 1998, and the United States and Britain did not develop other intelligence sources inside Iraq. According to David Kay, who was a weapons inspector for UNSCOM and the International Atomic Energy Association, "You had good, upright U.N. Inspectors doing the job [of collecting intelligence]. And the result is that there was essentially no effort after 1991 by National Intelligence Services to build an on-the-ground collection capability apart from the UN."[18]

Once UNSCOM was withdrawn, and there were no U.S. or British inspectors reporting their observations, there was no actual information about how the Iraqi regime was using refrigerators, or incubators, or yogurt makers. There was only imaginative speculation that these items could conceivably be used to produce weapons of mass destruction (WMD). This invented worst-case scenario then became the standard for determining policy.

One of the central technical experts in the U.S. review process, Robert von Tersch, was known for taking the most extreme of these positions. Von Tersch was a biochemist for the Army who worked for the State

Department's Nonproliferation Bureau, coordinating the weapons review of import contracts. He was the "point of contact" for Department of State technical experts that conducted review of oil-for-food contracts.[19] In an interview he described the possible misuse of a cheese factory: it included fermentation equipment, which in turn could be used to grow pathogens.[20] On one occasion he argued that Iraq should not be permitted to import chicken eggs. He found this contract suspicious on various grounds. He reasoned that eggs could be used to grow viruses for biological weapons and that the contract was questionable because the Iraqi government insisted that the eggs be certified to be free of pathogens. He also found it suspicious because the United States did not have evidence that Iraq had enough incubators to hatch the eggs.[21]

While it is true that egg yolks can be used as a growth medium in which to cultivate biological strains, Iraq was producing over 300 million eggs per year in 1998, and under the Oil-for-Food Programme that increased to over 600 million.[22] Presumably, Iraq had found some way to incubate the eggs, despite von Tersch's skepticism. And while the poultry production was not enough to meet Iraq's nutrition needs—600 million eggs per year meant that each Iraqi on average received about two dozen eggs annually—one would think that 600 million eggs already provided enough egg yolks for the government to grow whatever viruses it wanted to.

It is not hard to imagine the response in the 661 Committee if U.S. diplomats had argued that chicken eggs should not be allowed into Iraq because of the WMD risk they presented; and in the case of the suspicious egg contract, von Tersch was overruled. However, it was this reasoning that accounted for some of the more bizarre moments during the sanctions regime. One technical expert from the Department of Defense attended a meeting of U.S. and British officials with a vial of cat litter; to emphasize the difficulty of judging what was dual use, he informed them that cat litter could be used "to stabilize anthrax."[23] Likewise, the United States was concerned about toothpaste containing fluoride, on the grounds that the fluoride could conceivably be extracted from the toothpaste and used in chemical weapons.[24] The same reasoning resulted in the U.S. holds on contracts for laundry detergent containing bleach, on the grounds that the chlorine might conceivably be extracted and used in chemical weapons; or yogurt-making equipment could be used to grow viruses which in turn could be employed in biological weapons; and so forth.

A political officer at the U.S. mission to the UN acknowledged that for "items that can have a high impact on humanitarian grounds but little military use . . . the US tends to be pretty hard on these types of items and blocks contracts if there is any doubt."[25] Peter van Walsum, the chair of the 661 Committee in 1999 and 2000, attempted to raise this issue with U.S. officials:

> I wondered whether it would not be possible to weigh the proliferation risk against the humanitarian impact in such a way that a very remote dual-use potential might be winked at if the impact of an extended hold on, for example, the public health sector would evidently be disastrous . . . but the [U.S.] officials were not prepared to let humanitarian considerations override the principle that in the Iraqi context even the slightest risk of proliferation was unacceptable.[26]

In addition to outright denial, the United States deliberately adopted other practices that had the effect of denying goods. One was simply the length of time required for approval. The delays in reviewing contracts were due in part to the number of U.S. agencies involved, with the result that the approval of goods was a slow, cumbersome process. But the delays were also in part by design. According to Victor Comras, a former State Department official,

> For the Iraq sanctions, the US had in place a very laborious and time consuming process for granting exceptions or approving imports . . . This was a tactic we used for years. It was a way to kill transactions simply by putting them on hold. This slow approval process was not a formalized policy, but it was often used deliberately.[27]

In response to criticism for blocking contracts in the first half of the 1990s, the United States changed its language while maintaining the same practices. Instead of "blocking" goods, the United States began putting them "on hold," ostensibly a temporary status while the contract was under review. But the holds sometimes continued for months or even years, with no explanation other than "pending further evaluation."[28] The United States often made multiple requests for information, then waited months or years after all the information had been received before acting on the application.[29] This allowed U.S. officials to deflect criticism by claiming contracts were not blocked but were still "in process," while achieving the same result. According to Eugene Young, one of the State

Department officers who sat on the 661 Committee, "There was no out-right denial of a contract. Contracts that were never approved were in-definitely placed on hold."[30]

Equally damaging was the U.S. refusal to provide any clear criteria—to the UN, to Iraq, or to suppliers—about what the United States was willing to approve and what it was not. The result was that a contract for certain items would be approved on one occasion; then when Iraq sub-mitted another contract later on for the same type of goods, it would be rejected by the United States. This was a deliberate policy. In part the United States insisted on using vague, highly subjective criteria because U.S. officials looked at who the end user would be and then speculated about what sorts of goods, and in what amounts and prices, would (in the U.S. view) be "appropriate" for that end user. Von Tersch, for exam-ple, said that if the prices looked "weird" he would question the con-tract.[31] "We looked at where it was going, who it was going to, and the end user's past involvement with the program, to see if it made sense. Then assessment was done to judge the risk of diversion to prohibited purposes."[32] But the policy also meant that the U.S. criteria for approval were so unclear that neither Iraq nor the supplier nor the UN staff knew what contracts would be approved by the United States, making it im-possible to develop any coherent plan to meet Iraq's economic needs. The United States might object to water trucks on the basis that the lining of the tank was stainless steel of a certain specification. UN staff would ask the United States to say what specifications *were* permissible, so that the Iraqi government and the suppliers could provide contracts that con-formed to U.S. requirements. According to one UN official, "I met a num-ber of times with experts from Washington, and asked them for criteria. They'd say 'that's fair,' but never provided any."[33]

> For years, there was no definition of "dual use." For example, there would be trucks that were not on the 1051 list; UNMOVIC would approve of them; the US would say they were dual use; and we would ask "What's the threshold? What kind of trucks *will* you accept?" The US position was not consistent. If things heated up with the Iraqi regime, the US tightened up. There were too many agencies involved, and this generated inconsistencies. OIP presented the inconsistencies to the US; but the US made no attempt to re-solve them.[34]

198

To the extent that the U.S. goal was simply to cripple Iraq's economy, the refusal to state or abide by any criteria for approval was an extremely effective means of minimizing Iraq's access to humanitarian goods. The first time the United States actually agreed to abide by clear, publicly stated criteria was six years after the Oil-for-Food Programme began, and twelve years into the sanctions regime: when Security Council Resolution 1409 was passed in 2002, implementing the Goods Review List. At that juncture—when there were finally explicit standards, and when the United Nations Monitoring, Verification and Inspection Commission (UNMOVIC), not the United States, made the initial determination of risk—billions of contracts on hold by the United States were immediately approved and allowed into Iraq.

The U.S. Response to Criticism

Publicly, U.S. government officials maintained consistently that they were deeply committed to the welfare of the Iraqi population, that the terrible suffering in Iraq was due to Saddam Hussein's callous disregard for the condition of his people, and that it was entirely within his ability to improve their well-being. A State Department report maintained that "we will . . . continue our efforts to increase humanitarian relief for the people of Iraq, over the obstructions of the regime."[35] Madeleine Albright said similarly: "Had Saddam spent Iraq's money on humanitarian goods, his people's suffering would have been far less. Instead he squandered the country's assets rebuilding weapons factories and constructing lavish palaces for himself, his family, and his cronies."[36]

But while denying any role in the suffering in Iraq, U.S. government officials were sensitive to the growing criticisms of U.S. policy, viewing these criticisms as an increasingly serious public relations problem. In October 1999, one year into Hans von Sponeck's position as the UN's humanitarian coordinator in Iraq, the United States and Britain asked Secretary-General Kofi Annan to remove von Sponeck from his job on the grounds that he was reporting publicly on the impact of both U.S. air strikes and the sanctions.[37]

Philo Dibble, a senior State Department official, recalled that in the winter of 2000, "We were acutely conscious of the accusations."[38] An officer at the U.S. Mission to the UN commented that "We were routinely criticized in the 661 Committee and Security Council for denying access to critical humanitarian supplies, mostly by the Russian, French, and Chinese."[39] In Colin Powell's congressional testimony in March 2001, his rationale for pursuing sanctions reform was that

> We were being accused, and we were taking on the burden of hurting Iraqi people, hurting Iraqi children, and we needed to turn that around . . . we then had to take a look at the sanctions themselves. Were they being used to go after weapons of mass destruction . . . or, increasingly, were those sanctions starting to look as if they were hurting the Iraqi people.[40]

In her memoir, published in 2003, Madeleine Albright was still trying to undo the damage from her comment on *60 Minutes* in 1996. Lesley Stahl noted that some half a million children had died and asked if the price was worth it; Albright responded that it was. Years later she was still trying to explain her way out of her failure to respond more effectively to what she described as "our public relations problem":

> My reply had been a terrible mistake, hasty, clumsy and wrong. Nothing matters more than the lives of innocent people. I had fallen into a trap and said something that I simply did not mean. That was no one's fault but my own. There are many times in everyone's life when the mouth works faster than the brain; there was no more regrettable example in my own career than this ill-considered response to Leslie Stahl.[41]

Albright describes a panel presentation at Ohio State University in 1998 as both personally upsetting and deeply embarrassing:

> I tended to take things personally and got indignant when people said, for example, that I was responsible for murdering millions of people . . . Because the protestors succeeded in stealing the story, our appearance at Ohio State was a fiasco, my roughest day in office to that point . . . A cartoon showed the three of us stumbling into the Oval Office to report to the President looking as if we had just returned from a war.[42]

But while U.S. officials found it offensive or to some extent genuinely distressing when they were accused of having had a hand in the terrible damage done in Iraq, they rarely admitted in either public or private that the decisions they made and the policies they implemented were actually responsible. Instead, the documentation of Iraq's humanitarian crisis, including malnutrition, the collapse in health care, and the severe impoverishment of the society, was disparaged or dismissed in a variety of ways. Albright wrote that "[Saddam's] strategy was to publicize the hardships of Iraqi civilians in order to gain sympathy . . . and to an extent he succeeded. Anti-Americanism will always find a receptive audience in some circles."[43] Kael Weston, a political officer at the State Department, maintained that "the U.S. is conducting a public good which it has done a poor job of selling to other countries."[44]

Criticisms of U.S. policy were consistently framed as a political problem, for which the solution involved arm-twisting or political maneuvering, but never substantive reconsideration of the policy itself. Concerns raised by France, China, and Russia—not to mention those by elected members of the Security Council—were consistently dismissed out of hand as driven by naivete, political agendas, or economic interests. There was a deep-seated contentiousness, even antagonism, between the two factions of the Security Council's permanent members regarding the Iraq sanctions regime. In regard to the Iraq sanctions,

> the atmosphere between the delegations on the Security Council was aggressive and adversarial, as it remained until—and after—the invasion. Political divisions were allowed to degenerate into personal animosities. The Council, its chambers and corridors became a diplomatic battle zone where the more we fought, the more we entrenched our positions into competing blacks and whites.[45]

U.S. diplomats privately (half-jokingly) referred to France, Russia, and China as the "Evil 3." Rollover resolutions—the resolutions that extended the program for additional six-month periods—"often took a month to negotiate, deteriorating at times into screaming matches." According to a British diplomat,

> Political divisions were exacerbated by personal animosities; we argued all day. We often defined our position by opposing theirs—France would propose X and we would oppose it; six months later we would propose X and France would oppose it. The technical issues invariably became political issues—infant mortality rate, oil production—*everything* was politicized.[46]

The reports from the UN humanitarian coordinators in Iraq were not given credence. Instead, Halliday and von Sponeck were viewed by the United States and Britain as "politically tendentious." A senior State

Department official maintained that "some UN staff were unfortunately close to the Iraqi government's interpretation of the program, and discredited themselves by their association."[47] But according to von Sponeck, "as soon as I reported humanitarian damage from sanctions and air strikes, I was deemed to be naïve, politicized, rhetorical, and pro-Saddam."[48] The view of U.S. and British officials was that "his job was to do what he was told, not make speeches."[49] Similarly, the United States and Britain viewed Halliday as "completely biased and politicized."[50]

U.S. officials remained adamant that the Iraqi government was responsible for the humanitarian crisis, insisting that the UN staff had failed to see, for example, that the Iraqi government was warehousing goods rather than distributing them, failing to order goods promptly, and rejecting food deliveries. U.S. and British officials had little respect for either Halliday or von Sponeck: "We felt the problem was in the Iraqi obstruction of the distribution of goods, and we were unwilling to listen to emotional argument from Halliday and von Sponeck."[51] But according to UN staff, each accusation made by the United States or Britain was investigated. Regardless of how much information or documentation UN staff provided, U.S. officials dismissed it. In February 1999 U.S. ambassador Peter Burleigh criticized UN staff for failing to investigate whether goods were actually being distributed properly. When von Sponeck's staff looked into the warehousing issue they found that 90 percent of the goods were being distributed properly and the remaining 10 percent were stored for good reasons—for example, the equipment needed complementary parts that had not arrived. Von Sponeck's staff then began providing detailed information about the distribution of goods in their reports; and according to von Sponeck, "distribution was never referred to again by the U.S. and the British."[52]

Despite the repeated accusations of the United States and Britain, UN staff did follow up on their claims and did not find much evidence to support them. On one occasion, Britain accused Iraq of holding back $275 million in medical supplies without distributing them. But the World Health Organization (WHO) reported that it was appropriate and necessary for Iraq to maintain a certain amount of buffer stock. While the United States and Britain insisted that the Iraqi government was deliberately failing to order medical supplies for its people out of callousness, WHO documented that the Ministry of Health was in fact slow in ordering for other reasons, such as the lack of computerization and experienced people and lack of transport.[53] While the U.S. policy was grounded in an unshakable certainty that the Iraqi government was diverting humanitarian goods to military uses, as of 2002, "not one of the [UN monitors had] reported any major problem in humanitarian supplies being diverted, switched, or in any way misused."[54]

Regardless of what the UN staff observed and reported, in the eyes of the U.S. and British governments, the reports were not credible. They were certain that the Iraqi government was withholding goods or using them to rearm, and they maintained this certainty even though they had no reliable sources of information in Iraq after UNSCOM left, while UN officials were drawing on information collected from hundreds of national and international staff working in Iraq, in all parts of the country, and involved with every part of the economy and public services. All of this information was dismissed out of hand by the United States and Britain: "Any data coming out of Iraq relied on the government. We were generally internally quite dismissive of data. We felt there was a huge lack of empirical evidence—people banging on the table demanding changes without evidence."[55] To the contrary, there clearly was considerable empirical evidence presented repeatedly by UN agencies. Yet when UN staff met with the 661 Committee and gave detailed reports on the impact of holds on each sector in Iraq, U.S. and British staff saw this as "deteriorating into accusations."

But while dismissing data produced by UN agencies, U.S. and British officials themselves consciously distorted reports by UN staff. Former British diplomat Carne Ross described how he "produced one-sided arguments to justify sanctions by ignoring all contrary evidence":

There is . . . an invisible undertow at work on the civil servants who collate and analyse this information. If ministers want a particular story to emerge, it has a way of emerging: the facts are made to fit the policy. It takes a brave if not foolhardy civil servant to resist this tide. This is not to claim that there was some secret cubicle in Whitehall (or Washington) where evidence of Iraq's weapons was deliberately fabricated, but something more subtle. Evidence is selected from the available mass, contradictions are excised, and the selected data are repeated, rephrased, polished (spun, if you prefer), until it seems neat, coherent and convincing, to the extent that those presenting it may believe it fully themselves.[56]

Some have suggested that this in turn affected the reporting process by UN staff, who sometimes underreported those acts of the Iraq government that indicated corruption, favoritism, or measures that worsened the humanitarian situation. Claudia von Braunmühl, a UN consultant who analyzed the Iraq sanctions in 1995, found that the Iraqi government sometimes threatened to withhold food rations to obtain political submission; repairs and improvements to public services were focused on Baghdad, while the south—where the Shi'a uprising had taken place—was noticeably neglected; where health problems might have been remedied through public education programs, there were none; among some government officials there was irrational insistence that Iraq did not need to take measures to better address the impact of sanctions, because the sanctions were only temporary.[57] Yet von Braunmühl noted that the reports of the UN staff in Iraq at that time would not mention these things; they would include only the information documenting the negative impact of the economic sanctions themselves. The UN staff felt—quite correctly—that if any blame was attributed to the Iraqi government, the United States and Britain would seize on that particular item, ignoring all the other evidence of injury done by the sanctions, and use it to support their claim that Saddam Hussein was responsible for all the suffering in Iraq. At the same time, because the UN reports included no criticisms of the Iraqi government, the United States and Britain gave them no credibility, and the reports served to reinforce their view of UN staff as naïve and gullible, if not overtly pro-Saddam.

In the end, in the view of U.S. officials, the sanctions policy was successful, and the humanitarian impact was justified by the security concerns. In the view of a State Department officer at the UN,

> by the late 1990s, life had improved. It wasn't nearly as bad as it was in the first few years. The humanitarian situation—it was all used politically. This was also true of the UN agencies—they had their own agenda, to try to get sanctions reduced or eliminated. I'd like to believe they were purely interested in the well being of the Iraqi people; but they also weren't worrying about potential security risks.
>
> The humanitarian data was probably accurate, relatively accurate. But I don't think it told such a terrible story either. Could things have been better? Would life have been better without sanctions? Sure. But without allowing Saddam Hussein to rebuild?[58]

Ambassador Burleigh conceded that

> a Martian looking at the program would say the U.S. was respon-
> sible for all the humanitarian damage. The bottom line was that
> the U.S. was prepared to live with the horrible human impact. We
> gradually took steps to ameliorate it, but always slowly and reluc-
> tantly. But it's worth underscoring—everyone thought that there
> was a serious problem with WMD in Iraq—French, Germans,
> Israel. There was an issue of whether to close the nuclear portfolio;
> but there was no such attempt regarding biological and chemical
> weapons. Whatever you think of this in retrospect, our motivation
> at the time was based on that understanding.[59]

The Erosion of Support

While U.S. officials were satisfied with the trade-off they had made, it
was not surprising that the international community did not share their
view. The United States blamed the erosion of support on a variety of factors: that France, Russia, and China were pursuing their economic interests with Iraq, or for other reasons they and other nations were unwilling
to do their share to address the obvious and urgent threat that Iraq
presented.

Among U.S. policymakers there was little sense that the growing opposition to U.S. practices might be a legitimate reaction to U.S. over-
reaching. But much of the resistance was in fact due to the extreme policies of the United States and Britain and their willingness to ride roughshod
over the rest of the Council. The skepticism and resistance was evident
early on and increased over the course of the sanctions regime.

Starting in 1992, members of the Council questioned the U.S./British
insistence on regime change and their refusal to end the sanctions, should
Iraq agree to cooperate with the mandated disarmament measures. One
diplomat from an elected member of the Council said,

> while my delegation will insist that Iraq meet its obligations called
> for in Council resolutions, it is also important for the Security
> Council . . . to avoid the temptation to shift the goalposts. Where
> compliance has occurred, it must be accepted and recognized as
> having occurred. It is important for the prestige and credibility of
> the Security Council that the Council remain continuously focused
> on the legitimate goals and objectives for which the sanctions

205

regime was imposed on behalf of the international community as a whole.[60]

In 1994 Russia challenged the United States and Britain, insisting that if Iraq complied with the disarmament requirements, the sanctions regime should be lifted: the Council "must be ready to take 'Yes' for an answer."[61] By early 1995, China, France, and Russia circulated a draft resolution to lift the sanctions altogether, even though it was withdrawn in the face of veto threats by the United States and Britain.[62] In 1996 France stopped patrolling the northern no-fly zone. By December 1998 "there was growing exasperation with the inspections melodrama, and a sense on the part of [France, Russia, and China] that Iraq had mostly been disarmed."[63] Meanwhile, it became publicly known that the United States had used UNSCOM to gather intelligence about the Iraqi regime, compromising the organization's credibility and shocking many in the UN community.[64]

The United States and Britain, however, escalated the conflict with a bombing campaign. In December 1998 the United States conducted a massive, concentrated military attack against approximately 100 targets in Iraq—over 600 sorties in four days, as well as attacks by 300 Tomahawk missiles and 90 cruise missiles. From that point on, the United States lost all support from France. According to one French official, "December 1998 was a disaster." The French wanted to lift the sanctions in exchange for permanent monitors on the ground. According to the French, "in our view, sanctions helped the regime to find a culprit for all its difficulties."[65]

U.S. officials saw no legitimacy in these reactions and viewed them only with frustration. Ambassador Burleigh came to the UN in August 1997, seeking to persuade the Council to impose penalties on Iraq for its unwillingness to cooperate completely. There was little support; Russia, China, France, Egypt, and Kenya abstained. "It was a disaster for us, reflecting the already well-advanced dissolution of the council's consensus on Iraq. [It] was a prelude to those horrible years of 1998, 1999, and 2000 when France and Russia opposed every effort to get tough with the Iraqis."[66]

From the U.S. perspective, the situation kept deteriorating:

By the spring of 2000 UN sanctions on Iraq were unraveling. The sanctions were being violated openly and on a regular basis. The United States was under enormous international pressure to [scrap] or restructure them. Even our closest allies were critical of the unintended impact they were having on the Iraqi people. Three permanent Security Council members, France, Russia, and China, were pushing for agreement on an expanded list of exempted items. They also wanted a significant reduction in the list of red-lined goods (sensitive dual use and military items) that could not be exported at all to Iraq. By September 2000, Russia threatened to resume direct cargo flights to Baghdad in violation of sanctions.[67]

Iraq demanded that countries resume flying to Baghdad if they wanted a share of its oil-for-food contracts . . . Jordan followed the Russian lead, followed by planes from Yemen, Morocco, Tunisia, Turkey, the UAE, Algeria, Libya, Egypt, Lebanon, Ireland, Iceland, Greece, and France. By May 2001, Jordan announced resumption of regular commercial flights.[68]

From the U.S. perspective, the "sanctions fatigue" was not the only problem. By the mid-1990s there was deteriorating support as well for the disarmament process itself. When the Iraqi government went into northern Iraq in 1996, Saudi Arabia, Turkey, and Jordan would not permit the United States to launch air strikes from their territories.[69] At the same time, the Security Council was divided in its support for UNSCOM. In June 1996 Rolf Ekeus, the director of UNSCOM, agreed to limitations on the agency's authority in light of the Council's equivocation. In October 1997 three of the five permanent members—China, Russia, and France— refused to support UNSCOM's determination that Iraq was not in compliance with Council resolutions.[70]

It seems that there was never any sense on the part of U.S. officials that the loss of U.S. credibility within the Council occurred to some extent because the United States did not distinguish between its own goals and policies and those that in fact were authorized by the Security Council. What the United States saw as "erosion of support" was in part simply a refusal to grant legitimacy to unilateral decisions by the United States. While the international community had less and less support for the UN-authorized sanctions over time, its support for unilateral U.S. actions was even thinner.

This was illustrated vividly in regard to the U.S. bombing strikes over Iraq in January 1993. In the closing weeks of the George H. W. Bush presidency, the United States conducted over 100 bombing sorties in Iraq without any explicit authorization by the Security Council. Russia

objected and demanded that further military action be directly authorized.[71] The same was true of the no-fly zones. There were no Security
Council resolutions that explicitly authorized these, and the U.S. claim
that they were implicitly authorized—by language in an early resolution
inviting member states to provide humanitarian assistance—was shared
by almost no one. Russia and China, and later France, strongly took
issue with the United States' pronouncement and enforcement of the no-
fly zones. When the United States and Britain conducted bombing strikes
against Iraq in December 1998 without authorization from the Council,
France, Russia, and China were vocal in their opposition. France, which
had contributed to the enforcement of the no-fly zones, refused to participate any longer. Russia denounced the action as "a violation of the UN
Charter," and Qin Huasun of China said that "there is absolutely no ex-
cuse or pretext to use force against Iraq."[72]

The United States justified the bombing strikes on Iraq in December
1998 as a response to what was viewed as Iraq's groundless and illegitimate refusal to cooperate with UNSCOM as long as U.S. inspectors
were participating. Iraq claimed that the U.S. inspectors were passing on
information to U.S. intelligence services, which presumably would use
the information to support opposition movements and further the U.S.
efforts to remove Saddam Hussein from power. In fact, of course, that is
exactly what took place.[73] The comments of one scholar regarding the
no-fly zones were true in regard to many other things as well. He noted
that France and Britain supported the no-fly zones initially, and because
of the moral legitimacy and political expediency, no permanent members
objected. But the sense of unity deteriorated into acquiescence, until that
in turn gave way to overt defiance.[74]

The disputes over the bombing strikes and no-fly zones were significant not only because they illustrated how isolated the United States had
become in the Security Council on issues related to Iraq; they also pointed
to a profound failure on the part of U.S. officials to see any credibility in
those who viewed U.S. policy as illegitimate and wantonly destructive. It
seems there was simply no internal capacity to imagine and give credence
to how the rest of the international community saw the United States.

Publicly, the consistent position of the U.S. government was that the
United States had great concern for the Iraqi people and wanted to see
Iraq restored to a place of respectability within the international com-

munity. In fact, the internal process by which U.S. policy was formulated was quite different. There was a structural indifference to the well-being of the civilian Iraqi population. Civilian suffering literally counted for zero in the decision-making process, except indirectly from time to time, when the extent of the civilian harm created political problems for the United States. Among U.S. policymakers, "Saddam Hussein" and the people of Iraq were entirely conflated; denial of goods to the civilian population was seen as "denying Saddam."

While the U.S. government publicly maintained that it was blocking goods because of their military uses or that it was waiting for critical information, the internal policy was never anything other than to maximize denial and delay, irrespective of whether there was an actual cause for concern. While there may have been a legitimate need for more information in order to approve some goods, in many cases no amount of information was sufficient for the United States; for over a decade the United States refused to even identify what information it would need to render a decision.

Internally, the U.S. officials involved in the Iraq policy were often puzzled or indignant by the deterioration of support within the international community. U.S. officials often attributed this to hypocrisy and a failure of nerve on the part of other nations. But among U.S. officials it seems there was little sense that the rest of the international community found the United States to be overbearing and heavy handed, and was fundamentally uncomfortable with the U.S. efforts to go beyond the legitimate aims of the Council and to pursue its own goals, which were both illegitimate and unauthorized.

In the face of challenges to U.S. policies and their humanitarian impact, U.S. officials were unwilling to see any credibility, even from organizations and individuals that were deeply knowledgeable and internationally respected. By contrast, U.S. policymakers gave considerable credence to what was little more then speculation as to what might conceivably happen, under improbable circumstances, and then proceeded to act as though this were a reliable and credible basis for decision making. Anything that was conceivable, even events that were wildly implausible, were given more credibility than any information to the contrary, however extensive and well grounded.

Within the U.S. policy-making process, it seems that there was no internal source of self-restraint or any drive to limit the human damage from U.S. policies. The only points at which the U.S. government showed any hesitation were when its extreme practices became a political liability, where there was concerted pressure from the UN or from domestic political constituencies. What is clear is that, left to its own, there was simply no limit on how much harm the U.S. government was willing to do to Iraq.

11

INTERNATIONAL LAW AND THE SANCTIONS

Many have suggested that the sanctions imposed on Iraq violated international law. Denis Halliday, the former UN humanitarian coordinator in Iraq, called it genocide,[1] and one legal scholar maintained that "U.S. officials, in initiating and working tirelessly to maintain a program of comprehensive multilateral sanctions against the country and people of Iraq . . . have committed genocide."[2] Marc Bossuyt, the international law scholar, in his working paper for the UN's Commission on Human Rights, maintained that

> once clear evidence was available that thousands of civilians were dying . . . the deaths were no longer an unintended side effect—the Security Council was responsible for all known consequences of its actions. The sanctioning bodies cannot be absolved from having the "intent to destroy" the Iraqi people.[3]

Bossuyt and others have also maintained that the sanctions constituted war crimes in violation of the Geneva Convention[4] as well as violating treaties and UN Charter provisions concerning economic rights. Others have argued as well that the sanctions violated the peremptory norms of *jus cogens*, the fundamental principles of international law that are unwritten or customary.[5]

These are accusations that need to be taken seriously in light of the credibility of many of those making them, the magnitude of the damage, and the deliberate and systematic nature of the measures that brought about this damage.

To acknowledge the seriousness and importance of the accusations is not to say that there are judicial venues in which individuals or states, much less the Security Council itself, might be held accountable. It is very unlikely that there are any. Even if the United States were acting independently of

INVISIBLE WAR

the Council, it is not clear that there are legal venues where the U.S. policies could be challenged. The United States is not a signatory on some of the central treaties of human rights law, such as the International Covenant on Economic, Social, and Cultural Rights or the Convention on the Rights of the Child. In some cases, where the United States is a signatory, the document contains no provision for enforcement, as with the Universal Declaration of Human Rights.

But while it seems that no individuals could be prosecuted and no state could be found liable for the sanctions regime, or for the U.S. role in their implementation, we should consider how these policies stand with regard to principles of international human rights law, as a set of norms by which to judge the moral legitimacy of the sanctions.

International Human Rights Law and Economic Development

International law recognizes a right to economic development and to an adequate standard of living, and the necessity of these for the fundamental human dignity of the person.

The preamble to the Universal Declaration of Human Rights states that the members of the UN, in the Charter, indicated their determination "to promote social progress and better standards of life in larger freedom." Article 25 of the Declaration provides that "Everyone has the right to a standard of living adequate for the health and well-being of himself and of his family, including food, clothing, housing and medical care and necessary social services." The International Covenant on Economic, Social and Cultural Rights (ICESCR) provides that the states parties "recognize the right of everyone to an adequate standard of living for himself and his family, including adequate food, clothing and housing, and to the continuous improvement of living conditions."[6] The ICESCR also recognizes a right of all persons to be free from hunger. The states that are parties to the ICESCR agree to take measures to improve the production and distribution of food, to reform agrarian systems to achieve the best utilization of natural resources and specifically to ensure the equitable distribution of food on the basis of need.[7]

Yet when the sanctions were first imposed on Iraq—a country that imported two-thirds of its food—in August 1990, the United States insisted on making the importation of food conditional: Iraq could not import food except in "humanitarian circumstances." The Congressional

Research Service reported within weeks that Iraq's food availability was in crisis, and CIA Director William Webster reiterated this in December 1990. Despite this, the United States was intransigent in interpreting "humanitarian circumstances" in the most extreme way possible—that Iraq could not import food until there was irrefutable evidence of advanced stages of famine. On that basis, the United States, invoking the consensus decision-making rule, prevented Iraq from importing any food, including powdered milk for infants, for eight months.

Over the course of the entire sanctions regime, the United States also compromised Iraq's efforts to increase domestic food production by repeatedly and often unilaterally blocking Iraq from importing tractors, irrigation pipes, fertilizers, pesticides, and materials to manufacture fertilizer and pesticides. The United States blocked the Food and Agriculture Organization from bringing in parts to repair helicopters used for crop dusting. The United States blocked equipment to make yogurt and to mill flour, and then blocked Iraq from contracting to have its wheat milled outside the country. These practices continued in the face of near constant UN reports of severe and widespread malnutrition.

The right to health care is also widely recognized within international human rights law. The Universal Declaration provides that "Everyone has the right to a standard of living adequate for the health and well-being of himself and his family, including . . . medical care."[8] Under the ICESCR, the states parties "recognize the right of everyone to the enjoyment of the highest attainable standard of physical and mental health."[9] They agree to take steps to achieve this right, including measures necessary to reduce infant mortality rates, the prevention and treatment of epidemics, and the creation of conditions to ensure that medical services are available to all.[10] The Convention on the Rights of the Child provides that the states parties "shall ensure to the maximum extent possible the survival and development of the child."[11] The states parties agree to take measures to reduce infant and child mortality and to combat disease and malnutrition, including the provision of adequate foods and clean drinking water.[12]

Yet the U.S.-led bombing of water and sewage treatment plants in 1991 triggered epidemics of cholera, typhoid, and other water-borne diseases, exactly as anticipated by the Defense Department shortly before the bombing began; and the United States then consistently prevented Iraq from importing the necessary equipment and materials to restore adequate water treatment. The United States at various times objected to Iraq's import of drugs such as Ciprofloxacin, an antibiotic, and atropine,

213

a drug necessary for any surgery involving general anesthesia. The United States allowed ambulances, but then refused to allow Iraq to import the two-way radios that went with them, compromising their usefulness. For years the United States repeatedly blocked the equipment necessary to maintain the cold chain for pharmaceuticals and blood banks, including refrigerators and refrigerated trucks.

The Universal Declaration provides that "Everyone has the right to education."[13] The ICESCR provides that the states parties will institute various measures to provide educational institutions of all levels and shall actively pursue "the development of a system of schools" and the continuous improvement of "the material conditions of teaching staff."[14] The Convention on the Rights of the Child likewise includes a right of all children to education, at various levels.[15] But the United States at various points prevented Iraq from importing textbooks and also prevented it from importing the equipment needed to produce textbooks themselves, including the glue for the bindings. The United States blocked computers for secondary schools and universities as well as fabric for school uniforms. The travel restrictions and the compromised telecommunications facilities created an intellectual blockade that prevented Iraqi scholars and educators from attending conferences and communicating with their colleagues abroad. The bankrupting of the state was disastrous for the Iraqi educational system, which lost thousands of teachers at all levels. The deterioration of the schools and lack of materials prevented many schools from operating at all. Over the course of the 1990s some 40,000 teachers left their jobs, and there were chronic shortages of paper, books, and school supplies.

The Universal Declaration provides that "everyone has the right to work" and that "Everyone who works has the right to just and favourable remuneration ensuring for himself and his family an existence worthy of human dignity, and supplemented, if necessary, by other means of social protection."[16] Likewise, the ICESCR provides that the states parties recognize the right of everyone to conditions of work that ensure "a decent living for themselves and their families."[17] For years the United States invoked security concerns to block everything that might have contributed to restoring Iraq's manufacturing capacity, including nails, wire, paint, and window glass. The United States blocked Iraq from importing raw materials, or even unfinished products, that would have created employment—Iraq was permitted to import cigarettes but not cigarette paper, and shoes but not shoe leather—because these were considered "inputs to industry." The United States consistently blocked proposals for a cash component that would have allowed funds from the Oil-for-Food Programme to be used to buy locally produced goods and to hire Iraqi labor, both of which would have generated work and income for the population. The collapse of Iraq's industrial capacity, and the economy as a whole, triggered massive unemployment, the disappearance of Iraq's middle class, and a decline in the standard of living so extreme that, just to survive, engineers drove taxis and families sent their children to beg on the streets.

International law provides few means of enforcing rights of economic development. Even so, the basic documents of international human rights law create an expectation that international organizations, as well as nations working cooperatively, will undertake to promote economic well-being, not to undermine it. The UN Charter provides that the purposes of the UN include "achiev[ing] international co-operation in solving international problems of an economic, social, cultural, or humanitarian character."[18] The Universal Declaration provides that all persons have a right to social security and to the "economic, social and cultural rights indispensable for his dignity." But further, it provides that everyone is entitled to the realization of that right "through national effort and international co-operation."[19] The Convention on the Rights of the Child provides that the states parties will "undertake to promote and encourage international co-operation with a view to achieving progressively the full realization" of the rights of health care[20] and will do the same with regard to education.[21]

These documents speak of providing additional resources or attention to assist developing nations. The Convention on the Rights of the Child provides that "particular account shall be taken of the needs of developing countries" in promoting education[22] and health care.[23] The ICESCR provides that the states parties "shall take, individually and through international co-operation, the measures, including specific programmes" to increase food production.[24] The Universal Declaration states this explicitly: "Everyone is entitled to a social and international order in which the rights and freedoms set forth in this Declaration can be fully realized."[25] These provisions suggest that economic rights are not imperfect rights, which impose no obligations on anyone in particular. They impose an affirmative obligation on the international community to establish arrangements to achieve these rights, or at least, it would seem, not to undermine them. Yet in the case of the sanctions regime, it was international cooperation, within a system shaped at every juncture by the United States, that in fact created "problems of an economic ... or humanitarian character," rather than resolving them.

The Laws of Armed Conflict

The Geneva Conventions offer a clear statement of the internationally recognized norms for conduct during armed conflict. The parties to the Conventions are states, not the UN or any of its bodies, including the Security Council.[26] Consequently, it does not seem that any judicial venue could have jurisdiction over violations by the Council. However, war crimes have long been seen as serious violations of international law and norms. The provisions of the Rome Statute addressing war crimes include "grave breaches" of the Geneva Conventions, as well as other serious violations of customary and established international law.

The Geneva Conventions provide protections for goods and materials "indispensable to the survival of the civilian population."[27] Under this provision, "starvation of civilians as a method of warfare is prohibited."[28] Yet this is precisely what the United States did from August 1990 through March 1991 in blocking Iraq's requests for permission to import food under the "humanitarian circumstances" exemption in Security Council Resolution 661.

More broadly, Just War doctrine, as well as the treaties and customs that constitute international humanitarian law regarding situations of conflict, recognize a fundamental obligation to discriminate between civilians and combatants, to refrain from targeting civilians, and to provide protections for civilians from the damages of war. The Geneva Conventions generally prohibit attacks by military forces that affect civilians indiscriminately. "Attacks" are acts of violence against the adversary.[29] It can of course be argued that economic sanctions are not a form of violence. But in the case of Iraq they functioned in much the same way as a military siege. "Indiscriminate attacks" are defined as

> (a) Those which are not directed at a specific military objective;
> (b) Those which employ a method or means of combat which cannot be directed at a specific military objective; or
> (c) Those which employ a method or means of combat the effects of which cannot be limited as required by this Protocol; and consequently, in each such case, are of a nature to strike military objectives and civilians or civilian objects without distinction.[30]

It is hard to imagine that the impoverishment of an entire nation, the collapse of industry, agriculture, and infrastructure are anything other than "a means or method . . . which cannot be directed at a specific military objective." However, "indiscriminate attacks" are sometimes permitted, within certain parameters. Incidental harm to civilians is permitted, but in accordance with the principle of proportionality: the harm to civilians cannot be "excessive in relation to the concrete and direct military advantage anticipated."[31] Yet that is not at all reflected in the decision-making process by U.S. officials. Medical equipment, electrical generators, water treatment materials, and child vaccines were all critical to human well-being, and all were blocked by the United States on the basis of the speculative possibility that they might be used by the Iraqi government for military purposes. This was so even where it was extremely unlikely—because the Iraqis did not have the equipment or capacity to convert these goods into a serious military threat, because UN weapons inspectors saw no such risk, or because goods were subject to close monitoring by UN staff.

U.S. officials might argue that maintaining a state of massive, continuous devastation would achieve a direct and concrete military advantage. Certainly that was precisely the reasoning for the policy of containment. And it is true that eliminating a nation's science, technology, and manufacturing will prevent the state from rebuilding its military capacity; that crippling all industrial production will compromise military industries as well; and that crippling the nation's entire transportation system will also compromise military transportation. But insofar as the measures met the military necessity requirement, they were in gross violation of the principle of proportionality.

The Geneva Conventions also offers a framework for analyzing whether it is permissible to destroy or cripple the buildings, equipment, and goods that are necessary to sustain the civilian population. Article 54(2) provides:

> It is prohibited to attack, destroy, remove or render useless objects indispensable to the survival of the civilian population, such as food-stuffs, agricultural areas for the production of food-stuffs, crops, livestock, drinking water installations and supplies and irrigation works, for the specific purpose of denying them for their sustenance value to the civilian population or to the adverse Party, whatever the motive, whether in order to starve out civilians, to cause them to move away, or for any other motive.[32]

Certainly it was the case that the U.S.-led bombings of 1991, and then the extreme positions of the United States in blocking equipment and materials for water treatment, transportation of food and other goods, refrigeration for medicine and blood supplies, and inputs for agriculture, had the effect of "render[ing] useless objects indispensable to the survival of the civilian population." The motive may have been to prevent the Iraqi government from rebuilding its military, but Article 54 nevertheless prohibits these activities, "whatever the motive."

Article 54(3) provides limited exceptions. The destruction of civilian goods is permitted if they are used by the adverse party

(a) as sustenance solely for the members of its armed forces; or

(b) if not as sustenance, then in direct support of military action, provided, however, that in no event shall actions against these objects be taken which may be expected to leave the civilian population with such inadequate food or water as to cause its starvation or force its movement.[33]

Article 54(3)(a) permits the destruction of indispensable civilian goods, specifically those necessary to provide food and water, if they are "solely" for the military, not if they are "dual use." Even for goods that provide "direct support" for the military, it is not permissible to cause starvation to the civilian population. Yet while there was not complete famine, UNICEF as well as other agencies and public health experts documented the deaths of some 500,000 children under the age of five, primarily from dysentery combined with malnutrition; widespread and ongoing malnutrition such that as of 1997, a million children under age five were malnourished, and as of 1998, 70 percent of Iraqi women were anemic; and diseases from nutritional deficiencies, such as marasmus and kwashkior, were widespread.

Article 54(5) also allows an exception to the prohibition on destroying things indispensable to civilian survival: that in defense against the invasion of a country's own national territory, these provisions may be violated out of "imperative military necessity."[34] But this could not be said to apply here; neither the Security Council nor any of its member states was defending its own territory against invasion. Nor was there "imperative military necessity," for the same reasons that the sanctions could not meet the ordinary level of military necessity: the scenario in which flour mills or dump trucks or pencils would be used for military purposes rested entirely on speculation, with no certain "direct military advantage."

Article 52 also considers the circumstance in which something that is ordinarily a civilian object, such as a school, a place of worship, or a home, can be a legitimate military objective. It is a military objective if it by its "nature, location, purpose or use make[s] an effective contribution to military action and whose total or partial destruction, capture or neutralization, in the circumstances ruling at the time, offers a definite military advantage."[35] However, "in case of doubt whether an object which is normally dedicated to civilian purposes, such as a place of worship, a house or other dwelling or a school, is being used to make an effective contribution to military action, it shall be presumed not to be so used."[36]

After the departure of the United Nations Special Commission, the United States had no source of information, and it was in the absence of information that U.S. officials speculated about what could conceivably be done with aluminum foil, yogurt makers, and garbage trucks. But the presumption was not as the Geneva Conventions required—that "in case of doubt" it must be presumed that goods were being used for their usual civilian purposes. Instead, in the absence of information, the operating presumption was that the goods would be diverted for military purposes, and this presumption held, even when the technical requirements for doing this made such a claim wildly implausible.

The Problem of Jurisdiction

Regardless of the ways in which the policies of the Security Council, and the actions of the United States, may be in direct contravention of the principles and norms of international law, it seems that there is no venue in which a claim of such violations could be adjudicated. It is hard to imagine any circumstances in which the International Criminal Court (ICC) could prosecute individuals, however closely they were involved with the design or implementation of the sanctions. The Rome Statute binds only states parties, not institutions of international governance. The ICC can prosecute individuals only for violations committed on the territory of a state party or committed by a national of a state party,[37] and neither Iraq nor the United States is a party to the Rome Statute. In 2006 the ICC considered a request to prosecute U.S. nationals for abuses that took place at Abu Ghraib. It could not, because it had no jurisdiction.[38] Even if the ICC could prosecute acts committed on behalf of the Security Council, it is not at all clear whom the responsible agent would be. Is every nation that votes for a resolution responsible for the particulars of its implementation? If so, then what persons would be subject to prosecution: those in the government who support the resolution or the diplomat who states the vote on the record, or the staff of the Secretariat or UN agencies who implement it?

Nor is it likely that the matter could come before the International Court of Justice (ICJ). Neither the UN Charter nor the statute of the ICJ provide for judicial review of Security Council decisions. Adversarial cases can only be brought against states, not against organs of the UN; and while the ICJ could issue an advisory ruling regarding a decision of the Security Council, it could do so only on the request of the General Assembly or the Security Council itself. In the *Lockerbie* case, the ICJ ruled it would not overrule a Security Council decision even if it violated the treaty rights of a sovereign state.[39] Thus it is hard to see how either the ICJ or the ICC would even have jurisdiction to hear such a case, let alone find that there is liability, on the part of either a state or individuals acting under the auspices of Chapter VII resolutions. It is conceivable that there may be attempts by national courts to pursue prosecutions of individuals, invoking universal jurisdiction, along the lines of the prosecution in Spain against Chilean general Augusto Pinochet. But even the most ambitious of those have been directed at acts by officials of national governments, not at acts involved in the implementation of policies adopted by the UN.

But it is not only a matter of jurisdiction. There is also the question of whether any act or policy—regardless of the consequences or the intent of the parties—can be illegal if it is undertaken in accordance with Chapter VII of the UN Charter. Whatever the role of the United States might have been in shaping the sanctions, they were still a measure imposed by the Security Council. Article 41 provides that the Council may use whatever measures (not involving armed force) "are to be employed to give effect to its decisions"; Article 42 provides that the Council may use whatever force "may be necessary to maintain or restore international peace and security." The language of Chapter VII does not place any explicit limits on what the Council can authorize in this regard. Is it the case that any measure authorized by the Security Council under Chapter VII, however extensive or indiscriminate the harm, is legal?

Certainly the Security Council is not bound by the same limits that apply to states. If a state used force to invade another state, that would constitute aggression, in violation of international law, whereas the use of force by the Security Council is specifically permitted under Chapter VII. Hans Kelsen and others have argued that the Security Council is bound only by the Charter, not by international law in general, and that the Charter does not place limits on what measures the Council can pursue under Chapter VII.[40] Some have maintained that the Council is nevertheless bound by the broader principles of international law, since Article 24 of the UN Charter provides that, while the Council has "primary responsibility for the maintenance of international peace and security," the Charter also provides that "in discharging these duties the Security Council shall act in accordance with the Purposes and Principles of the United Nations."[41] Judge Lauterpacht of the ICJ suggested that to hold otherwise would be absurd: "One only has to state the proposition thus—that a Security Council Resolution may even require participation in genocide—for its unacceptability to be apparent."[42] In a dissent to the ICJ's *Lockerbie* decision, Judge Sir Robert Jennings noted that all authority to implement the law "flows itself from the law," and that it is not possible to both represent the power and authority of the law while claiming to be above it. Consequently, he maintained, the Security Council is not exempt from the law.[43] But in the end, it is not clear exactly what limits international law places on Security Council measures taken under Chapter VII.

Genocide and Crimes against Humanity

Even if there were a venue with jurisdiction, I do not believe that the sanctions on Iraq constitute genocide or crimes against humanity, as they are defined in international law. This is not to say the Security Council policies, as shaped by the United States, were benign or wise or, for that matter, minimally justifiable by any standard of morality. However appalling they were, it seems to me that the policies were not driven by the intent required for genocide or crimes against humanity. But it seems to me this does not constitute a vindication of the sanctions, but rather a failure of international law.

Many critics of the sanctions have maintained that they were genocidal. Under both the Genocide Convention and the Rome Statute, "genocide" includes "Deliberately inflicting on the [national, ethnic, racial or religious] group conditions of life calculated to bring about its physical destruction in whole or in part," where these acts are committed

221

with intent to destroy the group, in whole or in part.[44] "Deliberately inflicting on the group conditions of life calculated to bring about its physical destruction in whole or in part" was construed by the International Criminal Tribunal for Rwanda (ICTR) to include "subjecting a group of people to a subsistence diet, systematic expulsion from homes and the reduction of essential medical services below minimum vital standard."[45] In the *Kayeshima* case, the prosecution argued that the "conditions of life" provision "allows for the punishment of the perpetrator for the infliction of substandard conditions of life which, if left to run their course, could bring about the physical destruction of the group."[46] The Trial Chamber concurred with the interpretation that the provision included "circumstances which will lead to a slow death, for example, lack of proper housing, clothing, hygiene and medical care or excessive work or physical exertion."[47] The Trial Chamber held that the conditions of life envisioned included "the starving of a group of people, reducing required medical services below a minimum, and withholding sufficient living accommodation for a reasonable period, provided the above would lead to the destruction of the group in whole or in part."[48]

The sanctions imposed on Iraq, as shaped by the very extreme agenda of the United States, fit the acts described in the genocide provision: it was a policy and set of practices that deliberately inflicted conditions of life on the Iraqi people, specifically in the south and central governorates, which brought about their physical destruction in part. It is not hard to see why Halliday and Bossuyt, among others, would raise in a serious way the claim that the sanctions were genocidal.

But even if a prosecution were possible under the Rome Statute of the ICC, it does not seem that the *mens rea*, the mental component, for genocide is present. Genocide requires specific intent: the intent to destroy "a national, ethnical, racial or religious group, *as such*" means there must be an intent to destroy a racial or ethnic group because of its race or ethnicity, and not for, say, economic gain or political goals.[49] In addition, the acts must be "calculated to" bring about the destruction of the protected group, and they must be done with the "intent to destroy" the group, at least in part.

Genocidal intent does not have to be announced or explicitly acknowledged by the perpetrator. Intent can be inferred from circumstances, and some of the cases in the UN ad hoc tribunals on Rwanda and the former Yugoslavia took this route. In the *Akayesu* case before the ICTR, the Trial Chamber found that "in the absence of a confession from the accused, his intent can be inferred from a certain number of presumptions of fact," such as the context, other acts by the accused, the scale of the atrocities committed, and whether a particular group was targeted.[50]

Even so, I think that we cannot infer the required intent here. While the scale of the human damage was enormous and the damage was conducted systematically, the context suggests a willful blindness and a shockingly high tolerance for collateral damage; but these are not the same as the specific intent to destroy the Iraqi population.

To the extent that accusations of genocide have come before international courts, the specific intent provision has been interpreted very strictly. In the *Bashir* case, heard by the ICC, it was claimed that the government of Sudan had engaged in genocide in regard to the civilian population of Darfur, in part "by the subjection of a substantial part of the . . . civilian population of Darfur"—nearly 3 million people—to "unbearable conditions of life" within camps for internally displaced persons; then blocking aid from international organizations.[51] There was a lack of basic sanitation and restrictions on access to drinking water.[52] However, the court found that impeding humanitarian aid and cutting off food supplies and other essential goods "can be carried out for a variety of reasons other than intending to destroy in whole or in part the targeted group."[53] They found this was the case, for example, when the conditions in one of the camps were justified by the government of Sudan on security grounds.[54]

The ICJ ruled similarly when Bosnia brought an action against Serbia and Montenegro concerning the application of the Genocide Convention. Here, Bosnia argued that Serb forces surrounded civilian areas, then shelled them and cut off all supplies in order to starve the population.[55] There was also a report by a UN Special Rapporteur that electricity, water, and gas supplies to Sarajevo had been shut off and damage to supply lines was deliberate.[56] The court found that if there were any motive other than simply the destruction of the group in itself, there could not be a finding of the specific intent required to show genocide. If the purpose is to terrorize the civilian population, or drive them out in order to claim their land, then the specific intent requirement is not met. In the Bosnia case there was evidence that the siege was also a tactic to force civilians to flee; thus the Court found that the specific intent to destroy the protected group had not been conclusively proven.[57]

That the specific intent requirement is interpreted so strictly reflects a sense that "genocide has its own unique stigma and should not lightly be invoked."[58] Judge Patricia Wald, who served on the International Criminal

Tribunal for the former Yugoslavia, noted that "It comes down to the notion that the accused may have intended to destroy the group for several reasons—he may, for example, have been motivated to get rid of it in order to grab land, or even to promote himself in the eyes of his superiors."[59] But that is not sufficient because he must have the specific intent to destroy the group because of its race or ethnicity; it is not sufficient even to destroy the group in its entirety, if it is for some other motive. Wald notes that the Khmer Rouge defendants could well argue that the killings were motivated by programs of social and economic change; and however bloody those programs were, they were not driven by the specific intent required for genocide.[60]

It is clear that there is a trade-off: the strict interpretation may preserve the exclusivity of the notion of genocide; however, there will not be accountability for those who act knowingly and deliberately, but fall short of specific intent. Judge Wald noted:

> There is little doubt . . . that if a strict interpretation—requiring personal intent to destroy a group on the part of every person who may not have desired the extinction of the group on his own but is willing to go along and actively and substantially contribute to the genocide enterprise with full knowledge of its consequences and an ability to do something about it—becomes the norm, we will have fewer genocide convictions even though many genocides may occur.[61]

In light of the specific intent requirement for genocide, it seems to me that U.S. officials did not have the *mens rea* to be found responsible for genocide. The U.S. policy may have been deliberate and knowing, and deeply indifferent to the human consequences, but it does not seem that it was "calculated to" destroy the Iraqi population or that it was motivated by a drive to exterminate Iraqis specifically because they were Iraqis.

Certainly the public language of U.S. officials expressed no such intent. They almost always spoke in terms of legality and benevolence: that they harbored no animosity toward the Iraqi population, that they were deeply concerned about the children of Iraq, and that they wanted Iraq to be restored to a place among the free and law-abiding nations of the world. Internally, in the process of policy making, it was quite a different matter: there is absolutely no evidence of concern about Iraqi children or any other aspect of the suffering in Iraq. The singular preoccupation of U.S. officials was the possibility that Iraq might rebuild its military, and specifically that it might be producing weapons of mass destruction (WMD). It is true that U.S. officials found evidence of this when it seems that no rational person would have, and that they gave no weight at all to the humanitarian consequences of their decisions, except when the suffering in Iraq created political problems for the United States. But that is not quite the same thing as calculating the destruction of Iraqi civilians; nor is it the same as an intent to annihilate Iraqis, *because* they are Iraqis.

"Crimes against humanity" includes the crime of "extermination."[62] Extermination "includes the intentional infliction of conditions of life, *inter alia* the deprivation of access to food and medicine, calculated to bring about the destruction of part of a population."[63] Extermination can include the "creation of conditions of life that lead to mass killing" or the institution of circumstances that ultimately causes the mass death of others. This would include, for example, imprisoning a large number of people and withholding the necessities of life, which results in mass death, or introducing a deadly virus into a population and preventing medical care, which produces the same outcome.[64]

Crimes against humanity in general have a different *mens rea* than genocide: extermination and other acts listed constitute crimes against humanity "when committed as part of a widespread or systematic attack directed against any civilian population, *with knowledge of the attack.*"[65] In this regard, the *mens rea* requirement is lower than the specific intent required for genocide. But to meet the standard for extermination in particular, it is not enough to knowingly impose harsh conditions of life; it must also be shown that they were *intentionally* inflicted and *calculated* to destroy a part of the population.

The sanctions policies, as shaped and implemented by the United States, fit the acts described in the provision for crimes against humanity, in regard to extermination: they constituted conditions of life, including deprivation of access to food and medicine, which resulted in the destruction of part of a population. But just as the U.S. policies do not quite meet the intent standard for genocide, it can also be said that the infliction of conditions that brought about the destruction of so many people in Iraq was not actually "calculated" to accomplish the goal of extermination, which is a crime against humanity, but was rather just the consequence of the United States' very extreme interpretation of security concerns. It is

225

not a matter of legalistic hair-splitting. These distinctions go to the fundamental question of when government officials bear legal responsibility for enormous acts of destruction that result not from animosity, but from an ostensibly legitimate policy, however extreme the implementation; or from deep indifference, but not an explicit drive to exterminate a population.

In the cases of both genocide and crimes against humanity, we can see the influence of Raphael Lemkin's original model of the Nazi genocide, which explicitly and systematically sought to persecute, exile, and exterminate, and the language of "intent to destroy" and "calculated to bring about the destruction" reflect this. But certainly on the part of the Security Council, there were no such announcements. Most obviously, the Security Council resolutions establishing the sanctions invoked by Chapter VII of the UN Charter provide measures to address aggression, breaches of the peace, and threats to peace, but not to engage in genocide or extermination of populations. The resolutions themselves do not state any such intent; those establishing and modifying the sanctions regime are concerned with the need for Iraq to withdraw from Kuwait, then with disarmament, as well as various humanitarian measures intended for the well-being of the Iraqi population. Nor were there any such pronouncements by U.S. or British officials. Quite to the contrary, there were frequent expressions of concern for the well-being of the Iraqis, and indignation over their mistreatment at the hands of Saddam Hussein. But even if we dismiss these sorts of statements as public relations fodder, the motivations driving the Security Council policies, or the U.S. practices that were less visible, do not show the type of intent required for genocide, or crimes against humanity.

In Article 30, the Rome Statute does envision a different standard for *mens rea,* which is applicable where there are not other provisions that come into play. Consequently, it does not apply to genocide or crimes against humanity, which specify their own intent and knowledge requirements. Article 30 provides that for other violations of the statute, a person shall be criminally responsible if the material elements of the crime "are committed with intent and knowledge."[66] It holds that an individual has intent where "(a) in relation to conduct, that person means to engage in the conduct; (b) in relation to a consequence, that person means to cause that consequence or is aware that it will occur in the ordinary course of events."[67] "Knowledge" means "awareness that a circumstance exists or a consequence will occur in the ordinary course of events."[68]

Under this standard there would be culpability where "the perpetrators [are] aware that the action will result in the prohibited consequence (though not desired) with certainty . . . One could argue that in acting though aware of the prohibited consequences, the perpetrator was indeed willing to accept them."[69]

If that were the standard applicable to genocide or crimes against humanity, this standard would have certainly been met. Under this standard, it is clear that dozens of U.S. officials had the necessary intent and knowledge to be found criminally responsible under the Rome Statute, were there a prosecution. They meant to engage in the acts of denying humanitarian imports; these acts and decisions were conscious and deliberate, and not done under any form of coercion recognized by law. While there was a culture of suspicion regarding Saddam Hussein, and distrust and dislike of UN officials who documented the humanitarian situation, there are no grounds to believe that any of the U.S. officials who participated in this process were acting under duress or threat of harm. And while there may be a claim that those involved did not "mean to harm the innocent"—that perhaps they felt some reluctance or regret—there is no question that U.S. officials were aware "that a circumstance exists." The constant flow of UN reports ensured this, as well as the actual consequences—that blocking Iraq from importing equipment did "in the ordinary course of events" result in epidemics of water-borne diseases, did make it impossible to maintain the cold chain for medicines, did compromise the delivery of food supplies, did bring about increases in polio and other childhood diseases.

There is a terrible and obvious cost to using the higher level of intent that the Genocide Convention and the Rome Statute require for genocide and crimes against humanity, rather than the general intent standard contained in Article 30. While there are good reasons and considerable thought that went into the formulation of the intent requirement for these crimes, it is also the case that the specific intent standard is an invitation to disingenuous denials and casuistic reasoning. As Wald suggested, it may be that the specific intent requirement does not provide the means to punish genocidal murderers in general, but only tactically inept ones, who make stupid blunders in their public proclamations.

It is a question that emerged in the preliminary work for the Rome Statute. One of the working groups of the Preparatory Commission of the International Criminal Court suggested the language: "The accused knew or should have known that the conduct would destroy, in whole or in part, such group." William Schabas argues that this standard—essentially a negligence standard—was too low for genocide. But he maintains that the standard for criminal knowledge should include "wilful blindness," "where an individual deliberately fails to inquire into the consequences of certain behaviour, and where the person knows that such inquiry should be undertaken."[70] He cites Glanville Williams's treatise on criminal law—"The rule that wilful blindness is equivalent to knowledge is essential, and is found throughout the criminal law"—as well as a case from the International Criminal Tribunal for the former Yugoslavia that discussed "the requirement of either actual or 'constructive' knowledge that criminal acts were occurring on a widespread or systematic basis."[71]

Schabas also discusses Cherif Bassouni's criticism of the Genocide Convention on similar grounds, that the International Law Commission failed

> to progressively define article 2 of the 1948 Convention in light of the clearly perceived need for it considering all of the quasi-genocidal conduct that have taken place since 1948 ... It is not difficult to think of a number of contemporary conflicts such as those in Cambodia and the former Yugoslavia, where there is obviously no paper trail and where the specific intent can only be shown by the cumulative effect of the objective conduct to which one necessarily has to add the inference of specific intent deriving from omission.[72]

This question also arose in the early 1970s, when there was a great deal written by philosophers in response to the Vietnam War. Jean-Paul Sartre argued that the U.S. tactics, such as blanket bombing, the use of napalm, and the systematic burning of villages, amounted to genocide.[73] Hugo Bedau was sympathetic to the accusation, but in the end refuted it. He argued that however appalling the U.S. policies were, however deliberately and knowingly the atrocities were committed, it could not be shown that this met the specific intent required under the Genocide Convention. He concluded with "the Scottish verdict, Not proven, not quite."[74]

It seems that that is the case here as well, and for that we have good reason to be deeply disappointed in international law. There may not be a crime that could be prosecuted, for lack of a venue with jurisdiction, and because of the institutional context that authorized the sanctions overall. Yet it seems absolutely clear that the extreme way in which the sanctions were implemented violates the fundamental norms and principles of international human rights law. While international law gives us a framework to judge those acts driven by racial hatred, on the model of the Holocaust, it is not adequate to address atrocities that are deliberately implemented by indifferent officials for political or economic purposes. I do not use the term "atrocity" in a legal sense; David Scheffer uses the term "atrocity law" to refer to the acts that are recognized as international crimes, including genocide and crimes against humanity.[75] But I would use "atrocity" in the ordinary sense of the term, as evoking simply the shock and horror that most would feel in the face of such enormous and gratuitous human damage; a circumstance in which we would be hard-pressed not to disparage the justifications—"we believed that if Saddam had equipment to make cheese he would use it to produce weapons of mass destruction"—as disingenuous and shameful. It is not that the U.S. government is innocent; but rather that international law has failed to account for this kind of culpability.

International governance has failed us as well, in that it has been possible for an atrocity to be committed by the very body of international authority intended to intervene in the face of atrocities. It is a serious failure, and a serious risk, when the existing framework for international law does not envision the possibility that the very institutions that are charged with responding to these violations could themselves commit them, and does not envision the possibility that in the name of preventing aggression and threats to the peace the Security Council could implement a policy that would kill more people than all uses of weapons of mass destruction in the twentieth century combined.

International governance has also failed us in the way that this occurred: that the structure of the UN and the Security Council permitted a single nation to determine its decisions, and in some cases to override the will of nearly every other member of the Council, for years on end. The United States succeeded in using the Security Council, and binding all UN member states as well, first in order to impose its own agenda—regime change—in violation of the Council's resolutions, and arguably the UN Charter; and then to unilaterally impose its own standard—compromising the basic means to sustain life in an industrialized nation for an entire civilian population—in enforcing the measures the Security Council imposed.

As Arendt spoke about the bureaucratization of evil, the Iraq sanctions tell us about the legalization of atrocity. It may be that, in the end, there is a particular risk posed to humanity by international governance. As institutions of international governance extend their reach and legitimacy, they also entail the risk of a new form of global violence—not from terrorism or cruelty or racial or ethnic hatred, but rather from the possibility of a single nation hijacking an institution of international governance and substituting its own agenda in place of the interests and will of the international community.

12

This book was originally conceived as a discussion of the ethics of economic sanctions, for which the Iraq sanctions regime would serve as a case study. But in the course of researching and writing about the Iraq sanctions it became clear that they were about much more than Iraq, and much more than sanctions. Rather, what emerged from the documents and interviews concerning the Iraq sanctions was the story of how the United States projected influence within a central institution of international governance, as the Cold War ended, at the juncture when U.S. dominance was nearly absolute; in the decade that followed, when the international community, including most of our allies, became more reluctant to comply with U.S. desires; and finally, when the United States found itself in an intractable situation from which it had no viable exit strategy. Iraq did invade Kuwait; Iraq sometimes cooperated with weapons inspectors and sometimes not; Iraq sometimes instituted measures to lessen the impact of sanctions and sometimes not. However, it is also the case that the Security Council's policies were not simply a response to Iraq's actions, in conformity with international law. The fundamental decisions made by the Security Council and implemented by the Secretariat were at every turn shaped by the United States—many critical resolutions were drafted by the United States, and it was the United States who lined up the votes; although all of the permanent members had veto power, the United States used its veto far more than any other nation, including Britain, its most vocal ally. Within the operation of the 661 Committee, there was no other nation that was as dominant as the United States in shaping the committee's procedures, preventing urgently needed humanitarian goods from entering Iraq, undermining transparency, and blocking attempts at reform.

With the Security Council no longer paralyzed by the Cold War and with no other nation in a position to challenge the U.S. dominance, it was possible for the United States to pursue a project that would have the imprimatur of international governance as well as the mandatory participation of every member state of the UN. I am not suggesting that Iraq's invasion of Kuwait did not merit a response from international institutions. But there have been many acts of aggression and threats to peace in the history of the Security Council, and none were subject to the devastation of comprehensive measures, first in the form of a massive indiscriminate bombing campaign, then the strangulation of nearly the entire economy for over a decade. Directly or indirectly, that was the doing of the United States.

While these measures were concerned with Iraq, they also have a great deal to say about the shift in the relationship of the United States to the UN. Where the United States had often been marginalized and castigated within the General Assembly, and for forty years had been largely frustrated and paralyzed within the Security Council, in 1990 the United States was quite suddenly able to effectively commandeer the Council for any project it wished; and because Chapter VII measures require the participation of all member states, obtain the compliance of the rest of the world as well. And while the sanctions regime was imposed with the authorization of the Security Council, pursuant to the Charter, in fact the U.S. agenda, in critical aspects, was substituted for, and overrode, the decisions of the Council and the Charter.

In August 1990, when Iraq invaded Kuwait, the Security Council demanded that Iraq withdraw. At that point the U.S. position was consistent with the rest of the Council's and very much in accordance with Chapter VII of the Charter. A few months later, after the Gulf War, the Security Council resolutions required that Iraq submit to monitoring and partial disarmament. The Council's resolutions never demanded the removal of Saddam Hussein from power. To the contrary, many of the resolutions regarding Iraq reiterated the Council's commitment to Iraq's sovereignty. The United States, however, consistently maintained that the sanctions would not be lifted as long as Saddam Hussein was in power and until he was replaced by someone acceptable to the United States. Through the reverse veto the United States was able to impose its own conditions and maintain the sanctions indefinitely despite the opposition in the Council. While the United States insisted that its policies were in the service of international law, the preoccupation with regime change belied this. Whether in the U.S. administrations or in Congress, whether by Democrats or Republicans, it seems that what received not even fleeting consideration in the U.S. policy-making process was that such a demand was impermissible under international law; that one of the fundamental precepts of the UN Charter and international law is that one nation cannot determine the political leadership of another; that such action is aggression in one of its clearest forms; and that by substituting this agenda—regime change—for what was legitimately mandated by the Security Council, the United States fundamentally compromised the legality of the sanctions and the legitimacy of the Council.

While the United States consistently justified its policies in terms of preventing Iraq from developing weapons or threatening its neighbors, the U.S. policy went well beyond any rational concern with security. There was an elaborate architecture of policies that found a dozen other ways to simply do gratuitous harm that had not the least relation to the threat Iraq might have posed to its neighbors or to anyone else. This was apparent simply in the massive quantities of humanitarian goods that the United States unilaterally prevented Iraq from importing. As of July 2002, Iraq had received only about $20 billion in goods over the six years of the Oil-for-Food Programme, and by any standards was characterized by extreme poverty. Iraq could have had 25 percent more imports, were it not for the fact that the United States at that time was blocking over $5 billion of urgently needed goods. For thirteen years the United States unilaterally blocked nearly everything related to electricity, telecommunications, and transportation and blocked much of what was needed for agriculture and housing construction, even some equipment and materials necessary for health care and food preparation. Britain occasionally objected to goods, but the United States was much more extreme, blocking about twenty times more goods than Britain. Almost no one else on the Security Council vetoed humanitarian imports to Iraq. In the end, the holds were so extensive that the total goods Iraq legally imported under the Oil-for-Food Programme came to only $204 per person per year for all goods, including food, medicine, and the reconstruction of the infrastructure, or about one-half the per capita income of the poorest countries in the world.

Ironically, where the United States accused the Iraqi government of acting with incomprehensible perversity, such as failing to order needed medicines, it turns out that in many cases it was the U.S. positions that were incomprehensible and perverse, such as objecting to Iraq's import

233

of antibiotics and child vaccines. While in theory there were humanitarian exemptions in place to protect the civilian population, in fact the United States—sometimes with others, but often acting unilaterally—used procedural devices and political leverage to undermine them. These practices were in place from the beginning of the sanctions regime, when the United States invoked its extreme (and minority) interpretation of Resolution 661 to block Iraq from importing any food for its citizens for eight months. In 1991 and 1992, in the face of protests from the majority of Security Council members, the United States fought aggressively to prevent the articulation of clear criteria for approval of humanitarian goods. In the end, all that emerged was a "gentlemen's agreement" to "look favorably" on goods for health care, agriculture, foodstuffs, water treatment, and education. From that point on there were constant disputes as the United States vetoed many of these goods again and again, regardless of the agreement.

When the Security Council prohibited Iraq from importing goods "for industrial use," the United States interpreted this in the most extreme way possible: Iraq could buy finished clothing, but not sewing thread, because that was an "input to industry." Because Iraq was permitted to buy only finished products, Iraq lost the benefit of the value added in production while its own labor and manufacturing plants lay idle. These measures went well beyond any rational concern about dual-use goods or the use of Iraqi industry to rebuild its military.

Once the Oil-for-Food Programme began, giving Iraq a legal way to raise funds for imports, the United States consistently took measures to compromise Iraq's oil production and oil sales. Although industry experts retained by the UN reported time and again that Iraq's oil industry was in a "lamentable state" and badly needed equipment and repairs, the United States consistently prevented Iraq from obtaining the needed equipment, sometimes blocking even the most basic and standard equipment used in the industry, claiming possible military use. When UN staff found that Iraq was receiving illicit payments from oil purchasers, the United States and Britain responded with "retroactive pricing," requiring purchasers to sign blind contracts without knowing the price they were then committed to pay. This went well beyond merely curtailing any kickbacks. The U.S. and British pricing policy caused the collapse of Iraqi oil sales and nearly bankrupted the Oil-for-Food Programme as billions of dollars in humanitarian import contracts were cancelled or went unfunded.

While the United States claimed that Iraq was deliberately buying shoddy goods with Oil-for-Food funds, the Iraqi government in fact repeatedly asked to include commercial protections that would have ensured that imports met quality standards. It was not Iraq that deliberately purchased poor goods; it was the United States that opposed measures that would have provided quality assurances for Iraq's imports.

The sheer arbitrariness and unpredictability of the approval process constituted impediments in themselves. For years, when vendors submitted contracts for approval the majority were denied, with no stated criteria for approval and no reason given for the denial. Throughout the sanctions regime, as public pressure grew and there was increasing documentation of the crisis by nongovernmental organizations (NGOs) and the UN's humanitarian agencies, there were numerous attempts at reform, to implement transparent procedures and consistent standards to streamline the flow of goods. The United States resisted each of these in turn. When the 661 Committee implemented the "no-objection" procedure, requiring each nation to file its objection within forty-eight hours, the United States responded by simply filing blanket objections immediately, to nearly everything. Later on, when the "green list" was put in place, the United States fought strenuously to minimize its scope. On the occasions when the United States publicly agreed to transparent or streamlined procedures, behind the scenes the United States flatly refused to implement them.

Throughout the sanctions regime, U.S. practices were extreme and harsh, and often unilateral, going well beyond the mandate of the Security Council's resolutions, and well beyond the will of the rest of the Council members. The Security Council resolutions required the elimination of Iraq's weapons of mass destruction (WMD). However, the goal of the United States was the elimination of Iraq's *capacity* to produce WMD. While the production of nuclear weapons requires a large and sophisticated production facility, the production of biological and chemical weapons, or at least some of their components, can take place in nothing more than a college chemistry lab or in manufacturing facilities for things like fertilizers and pesticides. To eliminate a nation's *capacity* to produce biological and chemical weapons means eliminating all science education above the secondary school level, eliminating the capacity to produce yogurt and cheese, or, as Major von Tersch would have it, eliminating eggs, because egg yolks could possibly be used as a medium in which to grow viruses, which in turn could possibly be used for biological weapons.

235

Any industrialized nation relies continually on manufacturing processes that could possibly be converted to produce some aspect of a biological or chemical weapon. To eliminate this capacity, as opposed to the weapons themselves, would literally require reducing a nation to the most primitive possible condition and keeping it in those circumstances in perpetuity. That was not at all the policy adopted by the Security Council, which required only that Iraq be subject to partial disarmament and monitoring, but it was the policy of the United States.

The U.S. positions were so extreme they conflicted even with the judgment of international weapons inspectors. This was evident in the "1051 disagreements," where the United States invoked Security Council Resolution 1051 to block goods to which even the United Nations Monitoring, Verification and Inspection Commission (UNMOVIC) had no objection. At the same time, when it was politically convenient, the United States allowed goods that had long been decried as "WMD" or dual use, such as the occasion when the United States lifted its objections to China's sale of fiber-optic cables, which had a clear military use, to secure China's vote. This further undermined the credibility of the U.S. claim that its very extreme practices were grounded in a principled commitment to security and international law.

The deliberate and systematic nature of the U.S. policy was evident above all in the redundancy. The water treatment system was compromised first by the lack of equipment and chemicals for water purification; but if Iraq had somehow been able to produce or smuggle those, the water system would then have been compromised by the lack of electrical power, because electrical generators and related equipment had been bombed, and because the replacement equipment was blocked by the United States. If Iraq had been somehow able to generate sufficient electricity, then the clean water could not have been distributed because the bombings had caused so much breakage in the water pipes, and the United States then blocked the importation of water pipes. If Iraq had somehow been able to smuggle or manufacture water pipes, it did not have the bulldozers or cranes necessary to install them because those were blocked as well. The same was true in every area: agricultural production, manufacturing of basic goods, transportation, communication systems, education, and medical care. It was this terrible redundancy that ensured that nothing the Iraqi government did, that no amount of ingenuity or adaptation or targeting of resources, could have restored conditions fit to sustain human life.

While the humanitarian damage of the sanctions gradually received more international attention over the course of a dozen years, what received far greater attention, shortly after the invasion of Iraq in 2003, were the accusations of improprieties within the Oil-for-Food Programme. The U.S. Congress held dozens of hearings, and massive investigations were conducted by the Government Accountability Office, the Duelfer group, and a UN committee led by Paul Volcker. But in the end, there was little justification for the broad condemnation of the UN's program management. At the same time, there was little recognition that the United States had played a role in the bulk of the illicit trade that had taken place. Most of the illicit funds involved smuggling, unrelated to the Oil-for-Food Programme; and most of the smuggling concerned Jordan and Turkey, which the United States had explicitly protected. While there were illicit oil surcharges for a short time, it was UN staff—the oil overseers—who caught it almost immediately. The remainder involved kickbacks on import contracts. On dozens of occasions, UN staff notified the 661 Committee of pricing irregularities that could signal kickbacks. On none of these occasions did any member—including the United States—choose to block the contract in response.

The U.S. Internal Process

The policy of the U.S. government on Iraq sanctions was driven overwhelmingly by the U.S. administrations, with Congress playing only a marginal role. For the most part there was no substantive difference in the policies of the first Bush administration, the two terms of Clinton's administration, or the second Bush administration prior to September 2001. From the end of the Persian Gulf War in 1991 until September 2001, all three administrations adopted a policy of containment, which included strangling Iraq's economy in every possible way, at every juncture. By the late 1990s, when there was growing domestic protest within the United States, the State Department responded with greater efforts in public relations, but there was no substantive change in its actual policy.

The U.S. policy was in every sense a national policy, not a partisan one. The U.S. government's position was the same, regardless of whether the administration was Democratic or Republican, and regardless of whether Congress was controlled by Democrats or Republicans. However severe the humanitarian impact was, while a handful of members of Congress were outspoken, Congress as a body did nothing to press for measures that would require the administration to incorporate humanitarian concerns in its practices. Congress' lack of interest was in part because the mechanics of the sanctions regime all took place within the executive branch, and because the sanctions were seen as Security Council measures over which the United States had no control. But it was also the case that, as a body, Congress simply did not care. There was great involvement in the two decisions to go to war, in 1990 and 2003; considerable interest in whether Iraq was being disarmed; and an ongoing preoccupation with achieving regime change. But with the exception of a handful of senators and congressmen, there were few in Congress who showed any substantial interest in the humanitarian impact of the sanctions, or the role of the U.S. government, however extreme the impact was and however extensively it was documented.

Within the three administrations, while the overall policy remained largely unchanged for more than a decade, the particular decisions were made within a process that made it difficult to attribute responsibility or to even identify what the decision-making standards were. This was in part because the process was so diffuse. There were some sixty people involved in the process, from half a dozen different agencies. There were technical experts who analyzed the possible military uses of import items, ranging from pickup trucks to laundry detergent. But these technical reviewers were only analyzing, not deciding. The political officers, in turn, were not equipped to second-guess a biochemist's analysis of how particular chemicals could be used, and for the most part the political officers simply implemented the findings of the technical experts. There was no one in the U.S. process charged with evaluating the humanitarian impact, and when the UN agencies reported on the urgency of the humanitarian needs, their recommendations were routinely disparaged and dismissed.

Despite statements by State Department officials evincing their deep concern for the innocent Iraqi people, the fact is that the humanitarian cost was not a factor at any point in the decision-making process. In the end, it appears that the only factors that affected U.S. decision making were embarrassment and political pressure, either within the UN or in the media. This was apparent when the United States relented and allowed Iraq to import child vaccines after scathing criticism in the press and when the State Department rejected von Tersch's recommendation to block Iraq from importing eggs, something that would certainly have made a laughingstock of the United States within the Security Council.

The moral claim of the United States—that it was punishing a wrongdoer—was undermined as well by the consistent practice of equating Saddam Hussein with Iraq; by embracing the notion that depriving an entire population of plywood, telephones, light switches, and glue was a good way of punishing Saddam, and bringing about his downfall. Perhaps U.S. policymakers at some level justified this collective punishment by some notion of collective responsibility: the population as a whole permitted Saddam to remain in power, so there was at least tacit approval. But that was not true; there were numerous attempted coups and uprisings, all of which were brutally repressed. Perhaps the reasoning was that if Iraqis really wanted to signal their disapproval of the regime, they would leave the country. And in fact many did—there was a massive exodus of those who could afford to leave or had friends or families abroad who could take them in. But of course most Iraqis could not leave, for many reasons, and that did not signal their support of the regime, only the paucity of choices available to them.

While the United States framed its actions within the UN in terms of respect and enforcement of international law, in fact these measures, as shaped by the United States, systematically overrode many of the basic principles of international humanitarian law. Many have maintained that the magnitude of the suffering was such that the sanctions regime could properly be termed genocidal, among them Denis Halliday, the former humanitarian coordinator for the UN in Iraq. UN officials, as well as consultants and NGOs, documented the humanitarian impact of the sanctions from the beginning, starting with the Secretary-General's envoys in 1991. Once the humanitarian impact of the sanctions was apparent, scholars and activists began questioning their legitimacy. While there was ongoing debate for many years over the number of deaths caused by the sanctions, from early on it was clear that the human damage was considerable. Whether the number of child deaths was 200,000 or 500,000, the magnitude of the harm was enormous, and it was always known to be enormous. This was certainly true of the members of the Security Council, who received internal reports of the humanitarian situation frequently, from numerous agencies and envoys and from their own intelligence sources, as well as simply knowing what happens to an industrialized society if the electrical grid collapses and what happens to the health of a population if water and sewage are left untreated. All of this painted a consistent picture of terrible suffering.

It may well be that the international law questions will never be addressed by any judicial tribunal. It seems that no domestic or international criminal court would have jurisdiction to pursue a prosecution against a government for its actions within the Security Council. Yet if the standards articulated by international law were to apply here, then it would seem that the official policy of three U.S. administrations, and the acts of dozens of U.S. officials, were indeed tantamount to war crimes, even if there is no venue for prosecution; were indeed violations of human rights, even if they did not quite constitute crimes against humanity; were atrocities, even if these atrocities did not quite constitute genocide. The fact that these policies are unlikely to be examined in any judicial venue does not mean they are consistent with the norms of international human rights, much less that they are morally acceptable. It means only that the existing framework for international law is inadequate to address this particular kind of atrocity.

The sanctions regime on Iraq, as it was designed, interpreted, and enforced by the United States, evinced a willingness to see appalling things done in the name of security, and this requires us to consider that measures equally damaging and indiscriminate may be pursued in other circumstances, whether in the name of stopping aggression, drug trafficking, or terrorism. We must come to grips with the perversity of this. It is simply not good enough to say that atrocities committed for the right reasons, or by respected international organizations, are not really atrocities after all.

It is an odd thing, but it is the case that atrocities are neither morally nor empirically obvious. In this instance the humanitarian disaster that was brought about through the demands and devices of a superpower, using the vehicle of international governance, tells us something about how indecent policies can be not only legitimated but can be made invisible. In the case of the Iraq sanctions, this was very much what the United States sought, through the closed meetings of the 661 Committee and the restrictions on the circulation of its minutes and documents, in the attacks on the credibility of UN reports that documented the deterioration of living conditions, and through the obscurity of the process by which the United States prevented humanitarian goods from entering Iraq.

The genuine issues of the legality and morality of the sanctions were suppressed as well when U.S. administrations invoked the language of evil and monsters—"Saddam Hussein is just like Hitler." Within such a framework, there was little tolerance for hearing about the mixed actions

240

of the evil state—that it could do a fairly good job of providing food rations, even if there was also violent retribution against political enemies. There was even less tolerance for hearing about the mixed results of our state, the good one—that our measures to achieve security in fact caused suffering to an entire people. It was in the service of this intolerance that the United States sought to sanitize information, to discredit UN officials who spoke critically, and to use the frightening and vague language of "dual use" and "WMD" rather than stating plainly that the United States was unwilling for Iraqis to have refrigerators.

Because the U.S. government saw the situation in such stark terms, it in a sense painted itself into a corner. If Saddam was evil, then rehabilitation was impossible, and the only acceptable outcome was removal, which was not possible short of a full-scale military invasion. On the other hand, if the United States were to concede that compliance with the disarmament protocol in fact entitled Iraq to have the sanctions lifted, then such a position would have run counter to the U.S. claim that Saddam Hussein was irredeemably monstrous.

Ironically, while the United States could see no viable way out, Iraq was in the same position. While the U.S. government frequently said, "All Iraq has to do is comply," that was belied by the continual support for coup attempts and uprisings, the continual statements insisting on regime change, and the Iraq Liberation Act, which formalized that policy. Given the repeated U.S. commitment to regime change, Hussein and the Iraqi government had no incentive at all to comply with the demands made upon it. The fact that another nation was explicitly committed to seeing Hussein removed from power by any means possible would have given him little reason to cooperate with those forces that sought his political (or personal) elimination. While the U.S. government often portrayed Saddam Hussein as someone who functioned outside the bounds of both reason and morality, in fact it might have made more sense to view him as a rational decision maker in the face of an intransigent force committed to his destruction.

In a sense, Hussein's situation, in regard to both the problem of extrication and the calculus of decision making, paralleled that of the U.S. government. In the early 1990s, as the humanitarian situation in Iraq deteriorated, the United States struggled to contain the growing criticism and sustain the sanctions while waiting for the Iraqi regime to finally collapse. When it did not, despite the regime's increasingly precarious control, the United States agreed to the Oil-for-Food Programme as a concession that made it possible to keep the sanctions in place. During the same period, Hussein was struggling to retain control in the face of coup attempts, defections, and the growing desperation of the Iraqi population while calculating that the United States could not keep the sanctions in place much longer in the face of the international outcry against them. By 1995, when the sanctions were still in place despite five years of horrendous decline in living conditions, the Iraqi government agreed to the Oil-for-Food Programme as at least a measure that would prevent actual famine and an even worse collapse in living standards.

In the end, there were no options for Saddam Hussein that were both viable and acceptable. Perhaps for the duration of the decade-plus sanctions regime he continued to hope that the United States would somehow just relent and go away; from what is known of him, simply handing over power was not an option. Likewise, while the United States hoped that regime change would end the stalemate, it was clear from the beginning that that was quite unlikely; at the same time, conceding defeat and withdrawing was never a possibility.

While both the U.S. and Iraqi governments made concessions to hold on to their diminishing influence and retain their political alliances, it was also the case that when it came to implementing these agreements, both did whatever was in their power to undermine them at every turn. For Iraq, there were the well-known cat-and-mouse games with the weapons inspectors and the refusal to provide the full access to weapons sites and personnel that it had promised. For the United States, it was agreeing to the no-objection rule, the fast-track procedure, the elimination of the ceiling on oil sales, and the recommendations of the humanitarian panel, while at the same time implementing procedures to systematically undermine each of these.

For both Saddam Hussein and the U.S. government, one critical feature of the decision-making calculus was the same: it was that humanitarian needs, however extensive, urgent, and certain, were consistently subordinated to the state's overriding political agenda—for the United States, to achieve containment or regime change; for Saddam Hussein, to preserve his power and outlast the containment.

Having garnered control of the predominant institution of global governance, the United States showed no wisdom in its use. The tactics came easily enough: the closed meetings, the arm-twisting for votes, the endless delays, the opaque bureaucratic procedures. But at the same time,

242

the United States could not see a way out of its own dilemma, and this then became the UN's dilemma as well.

As the criticism grew, there is no sign that anyone in the U.S. administration, and only a tiny handful within Congress, actually took it to heart—actually questioned the sanity and legality of reducing an entire civilization to a preindustrial state, of bankrupting an entire nation for the purpose of containing one tyrannical man. Instead, however broad and insistent the objections were, however badly support was eroding, the situation was seen by the United States solely as a political problem, for which the only possible response was, "What concessions must be made at the margins, to maintain the policy as aggressively as possible?" As the criticism grew and the suffering continued on a massive scale, the U.S. administration stubbornly saw itself as alone in its moral leadership, never grasping the significance or thoroughness of its isolation and marginality. It seems that the United States simply could not see its policies the way the rest of the world did: not just Arab nations, or France or Russia, but nearly everyone—the General Assembly, NGOs, UNMOVIC, the UN's human rights rapporteur, every UN humanitarian agency, and nearly every member of the Security Council. The U.S. government continued to insist that it did nothing to contribute to the deterioration of living conditions, as though it were not completely transparent to every other nation involved in the process that the United States was doing precisely that. The U.S. government insisted that others share its view that Saddam was irredeemably evil, even as the rest of the world remembered perfectly well when the United States found Saddam's appalling acts to be perfectly tolerable.

U.S. officials did not act with the deliberate cruelty that is envisioned by international human rights law. It was not a hatred of Iraqis that led U.S. officials to act as they did; it was the decision that the Iraqis would bear the cost of the United States' intractable political dilemma. This particular catastrophe did not require actual hatred; it required only the capacity of U.S. officials to believe their own rationales, however implausible they might have been, and that there be no venue in which to challenge their reasoning as casuistic and disingenuous. Madeline Albright's memorable gaffe in response to the question "500,000 children—is it worth it?"—which she regretted for years—was always and only a public relations error. It made no difference that she and other State Department officials, from that point on, vigorously insisted that they cared deeply about Iraqi children. The more accurate answer, regardless of the public rhetoric, was: of course it was worth it. Blocking glue, water pipes, water tankers, thermos flasks, ambulance radios, irrigation equipment—all of this was worth it because the negligible imaginary possibility that these could be turned to nefarious purposes always outweighed the collapse of the Iraqi health system, Iraq's frantic efforts to increase agricultural production, the disappearance of Iraq's middle class, the hundreds of thousands of tons of untreated sewage that went daily into Iraq's rivers. However U.S. and British officials viewed their intent, however insistently they dismissed any possibility of their own guilt, they systematically ensured the conditions that would make Iraq unable to provide decent conditions for human life; and for all the blame directed at Saddam Hussein, it was the U.S. government that ensured that it would be simply impossible for anyone, including Saddam Hussein, to counter these measures with any effectiveness.

It is only the type of intent that prevents the Security Council measures, as shaped by the United States, from properly being labeled genocide or extermination. It is not the absence of intent, in the sense of mistake or ignorance. Certainly the U.S. policies were knowing, deliberate, systematic, planned; and the fact that this is not quite sufficient to show culpability tells us more about the limitations of international law than about the good will or good faith of the actors. It is profoundly troubling that planning and deliberation and awareness of the obvious are not sufficient; there must be the explicit desire to destroy. But it is almost always the case that this will be concealed or denied, in part because the intent of government officials will be so fundamentally shaped by a hunger to believe oneself to be good. Elizabeth Anscombe famously said, "If someone really thinks, in advance, that it is open to question whether such an action as procuring the judicial execution of the innocent should be quite excluded from consideration—I do not want to argue with him: he shows a corrupt mind."[1] No moral discussion is possible with one who has a corrupt mind. But, of course, that is the problem: it is so very unlikely that anyone does not. Those who formulated the U.S. policies were not shallow or ill-educated or coerced, nor driven by hatred for Iraqis or any impulse that they or we would identify as genocidal. Nevertheless, every act implementing this policy was knowing and deliberate and the consequences were known and recognized, even when they were contained within elaborate denials of responsibility.

In 1946 the German philosopher Karl Jaspers wrote:

We see the feelings of moral superiority and we are frightened: he who feels absolutely safe from danger is already on the way to fall victim to it. The German fate could provide all others with experience. If only they would understand this experience! We are no inferior race. Everywhere people have similar qualities . . . We may well worry over the victors' self-certainty.[2]

Jaspers was right to be worried about moral self-certainty. Above all, this study tells us much about the capacity of anyone, including those acting in the name of human rights and international law, to suspend both rational judgment and the capacity to recognize obvious moral truths when called upon to do so. In the end, history, and the rest of the world, will not judge the United States by its rhetoric or even by the intention of its leaders, but by its policies and its acts, and the magnitude of the suffering they have wrought.

I. THE POLICY OF CONTAINMENT

1. United Nations, Commission on Human Rights, "Question of the Violation of Human Rights and Fundamental Freedoms in Any Part of the World: Report of the Special Rapporteur on the Situation of Human Rights in Iraq, Mr. Andreas Mavrommatis," E/CN.4/2001/42, January 16, 2001, para. 12; see also United Nations, Commission on Human Rights, "Question of the Violation of Human Rights and Fundamental Freedoms in Any Part of the World: Report of the Special Rapporteur, Andreas Mavrommatis, on the Situation of Human Rights in Iraq," E/CN.4/2002/44, March 15, 2002, para. 87.

2. United Nations, Commission on Human Rights, "The Adverse Consequences of Economic Sanctions on the Enjoyment of Human Rights: Working Paper Prepared by Mr. Marc Bossuyt," E/CN.4/Sub.2/2000/33 (June 21, 2000).

3. United Nations, Sub-Commission on Human Rights, "Humanitarian Situation of the Iraqi Population, Sub-Commission on Human Rights Decision 2000/112," E/CN.4/2000/L.11/Add.2, August 18, 2000.

4. United Nations, "Convention on the Prevention and Punishment of the Crime of Genocide," Article 2; Rome Statute of the International Criminal Court, Article 6.

5. Neta C. Crawford, "Trump Card or Theater? An Introduction to Two Sanctions Debates," in *How Sanctions Work: Lessons from South Africa,* ed. Neta C. Crawford and Audie Klotz (New York: St. Martin's Press, 1999).

6. Johan Galtung, "On the Effects of International Economic Sanctions: With Examples from the Case of Rhodesia," *World Politics* 19, no. 3 (April 1967).

7. Gary Clyde Hufbauer, Jeffrey J. Schott, and Kimberly Ann Elliott, eds., *Economic Sanctions Reconsidered,* 2nd ed. (Washington, DC: Institute for International Economics, 1990).

8. Robert A. Pape, "Why Economic Sanctions Do Not Work," *International Security* 22, no. 2 (1997), p. 93.

9. "We began to see that sanctions are sometimes used (as in Iraq) as a stage or prelude to military action." Jack T. Patterson, "The Political and Moral Appropriateness of Sanctions," in *Economic Sanctions: Panacea or Peacebuilding in a Post–Cold War World?* edited by David Cortright and George A. Lopez (Boulder, CO: Westview Press, 1995), p. 90.

10. Ibid.

11. Andy Pasztor, "U.S. Sees Indications that Sanctions Are Seriously Hurting Iraq's Military," *Wall Street Journal,* October 22, 1990.

12. Edward Cody, "Iraq Feels Losses from Sanctions," *Washington Post,* October 21, 1990.

13. Joel Brinkley, "Iraq Rations Fuel as U.N. Sanctions Hinder Refineries," *New York Times,* October 19, 1990.

14. Peter Riddell, "US Believes Iraq May Be Able to 'Ride Out' Economic Sanctions," *Financial Times,* December 4, 1990.

15. George Lardner Jr. and R. Jeffrey Smith, "Iraq Sanctions Seen Working Slowly," *Washington Post,* November 24, 1990.

16. Kimberly Elliott, Gary Hufbauer, and Jeffrey Schott, "The Big Squeeze: Why the Sanctions on Iraq Will Work," *Washington Post,* December 9, 1990. Gary Hufbauer gave similar testimony at a hearing of the Senate Foreign Relations Committee on December 4, 1990.

17. U.S. Senate, Committee on Foreign Relations, "U.S. Policy in the Persian Gulf," Hearing on December 5, 1990, 101st Cong., 2nd sess., p. 122.

18. R. Jeffrey Smith, "Capitol Hill Hearings Seem to Be Setback for Bush's Policy," *Washington Post,* December 1, 1990.

19. U.S. Senate, Committee on Armed Services, "Crisis in the Persian Gulf Region: U.S. Policy Options and Implications," Hearing on November 27, 1990, 101st Cong., 2nd sess., p. 115.

20. U.S. Senate, Committee on Foreign Relations, "U.S. Policy in the Persian Gulf," Hearing on December 4, 1990, 101st Cong., 2nd sess.

21. U.S. House of Representatives, Committee on Armed Services, December 5, 1990, 101st Cong., 2nd sess., pp. 112–113, 115.

22. Robert L. Koenig, "Gephardt to Bush: Let Sanctions Work," *St. Louis Post-Dispatch,* January 4, 1991.

23. Walter Pincus and Thomas B. Edsall, "Debate in Congress Reshuffles Disparate Democrats," *Washington Post,* January 11, 1991.

24. U.S. Senate, Committee on Armed Services, "Crisis in the Persian Gulf Region: U.S. Policy Options and Implications," Hearing of the Senate Armed Services Committee, December 3, 1990, 101st Cong., 2nd sess., p. 681.

25. Brinton Whitall, "Sanctions Just May Avert War with Iraq," *New York Times,* December 23, 1990.

26. Robert F. Drinan, "Sanctions Not Yet Tried and Found Wanting," *National Catholic Reporter,* December 21, 1990.

27. William C. Wilbur, "U.S. Must Give Sanctions against Iraq Time to Work," *St. Petersburg Times,* January 7, 1991.

28. George Will, "Sanctions Preferable to Bombarding Iraq," *St. Louis Post-Dispatch,* November 21, 1990.

29. Tim Harper, "Give Iraq Sanctions Time to Work, 65% Say," *Toronto Star,* November 28, 1990.

30. Author's interview with David Welch, former senior State Department official, March 10, 2006.

31. Madeleine Albright, *Madam Secretary* (New York: Miramax, 2003). pp. 275, 287.

32. United Nations, "Report to the Secretary-General Dated 15 July 1991 on Humanitarian Needs in Iraq Prepared by a Mission Led by the Executive Delegate of the Secretary-General for Humanitarian Assistance in Iraq" (Aga Khan Report)" S/22799, para. 26.

33. Kenneth Pollack, *The Threatening Storm* (New York: Random House, 2002), p. 61.

34. Sarah Graham-Brown, "War and Sanctions: Cost to Society and Toll on Development," in *The Future of Iraq,* edited by John Calabrese (Washington, DC: Middle East Institute, 1997), p. 36.

35. Pollack, *The Threatening Storm,* p. 75.

36. Economist Intelligence Unit, "Country Report, Iraq," No. 1 (London: Economist Intelligence Unit, 1996), pp. 17–19; *Middle East Economic Survey,* January 8, 1996, p. A8.

37. Nicholas Arons, "U.S.-Supported Iraqi Opposition," *Foreign Policy in Focus* 6, no. 10 (April 2001).

38. Pollack, *The Threatening Storm.* p. 68.

39. Ibid.

40. Ibid., p. 71.

41. Ibid., p. 75.

42. Ibid., p. 76.

43. Kenneth Katzman, "Iraq: U.S. Efforts to Change the Regime" (Washington, DC: Congressional Research Service, March 22, 2002), p. 4.

44. Ibid.

45. See the accounts of this tension in Andrew Cockburn and Patrick Cockburn, *Out of the Ashes: The Resurrection of Saddam Hussein* (New York: HarperCollins, 1999); Bob Woodward, *Plan of Attack* (New York: Simon & Schuster, 2004); Albright, *Madam Secretary;* Nancy Soderberg, *The Superpower Myth: The Use and Misuse of American Might* (Hoboken, NJ: John Wiley and Sons, 2005); and Pollack, *The Threatening Storm.*

46. Pollack, *The Threatening Storm,* p. 57.

47. Ibid., p. 58.

48. Albright, *Madam Secretary,* p. 277.

49. Soderberg, *The Superpower Myth,* p. 211.

50. "It was widely believed that the administration [of George W. Bush] would make regime change in Iraq one of its first and highest priorities . . . However, prior to September 11, 2001, the Bush administration turned out to be not too dissimilar to the Clinton administration in its final days." Pollack, *The Threatening Storm,* pp. 104–105. "By the summer of 2001 it had become clear that the Bush administration was not going to pursue a radically new approach to Iraq . . . Instead the administration announced that while it would continue to study options for regime change, it would move ahead with an overhaul of the U.N. system known as 'smart sanctions.'" Pollack, *The Threatening Storm,* p. 106.

51. Pollack, *The Threatening Storm,* pp. 107–108.

52. Kenneth Katzman, "Iraq: U.S. Regime Change Efforts and Post-Saddam Governance" (Washington, DC: Congressional Research Service, March 7, 2006), p. 2.

53. "The United States has been attempting to change Iraq's regime since the 1991 Persian Gulf war, although achieving this goal was not declared policy until 1998. In November 1998, amid a crisis over UN weapons of mass destruction (WMD) inspections, the Clinton administration stated that the United States would seek not only to contain Iraq, but to promote a change of regime." Katzman, "Iraq: U.S. Efforts to Change the Regime," p. 1.

54. Katzman, "Iraq: U.S. Regime Change Efforts and Post-Saddam Governance," p. 2.

55. George Bush, "Remarks to the American Association of the Advancement of Science, February 15, 1991," in *Public Papers of the Presidents of the United States: Administration of George Bush, 1991* (Washington, DC: U.S. Government Printing Office, 1992), 1.145; Daniel Pipes, "Why America Can't Save the Kurds," *Wall Street Journal*, April 11, 1991, p. A15.

56. "Within days of the end of the Gulf War (February 28, 1991), opposition Shiite Muslims in southern Iraq and Kurdish factions in northern Iraq, emboldened by the regime's defeat and the hope of U.S. support, launched significant rebellions. The revolt in southern Iraq reached the suburbs of Baghdad." Katzman, "Iraq: U.S. Efforts to Change the Regime," p. 1.

57. Cockburn and Cockburn, *Out of the Ashes*, pp. 39–40.

58. "The uprisings materialized, but U.S. air cover never did . . . U.S. officials claimed that Bush favored a military coup within the regime, not a popular insurrection, which Washington feared would lead to a possible breakup of Iraq." Arons, "U.S.-Supported Iraqi Opposition."

59. "Many Iraqi Shiites blamed the United States for standing aside during Saddam's repression of the uprisings." Katzman, "Iraq: U.S. Regime Change Efforts and Post-Saddam Governance," p. 2.

60. "About two months after the failure of these uprisings, President George H. W. Bush reportedly sent Congress an intelligence finding that the United States would try to promote a military coup against Saddam Hussein . . . After a reported July 1992 coup failed, there was a U.S. decision to shift to supporting the Kurdish, Shiite, and other oppositionists." Katzman, "Iraq: U.S. Regime Change Efforts and Post-Saddam Governance," p. 2.

"[In May 1991], President Bush signed a presidential finding authorizing a covert action campaign to 'create the conditions for the removal of Saddam Hussein from power.' Five months later the administration increased the funding of this program from $15 million to $40 million." Pollack, *The Threatening Storm*, p. 59.

61. Congress more than doubled the budget for covert support to opposition groups from $15 million to $40 million for 1993. Elaine Sciolino, "Greater U.S. Effort Backed to Oust Iraqi," *New York Times*, June 2, 1992.

62. Arons, "U.S.-Supported Iraqi Opposition," p. 1.

63. The Iraq Liberation Act passed on October 7, 1998. In the House it passed by a vote of 360 to 38, and the Senate passed it unanimously.

64. United States Information Service, "Clinton on Signing the 'Iraqi Liberation Act of 1998,'" November 2, 1998.

65. In January 1999 Frank Ricciardone was named as the State Department's "Coordinator for the Transition in Iraq," the chief liaison with the opposition. Katzman, "Iraq: U.S. Efforts to Change the Regime," p. 5.

66. Pollack, *The Threatening Storm,* p. 95.

67. Total congressional funds appropriated were: FY1998, $10 million; FY1999, $8 million; FY2000, $10 million; FY2001, $25 million; FY2002, $25 million. Katzman, "Iraq: U.S. Efforts to Change the Regime," p. 13.

68. Cockburn and Cockburn, *Out of the Ashes,* p. 43.

69. Albright, *Madam Secretary,* p. 275.

70. Institute for Public Accuracy, "Iraq Sanctions: What's the Policy?" *Common Dreams Newswire,* November 12, 1998.

71. "To those who ask . . . how long we will insist that the international community's standards be met, our answer is—as long as it takes. We do not agree with the nations who argue that if Iraq complies with its obligations concerning weapons of mass destruction, sanctions should be lifted . . . Is it possible to [have peace] under Saddam Hussein? When I was a professor, I taught that you have to consider all possibilities. As Secretary of State, I have to deal with the realm of reality and probability. And the evidence is overwhelming that Saddam Hussein's intentions will never be peaceful." Madeleine Albright, "Preserving Principle and Safeguarding Stability: United States Policy toward Iraq," speech presented at Georgetown University, March 26, 1997.

72. Albright, *Madam Secretary,* p. 275.

73. Ibid.

74. United Nations, Security Council, Provisional Verbatim Record of the 3139th meeting, S/PV.3139, November 23, 1992, pp. 39–40.

75. United Nations, Security Council, Provisional Verbatim Record of the 3439th meeting, S/PV.3439, October 17, 1994, p. 3.

76. Claudia von Braunmühl, "Evaluating the Humanitarian Impact of Sanctions: Reflections on an Experience in 1995," paper presented at the Conference of the International Association for Contemporary Iraq Studies, London, September 2005, pp. 8–9.

2. HOW THE SANCTIONS WORKED

1. United Nations, Security Council Resolution 661 (1990), paragraph 3(c).

2. United Nations, Security Council, "Letter Dated 27 March 1999 from the Chairman of the Panels Established Pursuant to the Note by the President of the Security Council of 30 January 1999 (S/1999/100) Addressed to the President of the Security Council," S/1999/356, March 27, 1999, para. 11.

3. Ibid., para. 12.

4. Haris Gazdar and Athar Hussain, "Crisis and Response: A Study of the Impact of Economic Sanctions in Iraq" (London: Asia Research Centre, London School of Economics, December 1997), pp. 11–12.

5. Abbas Alnasrawi, *Iraq's Burdens: Oil, Sanctions, and Underdevelopment* (Westport, CT: Greenwood Press, 2002), p. 102.

6. Economist Intelligence Unit, "Country Profile: Iraq," 2002/2003, July 24, 2002.

7. UNICEF, "Iraq Watching Brief: Child Protection," prepared by Josi Salem-Pickartz, July 2003, p. 2.

8. Iraqi Economists Association, "Human Development Report: 1995" (Baghdad, 1995), p. 126.

9. Anthony H. Cordesman, *Iraq and the War of Sanctions* (Westport, CT: Praeger, 1999), p. xvi.

10. Barton Gellman, "Allied Air War Struck Broadly in Iraq; Officials Acknowledge Strategy Went Beyond Purely Military Targets," *Washington Post*, June 23, 1991.

11. Iraqi Economists Association, "Human Development Report: 1995," p. 66.

12. David M. Malone, *The International Struggle over Iraq: Politics in the UN Security Council, 1980–2005* (New York: Oxford University Press, 2006), p. 75.

13. U.S. Department of Energy, Energy Information Administration, "Iraq Country Analysis Brief," March 2002, http://www.mafhoum.com/press3/93E15.htm (accessed October 8, 2009).

14. United Nations, "Report to the Secretary-General on Humanitarian Needs in Kuwait and Iraq in the Immediate Post-crisis Environment by a Mission to the Area Led by Mr. Martti Ahtisaari, Under-Secretary-General for Administration and Management, Dated 20 March 1991," S/22366, annex (1991) (hereafter Ahtisaari Report), para 8.

15. United Nations, "Report to the Secretary-General Dated 15 July 1991 on Humanitarian Needs in Iraq Prepared by a Mission Led by the Executive Delegate of the Secretary-General for Humanitarian Assistance in Iraq" (hereafter Aga Khan Report), S/22788, annex (1991), para. 26.

16. United Nations, Security Council Resolution 705 (1991), para. 2.

17. Aga Khan Report, para. 29.

18. Paul Conlon, correspondence with the author, October 1, 2006.

19. Malone, *The International Struggle over Iraq*, p. 142n19.

20. United Nations, Security Council Resolution 661, para. 6.

21. Ibid., para. 6(a) and (b).

22. Sarah Graham-Brown, *Sanctioning Saddam: The Politics of Intervention in Iraq* (New York: I. B. Tauris, 1999), p. 262.

23. United Nations, Office of the Iraq Programme, "Oil-for-Food: About the Program," http://www.un.org/Depts/oip/background/chron.html (accessed July 15, 2009).

24. United Nations, General Assembly, Resolution 182, A/RES/46/182, December 19, 1991.

25. By February 2002, total international UN personnel came to 835, including 99 Cotecna and Saybolt inspection agents. The total number of national staff were 3,051. Statement by Benon V. Sevan at the informal consultations of the Security Council, February 26, 2002, http://www.un.org/Depts/oip/background/latest/bvs020226.html (accessed October 8, 2009).

26. Working Group established by the Independent Inquiry Committee, "The Impact of the Oil-for-Food Programme on the Iraqi People," September 7, 2005, p. 20.

27. United Nations, Security Council Resolution 986 (1995), para. 1.

28. In December 2000 the amount earmarked for Kuwait was reduced to 25 percent and the amount committed to the south/central area was increased to 59 percent. The amount earmarked for the UN's costs for disarmament and program administration was reduced to 3 percent. United Nations, Security Council Resolution 1330 (2000).

29. Gazdar and Hussain, "Crisis and Response," p. 8.

30. United Nations, Security Council Resolution 1153 (1998).

31. United Nations, Security Council Resolution 1284 (1999).

32. United Nations, Security Council Resolution 1284 (1999), para. 17.

33. United Nations, "Memorandum of Understanding between the Secretariat of the United Nations and the Government of Iraq on the Implementation of Security Council Resolution 986 (1995)," S/1996/356, May 20, 1996, Section VII; United Nations, Security Council Resolution 986, para. 11.

34. United Nations, Security Council Resolution 986, para. 1.

35. United Nations, Memorandum of Understanding, Annex II, para. 4.

36. Ibid.

37. See Thomas R. Stauffer, "Critical Review of UNCC Award for Lost Production and Lost Revenues," *Middle East Economic Survey* 44, no. 5 (2001).

38. United Nations, "UNSCOM: Chronology of Main Events," http://www.un.org/Depts/unscom/Chronology/chronology/htm.

39. United Nations Monitoring, Verification, and Inspection Commission (UNMOVIC), *Twelfth Quarterly Report of the Executive Chairman of the United Nations Monitoring, Verification and Inspection Commission in accordance with paragraph 12 of Security Council resolution 1284 (1999)*, S/2003/232, Annex, February 28, 2003.

40. Cordesman, *Iraq and the War of Sanctions*, p. xv.

41. Rear Admiral R. A. K. Taylor, 1991–1992; Vice-Admiral D. J. Katz, 1992–1994; Vice-Admiral J. S. Redd, 1994–1996; Vice-Admiral T. B. Fargo, 1996–1998; Vice-Admiral C. W. Moore Jr., 1998–2002; Vice-Admiral T. J. Keating, 2002–2003; Vice-Admiral D. C. Nichols, 2003. "Department of State Request for Information: Yearly Snapshot of the Multilateral Interception Force/Multinational Force," Central Command, U.S. Navy.

42. Sarah Graham-Brown, "No-Fly Zones: Rhetoric and Real Intentions," Middle East Research and Information Project, Press Information Note 49, February 20, 2001.

43. Manuelle Hurwitz and Patricia David, *The State of Children's Health in Pre-War Iraq* (London: Centre for Population Studies, London School of Hygiene and Tropical Medicine, 1992), p. 1. A WHO report found that in fact 90 percent of the population had access to safe water. World Health Organization, "The Health Conditions of the Population in Iraq since the Gulf Crisis" (March 1996), p. 3.

44. UNICEF, "Iraq Immunization, Diarrhoeal Disease, Maternal and Child-hood Mortality Survey." Evaluation Series no. 9 (Amman: UNICEF Regional Office for the Middle East and North Africa, 1990).

45. Hurwitz and David, *The State of Children's Health in Pre-War Iraq,* p. 15.

46. Peter L. Pellett, "Nutrition and Health in Iraq," *International Quarterly of Community Health Education* 17, no. 2 (1997–1998), p. 111.

47. World Health Organization, "The Health Conditions of the Population in Iraq since the Gulf Crisis," p. 9.

48. Cited in ibid., p. 4. "Calorie availability was 120% of actual requirements, nutritional deficiencies were at very low levels, while clinical disorders related to excessive and unbalanced consumption of food were increasingly encountered." Center for Economic and Social Rights, "Unsanctioned Suffering: A Human Rights Assessment of the United Nations Sanctions on Iraq" (New York: Center for Economic and Social Rights, 1996), p. 10.

49. UNICEF, "Situation Analysis of Children and Women in Iraq," April 30, 1998, p. 22.

50. World Health Organization, "The Health Conditions of the Population in Iraq since the Gulf Crisis," p. 3.

51. UNICEF, "Situation Analysis of Children and Women in Iraq," p. 7.

52. World Health Organization, "The Health Conditions of the Population in Iraq since the Gulf Crisis." p. 3. Ninety-seven percent of urban residents and 76 percent of rural residents had access to health care. UNICEF, "Situation Analysis of Children and Women in Iraq," p. 7.

53. Center for Economic and Social Rights, "Unsanctioned Suffering," p. 9.

54. UNICEF, "Situation Analysis of Children and Women in Iraq," pp. 8–9.

55. Graham-Brown, *Sanctioning Saddam,* p. 161.

56. Ibid.

57. UNICEF, "Situation Analysis of Children and Women in Iraq," p. 23.

58. International Federation of Red Cross and Red Crescent Societies, "World Disasters Report 1998," p. 100.

59. Graham-Brown, *Sanctioning Saddam,* p. 157.

60. Ibid., p. 158.

61. Alberto Ascherio et al., "Effect of the Gulf War on Infant and Child Mortality in Iraq," *New England Journal of Medicine* 327, no. 13 (1992). "The destruction of the supply of electrical power at the beginning of the war, with subsequent disruption of the electricity-dependent water and sewage systems, was probably responsible for the reported epidemics of gastrointestinal and other infections" (p. 935).

62. World Health Organization, "The Health Conditions of the Population in Iraq since the Gulf Crisis," p. 12.

63. Ahtisaari Report, para. 8.

64. Ibid., para. 37.

65. Aga Khan Report, para. 137.

66. Ibid., para. 14.

67. Ibid., para. 13.

68. Ibid., para. 28.

69. Ibid., para. 29.

70. Ibid., para. 30.

71. World Health Organization, "The Health Conditions of the Population in Iraq since the Gulf Crisis," p. 15.

72. "Iraq: Children, War and Sanctions," prepared by Eric Hoskins for UNICEF Baghdad, April 1993, p. 4.

73. Ibid., p. 14.

74. Ibid., p. 17.

75. Alnasrawi, *Iraq's Burdens*, p. 95.

76. United Nations, Food and Agriculture Organization, "Evaluation of Food and Nutrition Situation in Iraq, Terminal Statement" (Rome: Food and Agriculture Organization, 1993), p. 2.

77. Alnasrawi, *Iraq's Burdens*, p. 96,

78. United Nations, Food and Agriculture Organization, "Evaluation of Food and Nutrition Situation in Iraq," terminal statement prepared for the government of Iraq (Rome, 1995), p. 26.

79. UNICEF, "Situation Analysis of Children and Women in Iraq," p. 41.

80. Ibid., p. 32.

81. Ibid., pp. 32–33.

82. The degree to which the mortality rate of infants and of young children under age five rose during the sanctions was hotly disputed and highly politicized. Up through 1999, the Iraqi government, as well as critics of the sanctions, maintained that as many as a million children under age five had died as a result of the sanctions ("excess mortality"). However, opponents insisted that the data were unreliable for various reasons—any information coming from the Iraqi government was suspect, studies based on small sample sizes were questionable, and so on. Consequently, they maintained, it was not possible to tell how many children, if any, had died as a result of the sanctions. "No one seems to be able to agree on exactly how big the 'starvation' problem really is. UNICEF says that 4,500 Iraqi children die of malnutrition, starvation and disease every month; Iraq says 1.2 million people have died as a result of the embargo; a general UN report calculates that nearly one million Iraqi children suffer from malnutrition . . . Granted, none of these statistics is very rosy. But the discrepancies between them suggest there is really no reliable source of information about starving Iraqis." Editorial, *Washington Times*, December 5, 1997.

The collection of data regarding infant and child deaths was compromised by several factors. The Iraqi government was crippled in its capacity to perform the functions it had in the past, including gathering vital statistics. In addition, the usual reporting mechanisms were skewed for a variety of reasons. Because the hospitals were able to provide so little medical assistance, many Iraqis no longer came to the hospital for treatment, and deaths at home were not reported as consistently as deaths in the hospital. The ration system allotted food on the basis of the number of persons living in the household; if a child died the family had reason to withhold that information, in order to continue receiving the extra food.

However, despite the difficulties of data collection, several studies were done that tried to estimate how much child and infant mortality had risen during the sanctions period. In 1991, after the Persian Gulf War ended, a group of researchers based at Harvard University, the International Study Team, conducted a study that showed a sharp increase in child mortality. International Study Team, *Infant and Child Mortality and Nutritional Status of Iraqi Children after the Gulf Conflict* (Cambridge, MA: Center for Population and Development Studies, Harvard University, 1992). UN reports over the next several years showed growing malnutrition, deterioration in potable water, decline in health care, and other factors that correspond to increased child mortality. But many of the reports were partial or limited in various ways. In 1999 the Fourth Freedom Forum asked Richard Garfield, an epidemiologist, to look at the existing studies and articulate what, if anything, could be said with certainty about the excess mortality figures. Looking at several different sources of data, both from international agencies and from the Iraqi government, he concluded that between 1991 and 1998, it was likely that there were approximately 227,000 excess deaths of children under age five. Richard Garfield, "Morbidity and Mortality among Iraqi Children from 1990 through 1998: Assessing the Impact of the Gulf War and Economic Sanctions" (Goshen, IN and South Bend, IN: Fourth Freedom Forum and the Joan B. Kroc Institute for International Peace Studies at the University of Notre Dame, March 1999, http://www.fourthfreedom.org/Applications/cms.php?page_id=7).

Shortly after that, UNICEF released an extensive new study, based on new data collected in a national survey, in conjunction with Iraq's Ministry of Health. The UNICEF report found that infant mortality had more than doubled, from 47 deaths per thousand live births in the late 1980s to 107 deaths per thousand live births in the 1990s. Under age five mortality rates had more than doubled, from 56 per 1000 live births to 131 per thousand. UNICEF/Ministry of Health, "Child and Maternal Mortality Survey 1999: Preliminary Report," July 1999. UNICEF estimated that if the infant and child mortality patterns of the 1980s had continued without the intervention of the war and the sanctions, there would have been half a million fewer child deaths (http://www.fas.org/news/iraq/1999/08/irqu5est.pdf). The UNICEF report brought much of the controversy to a halt, and for some time the UNICEF figure of 500,000 for the eight-year period was widely used and carried considerable credibility. However, after the 2003 war in Iraq, there were other reports that revisited the dispute. A major study, called the "Iraq Living Conditions Survey," was done in 2004 by the United Nations Development Programme and the Fafo Institute for Applied International Studies, a Norwegian organization. Also in 2004, a "working group" was established to assess the impact of the Oil-for-Food Programme, in conjunction with the Volcker group (the Independent Inquiry Committee [IIC] established by the UN). Finally, there was a census done by the Iraqi government in 1997, from which the data became publicly available in 2005.

The IIC working group rejected the methodology of several of the prior studies and arrived at a very conservative conclusion: that excess child mortality from 1991 to 1995 totaled 45,000–68,000. For the period that followed, they maintained that there was no reliable estimate, although they expected that the rate would have gone down once the Oil-for-Food Programme came into operation. Independent Inquiry Commission into the United Nations Oil-for-Food Programme, "The Impact of the Oil-for-Food Programme on the Iraqi People," September 7, 2005, p. 53. Their estimates, in turn, were rejected on the grounds that the data on which *they* relied were questionable, whereas the studies the working group rejected were in fact based upon sound methods. John Blacker, Mohamed M. Ali, and Gareth Jones, "A Response to Criticism of Our Estimates of under-5 Mortality in Iraq, 1980–98," *Population Studies* 61, no. 1 (2007). Certainly the IIC working group's results are anomalous. In a review of all the major studies of this issue and their methodologies, Dyson argued that the IIC working group put far too much weight on the 1997 census data, which were quite flawed as a source of child mortality trends; for example, the surveys contained no information on dates of birth or dates of death. Tim Dyson, "Child Mortality in Iraq since 1990," *Economic and Political Weekly* 41, no. 42 (2006), p. 4493. He argued that there were no credible reasons to question the range of excess mortality generated by UNICEF, which was between 380,000 and 480,000 for the period of 1991–1998. Dyson, "Child Mortality in Iraq since 1990," p. 4495. Looking at the total body of research, Dyson noted that "the dominant picture is one of greatly elevated mortality between 1991 and 2003." He considered three counter-factuals: that the decline in child mortality from the 1970s and 1980s continued; that the child mortality rate at the end of the 1980s remained the same; and a mid-range. On this basis, he estimated under-5 excess mortality for the entire period of 1991 to 2003 was in the range of 670,000 to 880,000. Dyson, "Child Mortality in Iraq since 1990," p. 4495.

By the most conservative estimate, excess child mortality would be at least 100,000, while the majority of the studies conducted since 1991 have consistently placed the figure for the entire period somewhere between half a million and a million excess child deaths. The latter figures are far more consistent with the other information available concerning food availability and malnutrition, the continual shortages of water fit for human consumption, and the extreme deterioration of medical services. In this book I will assume that the number of excess child deaths over the course of the sanctions regime in Iraq was at least a half million.

83. Alnasrawi, *Iraq's Burdens,* p. 99.
84. Graham-Brown, *Sanctioning Saddam,* p. 187.
85. Ibid., p. 184.
86. Ibid., p. 182.
87. Ibid., p. 188.
88. Ibid.
89. Ibid., p. 190.

3. THE INFLUENCE OF THE UNITED STATES

1. In 1991 the Russian Federation took the seat held by the former Soviet Union.
2. United Nations, Charter, Art. 11.
3. Ibid., Arts. 39–42.

4. Ibid., Art. 25.

5. The Security Council has sought an advisory opinion only once since its inception: *Legal Consequences for States of the Continued Presence of South Africa in Namibia (South-West Africa) Notwithstanding Security Council Resolution 276 (1970), Advisory Opinion of 21 June 1971.*

6. United Nations, Charter, Art. 18.

7. See Samuel S. Kim, *The Quest for a Just World Order* (Boulder, CO: Westview Press, 1984), p. 217.

8. "On 21 March 1986, the Security Council President, making a 'declaration' and 'speaking on behalf of the Security Council,' stated that the Council members are 'profoundly concerned by the unanimous conclusion of the specialists that chemical weapons on many occasions have been used by Iraqi forces against Iranian troops . . . [and] the members of the Council strongly condemn this continued use of chemical weapons in clear violation of the Geneva Protocol of 1925 which prohibits the use in war of chemical weapons. The US voted against the issuance of this statement, and the UK, Australia, France, and Denmark abstained. However, the concurring votes of the other ten members of the Security Council ensured that this statement constituted the first criticism of Iraq by the Security Council. A similar Presidential statement was made on 14 May 1987, which noted that the Council was 'deeply dismayed' about the CW use against Iranian forces and civilians." Nathaniel Hurd and Glen Rangwala, "U.S. Diplomatic and Commercial Relationships with Iraq, 1980–2 August 1990," December 12, 2001, http://www.casi.org.uk/info/usdocs/usiraq80s90s.html (accessed October 12, 2009).

9. The United States was, for example, the principal architect of Security Council Resolution 661. Sarah Graham-Brown, *Sanctioning Saddam: The Politics of Intervention in Iraq* (New York: I. B. Tauris, 1999), p. 56.

10. Ibid., p. 347.

11. Phyllis Bennis wrote that:

Virtually every developing nation on the Security Council was offered new economic perks in return for a vote in favor of the U.S. war: Colombia, impoverished Ethiopia, and Zaire . . . were all offered new aid packages, access to World Bank credits or rearrangements of International Monetary Fund grants or loans.

Military deals were cut as well. Ethiopia's government was given access to new military aid after a long denial of arms to that civil war–wracked nation. Colombia was also offered a new package of military assistance.

China was the sole member of the Perm Five not toeing the U.S. line. It was common knowledge among UN-based journalists that China was looking for two major concessions in return for not opposing the U.S. resolution. One was Washington's support for Beijing's return to international diplomatic legitimacy after 18 months of isolation after the Tienanmen Square massacre. The second was economic development aid. On November 28, the day before the vote authorizing the use of force against Iraq, the White House announced a high-profile meeting between President Bush and Chinese Foreign Minister Qian Qichen, the first since Tienanmen Square, to be held the day after the vote . . . China abstained on the resolution. And less than one week later, the World Bank announced that China would be given access to $114 million in economic aid.

Phyllis Bennis, "False Consensus: George Bush's United Nations," in *Beyond the Storm: A Gulf Crisis Reader,* edited by Phyllis Bennis and Michel Moushabeck (New York: Olive Branch Press, 1991), pp. 119–120.

12. Legal scholar Burns Weston noted: "To ensure the votes of the Latin American and African delegations (Colombia, the Côte d'Ivoire, Ethiopia, Zaire), the United States is said to have promised long-sought financial help and attention. To win reliable Soviet support, the United States, according to news accounts, agreed to help keep Estonia, Latvia, and Lithuania out of the November 1990 Paris summit conference; and it additionally pledged to persuade Kuwait and Saudi Arabia to provide Moscow, as they ultimately did, with the hard currency that Moscow desperately needs to catch up on overdue payments to commercial creditors. And, it is reported, to secure a 'voluntary' Chinese abstention in lieu of a threatened Chinese veto, the United States, disregarding a then-current crackdown on political dissidents, consented to lift trade sanctions in place since the Tiananmen Square massacre of pro-democracy protesters . . . and to grant a long-sought Washington visit by the Chinese Foreign Minister, since realized, and the resumption of normal diplomatic intercourse between the two countries." Burns H. Weston, "Security Council Resolution 678 and Persian Gulf Decision Making: Precarious Legitimacy," *American Journal of International Law* 85 (1991), pp. 523–524 (citations omitted).

13. Weston, "Security Council Resolution 678 and Persian Gulf Decision Making," p. 524n48.

14. Bennis, "False Consensus," p. 120. Bennis reports that this statement was made immediately after the vote, and within earshot of the UN broadcasting system.

15. Arguably Britain could be said to have exercised the reverse veto as well. However, given its record, it seems unlikely that it would have invoked its veto separate from or in opposition to U.S. policies.

16. See, for example, a list of statements compiled by the Institute for Public Accuracy during the Clinton administration and the first Bush administration:

> May 20, 1991: James Baker, Secretary of State: "We are not interested in seeing a relaxation of sanctions as long as Saddam Hussein is in power."
>
> January 14, 1993: Clinton: "There is no difference between my policy and the policy of the present Administration . . . I have no intention of normalizing relations with him."
>
> March 26, 1997: Albright, in her first major foreign policy address as Secretary of State: "We do not agree with the nations who argue that if Iraq complies with its obligations concerning weapons of mass destruction, sanctions should be lifted. Our view, which is unshakable, is that Iraq must prove its peaceful intentions . . . And the evidence is overwhelming that Saddam Hussein's intentions will never be peaceful."
>
> November 14, 1997: Clinton: [When Iraq broke the inspections regime] "What he has just done is to ensure that the sanctions will be there until the end of time or as long as he lasts."

November 14, 1997: National Security Adviser Sandy Berger: "[Compliance is] a necessary condition. It may not be a sufficient condition."

August 20, 1997: Ambassador Bill Richardson: "Sanctions may stay on in perpetuity."

Institute for Public Accuracy, "Iraq Sanctions: What's the Policy?" November 13, 1998.

17. Madeleine Albright, "Preserving Principle and Safeguarding Stability: United States Policy toward Iraq," speech presented at Georgetown University, March 26, 1997.

18. See, e.g., Security Council Resolutions 1454 (2002), 1447 (2002), 1443 (2002), 1409 (2002), and 1382 (2001), all of which state that they are "Reaffirming the commitment of all Member States to the sovereignty and territorial integrity of Iraq."

19. The Security Council and General Assembly may request an advisory ruling on any matter. UN agencies may request advisory rulings on issues within their mandates.

20. United Nations, Charter, Arts. 40–42.

21. Ibid., Art. 1.

22. Paul Conlon, *United Nations Sanctions Management: A Case Study of the Iraq Sanctions Committee, 1990–1994* (Ardsley, NY: Transnational Publishers, 2000), pp. 8–9.

23. United Nations, Security Council Resolution 661, para. 6. Rule 28 provides that "The Security Council may appoint a commission or committee or a rapporteur for a specified question." By contrast, a committee established under Article 29 would have explicitly empowered the committee to perform the substantive work of the Council. "The Security Council may establish such subsidiary organs as it deems necessary for the performance of its functions." United Nations, Charter, Art. 29.

24. The language of the resolution provided that:

The Security Council . . . 6. *Decides* to establish, in accordance with rule 28 of the provisional rules of procedure, a Committee of the Security Council consisting of all the members of the Council, to undertake the following tasks and to report on its work to the Council with its observations and recommendations:

(a) To examine the reports on the progress of the implementation of the present resolution which will be submitted by the Secretary-General;

(b) To seek from all States further information regarding the action taken by them concerning the effective implementation of the provisions laid down in the present resolution . . .

Resolution 661 (1990), para. 6.

25. Conlon, *United Nations Sanctions Management,* p. 59.

26. Ibid., pp. 28–29.

27. Graham S. Pearson, *The UNSCOM Saga: Chemical and Biological Weapons Non-Proliferation* (New York: St. Martin's Press, 1999), p. 199.

28. As of November 1998. Ibid., p. 177.

29. Ibid., p. 176.

30. Ibid., pp. 198–199.

31. Ibid., p. 173.

32. Conlon, *United Nations Sanctions Management,* pp. 152–153.

33. Ibid., p. 31.

34. In a discussion in 1990, in which the United States opposed the view of the majority that the office of legal counsel should be consulted on a matter, the delegate from Yemen argued that "consensus was not the same as unanimity: it meant that a broad majority held a given opinion." Mr. Al-Ashtal, Security Council Committee established by Resolution 661, Summary Record, Meeting 6, S/AC.25/SR.6, October 8, 1990, in *The Kuwait Crisis: Sanctions and Their Economic Consequences,* Part II, edited by D. L. Bethlehem (Cambridge: Grotius Publications, 1991), p. 812.

35. Ibid., statement of Mr. Wilkinson, p. 810.

36. Ibid., statement of Mr. Richardson, p. 810.

37. Ibid., statement of Mr. Mr. Kirsch, p. 810.

38. Ibid., statements of Mr. Peñalosa, Mr. Alarcón de Quesada, and Mr. Al-Ashtal, pp. 810–812.

39. Ibid., statement of Mr. Redzuan, p. 811.

40. On another occasion, the Colombian delegation repeatedly asked the committee to seek an opinion from the UN's Legal Counsel regarding the delivery of food in Iraq by humanitarian agencies other than UN agencies—an increasingly urgent question—since Resolution 666 provided that "appropriate humanitarian agencies could provide food through the United Nations." When Mrs. Castaño, the Colombian representative, initially raised the question, no one objected, and she was asked to provide the request in writing (Security Council Committee established by Resolution 661, Summary Record, Meeting 14, S/AC.25/SR.14, September 27, 1990, in *The Kuwait Crisis,* p. 873). At the next meeting she brought the request, and the Legal Counsel also came to the meeting, prepared to inform the committee of his opinion. The United States objected strenuously, arguing that a draft of the request should first have been sent to all the committee members, and that it should also have been translated and circulated in all five working languages, and objected as well that the request should not be submitted to the Legal Counsel because it was unclear (statement of Mr. Wilkinson, in *The Kuwait Crisis,* p. 874). The delegates from Malaysia and China said that the question was perfectly clear. The Chairman invited Mrs. Castaño to read the request aloud. The United States again interfered, insisting that this procedure was "not acceptable" (*The Kuwait Crisis,* p. 875). Mrs. Castaño insisted on hearing the Legal Counsel's opinion, as the committee had agreed five days earlier. She "could not understand the fear which some members seemed to have of the Legal Counsel's opinion," which would help the committee in its deliberations. This fear, she said pointedly, suggested the "weakness of one particular delegation" (p. 877). The committee had already decided to hear the Legal Counsel's reply, she noted, but "unfortunately, one delegation seemed determined to override that decision." If the committee could not implement this decision, she said that the Colombian delegation would walk out (p. 878). Eventually the chair asked her to read the request for the legal interpretation. After the repeated efforts of the United States to derail the process, the Legal Counsel stated that Resolution 666 in fact permitted well-recognized

humanitarian agencies outside the UN to provide food to Iraq (pp. 879–880), an opinion that the United States presumably was not eager to have heard.

41. Paul Conlon, memorandum, "Historical Note on the Security Council's Disputed Right to Ban Supplies of Foodstuffs to a State under Sanction," June 26, 1998.

42. Security Council Committee established by Resolution 661, Summary Record, Meeting 4, S/AC.25/SR.4, August 28, 1990.

43. Security Council Committee established by Resolution 661, Summary Record, Meeting 5, S/AC.25/SR.5, August 31, 1990.

44. Security Council Committee established by Resolution 661, Summary Record, Meeting 19, S/AC.25/SR.19, November 8, 1990.

45. Security Council Committee established by Resolution 661, Summary Record, Meeting 24, S/AC.25/SR.24, January 14, 1991.

46. Security Council Committee established by Resolution 661, Summary Record, Meeting 22, S/AC.25/SR.22, December 20, 1990.

47. Lawrence Freedman and Efrain Karsh, *The Gulf Conflict: 1990–1991* (Princeton, NJ: Princeton University Press, 1993), p. 191.

48. Security Council Committee established by Resolution 661, "Decision of the Security Council Sanctions Committee Regarding Humanitarian Assistance to Iraq," S/22400, March 22, 1991, paras. 3–4.

49. United Nations, Security Council Committee established by Resolution 661, Summary Record, Meeting 82, S/AC.25/SR.82, November 30, 1992.

50. Security Council Committee established by Resolution 661, Summary Record, Meeting 71, S/AC.25/SR.71, June 1, 1992.

51. Security Council Committee established by Resolution 661, Summary Record, Meeting 74, S/AC.25/SR.74, July 24, 1992.

52. Security Council Committee established by Resolution 661, Summary Record, Meeting 85, S/AC.25/SR.85, January 12, 1993.

53. Geoff Simons, *The Scourging of Iraq: Sanctions, Law, and Natural Justice* (New York: St. Martin's Press, 1996), p. 118.

54. United Nations, Security Council Committee established by Resolution 661, Summary Record, Meeting 195, S/AC.25/SR.195, March 20, 2000, p. 2.

55. United Nations, Security Council Committee established by Resolution 661, Summary Record, Meeting 205, S/AC.25/SR.205, October 2, 2000, p. 6.

56. Ibid.

57. Security Council Committee established by Resolution 661, Summary Record, Meeting 61, S/AC.25/SR.61, January 9, 1992; Security Council Committee established by Resolution 661, Summary Record, Meeting 62, S/AC.25/SR.62, January 27, 1992.

58. Security Council Committee established by Resolution 661, Summary Record, Meeting 52, S/AC.25/SR.52, October 18, 1991.

59. Security Council Committee established by Resolution 661, Summary Record, Meeting 144, S/AC.25/SR.144, October 14, 1996.

60. Hans-C. von Sponeck, "Iraq Sanctions: What Options Did the UN Security Council Have?" paper presented at the Hiroshima Peace Institute, 2006, p. 3.

61. Security Council Committee established by Resolution 661, Summary Record, Meeting 1, S/AC.25/SR.1, August 9, 1990.

62. The 661 Committee gave no public statements to the press from 1991 to 1994. Paul Conlon, "Lessons from Iraq: The Functions of the Iraq Sanctions Committee as a Source of Sanctions Implementation Authority and Practice," *Virginia Journal of International Law* 35 (1995), p. 655n100.

63. Paul Conlon, memorandum to Martti Koskenniemi, "Confidential Non-Paper: Four Legal Issues Connected with United Nations Sanctions Management Practices in Recent Years," March 14, 1995, p. 6.

64. Conlon, *United Nations Sanctions Management,* pp. 34, 81.

65. Ibid., p. 28.

66. Ibid., p. 30.

67. Ibid., p. 31.

68. Ibid., p. 33.

69. Von Sponeck, "Iraq Sanctions," p. 16.

70. Tono Eitel, "Security Council Working Group on General Issues on Sanctions," November 14, 2000, pp. 1–2.

71. Conlon, memorandum to Martti Koskenniemi, pp. 9–10.

72. Memorandum from Paul Conlon to James C. Ngobi, "Desirability of Publishing Committee Decisions," May 16, 1994, p. 1.

73. Claudia von Braunmühl and Manfred Kulessa, "The Impact of UN Sanctions on Humanitarian Assistance Activities: Report on a Study Commissioned by the United Nations Department of Humanitarian Affairs" (Berlin: Gesellschaft für Communication Management Interkultur Training mbH—COMIT, 1995), p. 75.

74. Security Council Committee established by Resolution 661, Summary Record, Meeting 164, S/AC.25/SR.164, December 9, 1997. The French delegate commented upon the problem of ambiguity, in light of the U.S. interpretation of "dual use," saying that the 1051 list "applied to weapons of mass destruction and not to items like truck tires. Moreover, since the Secretary-General had approved the distribution plan, it should be possible for the Committee to approve the elements of that plan without passing judgment on the nature of certain items." Given the ambiguity, he suggested, the committee should specify what they consider dual use.

75. Security Council Committee established by Resolution 661, Summary Record, Meeting 186, S/AC.25/SR.186, May 27, 1999. In May 1999 Iraq requested to participate in formal committee meetings, in accordance with the note of the president of the Security Council, dated January 29, 1999, which called upon sanctions committees to offer targeted or affected countries better opportunities to explain or present their points of view. The French delegate suggested that if Iraq could not receive summary minutes, the chair could inform them informally of the outcome of each meeting. The delegate from Malaysia stated that request for participation was reasonable, and that since accountability and transparency were essential, the target country should be able to present its views. The United States insisted that Iraq should not receive minutes, and agreed only that "Iraq might be invited to give expert oral presentations in formal meetings on a case-by-case basis."

4. THE PROBLEM OF HOLDS

1. United Nations, Security Council Committee established by Resolution 661, Summary Record, Meeting 107, S/AC.25/SR.107, January 12, 1994.

2. United Nations, Security Council Committee established by Resolution 661, Summary Record, Meeting 115, S/AC.25/SR.115, August 26, 1994.

3. United Nations, Security Council Committee established by Resolution 661, Summary Record, Meeting 71, S/AC.25/SR.71, June 1, 1992.

4. United Nations, Security Council Committee established by Resolution 661, Summary Record, Meeting 81, S/AC.25/SR.81, November 11, 1992.

5. United Nations, Security Council Committee established by Resolution 661, Summary Record, Meeting 72, S/AC.25/SR.72, June 19, 1992.

6. United Nations, Security Council Committee established by Resolution 661, Summary Record, Meeting 73, S/AC.25/SR.73, July 9, 1992.

7. United Nations, Security Council Committee established by Resolution 661, Summary Record, Meeting 74, S/AC.25/SR.74, July 24, 1992.

8. United Nations, Security Council Committee established by Resolution 661, Summary Record, Meeting 82, S/AC.25/SR.82, November 30, 1992.

9. United Nations, Security Council Committee established by Resolution 661, Summary Record, Meeting 87, S/AC.25/SR.87, February 11, 1993.

10. United Nations, Security Council Committee established by Resolution 661, Summary Record, Meeting 92, S/AC.25/SR.92, April 22, 1993.

11. United Nations, "Report of the Secretary-General Pursuant to Paragraph 6 of Security Council Resolution 1210 (1998)," S/1999/187, Introductory Statement by Benon V. Sevan, February 25, 1999.

12. United Nations, "Report of the Secretary-General Pursuant to Paragraph 6 of Security Council Resolution 1242 (1999)," S/1999/896, August 19, 1999, para. 101.

13. United Nations, Office of the Iraq Programme, "Briefing by Benon Sevan, Executive Director of the Iraq Programme," April 20, 2000.

14. United Nations, "Report of the Secretary-General Pursuant to Paragraph 5 of Resolution 1302 (2000)," Introductory Statement by Benon V. Sevan, S/2000/1132, December 4, 2000.

15. Benon V. Sevan, Statement to the Security Council Committee established by Resolution 661 (1990), July 12, 2001.

16. Campaign Against Sanctions on Iraq, *CASI Newsletter,* July 2002, p. 5.

17. United Nations, Office of the Iraq Programme, "Weekly Update: Iraqi Oil Exports Plunge with Onset of War," March 25, 2003.

18. Letter from Carol Bellamy to Congressman Tony Hall, June 9, 2000.

19. Comm. nos. 7015841, 701586, and 701973. UNICEF, "Status of the Water and Sanitation Sector in South/Center Iraq," presentation to the 661 Committee, September 2001, Annex.

20. Comm. no. 800822. Ibid.

21. Comm. nos. 50123, 601616, 601659, and 801836. Ibid.

22. Ibid.

23. Health Sectoral Working Group, "Joint UN Team Field Report to the Arab Company for Antibiotics Industries (ACAI)," March 4, 2002, p. 4; United

Nations, Office of the Iraq Programme, Contracts Processing and Monitoring Division, "Applications 'On Hold,' Health Sector," March 4, 2002, comm. no. 901886.

24. United Nations Office of the Humanitarian Coordinator for Iraq, "Special Report on Observation Visit to Basrah Sewage Treatment Plant," May 29, 2001, p. 3.

25. Ibid., p. 2.

26. Ibid., p. 3; Office of the Iraq Programme, Contracts Processing and Monitoring Division, "Watsan/SA Applications on Hold," August 20, 2001, comm. no. 701973.

27. Werner Labi, "Consultancy Report: Water and Sanitation," United Nations, Office of the Iraq Programme, June 2000, p. 6.

28. Ibid., p. 7.

29. Ghulam R. Popal, World Health Organization, "Health Situation in Iraq: A Presentation to the UN Security Council 661 Committee," "Iraq after 1990," March 2002.

30. Ibid., "Major Surgical Operations (1989–2001)."

31. Ibid., "Laboratory Investigations in Iraq (1989–2001)."

32. Ibid., "Major Surgical Operations (1989–2001)."

33. Popal, "Health Situation in Iraq," "Items on Hold."

34. Ibid., "On Hold Items (as of 11 March 2002), 59% Account."

35. United Nations, Office of the Iraq Programme, Contracts Processing and Monitoring Division, "Applications 'on Hold,' Health Sector."

36. See, for example, Health Sectoral Working Group, "Report on Sterilizers and Autoclaves," July 30, 2001, comm. nos. 600318, 701485, and 801438; United Nations, Office of the Iraq Programme, Contracts Processing and Monitoring Division, "Applications 'On Hold,' Health Sector," March 4, 2002.

37. Health Sectoral Working Group, "Joint UN Team Field Report to the Arab Company for Antibiotics Industries (ACAI)," March 4, 2002, p. 3; Office of the Iraq Programme, Contracts Processing and Monitoring Division, "Applications 'On Hold,' Health Sector," March 4, 2002, comm. no. 901538.

38. Health Sectoral Working Group, "Joint UN Team Field Report to Samara Drug Industry (SDI), the State Enterprise for Drugs, Industries and Medical Appliances," June 23 and 27, 2001, p. 2.

39. Ibid.

40. Ibid., Annexes 2.1–2.5.

41. Health Sectoral Working Group, "Joint UN Team Field Report to the Arab Company for Antibiotics Industries (ACAI)," p. 4; Office of the Iraq Programme, Contracts Processing and Monitoring Division, "Applications 'On Hold,' Health Sector," March 4, 2002, comm. no. 901927.

42. Health Sectoral Working Group, "UN Team Field Report to Samara Drug Industries (SDI), Main Plant in Salah Al-Din," August 7, 2002, p. 1; United Nations, Office of the Iraq Programme, Contracts Processing and Monitoring Division, "Applications 'On Hold,' Health Sector," comm. no. 701110.

43. Health Sectoral Working Group, "UN Team Field Report to Samara Drug Industries," Main Plant in Salah Al-Din, p. 3.

44. United Nations, UNOHCI, Agriculture Sectoral Working Group, "Assessment of Agricultural Machinery in Iraq," March 8, 2001, p. 2.

45. United Nations, Office of the Iraq Programme, Contracts Processing and Monitoring Division, "Agriculture Sector: Holds Update," October 1, 2001, p. 2.

46. Ibid., p. 1.

47. Ibid., p. 2.

48. Ibid., p. 4.

49. United Nations, UNOHCI, Agriculture Sectoral Working Group, "Impact of SCR 986 Program Inputs on Rehabilitation of the Veterinary Cold Chain in Iraq," May 2001, p. 5; United Nations, Office of the Iraq Programme, Contracts Processing and Monitoring Division, "List of Holds as of 01/10/01, Annex 1: Agriculture," comm. no. 702533.

50. United Nations, Office of the Iraq Programme, Agriculture Sectoral Working Group, "Assessment of Impact of 986 Programme Inputs on Winter Vegetable Production in South/Center of Iraq," May 2001, p. 2.

51. United Nations, Office of the Iraq Programme, Contracts Processing and Monitoring Division, "Agriculture Sector: Holds Update," p. 2.

52. United Nations, Office of the Humanitarian Coordinator for Iraq, "Report: Executive Summary," January–February 2003, p. 19.

53. United Nations, Office of the Iraq Programme, Contracts Processing and Monitoring Division, "Enterotoxemia Vaccine Report," June 30, 2001, p. 2.

54. Ibid., p. 3; United Nations, Office of the Iraq Programme, "List of Holds as of 01/10/01, Annex 1: Agriculture," comm. nos. 700645, 801323, and 900641.

55. United Nations Office of the Humanitarian Coordinator for Iraq, "UNOHCI Monthly Implementation Report," May 2001, p. 16.

56. United Nations, Office of the Iraq Programme, Contracts Processing and Monitoring Division, "Electricity Sector: Holds Update," November 5, 2001, p. 1; United Nations, Office of the Iraq Programme, Contracts Processing and Monitoring Division, "Electricity Holds," August 14, 2002, comm. nos. 600620, 600630, 800701, 802151, and 802442.

57. For example, one contract was on hold from November 2000 to March 2002, with the United States at various points changing its reasons for the hold, requesting additional information, or simply not responding to OIP's reminders that all requested information had been provided and some sort of response was needed. United Nations, Office of the Iraq Programme, Contracts Processing and Monitoring Division, "Electricity Sector: Holds Update," p. 3; United Nations, Office of the Iraq Programme, Contracts Processing and Monitoring Division, "Electricity Holds," comm. no. 601695.

58. United Nations Office of the Humanitarian Coordinator for Iraq, "UNOHCI Monthly Implementation Report," p. 17.

59. Housing Sector Working Group, "Impact Assessment of Contracts on Hold for the Ministry of Housing and Construction of Iraq," September 15, 2001, p. 5; United Nations, Office of the Iraq Programme, Contracts Processing and Monitoring Division, "Housing Holds," August 14, 2002, comm. no. 901232.

60. Housing Sector Working Group, "Impact Assessment of Contracts on Hold for the Ministry of Housing and Construction of Iraq," p. 7; United Nations, Office of the Iraq Programme, Contracts Processing and Monitoring Division, "Housing Holds," comm. no. 802462.

61. Housing Sector Working Group, "Impact Assessment of Contracts on Hold for the Ministry of Housing and Construction of Iraq," pp. 5–6; United Nations, Office of the Iraq Programme, Contracts Processing and Monitoring Division, "Housing Holds," comm. nos. 901089, 901540, 901576, 901689, and 901542.

62. Housing Sector Working Group, "Impact Assessment of Contracts on Hold for the Ministry of Housing and Construction of Iraq," p. 2.

63. Ibid., p. 2.

64. Ibid., p. 4.

65. United Nations, Office of the Iraq Programme, Contracts Processing and Monitoring Division, "Housing Holds," comm. no. 901130.

66. International Telecommunications Union, "Telecommunication Sector within the 986 Program in Iraq: Presentation before the 661 Committee," May 4, 2001.

67. Ibid., p. 1.

68. A total of 188 contracts had been received as of April 2001, with a total value of $321.8 million. Ibid., "Status of Telecommunication Contracts as at 30 April 2001," p. 17.

69. Comm. no. 50476. Ibid., "Impact of Hold."

70. Ibid.

71. Ibid.

72. Ibid.

73. ITU identified the following equipment as particularly urgent: comm. nos. 50476, 50477, 50478, and 601308, which were all blocked by the United States alone; and comm. nos. 701688 and 701686, which were blocked by both the United States and Britain. "Telecommunication Sector within the 986 Program in Iraq," "Impact of Hold"; United Nations, Office of the Iraq Programme, Contracts Processing and Monitoring Division, "Applications on Hold—Telecom/Infrastructure," April 25, 2001.

74. United Nations Office of the Humanitarian Coordinator for Iraq, "UNOHCI Monthly Implementation Report," p. 13.

75. United Nations, Office of the Iraq Programme, Contracts Processing and Monitoring Division, "Food Handling Sector and Transportation Sub-Sector: Holds Update," February 4, 2002, p. 3.

76. United Nations Office of the Humanitarian Coordinator for Iraq, "UNOHCI Monthly Implementation Report," p. 14.

77. United Nations, Office of the Iraq Programme, Contracts Processing and Monitoring Division, "Watsan/SA Applications on hold," comm. nos. 702364, 702365, 701566, and 801853.

78. Transport and Food Handling Working Group, "Assessment of the Impact of Contracts on Hold: Report on Joint MDOU/WFP Visit to the Port of Um Qasr," April 2001, p. 2.

79. Ibid., pp. 1–2.

80. United Nations Office of the Humanitarian Coordinator for Iraq, "UNOHCI Monthly Implementation Report," p. 9.

81. United Nations, Office of the Iraq Programme, Contracts Processing and Monitoring Division, "Food Handling Sector and Transportation Sub-Sector: Holds Update," p. 3.

82. Ibid., p. 4.

83. Transport and Food Handling Working Group, "Assessment of the Impact of Contracts 'On Hold,'" April 2001, pp. 1–3.

84. Transport and Food Handling Working Group, "Assessment of the Impact of Contracts on Hold: Civil Aviation and Iraqi Airways," March 2001, pp. 1–7.

85. Ibid., pp. 2–6.

86. Transport and Food Handling Working Group, "Assessment of the Impact of Contracts 'On Hold': Railways," May 2001, p. 3.

87. Ibid., pp. 3–4.

88. United Nations, Office of the Iraq Programme, "The Humanitarian Programme in Iraq Pursuant to Security Council Resolution 986 (1995)," November 12, 2002, p. 32.

89. United Nations Humanitarian Office of Coordinator for Iraq, "December 2002 Report," p. 5.

90. Popal, "Health Situation in Iraq," p. 25.

91. Forty-four percent of the contracts blocked were on the 1051 list (goods raising security concerns, contained in the list established under Security Council Resolution 1051) and 11 percent were justified as dual use or WMD/dual use. United Nations, Office of the Iraq Programme, Contracts Processing and Monitoring Division, "Water and Sanitation Sector: Holds Update," August 20, 2001.

92. Total allocation in phases I–X was $3.37 billion. Total holds were $1.06 billion. Marcel Alberts, Chairperson, Electricity Working Group, "Sectoral Briefing to SC 661 Committee: Status of Electricity Sector," "Status of Applications," November 20, 2001.

93. Ibid., "Status of Holds."

94. Colum Lynch, "Mix of Uses Tangles Sanctions; U.S. Blocks Items to Iraq that Other Nations See as Benign," *Washington Post,* March 26, 2001, p. A21.

95. United Nations, Office of the Iraq Programme, Contracts Processing and Monitoring Division, "Electricity Sector: Holds Update."

96. Forty-one contracts, valued at $490.7 million, or 43.7 percent of all contracts on hold. Ibid.

97. United Nations, Office of the Iraq Programme, Contracts Processing and Monitoring Division, "Food Handling Sector and Transportation Sub-Sector: Holds Update," February 4, 2002, p. 1.

98. "Statement of Benon V. Sevan at the informal consultations of the Security Council," February 26, 2002.

99. United Nations, Office of the Iraq Programme, OKINFO Cumulative List, February 25, 2002.

100. Colin Rowat, "Iraq Sanctions Saga Continues amid Policy Confusion," *Middle East Economic Survey* 45, no. 23 (June 10, 2002), p. 2.

101. For example, the Telecommunications Sector Working Group, in its report to the 661 Committee, states, "The TSWG is ready to track and monitor every telecommunications item arriving in Iraq and to report on its utilisation." International Telecommunications Union, "Telecommunication Sector within the 986 Program in Iraq," p. 48. Similarly, the Electrical Sector Working Group, in its report to the 661 Committee, concludes by describing its observation mechanism: "Ability to track all the contracts from arrival to delivery to end users. Effective and efficient verification of all end use/user goods requested by the SC 661 committee. On random sampling basis effective and efficient verification that goods other than requested by the SC 661 committee are used for the intended purposes." Alberts, "Sectoral Briefing to SC 661 Committee."

102. For example, monitors reported that "UN observers conducted the physical verification of items requiring end-use/user observation, such as telephone exchanges, digital microwave systems, copper cables and accessories of various types and capacities, generating sets and floor-cleaning machines in 90 facilities." United Nations Office of the Humanitarian Coordinator for Iraq, "December 2002 Report," p. 11.

103. United Nations Office of the Humanitarian Coordinator for Iraq, "UNOHCI Monthly Implementation Report," p. 11.

104. United Nations Office of the Humanitarian Coordinator for Iraq, "Focus Observation Study on SCR 986 Programme Centrifugal Pumping Set," October 2000, p. 4.

105. United Nations Office of the Humanitarian Coordinator for Iraq, "UNOHCI Monthly Implementation Report," p. 13.

106. UNICEF, "Status of the Water and Sanitation Sector in South/Center Iraq."

107. Ibid., "Immediate Requirements: WatSan Sector South/Center Iraq."

108. Popal, "Health Situation in Iraq," p. 37.

109. United Nations, Office of the Iraq Programme, "Annex 6c (Health): Finished Products," communication from OIP to 661 Committee, January 2003, p. 6.

110. Ibid., p. 8.

111. United Nations, Office of the Iraq Programme, "Annex 6a (Health): Finished Products, Raw Materials and Growth Media: Indicators, Use and Annual Requirements," communication from OIP to 661 Committee, January 2003, table 27.

112. "Streptomycin with penicillin: This drug combination is a formulation of choice in animal health used to treat a wide range of diseases." United Nations, Office of the Iraq Programme, "Annex 2 (Agriculture): Estimation Methods for Animal and Poultry Drugs and Growth Media," communication from OIP to 661 Committee, January 2003, p. 2.

113. Ibid.

114. United Nations, Office of the Iraq Programme, "Annex 6c (Health): Finished Products," pp. 2–3.

115. United Nations, Office of the Iraq Programme, "Consumption Rates and Use Levels for the Implementation of Paragraph 20 of Annex B of Resolution 1454 (2002)," February 19, 2003, p. 4.

116. Ibid., p. 6.

117. Ibid., p. 5.

118. Ibid., p. 10.

119. Because nerve gas works very quickly, there is not time for a soldier to self-inject more than one ampule before death. A soldier would have to inject 2 mg/ml as an antidote, and almost all the atropine Iraq had imported was in ampules of 0.6 or 1.0 mg/ml. United Nations, Office of the Iraq Programme, "Atropine Sulphate: Intra-venous/Intramuscular Forms, Ordered under 'Oil for Food Programme,'" November 12, 2002.

120. United Nations, Office of the Iraq Programme, "Annex 6b (Health): Health Facilities in Centre/South Iraq that Could Use Items Subject to Quota Pursuant to SCR 1454 (2002)," communication from OIP to 661 Committee, January 23, table 28.

121. United Nations, Office of the Iraq Programme, "Consumption Rates and Use Levels for the Implementation of Paragraph 20 of Annex B of Resolution 1454 (2002)," p. 3.

122. Letter from Benon Sevan to the 661 Committee, August 5, 1999, S/AC.25/1999/COMM.68, discussed in Security Council Committee established by Resolution 661, Summary Record, Meeting 189, S/AC.25/SR.189, August 24, 1999, pp. 10–11.

123. Security Council Committee established by Resolution 661, Summary Record, Meeting 189, p. 11.

124. United Nations, Office of the Iraq Programme, "Briefing by Benon Sevan, Executive Director of the Iraq Programme."

125. Security Council Committee established by Resolution 661, Summary Record, Meeting 198, S/AC.25/SR.198, April 20, 2000, p. 3.

126. Ibid., p. 2.

127. See, for example, "Ruling Party Blasts US Over Vaccines," Agence France-Presse, March 13, 2001.

128. Colum Lynch, "Trade Deal Won Chinese Support of U.S. Policy on Iraq," *Washington Post,* July 6, 2001.

129. Campaign Against Sanctions on Iraq, *CASI Newsletter,* July 2002, p. 3.

130. They found that 171 contracts were legitimately on the 1051 list; another 83 contracts had one or more items from the new GRL list. They found that 40 percent of the contracts had no GRL items, and they asked for additional information on the balance. United Nations, Office of the Iraq Programme, "The Humanitarian Programme in Iraq Pursuant to Security Council Resolution 986 (1995)," November 12, 2002.

131. Ibid.

132. Ibid., Annex V, table 1, p. 1.

133. Security Council Committee established by Resolution 661, Summary Record, Meeting 151, S/AC.25/SR.151, March 17, 1997.

134. Security Council Committee established by Resolution 661, Summary Record, Meeting 185, S/AC.25/SR.185, April 22, 1999, pp. 4–5.

135. Ibid., p. 4.

136. Security Council Committee established by Resolution 661, Summary Record, Meeting 190, S/AC.25/SR.190, October 12, 1999, p. 5.

137. Ibid., p. 6.

138. Ibid., pp. 6–7.

139. Ibid., p. 3.

140. Ibid.

141. Ibid.

142. Security Council Committee established by Resolution 661, Summary Record, Meeting 192, S/AC.25/SR.192, January 19, 2000.

143. Security Council Committee established by Resolution 661, Summary Record, Meeting 244, S/AC.25/SR.244, January 22, 2003.

144. United Nations, Office of the Iraq Programme, "Briefing by Benon Sevan, Executive Director of the Iraq Programme," April 20, 2000.

5. THE MAGNITUDE OF THE CATASTROPHE

1. Abbas S. Mehdi, "Review of *The Iraqi Economy under Saddam Hussein: Development or Decline? By Muhammed-Ali Zainy," Middle East Policy* 10, no. 2 (2003), p. 140.

2. Abbas Alnasrawi, "Iraq: Economic Sanctions and Consequences, 1990–2000," *Third World Quarterly* 22, no. 2 (2001), p. 209.

3. U.S. Defense Intelligence Agency, "Iraq Water Treatment Vulnerabilities as of 18 Jan. 91—Key Judgments," January 18, 1991, para. 5.

4. Ibid., para. 14.

5. Ibid., para. 11.

6. Ibid., para. 3.

7. Ibid., para. 28.

8. World Health Organization, "Health Situation in Iraq," November 30, 2001, p. 1.

9. World Health Organization/UNICEF, "Special Mission to Iraq," February 1991, p. 12.

10. Ibid., p. 13.

11. Ibid., p. 12.

12. Alnasrawi, "Iraq: Economic Sanctions and Consequences, 1990–2000," p. 209.

13. World Health Organization/UNICEF, "Special Mission to Iraq," p. 12.

14. Ibid., p. 2.

15. Alnasrawi, "Iraq: Economic Sanctions and Consequences, 1990–2000," p. 210.

16. United Nations, "Report to the Secretary-General on Humanitarian Needs in Kuwait and Iraq in the Immediate Post-crisis Environment by a Mission to the Area Led by Mr. Martti Ahtisaari, Under-Secretary-General for Administration and Management, Dated 20 March 1991," S/22366, annex (1991) (Ahtisaari Report), para 8.

17. Alnasrawi, "Iraq: Economic Sanctions and Consequences, 1990–2000," p. 209.

271

18. UNICEF, "Iraq Watching Brief: Child Protection," prepared by Josi Salem-Pickartz, July 2003, p. 2.

19. Jonathan E. Sanford, "Iraq's Economy: Past, Present, Future" (Washington, DC: Congressional Research Service, 2003), p. 11.

20. "The difference between the GDP estimates made on the assumption of no sanctions and what was actually achieved, represents Iraq's loss in GDP opportunity as a result of the sanctions. The loss is estimated at about $265.3 billion in the period 1990–1995, of which $98.7 billions [were] in the oil sector and the remaining $166.6 billions in other sectors." Iraqi Economists Association, "Human Development Report" (Baghdad, 1995), p. 126.

21. Working Group established by the Independent Inquiry Committee, "The Impact of the Oil-for-Food Programme on the Iraqi People," September 7, 2005, p. 9.

22. Iraqi Economists Association, "Human Development Report," p. 66.

23. World Health Organization, "The Health Conditions of the Population in Iraq since the Gulf Crisis," WHO/EHA/96.1, March 1996, p. 15. "Prior to the Gulf war in 1990, Iraq had one of the highest per [capita] food availabilities in the region . . . The imposition of UN sanctions in August 1990 have, however, significantly constrained Iraq's ability to earn foreign currency needed to import sufficient quantities of food to meet needs. As a consequence, food shortages and malnutrition became progressively severe and chronic in the 1990s." United Nations, FAO/WFP, "Special Report: FAO/WFP Food Supply and Nutrition Assessment Mission to Iraq," October 3, 1997, p. 1.

24. Economist Intelligence Unit, "Country Profile: Iraq," 1998–1999, p. 14.

25. "Locally produced food items, including fruits, vegetables, poultry, eggs, meat and dairy products, have become increasingly available in markets throughout the country. Unfortunately, most Iraqis do not have the necessary purchasing power to buy these foods." United Nations, Secretary-General, "Report of the Secretary-General Pursuant to Paragraph 5 of Resolution 1302 (2000)," S/2000/857, September 8, 2000, para. 23.

26. UNICEF, "Iraq Watching Brief: Overview Report," prepared by Biswajit Sen, July 2003, p. iii.

27. Eric Hoskins, "The Humanitarian Impacts of Economic Sanctions and War in Iraq," in *Political Gain and Civilian Pain: Humanitarian Impacts of Economic Sanctions,* edited by Thomas G. Weiss et al. (Lanham, MD: Rowman & Littlefield, 1997), p. 111–112.

28. United Nations, "Special Topics on Social Conditions in Iraq: An Overview Submitted by the UN System to the Security Council Panel on Humanitarian Issues" (Baghdad, March 24, 1999), p. 13.

29. UNICEF, "Iraq Watching Brief: Child Protection," p. 2.

30. Sarah Graham-Brown, *Sanctioning Saddam: The Politics of Intervention in Iraq* (New York: I. B. Tauris, 1999), p. 161.

31. United Nations, Food and Agriculture Organization/World Food Programme, "Special Alert No. 237: FAO/WFP Crop and Food Supply Assessment Mission to Iraq," July 1993, "Overview," p. 1.

32. "Joint Government of Iraq–UNICEF Programme Review, 1990–2000, Sector Review Report, Health and Nutrition, Draft," November 1, 2000, p. 15.

33. World Health Organization, "Health Situation in Iraq," p. 3.

34. UNICEF, "The Situation of Children in Iraq," February 2002, p. 10.

35. Labi, "Consultancy Report: Water and Sanitation," p. 18.

36. Hans-C. von Sponeck, "Iraq Sanctions: What Options Did the UN Security Council Have?" paper presented at the Hiroshima Peace Institute, 2006, p. 13.

37. United Nations, FAO/WFP, "Special Report," p. 3.

38. United Nations, Security Council Resolution 661 (1990).

39. United Nations, "Report to the Secretary-General Dated 15 July 1991 on Humanitarian Needs in Iraq Prepared by a Mission Led by the Executive Delegate of the Secretary-General for Humanitarian Assistance in Iraq," S/22799, annex (1991) (hereafter Aga Khan report), p. 7, para. 14.

40. Ibid., para. 29.

41. United Nations, Security Council Resolutions 706 (1991) and 712 (1991).

42. United Nations, Security Council Resolution 986 (1995).

43. Ibid., para. 8.

44. United Nations, Security Council Resolution 1284 (1999).

45. United Nations, Security Council Resolution 1330 (2000).

46. United Nations, Office of the Iraq Programme, "The Humanitarian Programme in Iraq Pursuant to Security Council Resolution 986 (1995): Note by the Office of the Iraq Programme," November 12, 2002, Annex I, p. 1.

47. Hans-C. von Sponeck, "After Iraq—Reforming UN Sanctions," paper presented at a conference sponsored by the Hiroshima Peace Institute and the Center for International Conflict Resolution at Columbia University, March 21–23, 2007, pp. 10–11.

48. Thomas R. Stauffer, "Critical Review of UNCC Award for Lost Production and Lost Revenues," *Middle East Economic Survey* 44, no. 5 (2001). Stauffer notes, for example, that "the Panel included a large element of lost profits from the refineries. Those profits were predicated upon KPC's earning very large refining margins. It is far from obvious that such margins were in fact sustainable."

49. United Nations, Office of the Iraq Programme, "The Humanitarian Programme in Iraq Pursuant to Security Council Resolution 986 (1995)," November 12, 2002.

50. Statement by Riyadh Al-Qaysi, United Nations Security Council, Provisional Verbatim Record of the 4336th meeting, S/PV.4336 (Resumption 1), June 28, 2001, p. 17.

51. Michael E. Schneider, "How Fair and Efficient Is the UNCC System? A Model to Emulate?" *Journal of International Arbitration* 15, no. 1 (1998), p. 2.

52. Ibid., p. 6.

53. Ibid., p. 7.

54. United Nations, Office of the Iraq Programme, "The Humanitarian Programme in Iraq Pursuant to Security Council Resolution 986 (1995)," Annex I, para. 2c.

55. Schneider, "How Fair and Efficient Is the UNCC System?" p. 1.

56. "As a result of low world oil prices and lack of pumping capacity, it is expected that Iraq will only be able to export just over USD 3 billion worth of oil over the next six months—far short of the USD 5.25 billion approved by the UN Security Council under the oil-for-food agreement." United Nations, World Food Programme, "WFP Emergency Report 04: Iraq Update," January 29, 1999, para. E.1.2.

57. United Nations, Office of the Iraq Programme, "Report of the Group of United Nations Experts Established Pursuant to Paragraph 30 of the Security Council Resolution 1284 (2000)," March 2000: "The Iraqi oil industry is unable to sustain production at these levels due to its inability to replace the lost capacity of depleted strata and 'watered-out' wells. The suspension of drilling, well-workover and completion activities, and delays in the commissioning of wet-crude treatment plants, directly result from a lack of spare parts and equipment" (p. 11).

58. Ibid., p. 9.

59. Ibid., p. 15. A report by the Secretary-General reiterated this: "*Spare parts and equipment and the impact of holds on contract applications:* According to the group of experts, the recent decrease in the production and export of crude oil can be attributed to the failure to replenish depleted wells, the delays in implementing wet crude treatment projects and the loss of producing wells—56 in the south alone. Other contributing factors include the failure to carry out major plant and equipment overhauls, delays in the repair of the pipeline systems, the further decline in conditions on the Mina al-Bakr loading platform and limitations in the crude oil storage and transportation system. These are all factors that have arisen because of the lack of necessary spare parts and equipment." United Nations, "Report of the Secretary-General Pursuant to Paragraphs 28 and 30 of Resolution 1284 (1999) and Paragraph 5 of Resolution 1281 (1999)," S/2000/208, March 10, 2000, para. 49.

60. Statement by Selma Ashipala-Musavyi, delegate from Namibia. United Nations, Security Council, Provisional Verbatim Record of the 4120th meeting, S/PV.4120 (Resumption 1), March 24, 2000, p. 6. Indeed, a report from the Secretariat on the program's operation from December 1996 to November 1998 noted that "The oil spare parts and equipment required by Iraq are not always readily available and in some cases must be custom made; they often have long delivery periods, as stated in the relevant contracts submitted for approval. However, there have been considerable difficulties experienced in receiving approval of applications submitted to the Security Council committee established by Resolution 661 (1990). Inconsistencies have also been noted in the manner in which applications for spare parts have been placed on hold, depending on the geographical location of the installations concerned." United Nations, "Review and Assessment of the Implementation of the Humanitarian Programme Established Pursuant to Security Council Resolution 986 (1995) (December 1996–November 1998)," S/1999/481, April 28, 1999, para. 28.

61. "Report of the Secretary-General Pursuant to Paragraph 10 of Security Council Resolution 1153 (1998)," S/1998/1100, November 19, 1998, para. 13.

62. United Nations, "Report of the Secretary-General Pursuant to Paragraph 6 of Security Council Resolution 1210 (1998)," S/1999/187, February 22, 1999, para. 11.

63. "We welcome the increasingly flexible approach taken by members of the 661 Committee in reducing substantially the holds placed on oil spare parts and equipment. However, just as we welcome the decrease in numbers of holds, we face additional holds placed on new applications." Benon Sevan, "Introductory Statement by Benon V. Sevan, Executive Director of the Iraq Programme, at the Informal Consultations of the Security Council, on 25 February 1999," http://www.un .org/Depts/oip/background/latest/bvs990225.html (accessed July 19, 2009).

64. Of all the oil equipment contracts on hold, where the documentation specified the country imposing the hold, the United States alone had placed 124 of the holds; Britain alone had placed 4; 4 holds were placed by both the United States and Britain; and there were 9 holds where the documentation did not specify the country. United Nations, Office of the Iraq Programme, "Report of the Group of United Nations Experts Established Pursuant to Paragraph 30 of the Security Council Resolution 1284 (2000)," pp. 101–127.

65. Of 613 oil contracts on hold as of August 14, 2002, the United States alone had placed holds on 538; the United States and Britain had both placed holds on 71; and Britain alone had placed holds on 4 contracts. No other countries blocked any oil contracts. United Nations, Office of the Iraq Programme, Contracts Processing and Monitoring Division, "Oil Spares Holds as at 14 August 2002."

66. The oil experts for the UN documented all of this at length:

The lack of effectiveness of the spare parts and equipment program is now most apparent. The key problems are considered to be: . . .

• The long delays in obtaining approval of individual contracts, in some cases exceeding a year, after which contracted suppliers may not wish to perform as contracted, either on price or delivery . . .

• Large contracts placed on hold because one, or a few, items are considered unacceptable. Specific and timely advice on the unacceptable items would allow revised contracts to be raised for the balance of non-contentious items.

• The lack of specificity in reasons given for holds. Non-specific reasons, such as "dual-usage concern" and "not directly related to the repair of the Iraqi oil infrastructure for the purposes of increasing exports," effectively result in holds that cannot be removed and allocated funds that cannot be utilized for the other essential needs . . .

• The lack of time limits. Delays for evaluation for "mission clarification" and holds "pending further clarification" remain in place seemingly indefinitely.

• The lack of consistency regarding holds between phases. Spare parts and equipment approved, contracted and delivered in phase 4 are placed on hold in phases 5 and 6 . . .

• The lack of clarification of holds based on "1051" concerns. Without specificity, action cannot be taken to resolve such holds, nor can reordering of such items be avoided in subsequent contracts . . .

Proposals for approval mechanism modifications:

- Delays in approval to contracts for such reasons as "mission evaluation," "pending further clarification" and "pending further consideration" should be investigated by the OIP after a specific period (say 3 months maximum). If there is no likelihood of the hold being lifted, the purchaser should be advised of this, and the contract voided . . .
- Specific reasons should be given for holds for "dual use" and "items not directly related to the repair of the Iraqi oil infrastructure for purposes of increasing oil exports." This will allow the purchaser to either answer the questions raised, or re-consider the contract in light of the specific reason for the hold.
- Holds for "1051" reasons. The purpose of the "1051" list is understood to be to prevent the acquisition of equipment considered capable of utilization in the manufacture of weapons of mass destruction. The technical nature of many of the items required for the oil industry often result in contracts for spare parts and equipment that are included on the "1051" list. For example, corrosive resistant stainless steels are specified in pumps handling corrosive liquids, and certain items of laboratory equipment (such as gas-liquid chromatograms) are common to many scientific procedures. The use of such equipment cannot be avoided and should be accommodated within the existing monitoring function . . .
- Contracts on hold for "end use/user information" and "require technical specifications" should be released when this information is supplied; if information supplied is insufficient to release the hold, or incorrect, a request should be submitted specifying exactly what is required.
- The reason for a hold should not be changed from the original, after technical issues have been answered . . .
- Whilst reviewing the holds the group has noted that spare parts and equipment approved in phase 4 have been placed on hold in phases 5 and 6. In view of the need to increase the effectiveness of the spare parts program a consistent approach is recommended.

United Nations, Office of the Iraq Programme, "Report of the Group of United Nations Experts Established Pursuant to Paragraph 30 of the Security Council Resolution 1284 (2000)," March 2000, pp. 98–100. Note that the text of the report does not discuss the United States by name as the source of the holds. The United States is identified in the status list, annexed to the report, listing each of the holds, the length of the hold, the reasons given, and the country imposing it. There are 132 holds listed, identifying the source of the hold, and nine more without this information. Of the 132, the United States alone imposed 124, Britain alone imposed four, and the other four were imposed jointly by the United States and Britain (pp. 101–127).

67. United Nations, Office of the Iraq Programme, Contracts Processing and Monitoring Division, "Oil Industry Sector: Holds Update," April 10, 2002, p. 2; United Nations, Office of the Iraq Programme, Contracts Processing and Monitoring Division, "Oil Spares Holds," August 14, 2002, comm. nos. 53075, 630844, and 730507.

68. United Nations, Office of the Iraq Programme, Contracts Processing and Monitoring Division, "Oil Industry Sector: Holds Update," April 10, 2002, p. 2; United Nations, Office of the Iraq Programme, Contracts Processing and Monitoring Division, "Oil Spares Holds," August 14, 2002, comm. nos. 630747, 631026, 631031, 631038, 830058, 830293, 830593, 830683, 930096, 930367, 930394, 930414, 930435, and 930505.

69. For example, Anwarul K. Chowdhury of Bangladesh stated that while his delegation endorsed increasing funds available for oil equipment and spare parts, this would be "self-defeating if the requests for spare parts for Iraq's oil industry were stuck because of the holds placed on them. According to the Secretary-General's report, total value of contract applications on hold for oil spare parts and equipment as of 31 January 2000 was $291 million." United Nations, Security Council, 4120th meeting, Provisional Verbatim Record, S/PV.4120 (Resumption 1), March 24, 2000, p. 12.

70. "We are therefore far from a position where we could reach the target of the revenues authorized at $5.2 billion by resolution 1153 (1998) . . . There is no way, and can be no way for Iraq, to increase its capacity to export additional oil to finance both the humanitarian programme and to meet the demands for necessary spare parts and equipment." Sevan, "Introductory Statement by Benon V. Sevan."

71. United Nations, Security Council Resolution 1330 (2000), para. 15.

72. "Iran Oil-for-Food Deal Debated," News24, December 5, 2000.

73. Campaign Against Sanctions on Iraq, "Guide to Sanctions: 10—Why Is 'Oil for Food' Suffering a Funding Crisis?" http://www.casi.org/uk/guide/funding.html.

74. "Under retroactive pricing, the Security Council did not approve a price per barrel until the oil was delivered to the refinery. The Iraqi government signed contracts with suppliers without knowing the price it would have to pay until delivery. This allowed a fair market price to be set." General Accounting Office, "United Nations: Observations on the Management and Oversight of the Oil for Food Program," GAO-04-730T, April 28, 2004, p. 10, n. 6.

75. Kenneth Bredemeier and Peter Slevin, "US Companies Retreat from Iraq's Oil Market," *Alexander's Gas & Oil Connections* 7, No. 17 (September 5, 2002).

76. United Nations, Office of the Iraq Programme, discussion paper prepared by Oil Overseers for the 661 Committee, March 14, 2002.

77. United Nations. Security Council Committee established by Resolution 661, "Letter Dated 7 February 2002 from the Overseers Addressed to the Chairman of the Security Council Committee Established by Resolution 661 (1990) Concerning the Situation between Iraq and Kuwait," S/AC.25.2001/OIL/COMM.14, p. 4, table 2.

78. Estimates of these losses vary. According to the Congressional Research Service, retroactive pricing "reduced Iraq's oil sales by about 25%, although the UN noted a rebound to previous sales levels by September 2002." Jonathan E. Sanford, "Iraq's Economy: Past, Present, Future" (Washington, DC: Congressional Research Service, 2003), p. 35.

79. United Nations, Office of the Iraq Programme, "Statement by Benon V. Sevan, Executive Director of the Iraq Programme, at the Informal Consultations of the Security Council," "Revenue Generation," February 26, 2002.

80. United Nations, Office of the Iraq Progamme, "Statement by Benon V. Sevan, Executive Director of the Iraq Programme, at the Informal Consultations of the Security Council," September 25, 2002":

> The level of oil exports has dropped from an average of over 2 million barrels per day in the year 2000, to under one million barrels per day in recent months. Assuming a sustainable rate of export of 2.1 million barrels per day, between 1 June and 15 September, $3.2 billion in revenue has been lost, as a result of reduced levels of oil exports in this phase alone.
>
> The Government of Iraq has budgeted the humanitarian programme for the current phase XII at over $5 billion . . . Iraq would have to export $7 billion worth of oil during the present phase . . . it is now estimated that total revenue during the current phase would be at about $4.2 billion . . . only about $3.01 billion will, therefore, be made available for the implementation of the Programme, thus further compounding the dire funding shortfall.
>
> The situation is further exacerbated by the cumulative revenue shortfall from earlier phases, which has left over $2.3 billion worth of contracts for various humanitarian supplies approved by the United Nations, for which no funds are available . . .
>
> Several factors have contributed to the drop in the volume of Iraq oil exports under the Programme, including: Iraq's periodic unilateral suspension of its oil exports—such as the suspension of oil exports for 30 days during the previous phases, which resulted in over $1.2 billion in lost revenue—and the continued absence of an agreement between the Government of Iraq and the Security Council Committee (the 661 Sanctions committee) on the manner in which the price of Iraqi crude oil is set—the Committee has been pricing Iraqi oil retroactively amidst market reports of Iraq's demands for surcharge payments from its buyers—as well as concerns by traders over the reliability of uninterrupted Iraqi oil supplies and/or possible disruptions as a consequence of political developments.

81. United Nations, Office of the Iraq Programme, "The Humanitarian Programme in Iraq Pursuant to Security Council Resolution 986 (1995): Note by the Office of Iraq Programme," November 12, 2002, p. 4.

82. United Nations, Office of the Humanitarian Coordinator for Iraq, "Report: Executive Summary," January–February 2003, p. 4.

83. United Nations, Office of the Iraq Programme, "The Humanitarian Programme in Iraq Pursuant to Security Council Resolution 986 (1985)," p. 19.

84. Ibid., p. 20.

85. Ibid.

6. TENSIONS AT THE UNITED NATIONS

1. See, e.g., United Nations, Security Council Committee established by Resolution 661, Summary Record, Meeting 8, S/AC.25/SR.8, September 11, 1990.

2. Ibid.

3. See statements by Ecuador's representative, United Nations, Security Council Committee established by Resolution 661, Summary Record, Meeting 74, S/AC.25/SR.74, July 24, 1992; and statements by representatives of Zimbabwe, Ecuador, and Cape Verde, United Nations, Security Council Committee established by Resolution 661, Summary Record, Meeting 76, S/AC.25/SR.76, September 3, 1992.

4. United Nations, Security Council Committee established by Resolution 661, Summary Record, Meeting 77, S/AC.25/SR.77, September 17, 1992; United Nations, Security Council Committee established by Resolution 661, Summary Record, Meeting 80, S/AC.25/SR.80, October 29, 1992.

5. United Nations, Security Council Committee established by Resolution 661, Summary Record, Meeting 77, S/AC.25/SR.77, September 17, 1992.

6. United Nations, Security Council Committee established by Resolution 661, Summary Record, Meeting 105, S/AC.25/SR.105, December 22, 1993.

7. Ibid.

8. United Nations, Security Council Committee established by Resolution 661, Summary Record, Meeting 103, S/AC.25/SR.103, November 1, 1993.

9. United Nations Security Council, Provisional Verbatim Record of the 4336th meeting, S/PV.4336, June 26, 2001, p. 17.

10. Ibid., p. 12.

11. Ibid., pp. 23–24.

12. Ibid., p. 32.

13. United Nations, Security Council Committee established by Resolution 661, Summary Record, Meeting 76, S/AC.25/SR.76, September 3, 1992.

14. United Nations, Security Council Committee established by Resolution 661, Summary Record, Meeting 78, S/AC.25/SR.78, October 1, 1992.

15. United Nations, Security Council Committee established by Resolution 661, Summary Record, Meeting 115, S/AC.25/SR.115, August 26, 1994.

16. United Nations, Security Council Committee established by Resolution 661, Summary Record, Meeting 76, S/AC.25/SR.76, September 3, 1992.

17. Hans-C. von Sponeck, "After Iraq—Reforming UN Sanctions," paper presented at a conference sponsored by the Hiroshima Peace Institute and the Center for International Conflict Resolution at Columbia University, March 21–23, 2007, p. 13.

18. Paul Conlon uses this term in "Lessons from Iraq: The Functions of the Iraq Sanctions Committee as a Source of Sanctions Implementation Authority and Practice," *Virginia Journal of International Law* 35 (1995), p. 638.

19. Larry Minear, U. B. P. Chelliah, Jeff Crisp, John Mackinlay, and Thomas G. Weiss, "United Nations Coordination of the International Humanitarian Response to the Gulf Crisis, 1990–1992," Occasional Paper 13 (Providence, RI: Watson Institute, 1992), p. 15.

20. United Nations, Food and Agriculture Organization/World Food Programme, "Special Alert No. 237: FAO/WFP Crop and Food Supply Assessment Mission to Iraq," July 1993.

21. Ibid., "Overview."

22. See World Food Programme, "World Food Programme Emergency Reports," Center for International Disaster Information, http://www.cidi.org/humanitarian/wfp/.

23. Claudia von Braunmühl and Manfred Kulessa, "The Impact of UN Sanctions on Humanitarian Assistance Activities: Report on a Study Commissioned by the United Nations Department of Humanitarian Affairs" (Berlin: Gesellschaft für Communication Management Interkultur Training mbH—COMIT, 1995).

24. "The impact of sanctions on humanitarian activities and in particular on vulnerable groups has become a major concern of the humanitarian community. Various NGOs such as ICRC, WVI, Oxfam, War on Want etc. submitted penetrating papers on sanctions. Within the United Nations, DHA and the IASC made sanctions and 'the importance of shielding humanitarian assistance against the effects of sanctions' a key area to be given special attention . . . In the meantime the debate on sanctions and their humanitarian impact has gained considerable momentum. The Secretary-General, the General Assembly, the Security Council, and member states have expressed their concern. They have articulated the desire to work towards more satisfactorily formulated sanctions resolutions, to more professional structures of sanctions regime management, and to more efficient assessment and monitoring mechanisms." Ibid., p. 58.

25. Ibid., p. 2.

26. Ibid., Annex 3.

27. Ibid., Executive Summary, p. iii.

28. World Health Organization, "The Health Conditions of the Population in Iraq since the Gulf Crisis," WHO/EHA/96.1, March 1996, p. 2.

29. Ibid., p. 19.

30. World Health Organization, "Iraqi Health System Close to Collapse," Press Release WHO/16, February 27, 1997.

31. United Nations, World Food Programme, "Special Report: FAO/WFP Food Supply and Nutrition Assessment Mission to Iraq," October 3, 1997, "Overview."

32. "The agriculture sector has deteriorated significantly in the 1990s, due to a lack of investment and shortage of essential inputs . . . [S]ustainable improvement in the nutritional well-being of the population will require a substantial flow of resources into rehabilitation of the agriculture sector and the economy as a whole . . . Of major importance is the severe deterioration of the water and sanitation system in Iraq. Water availability in its widest sense involving drinking water, irrigation, water-logging, salinity and sewage disposal is absolutely fundamental to the future of agricultural productivity and health of the population. It is recommended that high priority be given to sustainable rehabilitation of the water and sanitation system, otherwise water-borne diseases, including nutritional marasmus, will remain a major problem despite improved food availability." The report found that, in the face of the food shortages, "widespread starvation was avoided due to an effective public rationing system, which provided minimum quantities of food to the population." Ibid.

33. United Nations, "Special Topics on Social Conditions in Iraq: An Overview Submitted by the UN System to the Security Council Panel on Humanitarian

Issues," Baghdad, March 24, 1999. The participating agencies were UNICEF, WHO, UNDP, WFP, the High Commissioner for Refugees, the Department of Economic and Social Affairs, the Office of the Humanitarian Coordinator for Iraq, UNESCO, and the United Nations Office for Project Services.

34. Sarah Graham-Brown, *Sanctioning Saddam: The Politics of Intervention in Iraq* (New York: I. B. Tauris, 1999), p. 281.

35. Ibid.

36. Ibid.

37. United Nations, Security Council Committee established by Resolution 661, Summary Record, Meeting 144, S/AC.25/SR.144, October 14, 1996.

38. United Nations, Security Council Committee established by Resolution 661, Summary Record, Meeting 148, S/AC.25/SR.148, January 23, 1997.

39. United Nations, Security Council Committee established by Resolution 661, Summary Record, Meeting 172, S/AC.25/SR.172, June 18, 1998.

40. United Nations, Security Council Committee established by Resolution 661, Summary Record, Meeting 134, S/AC.25/SR.134, March 1, 1996.

41. United Nations, Security Council Committee established by Resolution 661, Summary Record, Meeting 166, S/AC.25/SR.166, January 4, 1998.

42. United Nations, Security Council Committee established by Resolution 661, Summary Record, Meeting 132, S/AC.25/SR.132, February 1, 1996; United Nations, Security Council Committee established by Resolution 661, Summary Record, Meeting 133, S/AC.25/SR.133, February 7, 1996; United Nations, Security Council Committee established by Resolution 661, Summary Record, Meeting 134, S/AC.25/SR.134, March 1, 1996; United Nations, Security Council Committee established by Resolution 661, Summary Record, Meeting 160, S/AC.25/SR.160, August 27, 1997.

43. United Nations, Security Council Committee established by Resolution 661, Summary Record, Meeting 150, S/AC.25/SR.150, February 21, 1997; United Nations, Security Council Committee established by Resolution 661, Summary Record, Meeting 159, S/AC.25/SR.159, July 17, 1997.

44. United Nations, Security Council Committee established by Resolution 661, Summary Record, Meeting 143, S/AC.25/SR.143, August 28, 1996; United Nations, Security Council Committee established by Resolution 661, Summary Record, Meeting 144, S/AC.25/SR.144, October 14, 1996.

45. United Nations, Security Council Committee established by Resolution 661, Summary Record, Meeting 148, S/AC.25/SR.148, January 23, 1997.

46. United Nations, Security Council Committee established by Resolution 661, Summary Record, Meeting 133, S/AC.25/SR.133, February 7, 1996.

47. Ibid.

48. Paul Conlon, *United Nations Sanctions Management: A Case Study of the Iraq Sanctions Committee, 1990–1994* (Ardsley, NY: Transnational Publishers, 2000), pp. 47–48.

49. Ibid., p. 48n11.

50. Graham-Brown, *Sanctioning Saddam,* p. 90.

51. Ibid.

52. United Nations, "Report of the Secretary-General on the Work of the Organization: Supplement to an Agenda for Peace: Position Paper of the Secretary-General on the Occasion of the Fiftieth Anniversary of the United Nations, A/50/60 and S/1995/1, January 25, 1995, para. 70.

53. United Nations, "Report of the Secretary-General Pursuant to Paragraph 3 of Resolution 1111 (1997)," S/1997/935, November 28, 1997, para. 69.

54. Ibid., para. 70.

55. Ibid., para. 72.

56. United Nations, "Report of the Secretary-General Pursuant to Paragraph 7 of Security Council Resolution 1143 (1997)," S/1998/90, February 1, 1998, para. 29.

57. United Nations, "Report of the Secretary-General Pursuant to Paragraph 4 of Resolution 1143 (1997)," S/1998/194, March 4, 1998, para. 58.

58. Ibid., para. 59.

59. United Nations, Security Council, Provisional Verbatim Record of the 4120th meeting, S/PV.4120, March 24, 2000, p. 2.

60. Van der Stoel maintained that the Iraqi government prioritized military expenditures over health care and nutrition (United Nations, "Human Rights Questions: Human Rights Situations and Reports of Special Rapporteurs and Representatives: Situation of Human Rights in Iraq," A/49/651, November 8, 1994, para. 92); that it failed to cooperate with international humanitarian agencies (ibid., para. 99[l]); and that it placed internal embargoes on both the northern and southern areas of Iraq (ibid.). Van der Stoel repeatedly castigated the Iraqi government for its failure to accept the first Oil for Food program (ibid., para. 99[m]; United Nations, "Human Rights Questions: Human Rights Situations and Reports of Special Rapporteurs and Representatives: Situation of Human Rights in Iraq," A/51/496, October 15, 1996, para. 64; United Nations, Commission on Human Rights, "Report on the Situation of Human Rights in Iraq, Submitted by the Special Rapporteur, Mr. Max van der Stoel, in Accordance with Commission Resolution 1997/60," E/CN.4/1998/67, March 10, 1998, "Economic and Social Rights," para. 2; and United Nations, Commission on Human Rights, "Question of the Violation of Human Rights and Fundamental Freedoms in Any Part of the World: Situation of Human Rights in Iraq, Report Submitted by the Special Rapporteur, Mr. Max van der Stoel, in Accordance with Commission Resolution 1998/65," E/CN.4/1999/37, February 26, 1999, para. 29. Van der Stoel criticized the government of Iraq for failing to use available resources for the maximum benefit of the Iraqi population. United Nations, "Human Rights Questions: Human Rights Situations and Reports of Special Rapporteurs and Representatives: Situation of Human Rights in Iraq," A/52/476, October 15, 1997, para. 55; United Nations, "Report on the Situation of Human Rights in Iraq Prepared by the Special Rapporteur of the Commission on Human Rights in Accordance with Economic and Social Council Decision 1998/263 of 30 July 1998," A/53/433, September 24, 1998, para. 33.

61. United Nations, "Human Rights Questions: Human Rights Situations and Reports of Special Rapporteurs and Representatives: Situation of Human Rights in Iraq," A/51/496, October 15, 1996, para. 61.

62. United Nations, Commission on Human Rights, "Question of the Violation of Human Rights and Fundamental Freedoms in Any Part of the World: Report of the Special Rapporteur of the Situation of Human Rights in Iraq, Mr. Andreas Mavrommatis," E/CN.4/2001/42, January 16, 2001, para. 12. In Mavrommatis's later reports he also refers to the adverse effects of the embargo (see, e.g., United Nations, Commission on Human Rights, "Question of the Violation of Human Rights and Fundamental Freedoms in Any Part of the World: Report of the Special Rapporteur, Andreas Mavrommatis, on the Situation of Human Rights in Iraq," E/CN.4/2002/44, March 15, 2002, para. 87.

63. United Nations, "Situation of Human Rights in Iraq," A/56/340, September 13, 2001, paras. 20–21.

64. Emphasis added. United Nations, General Assembly, Resolution 50/191, "Situation of Human Rights in Iraq," A/RES/50/191, March 6, 1996, para. 6. Other resolutions adopting language similar to van der Stoel's were A/RES/48/144, December 20, 1993; A/RES/49/203, March 13, 1995; A/RES/51/106, March 3, 1997; and A/RES/52/141, March 6, 1998. The Human Rights Commission also passed a series of resolutions adopting language similar to van der Stoel's statements on Iraq's human rights practices. Several of those assert that the Iraqi government had imposed "internal embargoes" preventing the equitable distribution of food and medical supplies. "Situation of Human Rights in Iraq," Resolution 1993/74, March 10, 1993; "Situation of Human Rights in Iraq," Resolution 1994/74, March 9, 1994; "Situation of Human Rights in Iraq," Resolution 1995/76, March 8, 1995.

65. United Nations, General Assembly, "Situation of Human Rights in Iraq," Resolution 53/157, A/RES/53/157, February 25, 1999, para. 15 (emphasis added).

66. Ibid., para. 17 (emphasis added).

67. Ibid. (emphasis added).

68. United Nations, General Assembly, "Human Rights Situation in Iraq," Resolution 54/178. A/RES/54/178, February 24, 2000, para. 3(j) United Nations, General Assembly, "Situation of Human Rights in Iraq," Resolution 56/174, A/RES/ 56/174, February 27, 2002, para. 4(k) and 4(l).

69. See Resolution 1997/35 of the Commission on Human Rights, Sub-Commission on the Promotion and Protection of Human Rights, "Adverse Consequences of Economic Sanctions on the Enjoyment of Human Rights," E/CN.4/ SUB.2/RES/1997/35 (1997), as well as the Sub-Commission's decision in 1999, "Humanitarian Situation in Iraq," Decision 1999/110, E/CN.4/SUB.2/DEC/1999/ 110 (1999), and other resolutions that followed, such as "Adverse Consequences of Economic Sanctions," Resolution 2000/25, E/CN.4/SUB.2/RES/2000/25, and "Human Rights and Humanitarian Consequences of Sanctions, Including Embargoes," Resolution 2000/1 (2000), E/CN.4/SUB.2/RES/2000/1. See also "The Human Rights Impact of Economic Sanctions on Iraq: Background Paper Prepared by the Office of the High Commissioner for Human Rights for the Meeting of the Executive Committee on Humanitarian Affairs," September 5, 2000.

70. United Nations, Economic and Social Council, Committee on Economic, Social, and Cultural Rights, "Concluding Observations of the Committee on Economic, Social and Cultural Rights: Iraq." E/C.12/1/Add.17, December 12, 1997.

71. United Nations, Committee on the Rights of the Child, "Concluding Observations of the Committee on the Rights of the Child: Iraq," CRC/C/15/Add.94, October 26, 1998.

72. "Concluding Observations of the Committee on the Elimination of Racial Discrimination: Iraq," CERD/C/304/Add.80 (2001).

73. United Nations, Commission on Human Rights, Sub-Commission on the Promotion and Protection of Human Rights, "The Adverse Consequences of Economic Sanctions on the Enjoyment of Human Rights: Working Paper Prepared by Mr. Marc Bossuyt," E/CN.4/Sub.2/2000/33, 2000, para. 23.

74. Ibid., paras. 41–47.

75. United Nations, Sub-Commission on the Promotion and Protection of Human Rights, "Adverse Consequences of Economic Sanctions," Resolution 2000/25, August 14, 2000.

76. United Nations, Commission on Human Rights, Sub-Commission on the Promotion and Protection of Human Rights. "Humanitarian Situation of the Iraqi Population, Sub-Commission on Human Rights Decision 2000/112," E/CN.4/2000/L.11/Add.2, August 18, 2000.

77. Cornelio Sommaruga, Address at the United Nations General Assembly, 65th meeting, November 23, 1994, A/49/PV.65, p. 27.

78. Andrew Natsios, *U.S. Foreign Policy and the Four Horsemen of the Apocalypse: Humanitarian Relief in Complex Emergencies* (Westport, CT: Praeger, 1997), p. 71.

79. United Nations, Security Council Committee established by Resolution 661, Summary Record, Meeting 88, S/AC.25/SR.88, February 18, 1993.

80. Conlon, *United Nations Sanctions Management,* pp. 61–62.

81. See, for example, statements by Ecuador's representative in United Nations, Security Council Committee established by Resolution 661, Summary Record, Meeting 74, S/AC.25/SR.74, July 24, 1992; statements by representatives of Zimbabwe, Ecuador, Morocco, and Cape Verde, United Nations, Security Council Committee established by Resolution 661, Summary Record, Meeting 76, S/AC.25/SR.76, September 3, 1992; and by the Austrian delegate, United Nations, Security Council Committee established by Resolution 661, Summary Record, Meeting 77, S/AC.25/SR.77, September 17, 1992.

82. United Nations, Security Council Committee established by Resolution 661, Summary Record, Meeting 74, S/AC.25/SR.74, July 24, 1992.

83. United Nations, Security Council Committee established by Resolution 661, Summary Record, Meeting 76, S/AC.25/SR.76, September 3, 1992.

84. Ibid.

85. United Nations, Security Council Committee established by Resolution 661, Summary Record, Meeting 87, S/AC.25/SR.87, February 11, 1993.

86. United Nations, Security Council Committee established by Resolution 661, Summary Record, Meeting 85, S/AC.25/SR.85, January 12, 1993.

87. United Nations, Security Council Committee established by Resolution 661, Summary Record, Meeting 91, S/AC.25/SR.91, April 6, 1993.

88. von Braunmühl and Kulessa, "The Impact of UN Sanctions on Humanitarian Assistance Activities."

89. Ibid., p. 70.

90. Ibid., pp. 71–72.

91. Ibid., p. 73.

92. United Nations, Security Council, "Note by the President of the Security Council," S/1995/234, March 29, 1995; United Nations, Security Council, "Note by the President of the Security Council," S/1995/438, May 31, 1995; United Nations, Security Council, "Note by the President of the Security Council," S/1996/54, January 24, 1996.

93. The successor agency to DHA.

94. Minear et al., "Toward More Humane and Effective Sanctions Management."

95. Ibid., chap. 3, "Humanitarian Exemptions," "Recommendations."

96. United Nations, Security Council, "Note by the President of the Security Council: Work of the Sanctions Committees," S/1999/92, January 29, 1999.

97. United Nations, Security Council, "Note by the President of the Security Council," S/1999/100, January 30, 1999.

98. United Nations, Security Council, "Report of the Second Panel Established Pursuant to the Note by the President of the Security Council of 30 January 1999 (S/1999/100), Concerning the Current Humanitarian Situation in Iraq," S/1999/356, Annex II, March 30, 1999, p. 45.

99. Ibid., Annex II, p. 49.

100. Ibid., Annex II, pp. 51–52.

101. "More than a year ago the Council adopted the note of the President of 29 January 1999 containing a number of practical recommendations to improve the work of sanctions committees. Recently the Secretariat submitted to us information regarding the implementation of these recommendations. It clearly shows that not all of those recommendations, as moderate as they are, have been properly implemented, and there remains much to be done in this direction." Statement by Mr. Yel'chenko, United Nations, Security Council, Provisional Verbatim Record of the 4128th meeting, S/PV.4128, April 17, 2000, p. 10. The Iraqi ambassador listed these in detail at the open meeting of the Security Council: "Foremost among them were the following: a specific time-frame should be set for sanctions regimes; the Security Council should precisely set out the steps to be taken by the targeted country for sanctions against it to be lifted; and efforts should be made to enable targeted countries to obtain appropriate resources and procedures to finance humanitarian imports . . . The working group also recommended that there be consideration of the grave negative effects of sanctions on the abilities and activities of targeted countries in the field of development; the Security Council should submit regular reports to the General Assembly on the status of specific sanctions regimes; measures should be adopted in response to the expectations raised by Article 50 of the Charter; and, finally, targeted countries should be enabled to exercise their right to express their viewpoint before the sanctions committees." Ibid., pp. 41–42.

102. Eric Herring, "Between Iraq and a Hard Place: A Critique of the British Government's Case for UN Economic Sanctions," Review of International Studies 28, no. 1 (January 2002), p. 48.

103. Government Accountability Office, interview with Eugene Young, State Department, July 12, 2005, p. 2.

104. Hans-C. von Sponeck, "Reforming UN Sanctions," paper presented at a conference sponsored by the Hiroshima Peace Institute and the Center for International Conflict Resolution at Columbia University, March 21–23, 2007, p. 11.

105. The nations were Bangladesh, the United Kingdom, the United States, France, Ukraine, Namibia, Malaysia, Argentina, Tunisia, Mali, Jamaica, Russia, Portugal, Germany, Pakistan, Libyan Arab Jamihiriya, Italy, Sweden, Australia, Bulgaria, New Zealand, Cuba, Iraq, Macedonia, and Turkey. United Nations, Security Council, Provisional Verbatim Record of the 4128th meeting, S/PV.4128, April 17, 2000.

106. Mr. Levitte, France. Ibid, p. 8.

107. United Nations, Security Council, "Note by the President of the Security Council," S/2000/319, April 17, 2000.

108. "The United States and Britain this week barred two former U.N. officials who oppose sanctions against Iraq from testifying before a U.N. panel on guidelines to improve the use of embargoes, according to letters circulated on Wednesday. France, an opponent of sanctions, had requested that Hans von Sponeck and Denis Halliday, both coordinators of the U.N. humanitarian programme in Iraq, address a Security Council working group studying ways to impose sanctions but spare civilians. However, the U.S. and Britain, in separate letters to Anwarul Chowdhury, Bangladesh's ambassador who chairs the panel, [maintained that the panel was] looking at generic sanctions issues, not at individual sanctions regime before it recommended to the full council ways to improve them. 'It needs to focus on the tasks before it, and avoid getting side-tracked. A briefing by Mr. von Sponeck and Mr. Halliday would merely be an unhelpful distraction,' the British letter said, adding there was little time to hear even half the experts already on the committee's list. The United States said that previous experts before the panel have had a broad overview, generally academic. In contrast the two former U.N. officials are 'not sanctions experts and have narrow expertise in only one regime.'" "US, UK, Bar Testimony from Foes of Iraq Sanctions," *Reuters*, October 4, 2000.

109. United Nations, Security Council, Working Group on Sanctions, "Chairman's Proposed Outcome," February 14, 2001.

110. Ibid.

111. The U.S. efforts were described in some detail:

The US is fighting behind the scenes in New York to water down UN proposals aimed at overhauling sanctions policy.

The UN secretary general, Kofi Annan, set up a special committee last April to examine sanctions policy after a string of failures over the past decade, especially over Iraq. He was particularly concerned about the humanitarian impact of sanctions on civilian populations . . .

But the US, which is intent on maintaining tough sanctions against Iraq with the backing of Britain, will almost certainly succeed in cutting out two key recommendations: one setting a time limit on sanctions and the other introducing majority voting on sanctions committees . . .

The US is also opposed to a proposal that the UN sanctions committees, which oversee the embargoes, should "consider majority voting for reaching decisions either of a procedural nature or related to humanitarian exemptions." Decisions at present are by consensus: if the reform went ahead, Britain and the US would face the prospect of defeat on the Iraqi sanctions committee.

Ewen MacAskill, "US Tries to Head Off UN Plan to Reform Sanctions," *The Guardian*, February 9, 2001.

112. For example, the report does not suggest that sanctions committees should be required to clearly define the standards for invoking security concerns as the justification for preventing humanitarian imports. Instead, it recommends that sanctions committees shall define dual use "to the extent possible" and "as deemed feasible and appropriate." United Nations, Security Council, "Report of the Informal Working Group of the Security Council on General Issues of Sanctions," S/2006/997, December 22, 2006, Annex, II.A.3.(b).(i). Instead of recommending expiration dates on sanctions, which would require the Council to act affirmatively to renew them, the report recommends only that the committees "conduct periodic review and evaluation" (II.C.7.[a]). There is no requirement that holds be systematically reviewed, or that criteria be established for their removal. Instead, the report recommends that sanctions committees, "if they deem appropriate," may include provisions to review holds (IV.16.[f]).

113. United Nations, Security Council Committee established by Resolution 661, Summary Record, Meeting 190, S/AC.25/SR.190, October 12, 1999, pp. 2–3.

114. Ibid., p. 3.

115. At the meeting of the 661 Committee, "Mr. Mauriès (France) recalled that the representative of UNICEF in Baghdad had been requested to make a statement before the Committee in a formal meeting. Since she was currently in New York, it would be very appropriate to invite her to speak, especially about the humanitarian situation in the field. Mr. Young (United States of America) said that the proposal raised complications because it required a lot of preparation and study. Furthermore, it had been proposed to invite representatives of several agencies to a formal meeting, including UNICEF. In addition, it should be recalled that the Committee had decided to hear a number of personalities, including the Under-Secretary-General for Management, and that had not been done yet. Furthermore, since the Committee was still considering the possibility of holding an informational meeting on violations of the sanctions regime in the north of Iraq, it would be preferable to leave the proposal of the representative of France pending." United Nations, Security Council Committee established by Resolution 661, Summary Record, Meeting 194, S/AC.25/SR.194, March 17, 2000, p. 6.

116. United Nations, Security Council Committee established by Resolution 661, Summary Record, Meeting 190, S/AC.25/SR.190, October 12, 1999, p. 2.

117. United Nations, Office of the Iraq Programme, "Paper Dated 7 July 1999: Payment Mechanisms for the ESB (53 per cent) Account," p. 1, para. 1.

118. Ibid.

119. United Nations, Security Council Committee established by Resolution 661, Summary Record, Meeting 189, S/AC.25/SR.189, August 24, 1999, p. 5.

120. United Nations, Security Council Committee established by Resolution 661, Summary Record, Meeting 193, S/AC.25/SR.193, March 1, 2000, p. 2.

121. Campaign Against Sanctions on Iraq, *CASI Newsletter,* July 2002.

122. Hans-C. von Sponeck, "Iraq Sanctions: What Options Did the UN Security Council Have?" paper presented at the Hiroshima Peace Institute, 2006, pp. 12–13.

7. THE ROLE OF THE IRAQI GOVERNMENT

1. See, for example, U.S. Department of State, "Saddam Hussein's Iraq" (Washington, DC: U.S. Department of State, 1999).

2. Lee McClenny, Daily Press Briefing, U.S. Department of State, November 17, 1997.

3. Elizabeth Jones, Principal Deputy Assistant Secretary, Bureau of Near Eastern Affairs, U.S. Department of State, "State Department Briefing," August 13, 1999.

4. Alan Larson, Under Secretary for Economic, Business, and Agricultural Affairs, "Interview," CNBC, May 1, 2003,

5. Gen. Michael Delong, Interview, *The Command Post*, September 24, 2004. Another U.S. official referred to "the deteriorated infrastructure in Iraq created by years of neglect by the Ba'ath Party regime. Even before economic sanctions began, the regime failed to maintain essential power, water and sanitation systems. This neglect has had a disastrous effect on the health of Iraqis." Ambassador Roy L. Austin, "Giving Iraqis a Democratic Future," *The Trinidad Guardian,* May 9, 2003.

This claim was reiterated by an array of U.S. government officials: "Iraq's electrical system and other key infrastructure was all but ruined after years of neglect under Saddam Hussein's rule." Gerry J. Gilmore, "'Incredible Progress' Made Restoring Iraq's Infrastructure, Officials Say," *American Forces Press Service,* July 7, 2003. "In addition to these regulatory reforms, we're also working in what was a very vibrant agricultural economy. They have probably the best soils in the entire Arab world because of the flooding, periodic flooding, over the years, and the problem has been it has been neglected. Even the irrigation systems, the equipment has not been repaired in a very long time and we're doing that now. We're also introducing new seed varieties, improved seed varieties. The seed stock is among the worst I've ever seen in the world, only comparable probably to North Korea's. Their yields were the worst next to North Korea's I have ever seen in the world. African agriculture in the rural areas that has no science applied to it had higher production rates per hectare." Andrew Natsios, "Briefing on Reconstruction Progress in Iraq," U.S. Agency for International Development, December 3, 2004.

The Web site of the Coalition Provisional Authority (CPA) blamed the Hussein regime for the condition of the electricity system: "Saddam's Legacy: A reliable supply of electricity is essential to every functioning modern economy. The Saddam regime neglected all components of the electrical system—the generation, transmission, and distribution sub-sectors." http://govinfo.library.unt.edu/cpa

-iraq/ES/electric.html (accessed October 13, 2009). In a review of its accomplishments the CPA maintained that "The Baghdad sewage system suffers from decades of chronic neglect and underinvestment." Coalition Provisional Authority, "An Historic Review of CPA Accomplishments, Baghdad, Iraq," p. 27, http://www.cpa-iraq.org/pressreleases/20040628_historic_review_cpa.doc (accessed October 13, 2009).

Similarly, a CPA press release comments: "Repairing damages from more than 30 years of neglect under Saddam Hussein, Corps teams are restoring transmission lines, improving or replacing switching facilities and building or restoring more than two dozen power generation projects to produce a capacity not seen in this country before." "Rehabilitation of Turbine #5 Completed at Haditha, 110 MW Added to Grid," May 31, 2004, http://govinfo.library.unt.edu/cpa-iraq/pressreleases/20040605_Haditha5.html (accessed October 13, 2009).

A State Department report to Congress maintained that "Production problems associated with the southern oil fields are due primarily to years of neglect and a lack of investment, maintenance and inadequate water injection rates." *2207 Report to Congress*, July 2005, appendix I, p. 57. In another 2005 report the State Department similarly blamed Hussein's regime for the condition of the oil industry: "Infrastructure Security—A Continuing Concern: At the end of this quarter, insurgents markedly stepped up attacks on critical essential service infrastructure, targeting especially key electricity and oil linear infrastructure. Because of the fragile nature of the energy infrastructure due to years of neglect, poor maintenance and shoddy repairs, even a minor attack can have a large impact across the country." *2207 Report to Congress*, October 2005, p. 6. In that same report the State Department used similar language in reporting on the condition of the health system in Iraq: "Iraq faces a number of challenges in the health sector, many of which are consequences of neglect under Saddam Hussein. One of the most serious challenges is reducing Iraq's high infant mortality rate, which is a consequence in part of deteriorated health-care infrastructure, outbreaks of preventable diseases and low immunization coverage" (appendix I, p. I-87).

6. United Nations, World Food Programme, "Special Report: FAO/WFP Food Supply and Nutrition Assessment Mission to Iraq," October 3, 1997. "While full and effective implementation of SCR 986 will undoubtedly ease immediate food supply difficulties, sustainable improvement in the nutritional well-being of the population will require a substantial flow of resources into rehabilitation of the agricultural sector and economy as a whole . . . In light of this, the allocation of U.S.$94 million . . . for imports of urgently needed agricultural inputs in 1997, is considered by the Mission to be grossly inadequate in comparison to rehabilitation and investment needs in the sector" (p. 2).

7. The Office of the Iraq Programme criticized Iraq for spending too much on basic foods rather than on other sectors that have a complementary role in health and nutrition. United Nations, Office of the Iraq Programme, "Introductory Statement by Benon V. Sevan, Executive Director of the Iraq Programme, at the Informal Consultations of the Security Council," February 25, 1999.

8. "In general, implementation of the programme in the agricultural sector was constrained by a lack of proper prioritization in the preparation of distribution

plans [and] insufficiently coordinated contracting and submission." United Nations, "Report of the Secretary-General Pursuant to Paragraphs 28 and 30 of Resolution 1284 (1999) and Paragraph 5 of Resolution 1281 (1999)," S/2000/208, March 10, 2000, para. 146.

9. World Health Organization, "Health Update Iraq," November 24, 2000, p. 2.

10. Working Group established by the Independent Inquiry Committee, "The Impact of the Oil-for-Food Programme on the Iraqi People," September 7, 2005, p. 46.

11. Ibid.

12. For example, the 2000 mission of the Food and Agriculture Organization noted that the low levels of lysine were due in part to the lack of contracts for pulses (a type of legume) (ibid., p. 97). On another occasion, the Iraqi government was criticized for failing to follow the 661 Committee's procedures in ordering agricultural supplies (ibid., p. 27).

13. Ibid., p. 21.

14. Sarah Graham-Brown, *Sanctioning Saddam: The Politics of Intervention in Iraq* (New York: I. B. Tauris, 1999), p. 169.

15. An Office of the Humanitarian Coordinator for Iraq (UNOHCI) report in 2001 notes that nutrition observers were blocked from collecting statistics at ration distribution centers. In the same period, the water and sanitation observers complained that their work was interrupted for two weeks when no government escorts were made available to them (United Nations, UNOHCI, "Monthly Implementation Report," May 2000, p. 6), and education observers were prevented by government escorts from collecting statistics on school enrollment at about a third of the primary schools visited (p. 7). In 2001, a UN assessment of educational computers noted that "it was virtually impossible" to measure adequacy and equity in the educational sector because UN observers were denied essential statistics; they were only allowed to visit the schools that had received commodities; and they were not given access to the Department of Education's educational plans and priorities. United Nations, "Impact Assessment of Computers on Secondary Education," March 2001, Section 3.0.

16. Working Group established by the Independent Inquiry Committee, "The Impact of the Oil-for-Food Programme on the Iraqi People," p. 184.

17. Ibid., p. 25. There were many such measures. For example, the Iraqi government subsidized inputs by 80 percent and facilitated farmers' ability to acquire farm equipment through installment payments. United Nations, UNOHCI, Agriculture Sectoral Working Group, "Assessment of Agricultural Machinery in Iraq," March 8, 2001, p. 2.

18. UNICEF, "The Status of Children and Women in Iraq: A Situation Report," September 1995, p. 2.

19. Working Group established by the Independent Inquiry Committee, "The Impact of the Oil-for-Food Programme on the Iraqi People," p. 103.

20. See, for example, the testimony of William Webster, Hearing of the House Armed Services Committee, December 5, 1990: "We believe Baghdad's actions to

forestall shortages of food stocks, including rationing, encouraging smuggling and promoting agricultural production are adequate for the next several months." (U.S. Congress, House of Representatives, Committee on Armed Services, *Crisis in the Persian Gulf: Sanctions, Diplomacy and War,* 101st Cong., 2nd sess., December 5, 1990, p. 114); "To boost next year's food production, Baghdad has raised prices, paid the farmers for their produce, and decreed that farmers must cultivate all available land" (p. 115). See also United Nations, Food and Agriculture Organization/World Food Programme, "Special Alert No. 237: "FAO/WFP Crop and Food Supply Assessment Mission to Iraq," July 1993: "A massive starvation in the country has so far been averted by the provision of low-cost food, under the public rationing system, which is an indispensable means of sustenance for a majority of the population" ("Overview"). "While the rationing system has been instrumental in banishing the threat of a massive famine in the country so far, it has not [been able] to check the increasing malnutrition and morbidity rates, affecting large sections of the population" ("Current Food Supply Position"). See also United Nations, "Special Report: FAO/WFP Food Supply and Nutrition Assessment Mission to Iraq," October 3, 1997: "Prior to the Gulf war in 1990, Iraq had one of the highest per [capita] food availabilities in the region . . . The imposition of UN sanctions in August 1990 have, however, significantly constrained Iraq's ability to earn foreign currency needed to import sufficient quantities of food to meet needs. As a consequence, food shortages and malnutrition became progressively severe and chronic in the 1990s. Widespread starvation was avoided due to an effective public rationing system, which provided minimum quantities of food to the population" ("Overview").

21. Working Group established by the Independent Inquiry Committee, "The Impact of the Oil-for-Food Programme on the Iraqi People," p. 94.

22. However, two commentators noted that "Even if the present Iraqi regime's commitment to the ration system is motivated primarily by narrow political calculus, it needs to be stressed that this commitment to welfare is not new-found and that it must be viewed in the historical context of welfarist interventions by successive governments in Iraq. These interventions, which include action by the government on a variety of social and welfare issues, such as education (particularly the education of girls), public health care, development of infrastructure and indeed radical land reforms, have been consistent and substantial features of public policy at least since the late 1950s." Haris Gazdar and Athar Hussain, "Crisis and Response: A Study of the Impact of Economic Sanctions in Iraq" (London: Asia Research Centre, London School of Economics, December 1997), p. 34.

23. International Federation of Red Cross and Red Crescent Societies, "World Disasters Report 1998," p. 99.

24. Ibid., p. 98.

25. Gazdar and Athar, "Crisis and Response," p. 27.

26. In 1990 and 1991 "there had been a great deal of speculation outside Iraq that the ration system was used selectively as a reward and punishment device by the Iraqi regime against various sections of the population. The 1991 visit found no evidence for this. On the contrary, it was found that even people who privately expressed intense opposition to the regime were satisfied with the functioning of

the ration system" (ibid.). A 1996 survey had similar findings. "During our second visit, we covered fewer locations and interviewed a smaller number of households than in the 1991 visit. What we found is that the ration system, but for some details, operated exactly in the same way as observed in 1991" (ibid.). In one study, the researchers "did not find a single family which reported even a small difference between the quantities it received and the officially announced quantities. Furthermore, the ration agent was usually a local grocer and people faced little difficulty in obtaining the ration on time. It is fair to assume, therefore, that the ration system does function quite effectively" (ibid.). A Food and Agriculture Organization (FAO) study from 1993 found that the ration system was highly effective at reaching the population: errors of either duplication or omission occurred for only 1.7 percent of the cases. United Nations, Food and Agriculture Organization, "Evaluation of Food and Nutrition Situation in Iraq, Terminal Statement" (Rome: Food and Agriculture Organization, 1993), p. 5.

27. UNICEF and Government of Iraq, "Joint Government of Iraq–UNICEF Programme Review, Review Report, Center and South Iraq: Health and Nutrition, 1999–2000," p. 81.

28. "Iodisation itself had already began in 1990 using potassium iodate at a level of 50 ppm, and since that time only iodised salt was distributed in the food rations." Ibid., p. 80.

29. Ibid., p. 65.

30. For example, a UN report from 2001 notes that, in order to meet the May rations, the government of Iraq supplemented UN food supplies from national stock, providing 25 percent of the wheat flour, 25 percent of the vegetable oil, 75 percent of the tea, 50 percent of the soap, and 50 percent of the detergent. United Nations, Office of the Humanitarian Coordinator for Iraq, "Monthly Implementation Report," May 2001, p. 8.

31. UNICEF and World Health Organization, "Iraq Watching Briefs: Health and Nutrition," prepared by Juan Diaz and Richard Garfield, July 2003, p. 42.

32. UNICEF, "Iraq Watching Briefs: Overview Report," prepared by Biswajit Sen, July 2003, p. 13.

33. Eric Hoskins, "Children, War and Sanctions in Iraq," report for UNICEF-Baghdad, April 1993, p. 11.

34. United Nations, UNICEF, "Emergency Country Profile—Iraq: Health," May 1995.

35. Overall, "significant progress has been achieved for child survival in 1994 and 1995 particularly in immunization activities against the six antigens and efforts to curb mortality and morbidity associated with diarrhea." Ibid.

36. "National Immunization Days for polio were started in 1995. [A 1999] outbreak suggests that coverage during routine immunization and National Days had been sub-optimal. In response to the outbreak, Polio National Immunization Days were conducted during October and November 1999, while in 2000 an additional Immunization Day of two rounds was also carried out. The 2000 Days were reported successful due to good micro-planning and social mobilization. This included house-to-house campaigns, monitoring, and supervision. Health

workers prepared maps of their areas and plotted every under-five child on the map. These were used to plan the campaign and to ensure every child was vaccinated. About 9,500 volunteers (teachers, NGO members, community leaders, and local council and Ba'ath party members) participated in the campaign, helping to ensure 100% coverage. A pocket calculator or a diary and a certificate was given to them in recognition of their contribution. Supervisors from central, governorate, sector, and primary health care centers supported the teams through regular monitoring and supervision. TV spots and radio messages were produced to raise public health awareness. Loudspeakers were used for making announcements to educate the community and to ask them to bring their children for vaccination, and banners were displayed at public places to mobilize the community before and during the campaign." UNICEF, "The Situation of Children in Iraq: An Assessment Based on the United Nations Convention on the Rights of the Child," February 2002, p. 34.

37. United Nations, UNOHCI, "January–February 2003 Report," p. 11.

38. Working Group established by the Independent Inquiry Committee, "The Impact of the Oil-for-Food Programme on the Iraqi People," p. 44.

39. Ibid., p. 127.

40. United Nations, "Report to the Secretary-General Dated 15 July 1991 on Humanitarian Needs in Iraq Prepared by a Mission Led by the Executive Delegate of the Secretary-General for Humanitarian Assistance in Iraq" (hereafter Aga Khan Report), S/22788, annex (1991), para. 20.

41. Ibid.

42. Phebe Marr, "Iraq's Future: Plus Ça Change or Something Better?" in *The Gulf Crisis: Background and Consequences,* edited by Ibrahim Ibrahim (Washington, DC: Center for Contemporary Arab Studies, 1992), pp. 146–147.

43. Ibid., p. 147.

44. Elizabeth Stone, correspondence with the author, June 21, 2006.

45. Aga Khan Report, para. 20.

46. Sarah Graham-Brown, "War and Sanctions: Cost to Society and Toll on Development," in *The Future of Iraq,* edited by John Calabrese (Washington, DC: Middle East Institute, 1997), p. 34.

47. United Nations, UNOHCI, Agriculture Sectoral Working Group, "Assessment of Agricultural Machinery in Iraq," March 8, 2001, p. 2.

48. Ibid.

49. United Nations, UNOHCI, Agriculture Sectoral Working Group, "Impact of SCR 986 Program Inputs on Rehabilitation of the Veterinary Cold Chain in Iraq," May 2001, p. 8.

50. "Programme inputs have been effectively used for both construction and maintenance of the irrigation infrastructure ... A total of 45 deepwater wells were drilled at individual farmers' fields in 6 governorates; ... 1500km of streams and drains were cleared." United Nations, UNOHCI, "December 2002 Report," p. 8.

51. United Nations, UNOHCI, "January–February 2003 Report," p. 1.

52. United Nations, UNOHCI, "December 2002 Report," p. 9.

53. United Nations, UNOHCI, "Monthly Implementation Report," May 2001, p. 19.

54. United Nations, UNOHCI, "January–February 2003 Report," p. 2.

55. Ibid.

56. Werner Labi, "Consultancy Report: Water and Sanitation," United Nations, Office of the Iraq Programme, June 2000, p. 2.

57. United Nations, "Focus Observation Study on SCR 986 Programme Centrifugal Pumping Sets," December 2000, p. 1.

58. "Since the inception of the Programme, to respond to the needs of a growing population and the extensions of the network, the government of Iraq installed 81 low lift and 104 high lift pumps, alum dosing pumps, chlorinators and chlorine boosting pumps, as well as water purification chemicals (chlorine, aluminum sulphate and bleaching powder)." United Nations, UNOHCI, "January–February 2003 Report," p. 15.

59. United Nations, UNOHCI, "December 2002 Report," p. 7.

60. Ibid., p. 8.

61. Ibid.

62. UNICEF and World Health Organization, "Iraq Watching Briefs: Health and Nutrition," pp. 12–13.

63. Ibid., p. i.

64. UNICEF, "Iraq Watching Briefs: Education," prepared by Khalil Elain and Jamsheeda Parveen, July 2003, p. 3.

65. This was true as well after the 2003 war. "A case in point is that of the Ministry of Trade working together with the World Food Programme (WFP) to restore the food rations for the population and reaching such rations to many areas within Iraq." UNICEF, "Iraq Watching Briefs: Overview Report," p. 13.

66. Ibid., pp. 9–10.

67. UNICEF, "Iraq Watching Briefs: Water and Environmental Sanitation," prepared by Brendan Doyle, July 2003, p. 23.

68. UNICEF and World Health Organization, "Iraq Watching Briefs: Health and Nutrition," p. 4.

69. Graham-Brown, *Sanctioning Saddam*, p. 181.

70. Ibid.

71. Labi, "Consultancy Report: Water and Sanitation," p. 16.

72. UNICEF "Iraq Watching Briefs: Overview Report," p. 23.

73. UNICEF and World Health Organization, "Iraq Watching Briefs: Health and Nutrition," p. 31.

74. Gazdar and Hussain. "Crisis and Response," p. 15.

75. UNICEF, "Iraq Watching Briefs: Water and Environmental Sanitation," p. 9.

76. "Although public finance data were not available, it can be safely assumed that the main items of expenditure are salaries of government employees and consumer subsidies, notably through the ration system. It is clear that under its new and severe fiscal constraints Iraq could no longer afford to maintain its large public sector of old. All the evidence suggests that the government has maintained its fiscal commitment to subsidize the ration, and has preserved employment levels in

the public sector at the expense of the purchasing power of public sector salaries, by not adjusting them with the rise in prices." Gazdar and Hussain, "Crisis and Response," pp. 10–11.

77. United Nations, Food and Agriculture Organization, "Evaluation of Food and Nutrition Situation in Iraq," terminal statement prepared for the government of Iraq (Rome, 1995), p. 9.

78. UNICEF, "Iraq Watching Briefs: Water and Environmental Sanitation," p. 2.

79. UNICEF, "The Status of Children and Women in Iraq," Summary, December 1995, p. 2.

80. United Nations, Food and Agriculture Organization, "Evaluation of Food and Nutrition Situation in Iraq" (1995), p. 20.

81. Ibid., p. 22; Working Group established by the Independent Inquiry Committee, "The Impact of the Oil-for-Food Programme on the Iraqi People," p. 41.

82. UNICEF and World Health Organization, "Iraq Watching Briefs: Health and Nutrition," p. ii.

83. UNICEF, "The Situation of Children in Iraq," p. 42.

84. UNICEF, "Iraq Watching Briefs: Child Protection," prepared by Josi Salem-Pickart, July 2003, p. 2.

85. UNICEF, "Iraq Watching Briefs: Education," pp. 12–13.

86. United Nations, "Public Health Contribution to the MDOU Monthly Report," December 14, 1998, p. 2.

87. United Nations, UNICEF, "Fortnightly Report for the Period 13 to 27 September 1998," September 27, 1998, p. 4.

88. UNICEF, "Iraq Watching Briefs: Education," p. 5.

89. United Nations, "Impact Assessment of Computers on the Secondary Education Sector in Iraq," March 2001, para. 2.2.

90. UNICEF, "The Situation of Children in Iraq," p. 44. "The plain wooden desks are imported, since [Oil-for-Food Programme] funds are not released for local supplies."

91. Jonathan E. Sanford, "Iraq's Economy: Past, Present, Future" (Washington, DC: Congressional Research Service), June 3, 2003, p. 26.

92. United Nations, Security Council Committee established by Resolution 661, Summary Record, Meeting 144, S/AC.25/SR.144, October 14, 1996.

93. United Nations, "Special Topics on Social Conditions in Iraq: An Overview Submitted by the UN System to the Security Council Panel on Humanitarian Issues," Section 3, "Poverty Trends," March 24, 1999.

94. Ibid., Section 4, "Destitution."

95. Hoskins, "Children, War and Sanctions in Iraq," p. 7.

96. UNICEF, "Iraq Watching Briefs: Overview Report," p. 10.

97. Working Group established by the Independent Inquiry Committee, "The Impact of the Oil-for-Food Programme on the Iraqi People," p. 50.

98. UNICEF, "Iraq Watching Briefs: Water and Environmental Sanitation," p. 9.

99. UNICEF, "The Situation of Children in Iraq," p. 23.

100. UNICEF, "Iraq Watching Briefs: Water and Environmental Sanitation," p. 9.

101. Ibid.; UNICEF, "Iraq Watching Briefs: Overview Report," p. 26.

102. UNICEF, "Iraq Watching Briefs: Water and Environmental Sanitation," p. 11.

103. UNICEF, "The Situation of Children in Iraq," p. 23.

104. Labi, "Consultancy Report: Water and Sanitation," p. 8.

105. Eric Hoskins, "The Humanitarian Impacts of Economic Sanctions and War in Iraq," In *Political Gain and Civilian Pain*, ed. Thomas G. Weiss et al. (Lanham, MD: Rowman & Littlefield, 1997), p. 110.

106. World Health Organization, "Health Update Iraq," p. 2.

107. United Nations, "Profile of Children and Women in Iraq and UNICEF Country Programme of Cooperation," April 15, 2002, p. 2.

108. UNICEF, "Iraq Watching Briefs: Education," p. 11.

109. Ibid., p. 4.

110. UNICEF, "Iraq Watching Briefs: Overview Report," p. 33.

111. UNICEF, "Iraq Watching Briefs: Education," p. 19.

112. Ibid., p. 16.

113. UNICEF, "The Situation of Children in Iraq," p. 28.

114. United Nations, Food and Agriculture Organization, "Evaluation of Food and Nutrition Situation in Iraq, Terminal Statement" (1993), p. 19.

8. CONGRESS AND THE SANCTIONS

1. Kenneth Katzman, "Iraq: Compliance, Sanctions, and U.S. Policy" (Washington, DC: Congressional Research Service, July 5, 2002), p. 11.

2. U.S. Congress, *Congressional Record,* 101st Cong., 2nd sess., September 24, 1990/Legislative Day of September 10, 1990, Vol. 136, No. 119, p. S13542.

3. Ibid., p. S13543.

4. Ibid.

5. Ibid.

6. Susan B. Epstein, "The World Embargo on Food Exports to Iraq" (Washington, DC: Congressional Research Service, September 25, 1990), p. 8.

7. Ibid., p. 5.

8. Ibid., Summary.

9. "Because feed stocks (most of which is imported) will be severely reduced in the short run, the Iraqis may have to liquidate their livestock. Thus, more meat than usual may be available in the short run. Already hatching eggs are being sold for table eggs, so the next poultry cycle may well be minimal . . The livestock sector, if Iraq does liquidate it, will take months or even years to rebuild." Ibid., pp. 8–9.

10. Ibid., p. 8.

11. U.S. Congress, Joint Hearings before the Subcommittees on Arms Control, International Security and Science, Europe and the Middle East, and on International Operations of the Committee on Foreign Affairs and the Joint Economic Committee, "*The Persian Gulf Crisis,*" 101st Cong., 2nd sess., August 8, September 18 and 25, October 17, November 28, and December 11, 1990; U.S. Congress, Senate, Committee on Armed Services, *Crisis in the Persian Gulf Region: U.S. Policy Options and Implications,* 101st Cong., 2nd sess., September 11 and 13, November 27–30, and December 3, 1990; U.S. Congress, House of Representatives, Committee on Banking, Finance and Urban Affairs, *Economic Impact of the*

Persian Gulf Crisis, 101st Cong., 2nd sess., November 27 and 28, 1990; U.S. Congress, Subcommittee on Education and Health of the Joint Economic Committee, *Economic Sanctions against Iraq*, 101st Cong., 2nd sess., December 19, 1990; U.S. Congress, House of Representatives, Committee on Armed Services, *Crisis in the Persian Gulf: Sanctions, Diplomacy and War*, 101st Cong., 2nd sess., December 4, 5, 6, 12, 13, 14, 17, 19, and 20, 1990; U.S. Congress, Senate, Committee on Foreign Relations, *U.S. Policy in the Persian Gulf*, 101st Cong., 2nd sess., December 4 and 5, 1990, Pt. 1; U.S. Congress, Senate, Committee on Foreign Relations, *U.S. Policy in the Persian Gulf*, 101st Cong., 2nd sess., December 6, 12, and 13, 1990, Pt. 2; U.S. Congress, Senate, Committee on Foreign Relations, *U.S. Policy in the Persian Gulf*, 102nd Cong., 1st sess., January 8, 1991.

12. U.S. Congress, Senate, Committee on Foreign Relations, *U.S. Policy in the Persian Gulf*, 101st Cong., 2nd sess., December 6, 1990.

13. U.S. Congress, Subcommittee on Education and Health of the Joint Economic Committee, *Economic Sanctions against Iraq*, 101st Cong., 2nd sess., December 19, 1990.

14. U.S. Congress, House of Representatives, Committee on Armed Services, *Crisis in the Persian Gulf: Sanctions, Diplomacy and War*, 101st Cong., 2nd sess., December 5, 1990.

15. Senator Paul Wellstone, January 10, 1991/Legislative Day of January 3, 1991, 102nd Cong., 1st sess., *Congressional Record* 137, No. 6, p. S107.

16. Senator Pell argued,

As a result of the U.N. sanctions, Iraq can sell no oil. It can perform no financial transactions. Iraq's gross national product has fallen between 40 and 50 percent in just 4 months. There is also in place a virtually total ban on imports. Without spare parts, imported inputs, and foreign technicians, Iraq cannot operate most of the expensive infrastructure that it purchased in the oil boom years of the 1960's and 1970's. Iraq cannot manufacture tires for its transport. It will soon be unable to produce certain kinds of lubricants or to refine high quality aviation fuel.

Even more important, the sanctions are beginning to erode Iraq's military potential. Without spare parts it cannot fly its airplanes, replace its artillery, or maintain its tanks. The United States replaces its helicopter engines every 50 hours of flying time in the desert. Iraq cannot replace its helicopter engines.

Senator Claiborne Pell, January 10, 1991/Legislative Day of January 3, 1991, 102nd Cong., 1st sess., *Congressional Record* 137, No. 6, p. S125.

17. "This policy is working. Iraq has been deterred, ostracized and punished. Sanctions, unprecedented in their international solidarity and more massive in scope than any ever adopted in peacetime against any nation—I repeat—ever adopted against any nation, are inflicting painful costs on the Iraqi economy." Senator Sarbanes, January 10, 1991/Legislative Day of January 3, 1991, 102nd Cong., 1st sess., *Congressional Record* 137, No. 6, p. S153.

18. "CIA director William Webster said that sanctions are working and can further hurt Iraq. The administration knows that economic sanctions can work."

U.S. Congress, *Congressional Record*, 102nd Cong., 1st sess., January 12, 1991, Vol. 137, No. 8, p. H415.

19. Ibid., p. H414.

20. U.S. Congress, *Congressional Record*, 102nd Cong., 1st sess., January 10, 1991/Legislative Day of January 3, 1991, Vol. 137, No. 6, p. S141.

21. Ibid., p. S143.

22. "In the more than 5 months since the Iraqi invasion, Saddam Hussein has increased, rather than decreased his hold on Kuwait. Sanctions have produced no hint of a response from Iraq." Representative Dennis Hastert, January 12, 1991. 102nd Cong., 1st sess., *Congressional Record* 137, No. 8, p. H397.

"The sanctions have been somewhat effective but there has been universal agreement in congressional hearings that sanctions alone will not achieve Iraq's departure from Kuwait." Representative Sidney Morrison, January 12, 1991, 102nd Cong., 1st sess., *Congressional Record* 137, No. 8, p. H404.

"Even though the international community, in unprecedented unity, has rejected his immoral occupation and destruction of Kuwait—even though Iraq has been subjected to sanctions and a trade embargo—even though a 28-nation coalition has arrayed against him a military force of unquestionable power—Saddam Hussein has refused to budge." Representative Joe McDade, January 12, 1991, 102nd Cong., 1st sess., *Congressional Record* 137, No. 8, p. H422.

23. *Authorization for Use of Military Force against Iraq Resolution*, Public Law 1, 102nd Cong., 1st sess., January 12, 1991.

24. These included: U.S. Congress, House of Representatives, Committee on Armed Services, *Options for Dealing with Iraq*, 102nd Cong., 2nd sess., August 10–11, 1992; U.S. Congress, Senate, Committee on Armed Services, *Joint Chiefs of Staff Briefing on Current Military Operations in Somalia, Iraq, and Yugoslavia*, 103rd Cong., 1st sess., January 29, 1993; U.S. Congress, House of Representatives, Committee on Foreign Affairs, *U.S. Policy toward Iraq 3 Years after the Gulf War*, 103rd Cong., 2nd sess., February 23, 1994; U.S. Congress, Senate, Committee on Foreign Relations, *U.S. Policy toward Iran and Iraq*, 104th Cong., 1st sess., March 2 and August 3, 1995; U.S. Congress, House of Representatives, Committee on International Relations, *U.S. Policy toward Iraq* , 104th Cong., 2nd sess., March 28, 1996; U.S. Congress, Senate, Committee on Armed Services, *The Situation in Iraq*, 104th Cong., 2nd sess., September 12, 1996; U.S. Congress, Senate, Select Committee on Intelligence, *Iraq*, 104th Cong., 2nd sess., September 19, 1996; U.S. Congress, House of Representatives, Committee on National Security, *United States Policy toward Iraq*, 104th Cong., 2nd sess., September 26, 1996; U.S. Congress, House of Representatives, Committee on International Relations, *U.S. Options in Confronting Iraq*, 105th Cong., 2nd sess., February 25, 1998; U.S. Congress, Senate, Committee on Foreign Relations, *United States Policy in Iraq: Public Diplomacy and Private Policy*, 105th Cong., 2nd sess., September 9, 1998; U.S. Congress, House of Representatives, Committee on Armed Services, *United States Policy toward Iraq*, 106th Cong., 1st sess., March 10, 1999; U.S. Congress, Senate, Committee on Armed Services, *U.S. Policy toward Iraq*, 106th Cong., 2nd sess., September 19 and 28, 2000; U.S. Congress, House of Representatives, Com-

mittee on International Relations, *U.S. Policy toward Iraq,* 107th Cong., 1st sess., October 4, 2001; U.S. Congress, Senate, Committee on Governmental Affairs, *United States Policy in Iraq: Next Steps,* 107th Cong., 2nd sess., March 1, 2002; U.S. Congress, Senate, Committee on Foreign Relations, *Hearings to Examine Threats, Responses, and Regional Considerations Surrounding Iraq,* 107th Cong., 2nd sess., July 31 and August 1, 2002.

25. U.S. Congress, House of Representatives, Committee on International Relations, *U.N. Inspections of Iraq's Weapons of Mass Destruction Programs: Has Saddam Won?* 106th Cong., 2nd sess., September 26, 2000; U.S. Congress, Senate, Committee on Armed Services, *The Weapons of Mass Destruction Program of Iraq,* 107th Cong., 2nd sess., February 27, 2002.

26. U.S. Congress, House of Representatives, Committee on International Relations, *U.S. Policy toward Iraq,* 104th Cong., 2nd sess., March 28, 1996; U.S. Congress, Senate, Committee on Armed Services, *The Situation in Iraq,* 104th Cong., 2nd sess., September 12, 1996; U.S. Congress, House of Representatives, Committee on National Security, *United States Policy toward Iraq,* 105th Cong., 2nd sess., September 16, 1998; U.S. Congress, Senate, Committee on Armed Services, *U.S. Policy toward Iraq,* 106th Cong., 2nd sess., September 19 and 28, 2000; U.S. Congress, Senate, Committee on Foreign Relations, *United States Policy toward Iraq,* 107th Cong., 1st sess., March 1, 2001; U.S. Congress, House of Representatives, Committee on International Relations, *U.S. Policy toward Iraq,* 107th Cong., 1st sess., October 4, 2001; U.S. Congress, Senate, Committee on Governmental Affairs, *United States Policy in Iraq: Next Steps,* 107th Cong., 2nd sess., March 1, 2002.

27. U.S. Congress, House of Representatives, Committee on International Relations, *Disarming Iraq: The Status of Weapons Inspections,* 105th Cong., 2nd sess., September 15, 1998; U.S. Congress, House of Representatives, markup before the Committee on International Relations, *The Monitoring of Weapons Development in Iraq, as Required by U.N. Security Council Resolution 687 (April 3, 1991) and Reaffirming the Special Relationship between the U.S. and the Republic of the Philippines,* 107th Cong., 1st sess., December 12, 2001.

28. U.S. Congress, Senate, Committee on Foreign Relations, *United States Policy in Iraq: Public Diplomacy and Private Policy,* 105th Cong., 2nd sess., September 9, 1998; U.S. Congress, House of Representatives, Committee on National Security, *United States Policy toward Iraq,* 105th Cong., 2nd sess., September 16, 1998; U.S. Congress, House of Representatives, Committee on Armed Services, *United States Policy toward Iraq,* 106th Cong., 1st sess., March 10, 1999; U.S. Congress, Senate, Committee on Foreign Relations, *Facing Saddam's Iraq: Disarray in the International Community,* 106th Cong., 1st sess., September 28, 1999; U.S. Congress, Senate, Committee on Governmental Affairs, *United States Policy in Iraq: Next Steps,* 107th Cong., 2nd sess., March 1, 2002.

29. U.S. Congress, Senate, Select Committee on Intelligence, *Iraq,* 104th Cong., 2nd sess., September 19, 1996; U.S. Congress, House of Representatives, Committee on National Security, *United States Policy toward Iraq,* 104th Cong., 2nd sess., September 26, 1996; U.S. Congress, Senate, Committee on Foreign

Relations, *United States Policy toward Iraq,* 106th Cong., 1st sess., March 9, 1990; U.S. Congress, House of Representatives, Committee on Armed Services, *United States Policy toward Iraq,* 106th Cong., 1st sess., March 10, 1999; U.S. Congress, Senate, Committee on Armed Services, *U.S. Policy toward Iraq,* 106th Cong., 2nd sess., September 19 and 28, 2000; U.S. Congress, Senate, Committee on Foreign Relations, *United States Policy toward Iraq,* 107th Cong., 1st sess., March 1, 2001.

30. U.S. Congress, Senate, Committee on Foreign Relations, *Civil War in Iraq,* 102nd Cong., 1st sess., S. Prt. 102-27, May 1991.

31. U.S. Congress, Senate, Committee on Foreign Relations, *Iraq: Can Saddam Be Overthrown?* 105th Cong., 2nd sess., March 2, 1998.

32. U.S. Congress, Senate, Committee on Foreign Relations, *U.S. Policy toward Iraq: Mobilizing the Opposition,* 106th Cong., 1st sess., June 23, 1999.

33. U.S. Congress, Senate, Committee on Foreign Relations, *The Liberation of Iraq: A Progress Report,* 106th Cong., 2nd sess., June 28, 2000.

34. See, e.g., U.S. Congress, House of Representatives, Committee on Armed Services, *Options for Dealing with Iraq,* 102nd Cong., 2nd sess., August 10 and 11, 1992; U.S. Congress, House of Representatives, Committee on International Relations, *U.S. Policy toward Iraq,* 104th Cong., 2nd sess., March 28, 1996; U.S. Congress, Senate, Committee on Armed Services, *The Situation in Iraq,* 104th Cong., 2nd sess., September 12, 1996; U.S. Congress, Senate, Select Committee on Intelligence, *Iraq,* 104th Cong., 2nd sess., September 19, 1996; U.S. Congress, Senate, Committee on Foreign Relations, *United States Policy toward Iraq,* 106th Cong., 1st sess., March 9, 1990; U.S. Congress, Senate, Committee on Foreign Relations, *United States Policy toward Iraq,* 107th Cong., 1st sess., March 1, 2001; U.S. Congress, House of Representatives, Committee on International Relations, *U.S. Policy toward Iraq,* 107th Cong., 1st sess., October 4, 2001; U.S. Congress, Senate, Committee on Governmental Affairs, *United States Policy in Iraq: Next Steps,* 107th Cong., 2nd sess., March 1, 2002.

35. In 2001, for example, the United States provided about $25 million for opposition groups under the Iraq Liberation Act. Katzman, "Iraq: Compliance, Sanctions, and U.S. Policy" (Washington, DC: Congressional Research Service, February 27, 2002), p. 13.

36. Author's interview with Erik Gustafson, March 27, 2009.

37. U.S. Congress, Senate, Committee on Foreign Relations, *Civil War in Iraq,* 102nd Cong., 1st sess., S. Prt. 102-27, May 1991.

38. On April 11, 1991, the Senate passed Resolution 99, recognizing the United States' moral obligation to provide humanitarian relief for Kurdish and Shi'ite refugees. Raymond W. Copson, "Persian Gulf Conflict: Post-War Issues for Congress" (Washington, DC: Congressional Research Service, 1991), p. 3.

39. For example, H.R. 2251 provided some $236 million in humanitarian aid for Kurdish refugees and for international peacekeeping operations. U.S. Congress, *Congressional Record,* 102nd Cong., 1st sess., May 9, 1991, Vol. 137, No. 70, p. H2916.

40. Public Law 102-55, signed June 3, appropriated $556 million for relief for Kurds and other refugees. Copson, "Persian Gulf Conflict," p. 3.

41. U.S. Congress, Senate, Committee on the Judiciary, *Aftermath of War: The Persian Gulf Refugee Crisis*, 102nd Cong., 1st sess., May 20, 1991, p. v.

42. S. Res. 132, adopted May 29, 1991. Ibid., p. 35.

43. For example, H. Con. Res. 299 provided that it "is the sense of the Congress that . . . the United Nations presence in northern Iraq should be extended." U.S. Congress, *Congressional Record*, 102nd Cong., 2nd sess., June 2, 1992, Vol. 138, No. 77, p. H3934.

44. Senator Pell, for example, suggested that "The Security Council should also consider a partial lifting of the U.N. blockade for the Kurdish-held areas in northern Iraq, provided there is a verifiable commitment from the Kurdish leaders not to trade with Baghdad." U.S. Congress, *Congressional Record,* 103rd Cong., 1st sess., May 28, 1993, Vol. 139, No. 78, p. S6816.

45. "Implementation of the Helsinki Accords: Situation of Kurds in Turkey, Iraq and Iran," Briefing of the Commission on Security and Cooperation in Europe, Washington DC, May 17, 1993; U.S. Congress, House of Representatives, Committee on Foreign Affairs, *U.S. Policy toward Iraq 3 Years after the Gulf War.*

46. Regarding the ousting of Saddam and the selective relaxation of sanctions in the north to support the Kurds, there was a "sense of Congress statement to this effect . . . contained in the Senate version of the FY 1994 State Department authorization bill (H.R. 2333), and included in the conference report on that bill. The bill was passed by both houses and signed into law on April 30, 1994 (P.L. 103-236)." Kenneth Katzman, "Iraq: Current Sanctions, Long Term Threat, and U.S. Policy Options" (Washington, DC: Congressional Research Service, May 25, 1994), p. 24.

47. U.S. Congress, Senate, Committee on Foreign Relations, *U.S. Policy toward Iran and Iraq*, 104th Cong., 1st sess., March 2 and August 2, 1995; U.S. Congress, Senate, Committee on Armed Services, *The Situation in Iraq,* 104th Cong., 2nd sess., September 12, 1996; U.S. Congress, House of Representatives, Committee on International Relations, *U.S. Options in Confronting Iraq*, 105th Cong., 2nd sess., February 25, 1998.

48. "The Foreign Relations Authorization Act for FY 1992 (P.L. 102-138, October 28, 1991, section 301) stated the sense of Congress that the president should propose to the U.N. Security Council a war crimes tribunal for Saddam Husayn." Katzman, "Iraq: Compliance, Sanctions, and U.S. Policy," February 27, 2002, p. 6.

49. "As for my own amendment . . . it calls on the President of the United States to request the United Nations to establish a war crimes tribunal to hold Saddam Hussein and other officials in his regime accountable for their atrocities." Representative Jerry Solomon, April 28, 1994, 103rd Cong., 2nd sess., *Congressional Record* 140, No. 48, p. H2852.

50. Legislation on this issue that was passed by one or both chambers included H. Con. Res. 137, which passed the House in November 1997, and S. Con. Res. 78, which passed the Senate in March 1998. Katzman, "Iraq: Compliance, Sanctions, and U.S. Policy," February 27, 2002, p. 6.

51. U.S. Congress, Senate, Committee on Foreign Relations, *Iraq Claims Legislation,* 103rd Cong., 2nd sess., September 21, 1994; U.S. Congress, House of

Representatives, Committee on Foreign Affairs, *Iraq Claims Act of 1993,* 103rd Cong., 1st sess., October 13, 14, 20, and 28, 1993, hearings and markup of H.R. 3221.

52. David Bonior, introducing H. Res. 410, maintained that "all told, American claims against Iraq for losses, damages, and injuries suffered as a result of the [Gulf War] run to about $5 billion." U.S. Congress, *Congressional Record,* 103rd Cong., 2nd sess., April 28, 1994, Vol. 140, No. 48, p. H2850.

Similarly, Porter Goss argued that "H.R. 3221 provides a measured, technical process to help victims of the Persian Gulf war—private and public—recoup some of their serious losses. Clearly the available resources—$ 1.3 billion in frozen Iraqi assets—fall far short of covering the estimated $5 billion in total claims against the Iraqis resulting from the war." U.S. Congress, *Congressional Record,* 103rd Cong., 2nd sess., April 28, 1994, Vol. 140, No. 48, p. H2850.

In addition, H.R. 1632, which sought to compensate U.S. claimants against Iraq and use Iraq's frozen assets to pay U.S. claimants, was introduced in the 107th Congress. Katzman, "Iraq: Compliance, Sanctions, and U.S. Policy," February 27, 2002, p. 9.

53. U.S. Congress, Senate, Committee on Banking, Housing, and Urban Affairs, *United States Dual-Use Exports to Iraq and Their Impact on the Health of Persian Gulf War Veterans,* 103rd Cong., 2nd sess., May 25, 1994.

54. Author's interview with Carl LeVan, April 16, 2009.

55. Ibid.

56. U.S. Congress, Senate, Committee on the Judiciary, *Aftermath of War,* p. 4.

57. Ibid., p. 1.

58. Ibid., p. 19.

59. U.S. Congress, *Congressional Record,* House of Representatives, 102nd Cong., 1st sess., June 24, 1991, Vol. 137, No. 98, p. H4931.

60. Gonzalez's comments reiterated many of the observations of the Ahtisaari report, as well as international organizations and academic observers:

> Mr. Speaker, today I have introduced a resolution, House Resolution 180, that expresses a sense of the House that the economic embargo of Iraq should be lifted. . . .
>
> The United Nations, the International Red Cross, the Physicians for Human Rights, a Harvard study team, and Catholic Relief Services have all documented the fact that unless the economic sanctions imposed against Iraq are lifted immediately, tens of thousands, if not hundreds of thousands of Iraqi civilians will die in the next few months.

Ibid., p. H4930.

61. Representative Gonzalez introduced H. Res. 180, which provided:

> Whereas reports from the United Nations, the Physicians for Human Rights, the International Red Cross, a Harvard study team, other independent organizations, and private U.S. citizens have documented the fact that unless the economic sanctions imposed against Iraq are immediately lifted and Iraq is

allowed to buy and import food, medicine and equipment, especially for power generation, tens of thousands if not hundreds of thousands of Iraqi civilians will die in the upcoming months;

Whereas a Harvard study team estimates that at least 170,000 Iraqi children under the age of five will die within the next year from the delayed effects of the war in the Persian Gulf if the imposition of the sanctions continues;

Whereas this is a conservative estimate and does not include tens of thousands of Iraqi civilians above the age of five who are expected to die from similar causes;

Whereas the Catholic Relief Service estimates that more than 100,000 Iraqi children will die from malnutrition and disease in the upcoming months due to the economic embargo and destruction of the war, and the United Nations Children's Fund estimates that 80,000 Iraqi children may die from these causes;

Whereas malnutrition has become severe and widespread in Iraq since imposition of the embargo and the war due to severe food shortages and the inflation of food prices of up to 1000%, which has effectively priced many Iraqis, especially the poor and disadvantaged, out of the food market;

Whereas cholera, typhoid, and gastroenteritis have become epidemic throughout Iraq since the war due to the critical scarcity of medicine and the inability of Iraq to process sewage and purify the water supply;

Whereas the system of medical care has broken down in Iraq, resulting in the closure of up to 50% of Iraq's medical facilities due to acute shortages of medicines, equipment, and staff;

Whereas the incapacitation of 18 of Iraq's 20 power plants during the war is a principal cause of the deterioration in public health due to the resultant inability of Iraq to process sewage, purify its water supply, and supply electricity to health facilities;

Whereas the health care crisis cannot be addressed without the reconstruction of electrical facilities that enable the purification of water and treatment of sewage; . . .

Be it resolved by the House Of Representatives, That the United States should act on an emergency basis to lift the economic embargo of Iraq to save innocent Iraqi civilians, especially children, from death by disease and starvation.

Ibid., pp. H4936–H4937.

62. Senator Dodd, on behalf of himself and Senators Wellstone, Simon, Cranston, Pell, Jeffords, and Kennedy, introduced the following resolution:

Whereas medical teams from the United States, including a team of doctors from Harvard University and a team of doctors from the Arab-American Medical Association, have reported conditions in Iraq to be a "public health catastrophe";

Whereas widespread and severe acute malnutrition of children currently exist in Iraq due to acute shortages of food and infant formula that, if not relieved, could become a nationwide famine;

Whereas cholera, dysentery, typhoid, and gastroenteritis have reached epidemic proportions, and the incidence of all forms of water-borne diseases will increase during the summer months; . . .

Whereas basic infrastructure necessary to meet public health needs—water purification, sewage treatment, and electical power—has been substantially reduced;

Whereas the United Nations appealed to the world community for $400 million for emergency humanitarian assistance in Iraq, including assistance for the refugees on the border of Iraq and Turkey, of which less than 50 percent has been provided;

Whereas an estimate that $3.75 billion of foreign-held Iraqi state assets remain frozen, of which an estimated 40 percent is in United Sates banks; . . .

(1) the United Nations donor nations, including the United States, should fulfill their pledges made to the United Nations in response to its appeal for $400 million for emergency humanitarian assistance in Iraq, including assistance for the refugees; and

(2) the United States and other countries should immediately transfer a portion of Iraq's frozen state assets necessary to help meet the medical and humanitarian needs of Iraqi families and children in greatest need exclusively to the United Nations system, especially to its humanitarian and development assistance agencies, and to the International Committee of the Red Cross and other internationally recognized humanitarian relief organizations.

U.S. Congress, *Congressional Record*, 102nd Cong., 1st sess., July 16, 1991/Legislative Day of July 8, 1991, Vol. 137, No. 108, p. S10155.

Similarly, Senator Wellstone stated: "Mr. President, I rise today to offer a resolution with Senator Dodd and several others of my colleagues, which responds to the human tragedy unfolding daily in Iraq. I am pleased to be a member of the Subcommittee on Children and Families, chaired by Senator Dodd. Our shared concerns have motivated our efforts to find a means of alleviating the horrible suffering of the children and families of Iraq." Ibid., p. S10156.

63. H. Con. Res. 168, U.S. Congress, *Congressional Record*, 102nd Cong., 1st sess., November 26, 1991, Vol. 137, No. 177, Part 3, p. H11443.

64. U.S. Congress, House of Representatives, Select Committee on Hunger, *Humanitarian Crisis in Iraq: Challenge for U.S. Policy*, 102nd Cong., 1st sess., November 13, 1991; U.S. Congress, House of Representatives, Select Committee on Hunger, *The Future of Humanitarian Assistance in Iraq*, 102nd Cong., 2nd sess., March 18, 1992.

65. Testimony of Julia Devin, in U.S. Congress, House of Representatives, Select Committee on Hunger, *Humanitarian Crisis in Iraq*, p. 13.

66. U.S. Congress, House of Representatives, Select Committee on Hunger, *Humanitarian Crisis in Iraq*, p. 66.

67. "I saw the devastation of Iraq's infrastructure, wrought by the strategic bombing of the allied forces. The most essential aspects of a public health system in a society, water, electricity and a sewage system, were destroyed by our military

assault, and these systems have yet to be adequately reconstructed." Testimony of Jim McDermott, in U.S. Congress, House of Representatives, Select Committee on Hunger, *Humanitarian Crisis in Iraq*, p. 3.

68. Testimony of Richard Reid, UNICEF, in U.S. Congress, House of Representatives, Select Committee on Hunger, *Humanitarian Dilemma in Iraq*, 102nd Cong., 1st sess., August 1, 1991, pp. 5–7.

69. Ibid., p. 13.

70. Testimony of Julia Devin, in U.S. Congress, House of Representatives, Select Committee on Hunger, *Humanitarian Crisis in Iraq*, 102nd Cong., 1st sess., November 13, 1991, p. 14.

71. International Study Team, "Health and Welfare in Iraq after the Gulf Crisis: An In-Depth Assessment," October 1991, cited in U.S. Congress, House of Representatives, Select Committee on Hunger, *Humanitarian Crisis in Iraq*, p. 44.

72. Testimony of Julia Devin, in U.S. Congress, House of Representatives, Select Committee on Hunger, *Humanitarian Crisis in Iraq*, p. 14.

73. Ibid., p. 18.

74. Testimony of Jim McDermott, in ibid., p. 6.

75. Testimony of John Osgood Field, in U.S. Congress, House of Representatives, Select Committee on Hunger, *Humanitarian Dilemma in Iraq*, p. 32.

76. Testimony of Richard Reid, UNICEF, in U.S. Congress, House of Representatives, Select Committee on Hunger, *Humanitarian Dilemma in Iraq*, p. 24.

77. U.S. Congress, House of Representatives, Select Committee on Hunger, *Humanitarian Crisis in Iraq*, p. 14.

78. Referring to the Iraqi government, "They do not get in the way. You know, there are various levels of cooperation. Do we get our visas? Well, yes, but you have to wait sometimes and you wonder why. Can we move about? Everything that I hear from my colleagues, yes." Testimony of Alex Rondos, in U.S. Congress, House of Representatives, Select Committee on Hunger, *Humanitarian Crisis in Iraq*, p. 28.

79. Testimony of Charles LeMuniere, in U.S. Congress, House of Representatives, Select Committee on Hunger, *The Future of Humanitarian Assistance in Iraq*, 102nd Cong., 2nd sess., March 18, 1992, pp. 13 and 16.

80. Testimony of Melinda Kimble, in U.S. Congress, House of Representatives, Select Committee on Hunger, *Humanitarian Dilemma in Iraq*, p. 9.

81. Testimony of Jackie Wolcott, in U.S. Congress, House of Representatives, Select Committee on Hunger, *Humanitarian Crisis in Iraq*, p. 21.

82. Ibid., p. 16.

83. Ibid.

84. Testimony of Melinda Kimble, in U.S. Congress, House of Representatives, Select Committee on Hunger, *Humanitarian Dilemma in Iraq*, p. 9.

85. Testimony of Richard Reid, in U.S. Congress, House of Representatives, Select Committee on Hunger, *Humanitarian Dilemma in Iraq*, p. 16.

86. U.S. Congress, *Congressional Record*, 102nd Cong., 1st sess., November 26, 1991, Vol. 137, No. 177, Part 3, p. H11443 (introducing H. Con. Res. 168).

87. Ibid., p. H11444.

88. Ibid.

89. H. Res. 410, U.S. Congress, *Congressional Record*, 103rd Cong., 2nd sess., April 28, 1994, Vol. 140, No. 48, p. H2850.

90. U.S. Congress, *Congressional Record*, 103rd Cong., 2nd sess., April 12, 1994, Vol. 140, No. 38, p. H2199.

91. U.S. Congress, *Congressional Record*, 103rd Cong., 2nd sess., April 28, 1994, Vol. 140, No. 48, p. H2866.

92. Author's interview with Erik Gustafson, April 20, 2009.

93. Author's interview with Carl LeVan.

94. U.S. Congress, Senate, Committee on Armed Services, *Joint Chiefs of Staff Briefing on Current Military Operations*, 103rd Cong., 1st sess., June 24, 1993, p. 48.

95. U.S. Congress, House of Representatives, Committee on International Relations, *U.S. Policy toward Iraq*, 104th Cong., 2nd sess., March 28, 1996, pp. 50–51.

96. Testimony of Patrick Clawson, in U.S. Congress, House of Representatives, Committee on Armed Services, *Options for Dealing with Iraq*, 102nd Cong., 2nd sess., August 10–11, 1992, p. 8.

97. Ibid., p. 13.

98. U.S. Congress, House of Representatives, Committee on Foreign Affairs, *Developments in the Middle East, March 1993*, 103rd Cong., 1st sess., March 9, 1993, p. 25.

99. U.S. Congress, Senate, Committee on Armed Services, *The Situation in Iraq*, 104th Cong., 2nd sess., September 12, 1996, p. 35.

100. Representative Floyd D. Spence, U.S. Congress, House of Representatives, Committee on National Security, *United States Policy toward Iraq*, 104th Cong., 2nd sess., September 26, 1996, p. 2.

101. U.S. Congress, *Congressional Record*, 104th Cong., 2nd sess., May 21, 1996, Vol. 142, No. 72, pp. S5439–S5440.

102. Author's interview with Erik Gustafson, March 27, 2009.

103. Ibid.

104. "Representative Conyers Tells President Clinton: Food Not Bombs Will Topple Hussein," press release, office of John Conyers, September 4, 1996.

105. Author's interview with Carl LeVan.

106. Author's interview with Erik Gustafson, March 27, 2009.

107. Katzman, "Iraq: Compliance, Sanctions, and U.S. Policy," February 27, 2002, p. 2.

108. "U.N. Secretary-General Kofi Annan left for Iraq a few days ago. I am gratified that through his leadership and the world commitment to the United Nations, we were able to carve out the understanding that we might be able at this time to get a solution without war. Why not give peaceful negotiations an attempt? Why should we accuse someone of laying down with the enemy rather than standing up for peace?" U.S. Congress, *Congressional Record*, 105th Cong., 2nd sess., February 26, 1998, Vol. 144, No. 16, p. H654.

109. U.S. Congress, *Congressional Record*, 105th Cong., 2nd sess., February 27, 1998, Vol. 144, No. 17, p. S1134.

110. U.S. Congress, *Congressional Record*, 105th Cong., 2nd sess., July 31, 1998, Vol. 144, No. 106, p. S9656.

111. *Iraq Compliance with United Nations Resolutions*, Public Law 235, 105th Cong., 2nd sess., August 14, 1998.

112. Author's interview with Erik Gustafson, April 20, 2009.

113. U.S. Congress, *Congressional Record*, 105th Cong., 2nd sess., March 9, 1998, Vol. 144, No. 23, p. S1550. He repeated this a few days later: "Well, where are we? The teeth in Resolution 687 have effectively been removed with the expansion of the so-called oil-for-food exception to the sanctions. The first loosening of the sanctions occurred in 1995 when Security Council Resolution 986 allowed Iraq to export $1 billion in oil every 90 days, which is $4 billion over a year." U.S. Congress, *Congressional Record*, 105th Cong., 2nd sess., March 12, 1998, Vol. 144, No. 26, p. S1871.

114. U.S. Congress, *Congressional Record*, 106th Cong., 1st sess., February 3, 1999, Vol. 145, No. 19, pp. S1119–S1120.

115. "He is not stuck in an ever-constricting box; the box is full of holes. The resolution provides for infrastructure improvements such as sewers and electricity—all activities that would normally be undertaken by the Iraqi Government. To the extent this U.N. action quells citizen discontent with Iraqi leadership, we are just prolonging the life of this horrible regime." U.S. Congress, *Congressional Record*, 105th Cong., 2nd sess., March 9, 1998, Vol. 144, No. 23, p. S1551.

116. The resolution, S. Con. Res. 76,

(2) urges the Administration to oppose any further weakening of economic sanctions including extension of, or expansion of, United Nations Security Council Resolution 986;

(3) urges the President to propose to the United Nations Security Council measures to significantly tighten the international embargo on the sale of oil from Iraq . . .

U.S. Congress, *Congressional Record*, 105th Cong., 2nd sess., February 12, 1998, Vol. 144, No. 11, p. S770.

117. U.S. Congress, Senate, Committee on Foreign Relations and the Committee on Energy and Natural Resources, *New Proposals to Expand Iraqi Oil for Food: The End of Sanctions?* 106th Cong., 1st sess., March 17, 1999, p. 7.

118. "The Senator from Alaska said, 'Well, maybe we should curtail the flow of oil. We have a program that is called oil for food that has been going on for years now. Maybe if we tighten that up, it would put an economic squeeze on the Iraqis and maybe they would change their behavior and maybe we wouldn't need to drop bombs to have Saddam Hussein realize the errors of his way and that he needs to comply with the U.N. resolutions.'" U.S. Congress, *Congressional Record*, 105th Cong., 2nd sess., March 9, 1998, Vol. 144, No. 23, p. S1552.

119. "But what bothers me as much now, when we were discussing different options in lieu of a military strike, and one of the options was curtailing the flow of oil that was discussed in this Capitol with leaders of our Government, our leaders did not tell Congress that they had already agreed in the Security Council, or they were working on an agreement in the Security Council, on February 20, to

more than double the amount of oil that would be used in this oil-for-food program—more than doubled." Senator Don Nickles, ibid.

120. U.S. Congess, Senate, Committee on Foreign Relations and the Committee on Energy and Natural Resources, *Iraq: Are Sanctions Collapsing?* 105th Cong., 2nd sess., May 21, 1998, p. 4.

121. "New Proposals to Expand Iraqi Oil for Food: The End of Sanctions?" joint hearing before the Committee on Foreign Relations and the Committee on Energy and Natural Resources, U.S. Senate, 106th Congress, 1st sess., March 17, 1999, p. 3.

122. Ibid., p. 11.

123. Education for Peace in Iraq Center (EPIC), "EPIC Hosts Iraq Lobby Days," press release, June 23, 1999.

124. H. Con. Res. 39 (1999). Education for Peace in Iraq Center, "Congressional Voting Record on Iraq, Key to Legislative Actions Related to Iraq, 1991–2001."

125. U.S. Congress, *Congressional Record,* 107th Cong., 1st sess., July 12, 2001, Vol. 147, No. 97. p. S7592. Senator Murkowksi argued that:

Despite more than $15 billion available for [humanitarian] purposes, Iraq has spent only a fraction of that amount on its people's needs.

Instead, the Iraqi government spends that money on items of questionable, and often highly suspicious purposes. Why, when billions are available to care for the Iraqi people, who are malnourished, sick, and have inadequate medical care, would Saddam Hussein withhold the money available, and choose instead to blame the United States for the plight of his people?

Why is Iraq reducing the amount it spends on nutrition and pre-natal care, when millions of dollars are available?

Why does $200 million of medicine from the UN sit undistributed in Iraqi warehouses?

Why, given the urgent state of humanitarian conditions in Iraq, does Saddam Hussein insist that the country's highest priority is the development of sophisticated telecommunications and transportation infrastructure?

Why, if there are billions available, and his people are starving, is Iraq only buying $8 million of food from American farmers each year?

Murkowski repeated these accusations two weeks later. U.S. Congress, *Congressional Record*, 107th Cong., 1st sess., July 25, 2001, Vol. 147, No. 105, pp. S8177–S8178.

126. S. 1170. U.S. Congress, Senate, 107th Cong., 1st sess., July 12, 2001, Vol. 147, No. 97, p. S7592.

127. These included the ADAMS Islamic Center of Herndon, Virginia; the American-Arab Anti-Discrimination Committee; the American Muslim Council; American Muslims for Global Peace & Justice; the Arab-American Institute; the Bruderhof; the Catholic Worker movement; the Center for Economic and Social Rights; the Church of the Brethren (Washington, D.C., office); the Coordinating Council of Muslim Organizations; the Council on American Islamic Relations; the Dar Al-Hijrah Islamic Center; the Dominican Sisters; Education for Peace in Iraq; Fellowship of Reconciliation; the Friends Committee on National Legislation; Global Exchange;

Institute for Policy Studies; Life for Relief and Development; the Mennonite Central Committee; the Middle East Children's Alliance; Nonviolence International; Partners for Peace; Pax Christi USA; Peace Action; Veterans for Peace; Voices in the Wilderness; War Resisters League; Washington Peace Center; Washington Physicians for Social Responsibility; Women Against Military Madness; and Women's International League for Peace and Freedom. Correspondence with Erik Gustafson, July 14, 2009, and author's interview with Carl LeVan, April 10, 2009.

128. Statement of Representative John Conyers Jr., "Congressional Teach-In on Iraq," February 25, 1998.

129. John Conyers Jr. and Carolyn C. Kilpatrick, letter of announcement, "The Impact of Sanctions on Iraq: A Humanitarian, International, and U.S. Perspective," July 15, 1998.

130. "The Poverty of Civilian Sanctions: The Humanitarian Crisis in Iraq," letter of announcement, October 2, 1998.

131. Author's interview with Erik Gustafson, March 27, 2009.

132. U.S. Congress, House of Representatives, Committee on Ways and Means, *Use and Effect of Unilateral Trade Sanctions*, 105th Cong., 1st sess., October 23, 1997.

133. Ibid.

134. S. 327, S. 757, and H.R. 1244. Education for Peace in Iraq Center, "Congressional Analysis (Spring 2000)."

135. U.S. Congess, Senate, Committee on Foreign Relations and the Committee on Energy and Natural Resources, *Iraq: Are Sanctions Collapsing?* p. 6.

136. Ibid., p. 8.

137. U.S. Congress, *Congressional Record*, 105th Cong., 2nd sess., July 15, 1998, Vol. 144, No. 94, p. S8193.

138. Senator Hagel cited several different studies:

A CRS study, January 22, 1998—this year—listed 97, total, unilateral sanctions now in place. Since that report came out, we have added sanctions against India and Pakistan, for a total of at least 99 sanctions now in place . . .

A study by the National Association of Manufacturers found that from 1993 to 1996 we imposed, as I mentioned, another 61 sanctions. These 35 nations— these 35 nations—where we have imposed these sanctions make up 42 percent of the world population. Almost half of the 5.5 billion people on the Earth are included in these sanctions and 19 percent of the world's export market—$800 billion . . .

A new study by the International Institute of Economics estimates that, in 1995 alone, unilateral sanctions cost Americans $20 billion in lost exports, losing 200,000 jobs.

Ibid., p. S8191.

139. Ibid.

140. Ibid., p. S8192.

141. U.S. Congress, *Congressional Record—Extensions*, 107th Cong., 1st sess., July 26, 2001, Vol. 147, No. 106, p. E1452.

142. H. Res. 3140. Education for Peace in Iraq Center, "Congressional Voting Record on Iraq, Key to Legislative Actions Related to Iraq, 1991–2001."

143. S. 327. Education for Peace in Iraq Center, "Congressional Analysis" (2000).

144. U.S. Congress, *Congressional Record*, 106th Cong., 2nd sess., June 12, 2000, Vol. 146, No. 72, p. S4970.

145. U.S. Congress, House of Representatives, *Humanitarian Exports Leading to Peace Act of 2000*, H.R. 3825, 106th Cong., 2nd sess., *Congressional Record* 146, no. 22 (March 2, 2000), p. H641; U.S. Congress, House of Representatives, *Humanitarian Exports Leading to Peace Act of 2001*, H.R. 742, 107th Cong., 1st sess., *Congressional Record* 147, no. 24 (February 27, 2001), p. H441.

146. Letter from John Conyers Jr. to William Clinton, September 4, 1996.

147. Education for Peace in Iraq Center, "Congressional Voting Record on Iraq, Key to Legislative Actions Related to Iraq, 1991–2001."

148. Representative Kilpatrick noted that "In our letter to President Clinton, we urged the separation of humanitarian sanction from military sanctions. We also asked for improving the oversight and mechanisms for the oil-for-food trade, and the expeditious reform of the federal regulations impeding the flow of humanitarian goods to the people of Iraq. Like East Berlin before the airlift, we have heard several official and unofficial reports of the horrible starvation of children, medical deprivation of senior citizens, and general devastation faced by ordinary, everyday citizens in Iraq." U.S. Congress, *Congressional Record*, 105th Cong., 2nd sess., December 17, 1998, Vol. 144, No. 153, p. H11742.

149. Represenative Conyers noted that his proposed solution

does not depend on the suffering of thousands of vulnerable and innocent people. To this end I support the easing of the economic sanctions on Iraq while simultaneously tightening the military embargo. The cost of our containment policy does not have to be the death of 5000 children a month, and in fact the American role in the embargo that causes such devastation undermines any containment we hope to achieve . . .

Even after some limited reform, Oil-for-Food is still unable to meet the most basic needs of the people of Iraq. Some in Congress disagree with that, but I ask them where is their evidence? The World Health Organization, the United Nations Food and Agricultural Organization, UNICEF, and the Secretary General of the UN have all found otherwise.

The horror of this situation was brought to my attention most eloquently by Denis Halliday, who recently quit his job as the Assistant Secretary General of the United Nations and the director of Humanitarian Affairs in Iraq over this precise issue. The work that Halliday has undertaken along with Phyllis Bennis of the Institute for Policy Studies, has made an important contribution to bringing the indescribable human crisis in Iraq to America's attention. (I single out the United States because much of the world already knew how bad the situation in Iraq was.)

U.S. Congress, *Congressional Record—Extensions*, 106th Cong., 1st sess., March 24, 1999, Vol. 145, No. 47, p. E549.

150. Ibid., pp. E549–E550.

151. U.S. Congress, Senate, Committee on Foreign Relations, *U.S. Policy toward Iraq: Mobilizing the Opposition*, 106th Cong., 1st sess., June 23, 1999, p. 12.

152. U.S. Congress, Senate, Committee on Foreign Relations, *Facing Saddam's Iraq*, p. 18.

153. "Iraq Trip Report, Congressional Staff, 27 August–6 September 1999." Participating staff members were from the offices of Danny Davis, Sam Gejdenson, Earl Hilliard, Cynthia McKinney, and Bernard Sanders.

154. Education for Peace in Iraq Center, "Congressional Briefing to Present Grounds for Lifting Iraq Sanctions," media advisory, February 7, 2000.

155. Letter of February 18, 2000. U.S. Congress, House of Representatives, Committee on International Relations, *U.S. Policy toward Iraq*, 106th Cong., 2nd sess., March 23, 2000, Exhibit B.

156. Ibid., p. 26.

157. U.S. Congress, Senate, Committee on Foreign Relations, 107th Cong., 1st sess., *United States Policy toward Iraq*, March 1, 2001, pp. 4–7.

158. U.S. Congress, House of Representatives, Committee on International Relations, *U.S. Policy toward Iraq*, 106th Cong., 2nd sess., March 23, 2000, p. 3.

159. Ibid., p. 9.

160. U.S. Congress, Senate, Committee on Foreign Relations, *Saddam's Iraq: Sanctions and U.S. Policy*, 106th Cong., 2nd sess., March 22, 2000, pp. 13–14.

161. Education for Peace in Iraq Center, "Congressional Voting Record on Iraq, Key to Legislative Actions Related to Iraq, 1991–2001."

162. Letter from Representative Tony Hall to Madeleine Albright, May 31, 2000.

163. U.S. Congress, House of Representatives, Committee on International Relations, *U.N. Inspections of Iraq's Weapons of Mass Destruction Programs*, p. 18.

164. Ibid., p. 29.

165. U.S. Congress, Senate, Committee on Foreign Relations, *United States Policy toward Iraq*, 107th Cong., 1st sess., March 1, 2001, pp. 5–6.

166. Letter to Colin Powell, June 8, 2001.

167. U.S. Congress, *Congressional Record*, 107th Cong., 2nd sess., October 9, 2002, Vol. 148, No. 132, p. H7439.

168. Ibid., p. H7441.

169. Correspondence from the National Iraq Network to members of the House of Representatives, June 17, 1998.

170. Education for Peace in Iraq Center, letter to members of the Senate, April 9, 2000.

171. Education for Peace in Iraq Center, letter to members of the House of Representatives, June 25, 2000.

172. National Mobilization to End the Sanctions Against Iraq, press release, August 6, 2000.

173. Fellowship of Reconciliation, et al., "Letter from Religious Leaders, Faith-Based, Humanitarian, and Human Rights Organizations," to George Bush, May 29, 2001.

174. Campaign of Conscience for the Iraqi People, letter to members of Congress, June 5, 2001.

175. Education for Peace in Iraq Center, letter to members of the Senate, March 6, 2002.

176. Education for Peace in Iraq Center, lobbying report on Representative Judy Biggert, June 2, 1999.

177. Education for Peace in Iraq Center, lobbying report on Senator Blanche Lincoln, June 16, 1999.

178. Education for Peace in Iraq Center, lobbying report on Representative Paul Ryan, June 21, 1999.

179. Education for Peace in Iraq Center, lobbying report on Representative John Lewis, June 16, 1999.

180. Education for Peace in Iraq Center, lobbying report on Senator Carl Levin, June 2, 1999.

181. Education for Peace in Iraq Center, lobbying report on Representative Cynthia McKinney, June 16, 1999.

182. Education for Peace in Iraq Center, lobbying report on Representative William Clay, summer 1999.

183. Education for Peace in Iraq Center, lobbying report on Senator Russell Feingold, June 21, 1999.

184. Education for Peace in Iraq Center, lobbying report on Representative Anna Eshoo, September 14, 2001.

185. Education for Peace in Iraq Center, lobbying report on Representative Ileana Ros-Lehtinen, June 28, 1999.

186. Education for Peace in Iraq Center, lobbying report on Representative William Coyne, June 2, 1999.

187. Education for Peace in Iraq Center, lobbying report on Representative Joseph Hoeffel, June 2, 1999.

188. Education for Peace in Iraq Center, lobbying report on Representative Lee Terry, June 2, 1999.

189. Education for Peace in Iraq Center, lobbying report on Representative Robert Menendez, June 28, 1999.

190. U.S. Congress, Senate, Committee on Foreign Relations, *Hearings to Examine Threats, Responses, and Regional Considerations Surrounding Iraq*, 107th Cong., 2nd sess., July 31 and August 1, 2002, pp. 99–100.

191. U.S. Congress, House of Representatives, Committee on International Relations, *Authorization for Use of Military Force against Iraq*, 107th Cong., 2nd sess., October 2 and 3, 2002, p. 18.

192. Testimony of Dr. Eliot A. Cohen, U.S. Congress, House of Representatives, Committee on Armed Services, *United States Policy toward Iraq*, 107th Cong., 2nd sess., October 2, 2002, p. 345.

193. U.S. Congress, Senate, Committee on Armed Services, *U.S. Policy on Iraq*, 107th Cong., 2nd sess., September 19, 2002, pp. 28–29.

194. Ibid., p. 80.

195. U.S. Congress, House of Representatives, Committee on International Relations, *Authorization for Use of Military Force against Iraq*, 107th Cong., 2nd sess., October 3, 2002, p. 72.

196. Katzman, "Iraq: Current Sanctions, Long Term Threat, and U.S. Policy Options," p. 6.

197. Kenneth Katzman, Alfred Prados, and Clyde Mark, "Iraq-U.S. Confrontations" (Washington, DC: Congressional Research Service, December 5, 1996), p. 3.

198. U.S. Congress, House of Representatives, Committee on International Relations, *U.S. Options in Confronting Iraq*, 105th Cong., 2nd sess., February 25, 1998, p. 15.

199. Lois McHugh, "Iraq: Humanitarian Needs, Impact of Sanctions, and the 'Oil for Food' Program" (Washington, DC: Congressional Research Service, August 13, 1998), p. 9.

200. U.S. Congress, Senate, Committee on Foreign Relations, *Facing Saddam's Iraq*.

9. THE OIL-FOR-FOOD SCANDAL

1. "Oil for Scandal," *Wall Street Journal,* March 18, 2004, p. A16.

2. William Safire, "Kofigate Gets Going," *New York Times,* July 12, 2004.

3. U.S. Congress, House of Representatives, Committee on Energy and Commerce, *United Nations Oil for Food Program*, 108th Cong., 2nd sess., July 8, 2004, p. 2.

4. Now called the Government Accountability Office.

5. General Accounting Office, "United Nations: Observations on the Oil for Food Program," GAO-04-651T, April 7, 2004.

6. Charles Duelfer, *Comprehensive Report of the Special Advisor to the DCI on Iraq's WMD* (Washington, DC: Central Intelligence Agency, 2004).

7. Independent Inquiry Committee into the United Nations Oil-for-Food-Programme, "The Management of the United Nations Oil-for-Food Programme," September 7, 2005.

8. Working Group established by the Independent Inquiry Committee, "The Impact of the Oil-for-Food Programme on the Iraqi People," September 7, 2005.

9. Independent Inquiry Committee into the United Nations Oil-for-Food Programme, "Manipulation of the Oil-for-Food Programme by the Iraqi Regime," October 27, 2005, p. 1.

10. Independent Inquiry Committee into the United Nations Oil-for-Food Programme, "The Management of the United Nations Oil-for-Food Programme," p. 32.

11. Ibid., p. 33.

12. Ibid.

13. The GAO's April 2004 report stated that "from 1997 through 2002, we estimate that the former Iraqi regime acquired $10.1 billion in illegal revenues related to the Oil for Food Program." "United Nations: Observations on the Oil for Food Program," p. 2. Of this total, $5.7 billion came from oil smuggling and $4.4

billion from illicit surcharges on oil sales and commissions on imports. The report of the CIA's Iraq Study Group maintained that the bulk of Iraq's illicit funds came from government-to-government protocols—ongoing trade agreements between Iraq and other countries in violation of the sanctions. Iraq's income from these, according to the report, came to $8 billion, while kickbacks from import contracts were estimated at $1.5 billion, surcharges from oil sales at $229 million, and private-sector smuggling at $1.2 billion. "Comprehensive Report of the Special Advisor to the DCI on Iraq's WMD," "Regime Finance and Procurement" section, p. 23.

14. David Malone, *The International Struggle over Iraq: Politics in the UN Security Council, 1980–2005* (New York: Oxford University Press, 2006), p. 118.

15. Ibid., p. 131.

16. Ibid.

17. Ibid., p. 132.

18. It was so widely known that the trade accords were reported in industry periodicals, including updates on the negotiations and the actual terms of the agreements. For the extraordinary amount of detailed information that was publicly available, see for example, the following from *Alexander's Gas and Oil Connections*:

JORDAN TO RENEW OIL DEAL WITH IRAQ

Jan. 4, 1997. Senior Jordanian and Iraqi officials aided by technical experts are now busy working on details of renewing an oil agreement between the two countries. The agreement, under which Iraq is expected to increase by 7 % its oil supplies to Jordan, will be signed when Minister of Industry and Trade Ali Abul Ragheb visits Baghdad. At this moment technical experts from the two sides are working on the details. Abul Ragheb is scheduled to visit Baghdad for a meeting of the Joint Jordanian-Iraqi Economic Commission on January 6. During the visit, Jordan and Iraq are also expected to renew their annual trade protocol, which is tied with the oil agreement. Under the proposed agreement, Iraq will provide Jordan 4.5 mmt of crude oil and oil products in 1997. Since the end of the gulf war, Iraq has been meeting Jordan's oil needs by trucking 50,000 bpd of crude oil and 20,000 to 25,000 bpd of fuel oil to the country's only refinery at Zarqa. But Baghdad now owes Jordan $ 1.3 bn, representing debts accumulated in the 1980s as well as the unsettled payment of part of the Jordanian exports to Iraq. In 1996, Jordan cut the annual trade protocol by about half to $220mm. Officials have said that the amount is unlikely to be increased in 1997. Issues related to the outstanding Iraqi debts to Jordan and replacement of the present trucking system to pump Iraqi oil to Zarqa by the 500-kilometre pipeline are also expected to be discussed during the talks of Dabbas and Awad with Baghdad officials.

Alexander's Gas and Oil Connections 2, no. 1, January 15, 1997.

19. "Comprehensive Report of the Special Advisor to the DCI on Iraq's WMD," "Regime Finance and Procurement" section, p. 24.

20. Ibid., p. 26.

21. See, for example, correspondence from Barbara Larkin, Assistant Secretary, Legislative Affairs of the Department of State, to Benjamin Gilman, chair of the House Committee on International Relations, December 28, 1998, stating that the secretary of state was exercising the national interest waiver provision to permit assistance to the governments of Jordan and Turkey, along with the accompanying Memorandum of Justification, citing Jordan's "important role in buttressing the peace and security of the region," and noting that the restriction had been waived with respect to Jordan every year since its enactment in 1991. See also, for example, Richard Armitage, Deputy Secretary of State, "Determination under Section 531 of Foreign Operations, Export Financing and Related Programs Appropriation Act, 2002," finding that assistance to Jordan and Turkey was in the national interest of the United States, and accompanying memoranda, "Memorandum of Justification Regarding the Determination that Providing Assistance to Jordan is in the National Interest" and "Memorandum of Justification Regarding the Determination that Providing Assistance to Turkey is in the National Interest," October 17, 2002.

22. Testimony of Thomas Schweich, U.S. Congress, House of Representatives, Committee on Government Reform, *U.N. Oil-for-Food Program: The Inevitable Failure of U.N. Sanctions*, 109th Cong., 1st sess., April 12, 2005, p. 21.

23. The commanders of the MIF were Rear Admiral A. K. Taylor (1991–1992), Vice Admiral D. J. Katz (1992–1994), Vice Admiral J. S. Redd (1994–1996), Vice Admiral T. B. Fargo (1996–1998), Vice Admiral C. W. Moore Jr. (1998–2002), and Vice Admiral T. J. Keating (2002–2003).

24. In 2001 the United States contributed 90 vessels, Britain contributed 4, and all other participating countries contributed 1 or 2. In 2002 the United States contributed 99 vessels, five nations contributed 10 or more, and several other countries contributed less than 10. U.S. Naval Forces Central Command, "Department of State Request for Information: Yearly Snapshot of the MIF/MNF," correspondence with author, August 9, 2004.

25. Ibid. From 1994 to 2001 there were generally between 200 and 700 boardings per year; in 2002 and 2003 there were over 3,000 boardings per year.

26. Testimony of Robin Raphel, U.S. Congress, House of Representatives, Committee on Government Reform, *The Iraq Oil-for-Food Program: Starving for Accountability*, 108th Cong., 2nd sess., April 21, 2004, p. 43.

27. Testimony of Michael Thibault, Deputy Director, Defense Contract Audit Agency, U.S. Congress, Senate, Committee on Foreign Relations, *A Review of the United Nations Oil-for-Food Program*, 108th Cong., 2nd sess., April 7, 2004, p. 55.

28. According to the briefing memo of Thomas Costa of the committee staff, "In late 2000, allegations of a kickback scheme involving after-sale service fees on humanitarian contracts emerged. The US and UK raised the concern with OIP and the 661 Committee and in March 2001 submitted formal proposals to address these concerns. In the absence of evidence, the proposal received no support from the 661 Committee members." Costa, "The Iraq Oil for Food Program: Starving

for Accountability," memorandum to members of the Subcommittee on National Security, Emerging Threats, and International Relations, April 16, 2004.

29. Security Council Committee established by Resolution 661, Summary Record, Meeting 229, S/AC.25/SR.229, January 28, 2002.

30. Security Council Committee established by Resolution 661, Summary Record, Meeting 238, S/AC.25/SR.238, September 6, 2002.

31. Author's communications from former OIP staff, August 22, 2004.

32. "Although the flow of humanitarian and civilian goods to Iraq was a matter of strong interest to the U.S. Government, an even greater goal throughout the period of sanctions was to ensure that no items were imported which could in any way contribute to Iraq's WMD programs or capabilities. At the U.S. mission, we concentrated our efforts on this aspect of the sanctions." Testimony of Patrick F. Kennedy, U.S. Congress, House of Representatives, Committee on Government Reform, *The Iraq Oil-for-Food Program: Starving for Accountability*, pp. 30–31.

33. Testimony by John Ruggie, U.S. Congress, House of Representatives, Committee on International Relations, *The United Nations Oil-for-Food Program: Issues of Accountability and Transparency*, 108th Cong., 2nd sess., April 28, 2004, p. 59.

34. Iraq's official selling price plus the premia equals the market price. Office of the Iraq Programme, "Report of Oil Experts," March 20, 2002, p. 6.

35. According to the sources cited in the ISG report, purchasers were unwilling to pay surcharges of 50 cents per barrel. For the most part the surcharges varied between 10 and 15 cents per barrel. Duelfer, "Comprehensive Report of the Special Advisor to the DCI on Iraq's WMD," "Regime Finance and Procurement" section, p. 35.

36. Testimony of Patrick F. Kennedy, U.S. Congress, House of Representatives, Committee on Government Reform, *The Iraq Oil-for-Food Program: Starving for Accountability*, p. 38.

37. Office of the Iraq Programme, "Statement by Benon V. Sevan, Executive Director of the Iraq Programme, at the informal consultations of the Security Council," February 26, 2002.

38. Office of the Iraq Programme, "Statement by Benon V. Sevan, Executive Director of the Iraq Programme, at the informal consultations of the Security Council," May 29, 2002.

39. See, for example, United Nations, Office of the Iraq Programme, "Briefing by Benon Sevan, Executive Director of the Iraq Programme," April 20, 2000.

40. Office of the Iraq Programme, "Statement by Benon V. Sevan, Executive Director of the Iraq Programme, at the informal consultations of the Security Council," February 26, 2002.

41. Ibid.

42. Ibid.

43. The economist Ali Merza, using sources in both Arabic and English, estimated the cost of the food rations to the Iraqi government and identified the possible sources of financing. Because there are no direct figures available on the cost and finance, he made assumptions as indicated below.

I. Total cost of the rations (excluding Dhok, Arbil and Sulaimania in the north): the following figures are a backward extrapolation from actual figures on the cost of ration/person/month for 2000/2001 from the OFFP home page. The backward extrapolation connects 1991–1996 with 2000/2001 by first deflating the cost of 2000/2001 (by the import price index of the respective years 1991–1996) and then multiplying the deflated cost for each respective year by number of population in that respective year, 1991–1996:

1991 $1.56 billion
1992 $1.59 billion
1993 $1.61 billion
1994 $1.73 billion
1995 $1.96 billion
1996 $2.02 billion

II. Financing 1991–1996: three main sources were used in funding:

1. *Exports*: available data do not detail commodity groups involved for 1991–1996, but we can speculate that it was mainly smuggled oil and products plus other minor exports.

2. *Withdrawing from the reserves of foreign exchange.* Data indicate that throughout this period withdrawing from reserves was an important source. The reserves must have been accumulated prior to 1991 through, mainly, borrowing from abroad.

3. *Deficit financing.* During 1991–1996 the deficit of the budget had climbed steeply, and with it domestic public debt. Climbing domestic public debt was predominantly owed to the treasury and the central bank; in other words based on creating (printing) money. Consequently, inflation spiraled enormously during this period.

Correspondence with the author, July 31, 2008.

44. "Joint Government of Iraq–UNICEF Programme Review, 1990–2000, Sector Review Report, Health and Nutrition, Draft, November 1, 2000, pp. 44–45.

45. Hans-C. von Sponeck, "Iraq Sanctions: What Options Did the UN Security Council Have?" paper presented at the Hiroshima Peace Institute, 2006, pp. 13–14.

46. United Nations, Security Council Resolution 1483 (2003), para. 14.

47. Coalition Provisional Authority, "Development Fund for Iraq (DFI)—Financial Reporting Matrix," June 26, 2004.

48. "IRW Study of Recent Audits Shows Iraqi Fund Mismanagement," *Middle East Economic Survey* 47, no. 40, October 4, 2004.

49. U.S. Congress, House of Representatives, Committee on Government Reform, "Rebuilding Iraq: U.S. Mismanagement of Iraqi Funds," Minority Staff, Special Investigations Division, June 2005, pp. 19–20.

50. KPMG Bahrain, "Development Fund for Iraq: Report of Factual Findings in Connection with Disbursements for the Period from 1 January 2004 to 28 June 2004," September 2004, p. 18.

51. Ibid., p. 24.

52. Office of the Inspector General, Coalition Provisional Authority, "Coalition Provisional Authority's Contracting Processes Leading up to and Including Contract Award," Report no. 04-013, July 27, 2004, p. 2.

53. Iraq Revenue Watch, "Disorder, Negligence and Mismanagement: How the CPA Handled Iraq Reconstruction Funds," Report no. 7, September 2004, pp. 3–4.

54. Office of the Inspector General, Coalition Provisional Authority, "Coalition Provisional Authority's Contracting Processes Leading up to and Including Contract Award," p. 2.

55. International Advisory and Monitoring Board of Iraq, "Release of the KPMG Audit Reports on the Development Fund for Iraq," July 15, 2004, p. 2.

56. International Advisory and Monitoring Board of Iraq, "Report of the International Advisory and Monitoring Board on the Development Fund for Iraq: Covering the Period from the Establishment of the Development Fund of Iraq on May 22, 2003 until the Dissolution of the Coalition Provisional Authority on June 28, 2004," December 14, 2004, p. 3.

57. Ibid., p. 4.

58. Iraq Revenue Watch, "Disorder, Negligence and Mismanagement," p. 2.

59. Special Inspector General for Iraq Reconstruction, "Memorandum for Commander, U.S. Army Materiel Command," November 23, 2004, p. 3.

60. Iraq Revenue Watch, "Audit Finds More Irregularities and Mismanagement of Iraq's Revenues," Briefing no. 9, December 2004, pp. 3–4.

61. Office of the Inspector General, Coalition Provisional Authority, "Accountability and Control of Materiel Assets of the Coalition Provisional Authority in Kuwait," Report no. 05-002, October 25, 2004, p. i.

62. U.S. Congress, House of Representatives, Committee on Government Reform, Minority Staff, Special Investigations Division, "Rebuilding Iraq: U.S. Mismanagement of Iraqi Funds," June 2005, p. 14.

63. Open Society Institute, "Iraq in Transition: Post-Conflict Challenges and Opportunities," November 2004, p. 64.

64. Special Inspector General for Iraq Reconstruction, "Report to Congress," July 30, 2005, p. 62.

65. Ibid., pp. 65–66.

66. Special Inspector General for Iraq Reconstruction, "Shatt Al Arab Substation, Basrah, Iraq," PA-05-009, March 15, 2006, p. ii.

67. Special Inspector General for Iraq Reconstruction, "Management of Rapid Regional Response Program Contracts in South-Central Iraq," Report no. 05-023, January 23, 2006, p. 10.

68. U.S. Congress, House of Representatives, Committee on Oversight and Government Reform, "Cash Transfers to the Coalition Provisional Authority," memorandum from majority staff to committee members, February 6, 2007, p. 2.

69. Ibid., p. 17.

10. INSIDE THE U.S. POLICY

1. Author's interview with Peter Evans, desk officer, State Department, October 26, 2006.

2. Author's interview with Philo Dibble, former senior State Department official, March 29, 2006.

3. General Accounting Office, "Weapons of Mass Destruction: U.N. Confronts Significant Challenges in Implementing Sanctions against Iraq," GAO-02-625, May 2002, p. 18; Government Accountability Office, interview with Robert von Tersch, June 21, 2005.

4. General Accounting Office, "Weapons of Mass Destruction," p. 20; General Accounting Office, interview with Kael Weston and Lorraine Konzet, January 17–18, 2002, p. 1.

5. Author's interview with Kenneth Katzman, Congressional Research Service, May 5, 2006.

6. Ibid.

7. Government Accountability Office, interview with Eugene Young, State Department, March 21, 2005.

8. Bob Woodward, *Plan of Attack* (New York: Simon & Schuster, 2004), p. 15.

9. Author's interview with Robert Einhorn, former State Department official, March 15, 2006.

10. Author's interview with Ambassador Peter Burleigh, April 1, 2005.

11. Author's interview with David Welch, former senior State Department official, March 10, 2006.

12. Author's interview with State Department official, March 11, 2006.

13. Author's interview with Kenneth Katzman.

14. Author's interview with David Welch.

15. Author's interview with Peter Evans, October 26, 2006.

16. Author's interview with Kenneth Katzman.

17. Robert Baer, *See No Evil* (New York: Crown, 2002), p. 181.

18. David Kay, "Weapons of Mass Destruction: What's There, What's Not There, and What Does It All Mean?" presentation at United States Institute of Peace, Current Issues Briefing transcript, February 10, 2004, p. 24.

19. Government Accountability Office, interview with Robert von Tersch, p. 2.

20. Ibid.

21. Ibid.

22. United Nations, Office of the Humanitarian Coordinator for Iraq, "January–February 2003 Report," p. 18.

23. Carne Ross, correspondence with author, October 27, 2006.

24. Author's interview with former staff, Office of the Iraq Programme, January 30, 2005.

25. General Accounting Office, interview with the Norwegian Mission to the UN and Kael Weston, political officer, U.S. State Department, January 17, 2002, pp. 1–2.

26. Peter van Walsum, "The Iraq Sanctions Committee," in *The UN Security Council: From the Cold War to the 21st Century,* edited by David M. Malone (Boulder, CO: Lynn Rienner, 2004), p. 188.

27. Author's interview with Victor Comras, former State Department official, April 3, 2006.

28. For example, at one point over $100 million in telecommunications equipment was put on hold and kept there for periods ranging from six months to nearly two years, with no reason given other than "pending further evaluation." United Nations, Office of the Iraq Programme, Contracts Processing and Monitoring Division, "Telecommunications Sub-Sector: Holds Update," April 25, 2001. On another occasion, agriculture contracts were kept on hold for nearly a year, with no justification other than "pending further evaluation." United Nations, Office of the Iraq Programme, Contracts Processing and Monitoring Division, "Agriculture Sector: Holds Update," October 1, 2001.

29. For example, two months after all information had been provided, holds were still in place for $153 million in goods for food handling and distribution (United Nations, Office of the Iraq Programme, Contracts Processing and Monitoring Division, "Food Handling Sector and Transportation Sub-Sector: Holds Update," February 4, 2002); $130 million in medical equipment and supplies (United Nations, Office of the Iraq Programme, Contracts Processing and Monitoring Division, "Health Sector: Holds Update," March 4, 2002); $394 million in equipment for electricity production, some for over a year (Marcel Alberts, Electricity Sector Working Group, "Sectoral Briefing to SC 661 Committee: Status of Electricity Sector," Status of Holds," November 20, 2001); $318 million in equipment for the oil industry (United Nations, Office of the Iraq Programme, Contracts Processing and Monitoring Division, "Oil Industry Sector: Holds Update," April 10, 2002); and $21.7 million in supplies and equipment for education (United Nations, Office of the Iraq Programme, Contracts Processing and Monitoring Division, "Education Sector: Holds Update," November 28, 2001).

30. Government Accountability Office, interview with Eugene Young, State Department, p. 2.

31. Government Accountability Office, interview with Robert Von Tersch.

32. Author's interview with Peter Evans.

33. Author's interview with former staff, Office of the Iraq Programme, January 30, 2005.

34. Author's interview with former staff, Office of the Iraq Programme, December 28, 2005.

35. U.S. Department of State, "Saddam Hussein's Iraq," February 23, 2000, Executive Summary.

36. Madeleine Albright, *Madam Secretary* (New York: Miramax, 2003), p. 274.

37. "It was Wednesday, 27 October [1999], when the Secretary-General received me in his office with the words: 'Are you aware that the US and UK Governments have asked me for your removal?'" Hans C. von Sponeck, *A Different Kind of War: The UN Sanctions Regime in Iraq* (New York: Berghahn Books, 2006), p. 214; author's interview with Hans von Sponeck, September 1, 2005.

38. Author's interview with Philo Dibble.

39. Author's interview with State Department official.

40. U.S. Senate, Committee on Foreign Relations, "Overview of Foreign Policy Issues and Budget," 107th Cong., 1st sess., March 8, 2001, pp. 5–6.

41. Albright, *Madam Secretary,* pp. 274–275.

42. Ibid., pp. 282–283.

43. Ibid., p. 274. See also, for example, U.S. Department of State, "Saddam Hussein's Iraq," September 13, 1999.

44. General Accounting Office, interview with Kael Weston and Lorraine Konzet, p. 2.

45. Carne Ross, "War Stories," *Financial Times,* January 29, 2005.

46. Author's interview with Carne Ross, September 1, 2005.

47. Author's interview with David Welch.

48. Author's interview with Hans von Sponeck.

49. Author's interview with Carne Ross, September 30, 2005.

50. Ibid.

51. Ibid.

52. Author's interview with Hans von Sponeck.

53. Eric Herring, "Between Iraq and a Hard Place: A Critique of the British Government's Case for UN Economic Sanctions," *Review of International Studies* 28, no. 1 (January 2002), p. 50.

54. Ibid., p. 49.

55. Author's interview with Carne Ross, September 30, 2005.

56. Ross, "War Stories."

57. Claudia von Braunmühl, "Evaluating the Humanitarian Impact of Sanctions: Reflections on an Experience in 1995," paper presented at the conference of the International Association of Contemporary Iraq Studies, September 2005.

58. Author's interview with State Department official.

59. Author's interview with Ambassador Peter Burleigh.

60. Maciek Hawrylak, "Corrosion in the Council: Sanction in Iraq and the Effect on Security Council Unity and Authority," paper presented at the conference of the International Association of Contemporary Iraq Studies, September 2005, p. 8, citing the ambassador from Zimbabwe speaking at a meeting of the Security Council on November 23, 1992.

61. Ibid., p. 15.

62. Ibid., p. 16.

63. David Malone, *The International Struggle over Iraq: Politics in the UN Security Council, 1980–2005* (New York: Oxford University Press, 2006), p. 160.

64. Ibid., p. 161.

65. Nancy Soderberg, *The Superpower Myth: The Use and Misuse of American Might* (Hoboken, NJ: John Wiley and Sons, 2005), p. 210.

66. Ibid., p. 205.

67. Testimony of Victor Comras, U.S. Congress, House of Representatives, Committee on International Relations, "Syria and the United Nations Oil-for-Food Program," 109th Cong., 1st sess., July 27, 2005, p. 21.

68. Kenneth Pollack, *The Threatening Storm* (New York: Random House, 2002), p. 217.

69. Ibid., p. 83.

70. Maria Wahlberg, Milton Leitenberg, and Jean Pascal Zanders, "The Future of Chemical and Biological Weapon Disarmament in Iraq: From UNSCOM to UNMOVIC," paper presented at the Conference on Biosecurity and Bioterrorism (Villa Madama, Rome, Italy, 2000), pp. 8–9.

71. Lucia Mouat, "Iraq Probes Coalition in Search of Dialogue," *Christian Science Monitor,* January 22, 1993, p. 7.

72. Kristin Gazlay, "Russia, China Lead Opposition to Air Strikes," Associated Press, December 17, 1998.

73. Barton Gellman, "Annan Suspicious of UNSCOM Role: U.N. Official Believes Evidence Shows Inspectors Helped U.S. Eavesdrop on Iraq," *Washington Post,* January 6, 1999; Tim Weiner, "U.S. Used U.N. Team to Place Spy Devices in Iraq, Aides Say," *New York Times,* January 8, 1999; Gellman, "U.S. Spied on Iraqi Military Via U.N.; Arms Control Team Had No Knowledge of Eavesdropping," *Washington Post,* March 2, 1999; Tim Weiner, "US Explains How Spy Put Eavesdropping Device in Iraq," *International Herald Tribune,* January 9–10, 1999.

74. Hawrylak, "Corrosion in the Council," pp. 7–8.

II. INTERNATIONAL LAW AND THE SANCTIONS

1. Kimberly Gentile, "UN Official Tells U. Texas Crowd: Sanctions Killing Iraqis," *Daily Texan,* February 26, 1999.

2. George E. Basharat, "Sanctions as Genocide," *Transnational Law and Contemporary Problems* 11 (Fall 2001), p. 424. See also, e.g., Mary Ellen O'Connell, "Debating the Law of Sanctions," *European Journal of International Law* 13, no. 1 (2002), p. 72: "claims have even been made that the sanctions on Iraq violate the prohibition on genocide and that the Security Council has committed the gravest offense known to humanity."

3. United Nations, Commission on Human Rights, "The Adverse Consequences of Economic Sanctions on the Enjoyment of Human Rights: Working Paper Prepared by Mr. Marc Bossuyt," E/CN.4/Sub.2/2000/33 (2000), para. 72.

4. Ibid., para. 73.

5. See, for example, Cassandra LaRae-Perez, "Economic Sanctions as a Use of Force: Re-evaluating the Legality of Sanctions from an Effects-Based Perspective," *Boston University International Law Journal* 20 (2002), p. 176; Elias Davidsson, "Legal Boundaries to UN Sanctions," *International Journal of Human Rights* 7, no. 4 (Winter 2003).

6. International Covenant on Economic, Social and Cultural Rights, adopted and opened for signature, ratification and accession by General Assembly resolution 2200A (XXI) of 16 December 1966, *entry into force* 3 January 1976, Article 11.

7. Ibid.

8. Universal Declaration of Human Rights, Article 25(1).

9. International Covenant on Economic, Social and Cultural Rights, Article 12(1).

10. Ibid., Article 12.

11. Convention on the Rights of the Child, adopted and opened for signature, ratification and accession by General Assembly resolution 44/25 of 20 November 1989, *entry into force* 2 September 1990, Article 6.

12. Ibid., Article 24.

13. Universal Declaration of Human Rights, Article 26.

14. International Covenant on Economic, Social and Cultural Rights, Article 13.

15. Convention on the Rights of the Child, Article 28.

16. Universal Declaration of Human Rights, Article 23.

17. International Covenant on Economic, Social and Cultural Rights, Article 7.

18. United Nations Charter, Article 1(3).

19. Universal Declaration of Human Rights, Article 22.

20. Convention on the Rights of the Child, Article 24(4).

21. Ibid., Article 28(3).

22. Ibid.

23. Convention on the Rights of the Child, Article 24(4).

24. International Covenant on Economic, Social and Cultural Rights, Article 11(2).

25. Universal Declaration of Human Rights, Article 28.

26. "Recalling that every State has the duty . . . to refrain . . . from the threat or use of force against the sovereignty . . . of any State." Protocol Additional to the Geneva Conventions of 12 August 1949, and relating to the Protection of Victims of International Armed Conflicts (Protocol I), 8 June 1977, Preamble.

27. Ibid., Article 54.

28. Ibid., Article 54(1).

29. Ibid., Article 49(1).

30. Ibid., Article 51(4).

31. Ibid., Article 51(5)(b).

32. Ibid., Article 54(2).

33. Ibid., Article 54(3)(a) and (b).

34. Geneva Conventions, Protocol Additional I, Article 54(5): "In recognition of the vital requirements of any Party to the conflict in the defence of its national territory against invasion, derogation from the prohibitions contained in paragraph 2 may be made by a Party to the conflict within such territory under its own control where required by imperative military necessity."

35. Ibid., Article 52(2).

36. Ibid., Article 52(3).

37. Rome Statute of the International Criminal Court, UN DOC.A/CONF.183/9, opened for signature, July 17, 1998, Article 12.

38. International Criminal Court, "Letter from the Office of the Prosecutor Concerning the Situation in Iraq," February 9, 2006.

39. *Case Concerning Questions of Interpretation and Application of the 1971 Montreal Convention Arising from the Aerial Incident at Lockerbie (Libyan*

Arab Jamahiriya v. United Kingdom), Provisional Measures, Order of April 14, 1992.

40. See discussion by O'Connell in "Debating the Law of Sanctions," p. 71.

41. United Nations, Charter, Articles 24(1) and (2).

42. *Case Concerning Application of the Convention on the Prevention and Punishment of the Crime of Genocide* (Bosnia & Herzogovina v. Yugoslavia [Serbia and Montenegro]), International Court of Justice, Order of September 13, 1993, Separate Opinion of Judge Lauterpacht, p. 440.

43. *Case Concerning Questions of Interpretation and Application of the 1971 Montreal Convention Arising from the Aerial Incident at Lockerbie (Libyan Arab Jamahiriya v. United Kingdom)*, Judgment of February 27, 1998, Dissenting Opinion of Judge Sir Robert Jennings, p. 110.

44. International Criminal Court, Rome Statute, Article 6(c); Convention on the Prevention and Punishment of Genocide, Entry into force, January 12, 1951, Article II(c).

45. *Prosecutor v. Akayesu*, International Criminal Tribunal for Rwanda, ICTR 96-4-T, Judgement, September 2, 1998, para. 506.

46. *Prosecutor v. Kayeshima*, International Criminal Tribunal for Rwanda, ICTR-95-1-T, Judgement, para. 114.

47. Ibid., para. 115.

48. Ibid., para. 116.

49. Emphasis added. See Hugo Adam Bedau's discussion of this in the context of the Vietnam War: "Genocide in Vietnam?" *Boston University Law Review* 53, no. 3 (1973); see also Joy Gordon, "When Intent Makes All the Difference in the World: Economic Sanctions on Iraq and the Accusation of Genocide," *Yale Human Rights and Development Law Journal* 5 (2002).

50. *Prosecutor v. Akayesu*, Judgement, para. 523.

51. *Prosecutor v. Bashir*, ICC-02/05-01/09, March 4, 2009, Decision on the Prosecutor's Application for a Warrant of Arrest against Omar Hassan Ahmad Al Bashir, p. 65.

52. Ibid., p. 67.

53. Ibid., p. 69.

54. Ibid., p. 72.

55. *Case Concerning the Application of the Convention on the Prevention and Punishment of the Crime of Genocide (Bosnia and Herzegovina v. Serbia and Montenegro)*, International Court of Justice, February 26, 2007, Judgment, p. 116, para. 320.

56. Ibid., p. 117, para. 324.

57. Ibid., pp. 118–119, para. 328.

58. Patricia Wald, "Judging Genocide," *Justice Initiatives: The Extraordinary Chambers* (New York: Open Society Institute), April 2006, p. 86.

59. Ibid., p. 88.

60. Ibid., p. 89.

61. Ibid., p. 91.

62. Rome Statute of the International Criminal Court, Article 7(b).

63. Ibid., Article 7(2)(b).

64. *Prosecutor v. Kayeshima*, Judgement, para. 146.

65. Rome Statute of the International Criminal Court, Article 7(1). Emphasis added.

66. Ibid., Article 30(1).

67. Ibid., Article 30(2).

68. Ibid., Article 30(3).

69. Albin Eser, "Mental Elements—Mistake of Fact and Mistake of Law," in *The Rome Statute of the International Criminal Court*, vol. 1, ed. Antonio Cassese, Paola Gaeta, and John R. W. D. Jones (Oxford: Oxford University Press, 2002), p. 915.

70. William A. Schabas, *Genocide in International Law: The Crime of Crimes* (Cambridge: Cambridge University Press, 2000), pp. 212–213.

71. Ibid., p. 213.

72. Ibid., pp. 224–225.

73. Jean-Paul Sartre, "On Genocide," in *Crimes of War: A Legal, Political-Documentary, and Psychological Inquiry into the Responsibility of Leaders, Citizens, and Soldiers for Criminal Acts in Wars*, edited by Richard A. Falk et al. (New York: Random House, 1971), p. 534.

74. Bedau, "Genocide in Vietnam?" p. 622.

75. David Scheffer, "Genocide and Atrocity Crimes," *Genocide Studies and Prevention* 1, no. 3 (December 2006).

12. THE MORAL AND POLITICAL QUESTIONS

1. G. E. M. Anscombe, "Modern Moral Philosophy," *Philosophy* 33 (1958), p. 17.

2. Karl Jaspers, "The Question of German Guilt," in *Crimes of War*, ed. Richard A. Falk, Gabriel Kolko, and Robert Jay Lifton (New York: Random House, 1971), p. 483.

Writing this book turned out to be a much longer and more complicated process than I ever imagined. It involved far more documents, spreadsheets, and endnotes than I ever thought I would encounter in a single project. This book would not have been possible without the generosity and continuous support of a considerable number of people.

I want to begin by expressing my appreciation to a number of individuals whose deep friendship over many years has meant a great deal to me: Sam Schweber; Bruce Shapiro; Ruth Kliger; Fran Jeffries; Jim Bowler, S.J.; and Tom Regan, S.J. Each has contributed to my intellectual life in more ways than I can count. In addition, I want to thank my wonderful friends in New Haven and elsewhere, who have for many years now listened patiently to a nearly endless stream of information about Iraqi infrastructure and commercial protection clauses. I thank them for their great tolerance and good humor, along with the occasional emergency assistance.

I especially want to thank Kathleen McDermott, my editor at Harvard University Press, for her skill in working with me to shape the content of this book, for her advocacy and determination to see that this material would get a hearing, and for her support for this controversial project throughout a lengthy and complicated publication process. Were it not for Kathleen's extraordinary efforts, this book would not have been published. I have no words to express the depth of my gratitude to her.

I am also grateful to John Donohue of Westchester Book Group for his meticulous work and considerable patience and flexibility.

I want also to thank a group of friends and colleagues, all of them gifted scholars who work on issues in economic sanctions and related fields and who have given generously of their time, their expertise, and their insights. I want to express my gratitude to Paul Conlon, Rachel Connelly, Neta Crawford, Richard Garfield, Denis Halliday, Michael Levine, George Lopez, David Mapel, Colin Rowat, Claudia von Braun-mühl, and Hans von Sponeck.

A number of research assistants worked with me on this project at different points. All did splendid work, which was invaluable. I want to thank Carolyn Arnold, Eileen Arnold, Ryan Blair, Martin Connelly, Sydney Frey, Ben Manchak, Geoff Moseley, Steve Stafstrom, and Kyle Thompson-Westra.

Fairfield University has provided me with considerable resources of every sort. The Faculty Research Committee funded a sabbatical, summer research support on more than one occasion, and partial support for research assistance, all of which were enormously useful for the research and writing of this book. There were many occasions when I needed extra office space and summer housing for research assistants, additional computer equipment and technical support, flexibility in my teaching schedule, and support for conference travel. For finding ways to provide all of these things, I am grateful to Rick Dewitt and Dennis Keenan, my department chairs; to Tim Snyder, the former dean of the College of Arts and Sciences; to Mary Frances Malone, the associate academic vice president; and to Orin Grossman, the former academic vice president.

I am grateful to my colleagues in the philosophy department at Fairfield for their friendship and flexibility while I was pursuing research, and occasionally teaching courses, in an area that went far afield from philosophy. I have benefited as well from the expertise and insights of colleagues in other disciplines at Fairfield with whom I've had conversations on a wide range of questions in the course of writing this book. I particularly want to thank Charlene Wallace, Al Benney, Dina Franceschi, Curt Naser, and Kraig Steffen for their help in many ways, and on many occasions.

The philosophy department at Yale University provided me with an affiliation as a visiting fellow throughout the time I was writing this book, which gave me access to Yale's libraries. This was most helpful, and I want to thank the department chair, Michael Della Rocca. I also want to thank Pat Slatter for her friendship and encouragement for many years now, since my days as a graduate student at Yale.

I would like to thank Erik Gustafson, Janice O'Connell, and Carl LeVan for their thoughtful insights and suggestions on Chapter 8, and

Richard Falk, Liz Brundige, Ron Slye, and Christine Chung for theirs on Chapter 11. I want to express my appreciation as well to Harvard's reviewers and syndics, whose comments have made this a much better book than it would have been otherwise.

And while all of these people have contributed a great deal to this book, any mistakes are mine alone.

Albright, Madeleine. *Madam Secretary*. New York: Miramax, 2003.
———. "Preserving Principle and Safeguarding Stability: United States Policy toward Iraq." Speech presented at Georgetown University, March 26, 1997.
Alexander's Gas and Oil Connections. News & Trends: Middle East. Vol. 2, no. 1 (January 16, 1997).
Alnasrawi, Abbas. "Iraq: Economic Sanctions and Consequences, 1990–2000." *Third World Quarterly* 22, no. 2 (2001).
———. *Iraq's Burdens: Oil, Sanctions, and Underdevelopment*. Westport, CT: Greenwood Press, 2002.
Anglican Observer Office at the UN, et al. "Iraq Sanctions: Humanitarian Implications and Options for the Future." August 6, 2002.
Anscombe, G. E. M. "Modern Moral Philosophy." *Philosophy* 33 (1958).
Application of the Convention on the Prevention and Punishments of Crime of Genocide (Bosnia & Herz. v. Yugo. [Serbia and Montenegro]). ICJ Reports (1993) 325 (September 13).
Arons, Nicholas. "U.S.-Supported Iraqi Opposition." *Foreign Policy in Focus* 6, no. 10 (April 2001).
Ascherio, Alberto, et al. "Effect of the Gulf War on Infant and Child Mortality in Iraq." *New England Journal of Medicine* 327, no. 13 (1992).
Associated Press. "U.S., Russia Discuss Iraq Sanctions." March 29, 2002.
Austin, Ambassador Roy L. "Giving Iraqis a Democratic Future." *The Trinidad Guardian,* May 9, 2003.
Baer, Robert. *See No Evil*. New York: Crown, 2002.
Basharat, George E. "Sanctions as Genocide." *Transnational Law and Contemporary Problems* 11 (2001).
Bedau, Hugo Adam. "Genocide in Vietnam?" *Boston University Law Review* 53, no. 3 (1973).
Bellamy, Carol. Letter to Congressman Tony Hall, June 9, 2000.
Bennis, Phyllis. "False Consensus: George Bush's United Nations." In *Beyond the Storm: A Gulf Crisis Reader,* edited by Phyllis Bennis and Michel Moushabeck. New York: Olive Branch Press, 1991.
Bethlehem, D. L., ed. *The Kuwait Crisis: Sanctions and Their Economic Consequences*. Cambridge: Grotius Publications, 1991.

Blacker, John, Mohamed M. Ali, and Gareth Jones. "A Response to Criticism of Our Estimates of under-5 Mortality in Iraq, 1980–98." *Population Studies* 61, no. 1 (2007).

Bredemeier, Kenneth, and Peter Slevin. "US Companies Retreat from Iraq's Oil Market." *Alexander's Gas & Oil Connections* 7, no. 17 (September 5, 2002).

Brinkley, Joel. "Iraq Rations Fuel as U.N. Sanctions Hinder Refineries." *New York Times,* October 19, 1990.

Bush, George. "Remarks to the American Association of the Advancement of Science, February 15, 1991." In *Public Papers of the Presidents of the United States: Administration of George Bush, 1991,* vol. 1. Washington, DC: U.S. Government Printing Office, 1992.

Campaign Against Sanctions on Iraq. *CASI Newsletter,* July 2002.

———. "Guide to Sanctions: 10–Why Is 'Oil for Food' Suffering a Funding Crisis?" http://www.casi.org/uk/guide/funding.html.

Campaign of Conscience for the Iraqi People. Letter to members of Congress, June 5, 2001.

Case Concerning Questions of Interpretation and Application of the 1971 Montreal Convention Arising from the Aerial Incident at *Lockerbie (Libyan Arab Jamahiriya* v. *United Kingdom).* Judgment of 27 February 1998. Dissenting opinion of Judge Sir Robert Jennings.

Center for Economic and Social Rights. "Unsanctioned Suffering: A Human Rights Assessment of the United Nations Sanctions on Iraq." New York: Center for Economic and Social Rights, 1996.

Coalition Provisional Authority, Office of the Inspector General. "Accountability and Control of Material Assets of the Coalition Provisional Authority in Kuwait." Report no. 05-002, October 25, 2004.

———. "Coalition Provisional Authority's Contracting Process Leading up to and Including Contract Award." Report no. 04-013, July 27, 2004.

Cockburn, Andrew, and Patrick Cockburn. *Out of the Ashes: The Resurrection of Saddam Hussein.* New York: HarperCollins, 1999.

Cody, Edward. "Iraq Feels Losses from Sanctions." *Washington Post,* October 21, 1990.

Commission on Security and Cooperation in Europe. Implementation of the Helsinki Accords. "Situation of Kurds in Turkey, Iraq and Iran." May 17, 1993.

Conlon, Paul. "Lessons from Iraq: The Functions of the Iraq Sanctions Committee as a Source of Sanctions Implementation Authority and Practice." *Virginia Journal of International Law* 35 (1995).

———. Memorandum, "Historical Note on the Security Council's Disputed Right to Ban Supplies of Foodstuffs to a State under Sanction." June 26, 1998.

———. Memorandum to James C. Ngobi, "Desirability of Publishing Committee Decisions." May 16, 1994.

———. Memorandum to Martti Koskenniemi, "Confidential Non-Paper: Four Legal Issues Connected with United Nations Sanctions Management Practices in Recent Years." March 14, 1995.

————. *United Nations Sanctions Management: A Case Study of the Iraq Sanctions Committee, 1990–1994.* Ardsley, NY: Transnational Publishers, 2000.

Cordesman, Anthony H. *Iraq and the War of Sanctions.* Westport, CT: Praeger, 1999.

Costa, Thomas. "The Iraq Oil for Food Program: Starving for Accountability," Memorandum to members of the House of Representatives, Committee on Government Reform, Subcommittee on National Security, Emerging Threats and International Relations, April 16, 2004.

Cushman, John H., Jr. "Threats and Responses: Politics; Congressman Says Bush Would Mislead U.S." *New York Times.* September 30, 2002.

Davidsson, Elias. "Legal Boundaries to UN Sanctions." *International Journal of Human Rights* 7 (2003).

Drinan, Robert F. "Sanctions Not Yet Tried and Found Wanting." *National Catholic Reporter,* December 21, 1990.

Duelfer, Charles. "Comprehensive Report of the Special Advisor to the DCI on Iraq's WMD." Washington, DC: Central Intelligence Agency, 2004.

Dyson, Tim. "Child Mortality in Iraq since 1990." *Economic and Political Weekly* 41, no. 42 (2006).

Economist Intelligence Unit. "Country Profile: Iraq." London: Economist Intelligence Unit, 1998–1999.

————. "Country Report, Iraq." No. 1. London: Economist Intelligence Unit, 1996.

Education for Peace in Iraq Center (EPIC). "Congressional Analysis (2000)."

————. "Congressional Briefing to Present Grounds for Lifting Iraq Sanctions." Media advisory, February 7, 2000.

————. "Congressional Voting Record on Iraq, Key to Legislative Actions Related to Iraq, 1991–2001."

————. "EPIC Hosts Iraq Lobby Days." June 23, 1999.

————. Letter to members of the House of Representatives, June 25, 2000.

————. Letter to members of the Senate, April 9, 2000.

————. Letter to members of the Senate, March 6, 2002.

————. Lobbying report on Representative Ileana Ros-Lehtinen, June 28, 1999.

————. Lobbying report on Representative John Lewis, June 16, 1999.

————. Lobbying report on Representative Joseph Hoeffel, June 2, 1999.

————. Lobbying report on Representative Lee Terry, June 2, 1999.

————. Lobbying report on Representative Paul Ryan, June 21, 1999.

————. Lobbying report on Representative Robert Menendez, June 28, 1999.

————. Lobbying report on Representative William Coyne, June 2, 1999.

————. Lobbying report on Senator Blanche Lincoln, June 16, 1999.

Elliott, Kimberly, Gary Hufbauer, and Jeffrey Schott. "The Big Squeeze: Why the Sanctions on Iraq Will Work." *Washington Post,* December 9, 1990.

Epstein, Susan B. "The World Embargo on Food Exports to Iraq." Washington, DC: Congressional Research Service, 1990.

Fellowship of Reconciliation, et al. Letter from Religious Leaders, Faith-Based, Humanitarian, and Human Rights Organizations, to George Bush, May 29, 2001.

Freedman, Lawrence, and Efrain Karsh. *The Gulf Conflict: 1990–1991*. Princeton: Princeton University Press, 1993.

Galtung, Johan. "On the Effects of International Economic Sanctions: With Examples from the Case of Rhodesia." *World Politics* 19, no. 3 (April 1967).

Garfield, Richard. "Morbidity and Mortality among Iraqi Children from 1990 through 1998: Assessing the Impact of the Gulf War and Economic Sanctions." Goshen, IN and South Bend, IN: Fourth Freedom Forum and the Joan B. Kroc Institute for International Peace Studies at the University of Notre Dame, March 1999. http://www.fourthfreedom.org/Applications/cms.php?page_id=7.

Gazdar, Haris, and Athar Hussain. "Crisis and Response: A Study of the Impact of Economic Sanctions in Iraq." London: Asia Research Centre, London School of Economics, December 1997.

Gazlay, Kristin. "World Leaders Expressing Mixed Reactions to Bombardment." Associated Press, December 17, 1998.

Gellman, Barton. "Allied Air War Struck Broadly in Iraq; Officials Acknowledge Strategy Went Beyond Purely Military Targets." *Washington Post,* June 23, 1991.

———. "Annan Suspicious of UNSCOM Role; U.N. Official Believes Evidence Shows Inspectors Helped U.S. Eavesdrop on Iraq." *Washington Post,* January 6, 1999.

———. "U.S. Spied on Iraqi Military Via U.N.; Arms Control Team Had No Knowledge of Eavesdropping." *Washington Post,* March 2, 1999.

Gentile, Kimberly. "UN Official Tells U. Texas Crowd: Sanctions Killing Iraqis." *Daily Texan,* February 26, 1999.

Gilmore, Gerry J. "'Incredible Progress' Made Restoring Iraq's Infrastructure, Officials Say." *American Forces Press Service,* July 7, 2003.

Gordon, Joy. "When Intent Makes All the Difference in the World: Economic Sanctions on Iraq and the Accusation of Genocide." *Yale Human Rights & Development Law Journal* no. 5 (2002).

Graham-Brown, Sarah. "No-Fly Zones: Rhetoric and Real Intentions." Middle East Research and Information Project, Press Information Note 49, February 20, 2001.

———. *Sanctioning Saddam: The Politics of Intervention in Iraq*. New York: I. B. Tauris, 1999.

———. "War and Sanctions: Cost to Society and Toll on Development." In *The Future of Iraq*, edited by John Calabrese. Washington, DC: Middle East Institute, 1997.

Harper, Tim. "Give Iraq Sanctions Time to Work, 65% Say." *Toronto Star,* November 28, 1990.

Hawrylak, Maciek. "Corrosion in the Council: Sanction in Iraq and the Effect on Security Council Unity and Authority." Paper presented at the conference of the International Association of Contemporary Iraq Studies, September 2005.

Herring, Eric. "Between Iraq and a Hard Place: A Critique of the British Government's Case for UN Economic Sanctions." *Review of International Studies* 28, no. 1 (January 2002).

Hiro, Dilip. *Desert Shield to Desert Storm: The Second Gulf War.* New York: Routledge, 1992.

Hoskins, Eric. "Children, War and Sanctions." Report for UNICEF-Baghdad, April 1993.

———. "The Humanitarian Impacts of Economic Sanctions and War in Iraq." In *Political Gain and Civilian Pain: Humanitarian Impacts of Economic Sanctions,* edited by Thomas G. Weiss, David Cortright, George A. Lopez, and Larry Minear. Lanham, MD: Rowman & Littlefield, 1997.

Hoyos, Carola. "Block on Russia's Iraq Contracts Lifted." *Financial Times,* April 3, 2002.

Hufbauer, Gary Clyde, Jeffrey J. Schott, and Kimberly Ann Elliott, eds. *Economic Sanctions Reconsidered,* 2nd ed. Washington, DC: Institute for International Economics, 1990.

Hurd, Nathaniel, and Glen Rangwala. "U.S. Diplomatic and Commerical Relationships with Iraq, 1980–2 August 1990." Campaign against Sanctions on Iraq, December 12, 2001. http://www.casi.org/uk/info/usdocs/usiraq80s90s .html (accessed October 12, 2009).

Hurwitz, Manuelle, and Patricia David. *The State of Children's Health in Pre-War Iraq.* London: Centre for Population Studies, London School of Hygiene and Tropical Medicine, 1992.

Institute for Public Accuracy. "Iraq Sanctions: What's the Policy?" November 13, 1998.

International Criminal Court, Office of the Prosecutor. "Letter from the Office of the Prosecutor Concerning the Situation in Iraq." February 9, 2006.

International Federation of Red Cross and Red Crescent Societies. "World Disasters Report 1998." Oxford: International Federation of Red Cross and Red Crescent Societies, 1998.

International Study Team. "Health and Welfare in Iraq after the Gulf Crisis: An In-Depth Assessment." October 1991.

International Study Team. *Infant and Child Mortality and Nutritional Status of Iraqi Children after the Gulf Conflict.* Cambridge, MA: Center for Population and Development Studies, Harvard University, 1992.

Iraqi Economists Association. "Human Development Report 1995." Baghdad: Iraqi Economists Association, 1995.

"Iraq Oil-for-Food Deal Debated." *News24,* December 5, 2000.

Iraq Revenue Watch. "Audit Finds More Irregularities and Mismanagement of Iraq's Revenues." Briefing no. 9, December 2004.

———. "Disorder, Negligence and Mismanagement: How the CPA Handled Iraq Reconstruction Funds." Report no. 7, September 2004.

"IRW Study of Recent Audits Shows Iraqi Fund Mismanagement." *Middle East Economic Survey* 47, no. 40 (October 4, 2004).

Jaspers, Karl. "The Question of German Guilt." In *Crimes of War,* edited by Richard A. Falk, Gabriel Kolko, and Robert Jay Lifton. New York: Random House, 1971.

Kay, David. "Weapons of Mass Destruction: What's There, What's Not There, and What Does It All Mean?" Presentation at United States Institute of Peace, Current Issues Briefing transcript, February 10, 2004.

Kim, Samuel S. *The Quest for a Just World Order.* Boulder, CO: Westview Press, 1984.

Koenig, Robert L. "Gephardt to Bush: Let Sanctions Work." *St. Louis Post-Dispatch,* January 4, 1991.

LaRae-Perez, Cassandra. "Economic Sanctions as a Use of Force: Re-evaluating the Legality of Sanctions from an Effects-Based Perspective," *Boston University International Law Journal* 20 (2002).

Lardner, George, Jr., and R. Jeffrey Smith. "Iraq Sanctions Seen Working Slowly." *Washington Post,* November 24, 1990.

Legal Consequences for States of the Continued Presence of South Africa in Namibia (South-West Africa) Notwithstanding Security Council Resolution 276 (1970). International Court of Justice, Advisory Opinion of June 21, 1971.

Lewis, Jerry. "A Trip to Iraq Reveals the Need for U.S. Aid." *San Bernardino Sun,* September 11, 2001.

Lynch, Colum. "Mix of Uses Tangles Sanctions; U.S. Blocks Items to Iraq that Other Nations See as Benign." *Washington Post,* March 26, 2001.

———. "Trade Deal Won Chinese Support of U.S. Policy on Iraq." *Washington Post,* July 6, 2001.

MacAskill, Ewen. "US Tries to Head Off UN Plan to Reform Sanctions." *The Guardian,* February 9, 2001.

Malone, David M. *The International Struggle over Iraq: Politics in the UN Security Council, 1980–2005.* New York: Oxford University Press, 2006.

Marr, Phebe. "Iraq's Future: Plus Ça Change or Something Better?" In *The Gulf Crisis: Background and Consequences,* edited by Ibrahim Ibrahim. Washington, DC: Center for Contemporary Arab Studies, 1992.

Mehdi, Abbas S. "Review of *The Iraqi Economy under Saddam Hussein: Development or Decline?* By Muhammed-Ali Zainy." *Middle East Policy* 10, no. 2 (2003).

Merza, Ali. Correspondence with the author, July 31, 2008.

Middle East Economic Digest. April 5, 2002.

Middle East Economic Survey. January 8, 1996.

Minear, Larry, U. B. P. Chelliah, Jeff Crisp, John Mackinlay, and Thomas G. Weiss. "United Nations Coordination of the International Humanitarian Response to the Gulf Crisis, 1990–1992." Occasional Paper 13. Providence, RI: Watson Institue, 1992.

Minear, Larry, Thomas G. Weiss, George A. Lopez, David Cortright, and Julia Wagler. "Toward More Humane and Effective Sanctions Management: Enhancing the Capacity of the United Nations System." Occasional Paper 31. Providence, RI: Watson Institue, 1998.

Mouat, Lucia. "Iraq Probes Coalition in Search of Dialogue." *Christian Science Monitor,* January 22, 1993.

National Mobilization to End the Sanctions against Iraq. Press release, August 6, 2000.

National Network on Iraq. Letter to members of the House of Representatives, June 17, 1998.

Natsios, Andrew. *U.S. Foreign Policy and the Four Horsemen of the Apocalypse: Humanitarian Relief in Complex Emergencies.* Westport, CT: Praeger, 1997.

O'Connell, Mary Ellen. "Debating the Law of Sanctions." *European Journal of International Law* 13, no. 1 (2002).

"Oil for Scandal." *Wall Street Journal,* March 18, 2004.

Open Society Institute. "Iraq in Transition: Post-Conflict Challenges and Opportunities." November 2004.

Pape, Robert. "Why Economic Sanctions Do Not Work." *International Security* 22, no. 2 (1997).

Pasztor, Andy. "US Sees Indications that Sanctions Are Seriously Hurting Iraq's Military." *Wall Street Journal,* October 22, 1990.

Patterson, Jack T. "The Political and Moral Appropriateness of Sanctions." In *Economic Sanctions: Panacea or Peacebuilding in a Post–Cold War World?* edited by David Cortright and George A. Lopez, 89–96. Boulder, CO: Westview Press, 1995.

Pearson, Graham S. *The UNSCOM Saga: Chemical and Biological Weapons Non-Proliferation.* New York: St. Martin's Press, 1999.

Pellett, Peter. "Nutrition and Health in Iraq." *International Quarterly of Community Health Education* 17, no. 2 (1997–1998).

———. "Sanctions, Food, Nutrition, and Health in Iraq." In *Iraq under Siege: The Deadly Impact of Sanctions and War,* ed. Anthony Arnove. Cambridge, MA: South End Press, 2002.

Pincus, Walter, and Thomas B. Edsall. "Debate in Congress Reshuffles Disparate Democrats." *Washington Post,* January 11, 1991.

Pipes, Daniel. "Why America Can't Save the Kurds." *Wall Street Journal,* April 11, 1991.

Pollack, Kenneth. *The Threatening Storm.* New York: Random House, 2002.

Prosecutor v. Akayesu. International Criminal Tribunal for Rwanda, ICTR 96-4-T, Trial Chamber I, September 2, 1998.

Prosecutor v. Bashir. ICC-02/05–01/09, March 4, 2009. Decision on the Prosecutor's Application for a Warrant of Arrest against Omar Hassan Ahmad Al Bashir.

Prosecutor v. Kayeshima. Judgment.

Prosecutor v. Rutaganda. International Criminal Tribunal for Rwanda, ICTR-96-3-T, Judgment and Sentence.

Riddell, Peter. "US Believes Iraq May Be Able to 'Ride out' Economic Sanctions." *Financial Times,* December 4, 1990.

Ross, Carne. Correspondence with the author, October 27, 2006.

———. "War Stories." *Financial Times,* January 29, 2005.

Rowat, Colin. "Iraq Sanctions Saga Continues amid Policy Confusion." *Middle East Economic Survey* 45, no. 23 (June 10, 2002).

Safire, William. "Kofigate Gets Going." *New York Times,* July 12, 2004.

Sartre, Jean-Paul. "On Genocide." In *Crimes of War: A Legal, Political-Documentary, and Psychological Inquiry into the Responsibility of Leaders, Citizens, and Soldiers for Criminal Acts in Wars,* ed. Richard A. Falk et al. New York: Random House, 1971.

Scheffer, David. "Genocide and Atrocity Crimes." *Genocide Studies and Prevention* 1, no. 3 (December 2006).

Schneider, Michael E. "How Fair and Efficient Is the UNCC System? A Model to Emulate?" *Journal of International Arbitration* 15, no. 1 (1998).

Sciolino, Elaine. "Greater US Effort Backed to Oust Iraqi." *New York Times,* June 2, 1992.

Simons, Geoff. *The Scourging of Iraq: Sanctions, Law, and Natural Justice.* New York: St. Martin's Press, 1996.

Smith, R. Jeffrey. "Capitol Hill Hearings Seem to Be Setback for Bush's Policy." *Washington Post,* December 1, 1990.

Soderberg, Nancy. *The Superpower Myth: The Use and Misuse of American Might.* Hoboken, NJ: John Wiley and Sons, 2005.

Sommaruga, Cornelio. "Strengthening the Coordination of Emergency Humanitarian Assistance: Address by Cornelio Sommaruga, President of the ICRC." UN General Assembly, 49th session, 1994.

Stauffer, Thomas R. "Critical Review of UNCC Award for Lost Production and Lost Revenues." *Middle East Economic Survey* 44, no. 5 (2001).

Stone, Elizabeth. Correspondence with the author, June 21, 2006.

"US, UK, Bar Testimony from Foes of Iraq Sanctions." Reuters, October 4, 2000.

van Walsum, Peter. "The Iraq Sanctions Committee." In *The UN Security Council: From the Cold War to the 21st Century,* edited by David M. Malone. Boulder, CO: Lynn Rienner, 2004.

von Braunmühl, Claudia. "Evaluating the Humanitarian Impact of Sanctions: Reflections on an Experience in 1995." Paper presented at the conference of the International Association of Contemporary Iraq Studies, September 2005.

von Braunmühl, Claudia, and Manfred Kulessa. "The Impact of UN Sanctions on Humanitarian Assistance Activities: Report on a Study Commissioned by the United Nations Department of Humanitarian Affairs." Berlin: Gesellschaft für Communication Management Interkultur Training mbH—COMIT, 1995.

von Sponeck, Hans C. "After Iraq—Reforming UN Sanctions." Paper presented at a conference sponsored by the Hiroshima Peace Institute and the Center for International Conflict Resolution at Columbia University, March 21–23, 2007.

———. *A Different Kind of War: The UN Sanctions Regime in Iraq.* New York: Berghahn Books, 2006.

———. "Iraq Sanctions: What Options Did the UN Security Council Have?" Paper presented at the Hiroshima Peace Institute, 2006.

Wahlberg, Maria, Milton Leitenberg, and Jean Pascal Zanders. "The Future of Chemical and Biological Weapon Disarmament in Iraq: From UNSCOM to UNMOVIC." Paper presented at the Conference on Biosecurity and Bioterrorism, Villa Madama, Rome, Italy, 2000.

Wald, Patricia. "Judging Genocide." In *Justice Initiatives: The Extraordinary Chambers.* New York: Open Society Institute, 2006.

Washington Times. Editorial, December 5, 1997.

Weiner, Tim. "US Admits Spies Worked as Inspectors of Iraqi Arms." *International Herald Tribune,* January 8, 1999.

———. "US Explains How Spy Put Eavesdropping Device in Iraq." *International Herald Tribune,* January 9–10, 1999.

Weston, Burns H. "Security Council Resolution 678 and Persian Gulf Decision Making: Precarious Legitimacy." *American Journal of International Law* 85 (1991).

Whitall, Brinton. "Sanctions Just May Avert War with Iraq." *New York Times,* December 23, 1990.

Wilbur, William C. "U.S. Must Give Sanctions against Iraq Time to Work." *St. Petersburg Times,* January 7, 1991.

Will, George. "Sanctions Preferable to Bombarding Iraq." *St. Louis Post-Dispatch,* November 21, 1990.

Woodward, Bob. *Plan of Attack.* New York: Simon & Schuster, 2004.

AUTHOR INTERVIEWS

Phyllis Bennis, April 15, 2009.
Peter Burleigh, U.S. ambassador, April 1, 2005.
Victor Comras, former State Department official, April 3, 2006.
Philo Dibble, former senior State Department official, March 29, 2006.
Robert Einhorn, former senior State Department official, March 15, 2006.
Peter Evans, State Department, October 26, 2006.
Erik Gustafson, March 27, 2009.
Erik Gustafson, April 20, 2009.
Kenneth Katzman, Congressional Research Service, May 5, 2006.
Carl LeVan, April 10, 2009.
Carl LeVan, April 16, 2009.
Former staff, Office of the Iraq Programme, August 22, 2004.
Former staff, Office of the Iraq Programme, January 30, 2005.
Former staff, Office of the Iraq Programme, December 28, 2005.
Carne Ross, September 1, 2005.
Carne Ross, September 30, 2005.
State Department official, March 11, 2006.
Hans von Sponeck, September 1, 2005.
David Welch, former senior State Department official, March 10, 2006.

UNITED NATIONS AND RELATED DOCUMENTS

Alberts, Marcel. Electricity Working Group. "Sectoral Briefing to SC 661 Committee: Status of Electricity Sector." November 20, 2001.

Coalition Provisional Authority. "Development Fund for Iraq (DFI)—Financial Reporting Matrix." June 26, 2004.

Convention on the Rights of the Child. Adopted and opened for signature, ratification and accession by General Assembly resolution 44/25 of 20 November 1989, *entry into force* 2 September 1990.

Food and Agriculture Organization. "Evaluation of Food and Nutrition Situation in Iraq." Rome: Food and Agriculture Organization, 1995.

———. "Evaluation of Food and Nutrition Situation in Iraq, Terminal Statement." Rome: Food and Agriculture Organization, 1993.

Food and Agriculture Organization/World Food Programme. "Special Alert No. 237: FAO/WFP Crop and Food Supply Assessment Mission to Iraq." July 1993.

———. "Special Report: FAO/WFP Food Supply and Nutrition Assessment Mission to Iraq," October 3, 1997.

Independent Inquiry Committee. "The Management of the United Nations Oil-For-Food Programme." September 7, 2005.

———. "Report on the Manipulation of the Oil-for-Food Programme by the Iraqi Regime." October 27, 2006.

International Advisory and Monitoring Board for Iraq. "Report of International Advisory and Monitoring Board of the Development Fund for Iraq: Covering the Period from the Establishment of the DFI on May 22, 2003 until the Dissolution of the CPA on June 28, 2004." December 14, 2004.

———. "Statement of the IAMB—Release of the KPMG Audit Reports on the Development Fund of Iraq." July 15, 2004.

International Covenant on Economic, Social and Cultural Rights. Adopted and opened for signature, ratification and accession by General Assembly, resolution 2200A (XXI) of 16 December 1966, *entry into force* 3 January 1976.

International Telecommunications Union. "Telecommunication Sector within the 986 Program in Iraq: Presentation before the 661 Committee." "Present Status of the Telecommunication Network." May 4, 2001.

KPMG Bahrain. "Development Fund for Iraq: Report of Factual Findings in Connection with Disbursements for the Period from 1 January 2004 to 28 June 2004." September 2004.

Labi, Werner. "Consultancy Report: Water and Sanitation." United Nations, Office of Iraq Programme, June 2000.

Popal, Ghulam R., World Health Organization. "Health Situation in Iraq: A Presentation to the UN Security Council 661 Committee." March 2002.

Protocol Additional to the Geneva Conventions of 12 August 1949, and relating to the Protection of Victims of International Armed Conflict (Protocol I), 8 June 1977.

UNICEF. "Emergency Country Profile—Iraq: Health." May 1995.

———. "Fortnightly Report for the Period 13 to 27 September 1998." September 27, 1998.

———. "Iraq Immunization, Diarrhoeal Disease, Maternal and Childhood Mortality Survey." Evaluation Series no. 9. Amman: UNICEF Regional Office for the Middle East and North Africa, 1990.

———. "Iraq Watching Brief: Child Protection," prepared by Josi Salem-Pickartz. July 2003.

———. "Iraq Watching Brief: Education," prepared by Khalil Elain and Jamsheeda Parveen. July 2003.

———. "Iraq Watching Brief: Overview Report," prepared by Biswajit Sen. July 2003.

———. "Iraq Watching Brief: Water and Environmental Sanitation," prepared by Brendan Doyle. July 2003.

———. "Profile of Children and Women in Iraq and UNICEF Country Programme of Cooperation." April 15, 2002.

———. "Situation Analysis of Children and Women in Iraq." Baghdad: UNICEF/Iraq, April 30, 1998.

———. "The Situation of Children in Iraq: An Assessment Based on the United Nations Convention on the Rights of the Child," New York: UNICEF, February 2002.

———. "The Status of Children and Women in Iraq." Baghdad, December 1995.

———. "The Status of Children and Women in Iraq: A Situation Report." September 1995.

———. "Status of the Water and Sanitation Sector in South/Center Iraq." Presentation to the 661 Committee, September 2001.

UNICEF and Government of Iraq. "Joint Government of Iraq–UNICEF Programme Review, 1990–2000, Sector Review Report, Health and Nutrition." Draft, November 1, 2000.

UNICEF and World Health Organization. "Iraq Watching Brief: Health and Nutrition," prepared by Juan Diaz and Richard Garfield. July 2003.

UNICEF/Ministry of Health. "Child and Maternal Mortality Survey 1999: Preliminary Report." July 1999.

United Nations. Charter.

———. "Convention on the Prevention and Punishment of the Crime of Genocide."

———. "Human Rights Questions: Human Rights Situations and Reports of Special Rapporteurs and Representatives: Situation of Human Rights in Iraq." A/49/651, November 8, 1994.

———. "Human Rights Questions: Human Rights Situations and Reports of Special Rapporteurs and Representatives: Situation of Human Rights in Iraq." A/51/496, October 15, 1996.

———. "Human Rights Questions: Human Rights Situations and Reports of Special Rapporteurs and Representatives: Situation of Human Rights in Iraq." A/52/476, October 15, 1997.

———. "Impact Assessment of Computers on Secondary Education." March 2001.

———. "Memorandum of Understanding between the Secretariat of the United Nations and the Government of Iraq on the Implementation of Security Council Resolution 986 (1995)." S/1996/356, May 20, 1996.

———. "Report of the Secretary-General on the Work of the Organization, Supplement to an Agenda for Peace: Position Paper of the Secretary-General on the Occasion of the Fiftieth Anniversary of the United Nations." A/50/60 and S/1995/1, January 25, 1995.

———. "Report of the Secretary-General Pursuant to Paragraph 3 of Resolution 1111 (1997)." S/1997/935, November 28, 1997.

———. "Report of the Secretary-General Pursuant to Paragraph 4 of Resolution 1143 (1997)." S/1998/194, March 4, 1998.

———. "Report of the Secretary-General Pursuant to Paragraph 5 of Resolution 1302 (2000)." S/2000/1132, December 4, 2000.

———. "Report of the Secretary-General Pursuant to Paragraph 6 of Security Council Resolution 1210 (1998)." S/1999/187, February 22, 1999.

———. "Report of the Secretary-General Pursuant to Paragraph 7 of Security Council Resolution 1143 (1997)." S/1998/90, February 1, 1998.

———. "Report of the Secretary-General Pursuant to Paragraph 10 of Security Council Resolution 1153 (1998)." S/1998/1100, 1998.

———. "Report of the Secretary-General Pursuant to Paragraph 11 of Security Council Resolution 986 (1995)." S/1997/206, March 10, 1997.

———. "Report of the Secretary-General Pursuant to Paragraphs 28 and 30 of Resolution 1284 (1999) and Paragraph 5 of Resolution 1281 (1999)." S/2000/208, March 10, 2000.

———. "Report on the Situation of Human Rights in Iraq Prepared by the Special Rapporteur of the Commission on Human Rights in Accordance with Economic and Social Council Decision 1998/263 of 30 July 1998." A/53/433, September 24, 1998.

———. "Report to the Secretary-General Dated 15 July 1991 on Humanitarian Needs in Iraq, Prepared by a Mission Led by Sadruddin Agh Khan, Executive Delegate of the Secretary General." S/22788, annex (1991).

———. "Report to the Secretary-General on Humanitarian Needs in Kuwait and Iraq in the Immediate Post-crisis Environment by a Mission to the Area Led by Mr. Martti Ahtisaari, Under-Secretary-General for Administration and Management." S/22366, annex, March 20, 1991.

———. "Review and Assessment of the Implementation of the Humanitarian Programme Established Pursuant to Security Council Resolution 986 (1995) (December 1996–November 1998)," S/1999/481, April 28, 1999.

———. Rome Statute of the International Criminal Court. UN DOC.A/CONF.183/9, opened for signature July 17, 1998.

———. "Special Topics on Social Conditions in Iraq: An Overview Submitted by the UN System to the Security Council Panel on Humanitarian Issues." Baghdad, March 24, 1999.

———. "Weekly Update: Iraqi Oil Exports Plunge with Onset of War." March 25, 2003.

United Nations. Commission on Human Rights. "The Adverse Consequences of Economic Sanctions on the Enjoyment of Human Rights: Working Paper Prepared by Mr. Marc Bossuyt." E/CN.4/Sub.2/2000/33, 2000.

———. "Question of the Violation of Human Rights and Fundamental Freedoms in Any Part of the World: Report of the Special Rapporteur, Andreas Mavrommatis, on the Situation of Human Rights in Iraq." E/CN.4/2002/44, March 15, 2002.

———. "Question of the Violation of Human Rights and Fundamental Freedoms in Any Part of the World: Report of the Special Rapporteur on the Situation of

Human Rights in Iraq, Mr. Andreas Mavrommatis." E/CN.4/2001/42, January 16, 2001.

———. "Question of the Violation of Human Rights and Fundamental Freedoms in Any Part of the World: Report of the Special Rapporteur, Andreas Mavrommatis, on the Situation of Human Rights in Iraq." E/CN.4/2002/44, March 15, 2002.

———. "Question of the Violation of Human Rights and Fundamental Freedoms in Any Part of the World: Situation of Human Rights in Iraq, Report Submitted by the Special Rapporteur, Mr. Max van der Stoel, in Accordance with Commission Resolution 1998/65." E/CN.4/1999/37, February 26, 1999.

———. "Situation of Human Rights in Iraq." Resolution 1993/74, March 10, 1993.

———. "Situation of Human Rights in Iraq." Resolution 1994/74, March 9, 1994.

———. "Situation of Human Rights in Iraq." Resolution 1995/76, March 8, 1995.

United Nations. Commission on Human Rights. Sub-Commission on the Promotion and Protection of Human Rights. "Adverse Consequences of Economic Sanctions." Resolution 2000/25, E/CN.4/SUB.2/RES/2000/25, 2000.

———. "Adverse Consequences of Economic Sanctions on the Enjoyment of Human Rights." Resolution 1997/35, E/CN.4/SUB.2/RES/1997/35, 1997.

———. "Humanitarian Situation in Iraq." Decision 1999/110, E/CN.4/SUB.2/DEC/1999/110, 1999.

———. "Humanitarian Situation of the Iraqi Population, Sub-Commission on Human Rights Decision 2000/112." E/CN.4/2000/L.11/Add.2, August 18, 2000.

———. "Human Rights and Humanitarian Consequences of Sanctions, Including Embargoes." Resolution 2000/1, E/CN.4/SUB.2/RES/2000/1, 2000.

United Nations. Committee on the Rights of the Child: Iraq. "Concluding Observations of the Committee on the Rights of the Child: Iraq." CRC/C/15/Add.94, October 26, 1998.

United Nations. Economic and Social Council. "Concluding Observations of the Committee on Economic, Social, and Cultural Rights: Iraq." E/C.12/1/Add.17, December 12, 1997.

United Nations. General Assembly. Resolution 106. A/RES/51/106. March 3, 1997.

———. Resolution 141. A/RES/52/141, March 6, 1998.

———. Resolution 144. A/RES/48/144. December 20, 1993.

———. Resolution 157. A/RES/53/157. February 25, 1999.

———. Resolution 174. A/RES/56/174. February 27, 2002.

———. Resolution 178. A/RES/54/178. February 24, 2000.

———. Resolution 182. A/RES/46/182. December 19, 1991.

———. Resolution 191. A/RES/50/191. March 6, 1996.

———. Resolution 203. A/RES/49/203. March 13, 1995.

United Nations. Human Rights Committee. "Concluding Observations of the Human Rights Committee: Iraq." CCPR/C/79/Add.84, November 19, 1997.

United Nations. Office for the Coordination of Humanitarian Affairs. "United Nations Consolidated Inter-Agency Humanitarian Programme in Iraq." April 1, 1996.

United Nations. Office of the High Commissioner for Human Rights. "The Human Rights Impact of Economic Sanctions on Iraq: Background Paper Prepared by the Office of the High Commissioner for Human Rights for the Meeting of the Executive Committee on Humanitarian Affairs." September 5, 2000.

United Nations. Office of the Humanitarian Coordinator for Iraq. "Monthly Implementation Report." May 2000.

———. "Monthly Implementation Report." May 2001.

———. "Monthly Implementation Report." December 2002.

———. "Monthly Implementation Report." January–February 2003.

———. "Special Report on Observation Visit to Basrah Sewage Treatment Plant." May 29, 2001.

United Nations. Office of the Humanitarian Coordinator for Iraq, Agriculture Sectoral Working Group. "Assessment of Agricultural Machinery in Iraq." March 8, 2001.

———. "Impact of SCR 986 Program Inputs on Rehabilitation of the Veterinary Cold Chain in Iraq." May 2001.

United Nations. Office of the Iraq Programme. "About the Programme." http://www.un.org/depts/oip/background/latest/bvs010712.html (accessed July 15, 2009).

———. "Annex 2 (Agriculture): "Estimation Methods for Animal and Poultry Drugs and Growth Media." Communication from OIP to 661 Committee, January 2003.

———. "Annex 6a (Health): Finished Products, Raw Materials and Growth Media: Indicators, Use and Annual Requirements." Communication from OIP to 661 Committee, January 2003.

———. "Annex 6b (Health): Health Facilities in Centre/South Iraq that Could Use Items Subject to Quota Pursuant to SCR 1454 (2002)." Communication from OIP to 661 Committee, January 23, 2003.

———. "Annex 6c (Health): Finished Products." Communication from OIP to 661 Committee, January 2003.

———. "Atropine Sulphate: Intra-venous/Intramuscular Forms, Ordered under 'Oil for Food Programme.'" November 12, 2002.

———. "Briefing by Benon Sevan, Executive Director of the Iraq Programme." April 20, 2000.

———. "Chronology of Main Events." http://www.un.org/Depts/unscom/Chronology/chronology/htm.

———. "Consumption Rates and Use Levels for the Implementation of Paragraph 20 of Annex B of Resolution 1454 (2002)." February 19, 2003.

———. "Focus Observation Study on SCR 986 Programme Centrifugal Pumping Sets." December 2000.

———. "The Humanitarian Programme in Iraq Pursuant to Security Council Resolution 986 (1995): Note by the Office of the Iraq Programme." November 12, 2002.

———. "Implementation of Oil-for-Food: A Chronology." http://www.un.org/Depts/oip/background/chron.html (accessed July 15, 2009).

———. "Introductory Statement by Benon V. Sevan, Executive Director of the Iraq Programme, at the Informal Consultations of the Security Council on 25 February 1999." http://www.un.org/Depts/oip/background/latest/bvs9902255.html (accessed July 15, 2009).

———. "Paper Dated 7 July 1999: Payment Mechanisms for the ESB (53 Percent) Account."

———. "Report of Oil Experts." March 20, 2002.

———. "Report of the Group of United Nations Experts Established Pursuant to Paragraph 30 of the Security Council Resolution 1284 (2000)." March 2000.

———. "Statement by Benon V. Sevan, Executive Director of the Iraq Programme, at the Informal Consultations of the Security Council." February 26, 2002.

———. "Statement by Benon V. Sevan, Executive Director of the Iraq Programme, at the Informal Consultations of the Security Council." May 29, 2002.

———. "Statement by Benon V. Sevan, Executive Director of the Iraq Programme, at the Informal Consultations of the Security Council." September 25, 2002.

United Nations. Office of the Iraq Programme, Agriculture Sectoral Working Group. "Assessment of Impact of 986 Programme Inputs on Winter Vegetable Production in South/Center of Iraq." May 2001.

United Nations. Office of the Iraq Programme, Contracts Processing and Monitoring Division. "Agriculture Sector, Holds Update." October 1, 2001.

———. "Applications 'On Hold,' Health Sector." March 4, 2002.

———. "Education Sector: Holds Update." November 28, 2001.

———. "Electricity Sector: Holds Update." November 5, 2001.

———. "Enterotoxemia Vaccine Report." June 30, 2001.

———. "Food Handling Sector and Transportation Sub-Sector: Holds Update." February 4, 2002.

———. "Health Sector: Holds Update." March 4, 2002.

———. "Oil Industry Sector: Holds Update." April 10, 2002.

———. "Oil Spares Holds as at 14 August 2002."

———. "Telecommunications Sub-Sector: Holds Update." April 25, 2001.

———. "Water and Sanitation Sector: Holds Update." August 20, 2001.

United Nations. Office of the Iraq Programme, Health Sectoral Working Group. "Joint UN Team Field Report to Samara Drug Industry (SDI), the State Enterprise for Drugs, Industries and Medical Appliances." June 23 and 27, 2001.

———. "Joint UN Team Field Report to the Arab Company for Antibiotics Industries (ACAI)." March 4, 2002,

———. "Report on Sterilizers and Autoclaves." July 30, 2001.

———. "UN Team Field Report to Samara Drug Industries (SDI), Main Plant in Salah Al-Din." August 7, 2002.

United Nations. Office of the Iraq Programme, Housing Sector Working Group. "Impact Assessment of Contracts on Hold for the Ministry of Housing and Construction of Iraq." September 15, 2001.

United Nations. Office of the Iraq Programme, Multidisciplinary Observation Unit. "Public Health Contribution to the MDOU Monthly Report." December 14, 1998.

United Nations. Office of the Iraq Programme, Oil Overseers for the 661 Committee. Discussion paper prepared for the 661 Committee, March 14, 2002.

United Nations. Office of the Iraq Programme, Transport and Food Handling Working Group. "Assessment of the Impact of Contracts 'On Hold': Railways." May 2001.

———. "Assessment of the Impact of Contracts on Hold: Report on Joint MDOU/WFP Visit to the Port of Um Qasr." April 2001.

United Nations. Security Council. "Note by the President of the Security Council." S/1995/234, March 29, 1995.

———. "Note by the President of the Security Council." S/2000/319, April 17, 2000.

———. "Note by the President of the Security Council: Improvements to the Procedures of the Sanctions Committee." S/1995/438, May 31, 1995.

———. "Note by the President of the Security Council: Improvements to the Procedures of the Sanctions Committee." S/1996/54, January 24, 1996.

———. "Note by the President of the Security Council: Work of the Sanctions Committees." S/1999/92, January 29, 1999.

———. Provisional Verbatim Record of the 3139th meeting, S/PV.3139, November 23, 1992.

———. Provisional Verbatim Record of the 3439th meeting, S/PV.3439, October 17, 1994.

———. Provisional Verbatim Record of the 4120th meeting, S/PV.4120 (Resumption 1), March 24, 2000.

———. Provisional Verbatim Record of the 4128th meeting, S/PV.4128, April 17, 2000.

———. Provisional Verbatim Record of the 4241st meeting, S/PV.4241, December 5, 2000.

———. "Report of the Informal Working Group of the Security Council on General Issues of Sanctions." S/2006/997, December 22, 2006.

———. "Report of the Second Panel Established Pursuant to the Note by the President of the Security Council of 30 January 1999 (S/1999/100), Concerning the Current Humanitarian Situation in Iraq." S/1999/356, March 30, 1999.

———. Resolution 661 (1990).

———. Resolution 705 (1991).

———. Resolution 706 (1991).

———. Resolution 712 (1991).

———. Resolution 986 (1995).

———. Resolution 1153 (1998).

———. Resolution 1284 (1999).

———. Resolution 1330 (2000).

———. Resolution 1382 (2001).

———. Resolution 1441 (2002).

———. Resolution 1443 (2002).

———. Resolution 1447 (2002).

———. Resolution 1454 (2002).

———. Resolution 1483 (2003).

———. "Working Group on Sanctions: Chairman's Proposed Outcome—Draft Report." February 14, 2001.

United Nations. Security Council. Working Group on Sanctions. "Chairman's Proposed Outcome." February 14, 2001.

United Nations. Security Council Committee established by Resolution 661. "Decision of the Security Council Sanctions Committee Regarding Humanitarian Assistance to Iraq." S/22400, March 22, 1991.

———. "Letter Dated 7 February 2002 from the Overseers Addressed to the Chairman of the Security Council Committee Established by Resolution 661 (1990) Concerning the Situation between Iraq and Kuwait." S/AC.25.2001/OIL/COMM.14.

———. Summary Record, Meeting 4. S/AC.25/SR.4, August 28, 1990.

———. Summary Record, Meeting 5. S/AC.25/SR.5, August 31, 1990.

———. Summary Record, Meeting 19. S/AC.25/SR.19, November 8, 1990.

———. Summary Record, Meeting 22. S/AC.25/SR.22, December 20, 1990.

———. Summary Record, Meeting 24. S/AC.25/SR.24, January 14, 1991.

———. Summary Record, Meeting 47. S/AC.25/SR.47, August 14, 1991.

———. Summary Record, Meeting 52. S/AC.25/SR.52, October 18, 1991.

———. Summary Record, Meeting 61. S/AC.25/SR.61, January 9, 1992.

———. Summary Record, Meeting 62. S/AC.25/SR.62, January 27, 1992.

———. Summary Record, Meeting 63. S/AC.25/SR.63, February 6, 1992.

———. Summary Record, Meeting 66. S/AC.25/SR.66, March 6, 1992.

———. Summary Record, Meeting 71. S/AC.25/SR.71, June 1, 1992.

———. Summary Record, Meeting 72. S/AC.25/SR.72, June 19, 1992.

———. Summary Record, Meeting 73. S/AC.25/SR.73, July 9, 1992.

———. Summary Record, Meeting 74. S/AC.25/SR.74, July 24, 1992.

———. Summary Record, Meeting 76. S/AC.25/SR.76, September 3, 1992.

———. Summary Record, Meeting 77. S/AC.25/SR/77, September 17, 1992.

———. Summary Record, Meeting 80. S/AC.25/SR.80, October 29, 1992.

———. Summary Record, Meeting 81. S/AC.25/SR.81, November 11, 1992.

———. Summary Record, Meeting 82. S/AC.25/SR.82, November 30, 1992.

———. Summary Record, Meeting 85. S/AC.25/SR.85, January 12, 1993.

———. Summary Record, Meeting 87. S/AC.25/SR.87, February 11, 1993.

———. Summary Record, Meeting 88. S/AC.25/SR.88, February 18, 1993.

———. Summary Record, Meeting 91. S/AC.25/SR.91, April 6, 1993.

———. Summary Record, Meeting 92. S/AC.25/SR.92, April 22, 1993.

———. Summary Record, Meeting 103. S/AC.25/SR.103, November 1, 1993.

———. Summary Record, Meeting 105. S/AC.25/SR.105, December 22, 1993.

———. Summary Record, Meeting 107. S/AC.25/SR.107, January 27, 1994.

———. Summary Record, Meeting 115. S/AC.25/SR.115, August 26, 1994.

———. Summary Record, Meeting 116. S/AC.25/SR.116, October 11, 1994.

————. Summary Record, Meeting 117. S/AC.25/SR.117, November 10, 1994.
————. Summary Record, Meeting 118. S/AC.25/SR.118, December 16, 1994.
————. Summary Record, Meeting 132. S/AC.25/SR.132, February 1, 1996.
————. Summary Record, Meeting 133. S/AC.25/SR.133, February 7, 1996.
————. Summary Record, Meeting 134. S/AC.25/SR.134, March 1, 1996.
————. Summary Record, Meeting 141. S/AC.25/SR.141, July 31, 1996.
————. Summary Record, Meeting 142. S/AC.25/SR.142, August 8, 1996.
————. Summary Record, Meeting 143. S/AC.25/SR.143, August 28, 1996.
————. Summary Record, Meeting 144. S/AC.25/SR.144, October 14, 1996.
————. Summary Record, Meeting 148. S/AC.25/SR.148, January 23, 1997.
————. Summary Record, Meeting 150. S/AC.25/SR.150, February 21, 1997.
————. Summary Record, Meeting 151. S/AC.25/SR.151, March 17, 1997.
————. Summary Record, Meeting 155. S/AC.25/SR.155, May 14, 1997.
————. Summary Record, Meeting 159. S/AC.25/SR.159, July 17, 1997.
————. Summary Record, Meeting 160. S/AC.25/SR.160, August 27, 1997.
————. Summary Record, Meeting 166. S/AC.25/SR.166, January 4, 1998.
————. Summary Record, Meeting 172. S/AC.25/SR.172, June 18, 1998.
————. Summary Record, Meeting 175. S/AC.25/SR.175, February 24, 1999.
————. Summary Record, Meeting 180. S/AC.25/SR.180, February 26, 1999.
————. Summary Record, Meeting 181. S/AC.25/SR.181, March 8, 1999.
————. Summary Record, Meeting 184. S/AC.25/SR.184, March 18, 1999.
————. Summary Record, Meeting 185. S/AC.25/SR.185, May 27, 1999.
————. Summary Record, Meeting 189. S/AC.25/SR.189, August 24, 1999.
————. Summary Record, Meeting 190. S/AC.25/SR.190, October 12, 1999.
————. Summary Record, Meeting 192. S/AC.25/SR.192, January 19, 2000.
————. Summary Record, Meeting 193. S/AC.25/SR.193, March 1, 2000.
————. Summary Record, Meeting 194. S/AC.25/SR.194, March 17, 2000.
————. Summary Record, Meeting 195. S/AC.25/SR.195, March 20, 2000.
————. Summary Record, Meeting 205. S/AC.25/SR.205, October 2, 2000.
————. Summary Record, Meeting 229. S/AC.25/SR.229, January 28, 2002.
————. Summary Record, Meeting 231. S/AC.25/SR.231, February 8, 2002.
————. Summary Record, Meeting 238. S/AC.25/SR.238, September 6, 2002.
————. Summary Record, Meeting 244. S/AC.25/SR.244, January 22, 2003.
United Nations Development Programme and the Fafo Institute for Applied International Studies. "Iraq Living Conditions Survey." 2004.
United Nations Special Commission (UNSCOM). "UNSCOM: Chronology of Main Events." http://www.un.org/Depts/unscom/Chronology/chronology.htm (accessed July 15, 2009).
Universal Declaration of Human Rights. G.A. Res. 217A (III), U.N. Doc. A/810 at 71 (1948).
Working Group established by the Independent Inquiry Committee. "The Impact of the Oil-for-Food Programme on the Iraqi People." September 7, 2005.
World Food Programme. "WFP Emergency Report 04: Iraq Update." January 29, 1999.
————. "World Food Programme Emergency Reports." Center for International Disaster Information, http://www.cidi.org/humanitarian/wfp/.

World Health Organization. "The Health Conditions of the Population in Iraq since the Gulf Crisis." WHO/EHA/96.1, March 1996.

———. "Health Situation in Iraq." November 30, 2001.

———. "Health Update Iraq." November 24, 2000.

———. "Iraqi Health System Close to Collapse." Press Release WHO/16, February 27, 1997.

World Health Organization/UNICEF. "Special Mission to Iraq." February 1991.

U.S. GOVERNMENT AND RELATED DOCUMENTS

Congressional Staff. "Iraq Trip Report." August 27–September 6, 1999.

Conyers, John, Jr. Letter to William Clinton, September 4, 1996.

———. "Representative Conyers Tells President Clinton: Food Not Bombs Will Topple Hussein." Press release, September 4, 1996.

———. Statement of Representative John Conyers, Jr., "Congressional Teach-In on Iraq." February 25, 1998.

Conyers, John, Jr., and Carolyn C. Kilpatrick. "The Impact of Sanctions on Iraq: A Humanitarian, International, and U.S. Perspective." July 15, 1998.

Conyers, John, Jr., et al. "The Poverty of Civilian Sanctions: The Humanitarian Crisis in Iraq." October 2, 1998.

Copson, Raymond W. "Persian Gulf Conflict: Post-War Issues for Congress." Washington DC: Congressional Research Service, 1991.

Epstein, Susan B. "The World Embargo on Food Exports to Iraq." Washington DC: Congressional Research Service, September 25, 1990.

General Accounting Office. Interview with the Norwegian Mission to the UN and Kael Weston, political officer, U.S. State Department, January 17, 2002.

———. Interview with Kael Weston and Lorraine Konzet, January 17–18, 2002.

———. "United Nations: Observations on the Oil for Food Program." GAO-04-651T. April 7, 2004.

———. "Weapons of Mass Destruction: U.N. Confronts Significant Challenges in Implementing Sanctions against Iraq." GAO-02-625, May 2002.

Government Accountability Office. Interview with Robert Von Tersch, June 21, 2005.

———. Interview with Eugene Young, State Department, July 12, 2005.

Hall, Tony. Letter to Madeleine Albright, May 31, 2000.

"Iraq Compliance with United Nations Resolutions." Public Law 235, 105th Cong., 2nd sess., August 14, 1998.

"Iraq Liberation Act of 1998." Public Law 338, 105th Cong., 2nd sess., October 31, 1998.

Jones, Elizabeth, Principal Deputy Assistant Secretary, Bureau of Near Eastern Affairs. "State Department Briefing." August 13, 1999.

Katzman, Kenneth. "Iraq: Compliance, Sanctions, and U.S. Policy." Washington, DC: Congressional Research Service, February 27, 2002.

———. "Iraq: Compliance, Sanctions, and U.S. Policy." Washington, DC: Congressional Research Service, July 5, 2002.

———. "Iraq: Current Sanctions, Long Term Threat, and U.S. Policy Options." Washington DC: Congressional Research Service, March 25, 1994.

———. "Iraq: U.S. Efforts to Change the Regime." Washington, DC: Congressional Research Service, March 22, 2002.

———. "Iraq: U.S. Regime Change Efforts and Post-Saddam Governance." Washington, DC: Congressional Research Service, March 7, 2006.

Katzman, Kenneth, Alfred Prados, and Clyde Mark. "Iraq-U.S. Confrontations." December 5, 1996.

Larson, Alan, Under Secretary for Economic, Business, and Agricultural Affairs, U.S. Department of State. Interview, CNBC, May 1, 2003.

McClenny, Lee. Daily Press Briefing, U.S. Department of State. November 17, 1997.

McHugh, Lois. "Humanitarian Needs, Impact of Sanctions, and the 'Oil for Food' Program." Washington, DC: Congressional Research Service, 1998.

Moltzen, Ed. "Interview with Gen. Michael Delong." *The Command Post*, http://www.command-post.org/oped/2_archives/015496.html, 2004.

Natsios, Andrew, U.S. Agency for International Development. "Briefing on Reconstruction Progress in Iraq." December 3, 2004.

Sanford, Jonathan E. "Iraq's Economy: Past, Present, Future." Washington, DC: Congressional Research Service, 2003.

Special Inspector General for Iraq Reconstruction. "Management of Rapid Regional Response Program Contracts in South-Central Iraq." Report no. 05-023, January 23, 2006.

———. "Memorandum for Commander, U.S. Army Materiel Command," November 23, 2004.

———. "Report to Congress," July 30, 2005.

———. "Shatt Al Arab Substation, Basrah, Iraq." PA-05-009, March 15, 2006.

U.S. Congress. *Congressional Record*. House of Representatives, 102nd Cong., 1st sess., Vol. 137, No. 8. January 12, 1991.

———. *Congressional Record*. House of Representatives, 102nd Cong., 1st sess., Vol. 137, No. 70. May 9, 1991.

———. *Congressional Record*. House of Representatives, 102nd Cong., 1st sess., Vol. 137, No. 98. June 24, 1991.

———. *Congressional Record*. House of Representatives, 102nd Cong., 1st sess., Vol. 137, No. 177. November 26, 1991.

———. *Congressional Record*. House of Representatives, 102nd Cong., 2nd sess., Vol. 138, No. 77. June 2, 1992.

———. *Congressional Record*. House of Representatives, 103rd Cong., 2nd sess., Vol. 140, No. 38. April 12, 1994.

———. *Congressional Record*. House of Representatives, 103rd Cong., 2nd sess., Vol. 140, No. 48. April 28, 1994.

———. *Congressional Record*. House of Representatives, 105th Cong., 2nd sess., Vol. 144, No. 16. February 26, 1998.

———. *Congressional Record*. House of Representatives, 105th Cong., 2nd sess., Vol. 144, No. 153. December 17, 1998.

———. *Congressional Record*. House of Representatives, 107th Cong., 2nd sess., Vol. 148, No. 132. October 9, 2002.

———. *Congressional Record*. Senate, 101st Cong., 2nd sess., Vol. 136, No. 119. September 24, 1990/Legislative Day of September 10, 1990.

————. *Congressional Record.* Senate, 102nd Cong., 1st sess., Vol. 137, No. 6. January 10, 1991/Legislative Day of January 3, 1991.

————. *Congressional Record.* Senate, 102nd Cong., 1st sess., Vol. 137, No. 79. May 23, 1991/Legislative Day of April 25, 1991.

————. *Congressional Record.* Senate, 102nd Cong., 1st sess., Vol. 137, No. 108. July 16, 1991/Legislative Day of July 8, 1991.

————. *Congressional Record.* Senate, 103rd Cong., 1st sess., Vol. 139, No. 78. May 28, 1993.

————. *Congressional Record.* Senate, 104th Cong., 1st sess., Vol. 141, No. 129. August 4, 1995/Legislative Day of July 10, 1995.

————. *Congressional Record.* Senate, 104th Cong., 2nd sess., Vol. 142, No. 72. May 21, 1996.

————. *Congressional Record.* Senate, 105th Cong., 2nd sess., Vol. 144, No. 11. February 12, 1998.

————. *Congressional Record.* Senate, 105th Cong., 2nd sess., Vol. 144, No. 17. February 27, 1998.

————. *Congressional Record.* Senate, 105th Cong., 2nd sess., Vol. 144, No. 23. March 9, 1998.

————. *Congressional Record.* Senate, 105th Cong., 2nd sess., Vol. 144, No. 26. March 12, 1998.

————. *Congressional Record.* Senate, 105th Cong., 2nd sess., Vol. 144, No. 94. July 15, 1998.

————. *Congressional Record.* Senate, 105th Cong., 2nd sess., Vol. 144, No. 106. July 31, 1998.

————. *Congressional Record.* Senate, 106th Cong., 1st sess., Vol. 145, No. 19. February 3, 1999.

————. *Congressional Record.* Senate, 106th Cong., 2nd sess., Vol. 146, No. 72. June 12, 2000.

————. *Congressional Record.* Senate, 107th Cong., 1st sess., Vol. 147, No. 97. July 12, 2001.

————. *Congressional Record.* Senate, 107th Cong., 1st sess., Vol. 147, No. 105. July 25, 2001.

————. *Congressional Record—Extensions.* House of Representatives, 106th Cong., 1st sess., Vol. 145, No. 47, March 24, 1999.

————. *Congressional Record—Extensions.* 107th Cong., 1st sess., Vol. 147, No. 106. July 26, 2001.

U.S. Congress. House of Representatives. *Humanitarian Exports Leading to Peace Act of 2000.* H.R. 3825, 106th Cong., 2nd sess., *Congressional Record* 146, no. 22 (March 2, 2000): H641.

————. *Humanitarian Exports Leading to Peace Act of 2010.* H.R. 742, 107th Cong., 1st sess., *Congressional Record* 147, no. 24 (February 27, 2001): H441.

————. Letter to William Clinton, October 6, 1998.

————. Letter to Colin Powell, June 8, 2001.

U.S. Congress. House of Representatives. Committee on Armed Services. *Crisis in the Persian Gulf: Sanctions, Diplomacy and War.* 101st Cong., 2nd sess., December 4, 5, 6, 12, 13, 14, 17, 19, and 20, 1990.

———. *Options for Dealing with Iraq.* 102nd Cong., 2nd sess., August 10 and 11, 1992.

———. *United States Policy toward Iraq.* 106th Cong., 1st sess., March 10, 1999.

———. *United States Policy toward Iraq.* 107th Cong., 2nd sess., September 10, 18, 19, and 26, and October 2, 2002.

U.S. Congress. House of Representatives. Committee on Banking, Finance and Urban Affairs. *Economic Impact of the Persian Gulf Crisis.* 101st Cong., 2nd sess., November 27 and 28, 1990.

U.S. Congress. House of Representatives. Committee on Energy and Commerce. *U.N. Oil-For-Food Program.* 108th Cong., 2nd sess., July 8, 2004.

U.S. Congress. House of Representatives. Committee on Foreign Affairs. *Developments in the Middle East.* 103rd Cong., 1st sess., March 9, 1993.

———. *Iraq Claims Act of 1993.* 103rd Cong., 1st sess., October 13, 14, 20, and 28, 1993.

———. *U.S. Policy toward Iraq 3 Years after the Gulf War.* 103rd Cong., 2nd sess., February 23, 1994.

U.S. Congress. House of Representatives. Committee on Government Reform. *The Iraq Oil-for-Food Program: Starving for Accountability.* 108th Cong., 2nd sess., April 21, 2004,

———. "Rebuilding Iraq: U.S. Mismanagement of Iraqi Funds." Minority Staff, Special Investigations Division, June 2005.

———. *U.N. Oil-for-Food Program: The Inevitable Failure of U.N. Sanctions.* 109th Cong., 1st sess., April 12, 2005.

U.S. Congress. House of Representatives. Select Committee on Hunger. *The Future of Humanitarian Assistance in Iraq.* 102nd Cong., 2nd sess., March 18, 1992.

———. *Humanitarian Crisis in Iraq: Challenge for U.S. Policy.* 102nd Cong., 1st sess., November 13, 1991.

———. *Humanitarian Dilemma in Iraq.* 102nd Cong., 1st sess., August 1, 1991.

U.S. Congress. House of Representatives. Committee on International Relations. *Authorization for Use of Military Force against Iraq.* 107th Cong., 2nd sess., October 2 and 3, 2002.

———. *Disarming Iraq: The Status of Weapons Inspections.* 105th Cong., 2nd sess., September 15, 1998.

———. *The Monitoring of Weapons Development in Iraq, as Required by U.N. Security Council Resolution 687 (April 3, 1991); and Reaffirming the Special Relationship Between the U.S. and the Republic of the Philippines.* 107th Cong., 1st sess., December 12, 2001.

———. *Syria and the Oil for Food Program.* 109th Cong., 1st sess., July 27, 2005.

———. *U.N. Inspections of Iraq's Weapons of Mass Destruction Programs: Has Saddam Won?* 106th Cong., 2nd sess., September 26, 2000.

———. *U.S. Options in Confronting Iraq.* 105th Cong., 2nd sess., February 25, 1998.

———. *U.S. Policy toward Iraq.* 104th Cong., 2nd sess., March 28, 1996.

———. *U.S. Policy toward Iraq.* 106th Cong., 2nd sess., March 23, 2000.

———. *U.S. Policy toward Iraq.* 107th Cong., 1st sess., October 4, 2001.

U.S. Congress. House of Representatives. Committee on National Security. *United States Policy toward Iraq.* 104th Cong., 2nd sess., September 26, 1996.

————. *United States Policy toward Iraq.* 105th Cong., 2nd sess., September 16, 1998.

U.S. Congress. House of Representatives. Committee on Oversight and Government Reform. "Cash Transfers to the Coalition Provisional Authority." Memorandum from majority staff to committee members, February 6, 2007.

U.S. Congress. House of Representatives. Committee on Ways and Means. *Use and Effect of Unilateral Trade Sanctions.* 105th Cong., 1st sess., October 23, 1997.

U.S. Congress. Joint Economic Committee. *Economic Sanctions against Iraq.* 101st Cong., 2nd sess., December 19, 1990.

U.S. Congress. Joint Hearings. Committee on Foreign Affairs and the Join Economic Committee. *The Persian Gulf Crisis.* 101st Cong., 2nd sess., August 8, September 18, September 25, October 17, November 28, and December 11, 1990.

U.S. Congress. Senate. Committee on Armed Services. *Crisis in the Persian Gulf Region: U.S. Policy Options and Implications.* 101st Cong., 2nd sess., September 11, 13; November 27, 28, 29, 30; December 3, 1990.

————. *Joint Chiefs of Staff Briefing on Current Military Operations.* 103rd Cong., 1st sess., June 24, 1993.

————. *Joint Chiefs of Staff Briefing on Current Military Operations in Somalia, Iraq, and Yugoslavia.* 103 Cong., 1st sess., January 29, 1993.

————. *The Situation in Iraq.* 104th Cong., 2nd sess., September 12, 1996.

————. *U.S. Policy on Iraq.* 107th Cong., 2nd sess., September 19, 23, and 25, 2002.

————. *U.S. Policy toward Iraq.* 106th Cong., 2nd sess., September 19 and 28, 2000.

————. *The Weapons of Mass Destruction Program of Iraq.* 107th Cong., 2nd sess., February 27, 2002.

U.S. Congress. Senate. Committee on Banking, Housing, and Urban Affairs. *United States Dual-Use Exports to Iraq and Their Impact on the Health of the Persian Gulf War Veterans.* 103rd Cong., 2nd sess., May 25, 1994.

U.S. Congress. Senate. Committee on Foreign Relations. *Civil War in Iraq.* 102nd Cong., 1st sess., S. Prt. 102-27, May 1991.

————. *Facing Saddam's Iraq: Disarray in the International Community.* 106th Cong., 1st sess., September 28, 1999.

————. *Hearings to Examine Threats, Responses, and Regional Considerations Surrounding Iraq.* 107th Cong., 2nd sess., July 31 and August 1, 2002.

————. *Iraq: Can Saddam Be Overthrown?* 105th Cong., 2nd sess., March 2, 1998.

————. *Iraq Claims Legislation.* 103rd Cong., 2nd sess., September 21, 1994.

————. *The Liberation of Iraq: A Progress Report.* 106th Cong., 2nd sess., June 28, 2000.

————. *Overview of Foreign Policy Issues and Budget.* 107th Cong., 1st sess., March 8, 2001,

————. *Saddam's Iraq: Sanctions and U.S. Policy.* 106 Cong., 2nd sess., March 22, 2000.

————. *United States Policy in Iraq: Public Diplomacy and Private Policy.* 105th Cong., 2nd sess., September 9, 1998.

————. *United States Policy toward Iraq.* 106th Cong., 1st sess., March 9, 1999.

————. *United States Policy toward Iraq.* 107th Cong., 1st sess., March 1, 2001.

————. *U.S. Policy in the Persian Gulf.* 101st Cong., 2nd sess., December 4 and 5, 1990.

————. *U.S. Policy in the Persian Gulf.* 101st Cong., 2nd sess., December 6, 12, and 13, 1990.

————. *U.S. Policy in the Persian Gulf.* 102nd Cong., 1st sess., January 8, 1991.

————. *U.S. Policy toward Iran and Iraq.* 104th Cong., 1st sess., March 2 and August 3, 1995.

————. *U.S. Policy toward Iraq: Mobilizing the Opposition.* 106th Cong., 1st sess., June 23, 1999.

U.S. Congress. Senate. Committee on Foreign Relations and Committee on Energy and Natural Resources. *Iraq: Are Sanctions Collapsing?* 105th Cong., 2nd sess., May 21, 1998.

————. *New Proposals to Expand Iraqi Oil for Food: The End of Sanctions?* 106th Cong., 1st sess., March 17, 1999.

U.S. Congress. Senate. Committee on Governmental Affairs. *United States Policy in Iraq: Next Steps.* 107th Cong., 2nd sess., March 1, 2002.

U.S. Congress. Senate. Committee on the Judiciary. *Aftermath of War: The Persian Gulf Refugee Crisis.* 102nd Cong., 1st sess., May 20, 1991.

U.S. Congress. Senate. Select Committee on Intelligence. *Iraq.* 104th Cong., 2nd sess., September 19, 1996.

U.S. Defense Intelligence Agency. "Iraq Water Treatment Vulnerabilities as of 18 January 91—Key Judgments." January 18, 1991.

U.S. Department of Energy. Energy Information Administration. "Iraq Country Analysis Brief." March 2002. http://www.mafhoum.com/press3/93E15.htm (accessed October 8, 2009).

U.S. Department of State. "Request for Information—Yearly Snapshot of the Multilateral Interception Force/Multinational Force." Correspondence with the author, August 9, 2004.

————. *Saddam Hussein's Iraq.* September 13, 1999.

————. *Saddam Hussein's Iraq.* Update, November 1999.

————. *Saddam Hussein's Iraq.* Update, March 24, 2000.

International Covenant on Economic, Social
and Cultural Rights, 212, 213, 214, 215
International Criminal Court, 219, 220, 223
International Criminal Tribunal for
Rwanda, 222–223
International Criminal Tribunal for the
former Yugoslavia, 223–224, 228
International Study Team, 150, 256n82
Iraq: condition of oil industry, 96–97;
conditions prior to 1990, 32–33;
economy, 33, 91–92; impact of sanctions
on, 35–38, 89–91; infant and child
mortality rates, 164, 201, 255n82
Iraq, disarmament of, 30, 31, 45, 118, 206;
Congress and, 146, 158, 164; as require-
ment for lifting sanctions, 12, 170, 205,
241; as Security Council objective, 17, 45,
50, 106, 170, 205, 206, 207, 232, 236;
U.S. interpretation of, 4, 11, 104
Iraq, government of: efforts to mitigate
impact of sanctions, 127–132; failures to
respond to humanitarian crisis, 132–134;
impoverishment of, 92–94, 135–137
Iraq, Kurdish population, 13, 16, 25, 26,
42; attention by Congress, 146, 147, 149
Iraq, Shi'a population, 16, 147, 204
Iraqi National Accord, 13
Iraq Liberation Act. See U.S. Congress, Iraq
Liberation Act

Jaspers, Karl, 244–245
Jordan, illicit trade with, 91, 105, 152, 175,
176, 177, 207

Kay, David, 195
Kilpatrick, Carolyn C., 161, 163, 172
KPMG, 184, 185
Kuwait, Iraqi invasion of, 1, 6, 7, 20, 21,
30, 41, 125, 145, 232
Kuwait compensation fund, 22, 25, 29, 94,
95–96, 118, 119, 148
Kuwait Petroleum Company, 95, 96

Mavrommatis, Andreas. See United
Nations, human rights rapporteurs
McDermott, Jim, 150, 151

McNamara, Robert, 8, 145
Moynihan, Daniel Patrick, 143, 144
Multinational Interception Force, 30, 32,
177–178
Murkowski, Frank, 159, 160

No-fly zones, 23, 43, 104, 141, 146, 208;
U.S. interpretation of, 31, 32, 39

Office of the Humanitarian Coordinator for
Iraq, 25, 56, 68, 93, 120, 122, 161, 199,
201, 211
Office of the Iraq Programme, 24, 27, 30,
63, 67, 71, 74, 78, 107, 116, 122, 123,
174, 179, 180, 198
Oil-for-Food Programme: accusations of
improprieties, 126, 173–176, 178–180,
181–182; adequacy, 113, 118, 136; cash
component, lack of, 91–93, 98; commercial protections, 122–123; congressional
opposition to, 142, 158, 159, 163;
financial crisis (see Retroactive oil
pricing); first oil-for-food proposal, 12,
95; Goods Review List, 30, 75, 80, 81,
83, 199; holds on humanitarian contracts
(see Holds); impact of, 67, 91; in northern
governorates, 26

Penny, Timothy, 150, 152, 153
Persian Gulf War: bombing campaign, 12,
21, 32, 89–91, 94, 129; uprising after, 15,
16, 31, 146, 147, 204
Pollack, Kenneth, 16
Powell, Colin, 9, 15, 193, 200

Rao Singh, Anupama, 55, 121
Reform attempts: "gentlemen's agreement,"
104, 116, 234; Goods Review List, 30,
75, 80, 81, 83, 199, 244; green list, 27,
28, 30, 81, 119; "smart sanctions," 29,
80, 83, 100
Regime change: opposition groups, 13,
16, 17, 44, 45, 146, 147, 158, 208;
U.S. insistence on, 11, 12, 14, 15, 17, 18,
46, 146, 158, 170, 229, 232–233, 241,
242